Yale Library of Medieval Philosophy

GENERAL EDITORS

Norman Kretzmann

Cornell University

Eleonore Stump

St. Louis University

John F. Wippel

Catholic University of America

The Yale Library of Medieval Philosophy is a series of commissioned translations of philosophical texts from the Latin Middle Ages. The series is intended to make available in English complete works of philosophical and historical importance, translated by scholars whose linguistic abilities are complemented by a philosophical understanding of the subject matter. Each translation published in the series will be accompanied by a brief introduction, sparse notes (confined to indispensable explanations and references), and an index.

Previously published

William of Ockham, *Quodlibetal Questions*

VOLUME 1

Quodlibets 1–4

translated by Alfred J. Freddoso

and Francis E. Kelley

VOLUME 2

Quodlibets 5–7

translated by Alfred J. Freddoso

Francisco Suarez, S.J.

On Efficient Causality

METAPHYSICAL

DISPUTATIONS

17, 18, AND 19

Translated by Alfred J. Freddoso

YALE UNIVERSITY PRESS

New Haven & London

Published with the assistance of the Ernst Cassirer Publications Fund.

Set in type by Tseng Information Systems, Inc., Durham, North Carolina.
Printed in the United States of America by
Lightning Source

Library of Congress Cataloging-in-Publication Data
Suárez, Francisco, 1548–1617.
[Disputationes metaphysicae. Disputation 17–19. English]
On efficient causality : metaphysical disputations 17, 18, and 19 /
Francisco Suárez ; translated by Alfred J. Freddoso.
p.   cm. — (Yale library of medieval philosophy)
Includes bibliographical references and indexes.
ISBN 0-300-06007-6
ISBN -13: 978-0-300-06007-2

1. Causation—Early works to 1800.   2. Necessity (Philosophy)—
Early works to 1800.   3. Aristotle—Influence—Philosophy,
Renaissance.   4. Philosophy, Renaissance.   I. Freddoso, Alfred J.
II. Title.   III. Series.
B4568.S83D5713   1994
122—dc20
94-12480
CIP

The paper in this book meets the guidelines for permanence and
durability of the Committee on Production Guidelines for Book
Longevity of the Council on Library Resources.

Mulieris bonae beatus vir;
numerus enim annorum illius duplex

Contents

Introduction

The Historical Importance of the Disputationes Metaphysicae

Francisco Suarez, S.J. (1548–1617), was a preeminent figure in the remarkable scholastic revival that took place on the Iberian peninsula in the sixteenth and early seventeenth centuries.[1] The *Disputationes Metaphysicae*, a set of fifty-four disputations occupying two complete volumes of Suarez's *Opera Omnia*, were first published in Spain in 1597 and within the next few years were reprinted more than ten times in France, Italy, Germany, and Belgium. Widely read in the seventeenth and early eighteenth centuries, they were used extensively not only in Jesuit-run schools but even in the Protestant universities of Germany.

It is not difficult to discern why the *Disputationes Metaphysicae* should have been so influential. First of all, Suarez was a brilliant, technically proficient, and profound metaphysician; many rank him second only to St. Thomas Aquinas among the Christian scholastics. A near contemporary of Galileo and Descartes, he came quickly to be regarded in the seventeenth century as the leading champion of Aristotelian scholasticism, the one who would have to be confronted if a reasoned case were to be made against Aristotelianism by the practitioners of the new science and of the new "way of ideas" in philosophy. Directly through his own writings and indirectly through the writings of his followers, Suarez thus became an important background figure in the scientific and philosophical revolutions of the seventeenth century.

Second, Suarez deliberately chose to write the *Disputationes Metaphysicae* as a "purely philosophical" propaedeutic to the study of revealed theology; so it was not necessary in his case, as it was in the case of his scholastic predecessors, to search far and wide through his theological works in order to piece together a cohesive and exhaustive treatment of one or another important metaphysical topic. What's more, the *Disputationes Metaphysicae* taken as a whole are truly comprehensive; there is hardly a metaphysical topic of any importance that they do not deal with systematically and at length.[2]

1. For sympathetic treatments of Suarez's life and times, see R. de Scorraille, S.J., *François Suárez de la Compagnie de Jésus*, 2 vols. (Paris: Lethiellieux, 1912–13), and Joseph H. Fichter, S.J., *Man of Spain: Francis Suarez* (New York: Macmillan, 1940). For a briefer overview, less enamored with the Society of Jesus, see Carlos Noreña, "Suárez and the Jesuits," *American Catholic Philosophical Quarterly* 65 (1991):267–286.

2. The one exception is that certain metaphysical issues in the philosophy of mind are

Third, Suarez was not only an outstanding philosopher in his own right; he was also a gifted and erudite student of philosophy who was familiar with Hellenistic, Patristic, Jewish, and Islamic sources, as well as with all of his most important scholastic predecessors. The resulting synthesis is truly extraordinary. On one topic after another, problematics are lucidly delineated, and the best arguments proposed thus far for the main competing positions are laid out sympathetically and in depth. In short, the *Disputationes Metaphysicae* gave early modern philosophers access to all the diverse strains of classical and medieval Aristotelianism as well as to the various anti-Aristotelian positions that Suarez and his forebears had been forced to contend with. This also explains why Suarez's works, though written in the late sixteenth and early seventeenth centuries, are normally classified as medieval and are thus properly included in a series of translations of medieval philosophy.

Unfortunately, in our own time Suarez's metaphysical writings have been almost entirely overlooked by English-speaking philosophers and historians of philosophy. This neglect is in large part a by-product of the general disdain for both metaphysics and medieval philosophy that infected mainstream Anglo-American philosophy for the first several decades of this century. Yet this antimetaphysical bias cannot be the whole story; for despite the recent reawakening of interest in medieval metaphysics among some prominent analytic philosophers, Suarez's metaphysical writings have still not received the attention they merit. And in fairness to non-Catholic philosophers, it should be pointed out that Suarez has received short shrift even from Catholic philosophers during the scholastic revival that began in the late nineteenth century under the inspiration of Pope Leo XIII's encyclical *Aeterni Patris*, reached its zenith in the middle decades of the twentieth century, and is even now showing signs of vitality despite having been repudiated by many academically influential Catholic intellectuals.

The net result is that both inside and outside the tradition of Aristotelian scholasticism, few of today's English-speaking philosophers have read even small chunks of the *Disputationes Metaphysicae*. Indeed, not counting the present volume, only six of the fifty-four disputations have thus far been published in English translation.[3]

There are, however, some hopeful signs that this deplorable situation is being rectified, albeit slowly. To begin with, over half the disputations that have been translated into English have appeared within the last ten years or

---

dealt with most thoroughly in the six books of the tract *De Anima*, which is found in Suarez's commentary on *Summa Theologiae* 1.

3. See Bibliography for a list of these translations.

so—this in large measure due to the efforts of Jorge J. E. Gracia. In addition, discussions of Suarez's distinctive contributions to various metaphysical debates have become somewhat more frequent in the scholarly literature.

Even more encouraging is the increasing attention being paid to Suarez by Anglo-American scholars working on early modern philosophy. All things considered, this should come as no surprise. Earlier this century Etienne Gilson argued convincingly that Descartes's philosophical writings can be understood deeply only against the backdrop of the scholastic influence on his thought, an influence that stemmed in large measure either directly or indirectly from Suarez. A similar case can be made, to greater or lesser degrees, for other important seventeenth- and eighteenth-century philosophers and scientists.

The Systemic Importance of the Disputationes Metaphysicae

Still, I do not mean to give the impression that Suarez's importance for contemporary philosophers is exhausted by the promise that a close reading of the *Disputationes Metaphysicae* will help us to understand better the writings of one or another late medieval or early modern philosopher. For despite some lean times of late, Aristotelian metaphysics is far from dead. Indeed, for those of us who think of ourselves as Aristotelians in some broad but substantive sense, the recent history of mainstream Anglo-American philosophy has been, relatively speaking, a joy to behold. Across the board—in ethics, epistemology, and metaphysics—philosophers have articulated and defended positions that can justifiably be described as Aristotelian, whether or not their authors have always recognized them as such.[4] This is not to say, of course, that the positions in question have gained widespread acceptance. Nonetheless, after decades of what, from an Aristotelian perspective,

---

4. In ethics I have in mind, e.g., the writings of Alasdair MacIntyre, beginning with his ground-breaking book *After Virtue* (Notre Dame, Ind.: University of Notre Dame Press, 1981). The best example in the area of analytic epistemology is Alvin Plantinga's newly published 2-vol. work *Warrant* (New York: Oxford University Press, 1993), in which a central role is played by the teleological notion of proper cognitive functioning. In metaphysics, Elizabeth Anscombe and Peter Geach have championed Aristotelian conceptions of substance and causality, while Peter van Inwagen's important book on substance, *Material Beings* (Ithaca, N.Y.: Cornell University Press, 1990), has about it a distinctly Aristotelian aura, as does Nancy Cartwright's *Nature's Capacities and their Measurement* (Oxford: Clarendon Press, 1989), which has to do with scientific explanation and causal action in nature. Another notable contribution, this in the area of philosophy of mind, is David Braine's *The Human Person: Animal and Spirit* (Notre Dame, Ind.: University of Notre Dame Press, 1993).

can only be seen as the regrettable, even if by no means fruitless or unin-
structive, domination of Anglo-American philosophy by movements deeply
inimical to the classical metaphysical traditions, Aristotelianism of various
stripes has attained at least a modicum of respectability—something that
would have seemed highly unlikely just twenty years ago.

A case in point is the very topic of the three disputations presented here:
namely, efficient causality. Today it is not at all uncommon to find typically
Aristotelian notions such as agency, power, tendency, disposition, impediment, interference, and *de re* causal necessity insinuating themselves into the
discussion of causality and scientific explanation—and this in both of the
(relatively independent) branches of that discussion, that carried on among
metaphysicians and that among philosophers of science. To be sure, in many
cases the full import of the use of these notions is not well understood—
mainly because in our self-proclaimed "post-positivistic" philosophical era,
many philosophers still cling, oftentimes inadvertently, to deep-seated posi-
tivistic presuppositions. But this is just where a close study of Suarez on
efficient causality might prove to be beneficial in opening up new conceptual
vistas.

So in presenting this translation of Suarez's treatise on efficient causality,
I hope to contribute to the current resuscitation of Aristotelian metaphysics.
Of course, like the other parts of the *Disputationes Metaphysicae*, Disputations
17–19 are dense and difficult and chock full of intricate arguments of the sort
that those with antimetaphysical proclivities have always been fond of ridi-
culing. Still, for anyone who sees a deep congruence between the perennial
pursuit of wisdom and close metaphysical analysis, these disputations are a
veritable treasure chest. And for those of us sympathetic to Aristotelianism,
they offer a systematic background against which to try to present a broadly
Aristotelian metaphysics more convincingly to present-day philosophers.

Description of Disputations 17, 18, and 19

In order to situate Disputations 17–19 within their proper context, I will
first present an outline of the *Disputationes Metaphysicae* that will help make
clear the overall structure of the work. The individual disputations are designated in parentheses, with asterisks to indicate those disputations currently
available in English translation.

   I. The nature of metaphysics (1)
   II. The transcendentals: being and its attributes (2–11)
       A. Being (2, 3)
       B. One (4, 5˙–7˙)

Of the six disputations dealing with efficient causality, the first triad (17–19), contained in the present volume, is concerned mainly with creaturely efficient causality, while the second triad (20–22) deals with the three modes of God's efficient causality: namely, creation, conservation, and general concurrence. Disputations 17–19 constitute, as far as I know, the longest, most profound, and most thorough tract ever written on creaturely efficient causality from an Aristotelian perspective. Let me briefly describe each of these disputations.

Disputation 17, entitled "On the Efficient Cause in General," provides a general characterization of efficient causality and its various modes. In section 1 Suarez expounds and modifies Aristotle's definition of an efficient or agent cause as that "whence there is a first beginning of change or rest," carefully distinguishing the efficient cause from the other three Aristotelian causes: namely, the formal, material, and final causes. He concludes that an efficient cause is an extrinsic *per se* principle that communicates *esse*, or being of some sort, to an effect by the mediation of an action. In section 2 Suarez goes on to discuss the main divisions of efficient causes: namely, (i) *per se* versus *per accidens*, (ii) physical versus moral, (iii) principal versus instrumental, (iv) univocal versus equivocal, and (v) primary versus secondary. Along the way he also makes some illuminating remarks about the important distinction between agent causes or principles properly speaking and the *sine qua non* conditions required in order for those agents to exercise their causal power.

Disputation 18, entitled "On the Proximate Efficient Cause and on its Causality and on All the Things that it Requires in order to Cause," deals with the metaphysics of creaturely causation in general and especially with the efficient causality proper to material substances and their accidents. Section 1 contains Suarez's reply to occasionalism and other theories that either deny that material substances are efficient causes at all or else severely limit the general range of effects that can be produced by them. Sections 2–6 treat general metaphysical issues concerning the efficient principles involved in the production of new substances and accidents. Then in sections 7–9 Suarez discusses the three most disputed *sine qua non* conditions for efficient causality: namely (i) the condition that the thing acting (agent) be distinct from the thing acted upon (patient), (ii) the condition that the agent be spatially proximate to the patient, and (iii) the condition that the agent be initially dissimilar to the patient. Having completed his treatment of the principles and prerequisites of efficient causality, he next (section 10) takes up the ontological question of what it is that formally constitutes a substance or accident as an actual efficient cause. Finally, in section 11 he lays out the metaphysics of destructive or corrupting efficient causality.

Disputation 19, entitled "On Causes that Act Necessarily and Causes that Act Freely or Contingently; also on Fate, Fortune, and Chance," turns to issues concerning causal necessity and contingency. In sections 1–3 Suarez gives a precise characterization of the distinction between causes that act by a necessity of nature and causes that act without necessity; in addition, he takes up the disputed question of whether there could be any causal contingency in the created world if, contrary to fact, God acted only by a necessity of nature. Sections 4–9 go into great depth on the nature of free choice and include an extended treatment of controversial issues surrounding the relationship between intellect and will in free action. Finally, sections 10–12 take up a series of questions concerning fate, fortune, and chance.

On the Translation and Notes

The copy of the *Disputationes Metaphysicae* I have used in preparing the translation is a reprint (Hildesheim: Georg Olms, 1965) of volumes 25 and 26 of Carolo Berton's edition of Suarez's *Opera Omnia* (Paris, 1866). Disputations 17–19 occupy 166 double-columned pages of volume 25, specifically pages 580–745. For ease of reference, within the translation itself I have included page and column designations from the Berton edition; for instance, the designation /592b/ indicates the second column on page 592. The Berton edition, including Berton's own suggested revisions, is generally regarded as eminently reliable, though in certain problematic spots I have consulted the Latin text published with the seven-volume Spanish translation of the *Disputationes Metaphysicae* made by Sergio Rábade, Salvador Caballero, and Antonio Puigcerver (Madrid: Biblioteca Hispanica de Filosofia, 1960–66). When I depart from the Berton text, whether or not in ways consistent with Berton's own suggested emendations, I indicate this by means of asterisks appended to the words in question. Interpolated words and phrases are bracketed only when their appropriateness is not wholly obvious. As a general rule, I have tried to minimize the use of brackets.

As for Suarez's references to the works of other authors, I have adopted the following conventions. The titles of Greek works, along with ancient and medieval commentaries on those works, are rendered in English. When a work of Aristotle's is cited with some other author, the reference is to that author's commentary on the relevant Aristotelian work. The titles of Latin works that are not commentaries on Aristotle are retained in the original language—the lone exception being commentaries on Peter Lombard's *Sentences*, which are signalled simply by the English title *Sentences*. When St. Thomas's *Summa Theologiae* or *Summa Contra Gentes* is cited with another author, the reference is to that author's commentary on St. Thomas's work. Lastly, for the sake of convenience, references to an author's quodlibetal questions are given under the title *Quodlibeta*.

In keeping with the general policy set for the Yale Library of Medieval Philosophy, I have kept the notes to a minimum. Most of them involve simple cross-references to other sections of the *Disputationes Metaphysicae*, while a few are explanatory in nature. In most of the cross-references the first number designates the disputation, the second the section, and the third the subsection. So, for example, *DM* 23. 4. 5 refers to Disputation 23, section 4 subsection 5. In cross-references to other places within the current section and disputation, the first number refers to a subsection and the second (if any) to a paragraph within that subsection. So, for instance, §6, par. 3 refers to the third paragraph of subsection 6 of the current section and disputation.

Alfred J. Freddoso

On Efficient Causality

Disputation 17

On the Efficient Cause in General

Now that we have considered the material cause and the formal cause, which are intrinsic causes, we have to follow this up with a discussion of the extrinsic causes: namely, the final cause and the efficient cause. Even though the final cause is considered the prior and more noble of these extrinsic causes, nonetheless, the efficient cause's causality is better known to us and should thus be discussed first.

It is unnecessary to ask whether this sort of cause exists, because this was adequately proved above when we discussed how many causes there are[1] and also because nothing is more evident or better known through experience. For the transmutations and generations that we have experience of cannot be brought about except by some effecting thing that is a cause of both the transmutation and the effect, since nothing can bring itself from not existing to existing. Therefore, assuming that this genus of cause exists in reality, we must ascertain what it is, what its causality consists in, and what

1. See DM 12. 3.

it requires in order to be able to cause. However, since within this genus there are many species and modes of causes, we will first explain, in general, what this cause is, how many kinds it subsumes under itself, and what is common to all of them. After that, we will discuss one by one, to the extent that we judge expedient for the full treatment of this subject matter, each of the species of efficient cause and their various modes of causing.

Section 1

What an Efficient Cause Is

1. *Aristotle's definition; what the genus is in this definition.* In *Metaphysics* 5.2 [1013a29–32] and *Physics* 2.3 [194b29–32] Aristotle defines the efficient cause in general, claiming that it is that "whence there is a first beginning of change or rest." This definition needs a lot of interpretation and supplementation to be reduced to a true sense, so that it might encompass every efficient cause and make clear the causality proper to an efficient cause.

First of all, there seems to be nothing occupying the genus-place in the definition. For the term 'whence', which Aristotle posits by itself, is not properly posited in the genus-place and is exceedingly ambiguous as well, since both the time and the place can be said to be that 'whence' a motion begins. For this reason, the term '*per se* principle' must, it seems, be supplied in the genus-place. However, lest it appear that a truism is being conveyed by the claim that an efficient cause is a *per se* principle (*principium*) whence there is a first beginning (*principium*) of motion, one will have to say that an efficient cause is a *per se* principle /581a/ from which a change first exists or comes to exist. So it follows that Aristotle's description implicitly contains the genus '*per se* principle', by means of which the efficient cause can be defined.

2. *The sense in which the definition is fitted just to the thing defined.* But then a second difficulty arises, since the definition so expounded applies to the other causes as well. For within its own genus the matter is a *per se* principle of change and rest. Nor is it sufficient to reply that the matter is excluded by the term 'first'. For even though the formal cause can be excluded by that term (since in fact it is not a first principle of change but is rather the terminus of a change, in view of which we claimed above that the form is properly a cause not of the generation but of the thing that is generated[1]), nonetheless, the material cause is not excluded by that term. For within its own genus the material cause concurs just as primarily with respect to a change as the efficient cause does, and so it is also a *per se* principle whence a change first begins.

Perhaps someone will assert that even though, with respect to some effect-ings, the matter causes the change simultaneously with the efficient cause, still, if one compares the material and efficient causes absolutely, the latter

---

1. See *DM* 15. 7.

is prior because the matter itself must be brought into existence before it is a cause. However, this point is irrelevant in the present context, since the priority in question is remote and has to do with another action that Aristotle made no mention of; nor is it clear whether he even knew of it.[2] Hence, this priority is, as it were, accidental as regards the matter's concurrence with the efficient cause in a natural change. The point in question, then, is not sufficient to exclude the matter's causality. Otherwise, the secondary efficient cause would be excluded as well. For a secondary efficient cause is not first, absolutely speaking, with respect to any effecting, since it itself must first be effected.

To resume, there are two possible replies. One is that even though in reality a natural change is simultaneously from both the efficient cause and the material cause, nonetheless, the efficient cause's influence is conceptually prior to that of the material cause. Hence, to speak in accord with the precise formal concepts, the passion is from the action, and not vice versa, and so "Because the agent acts, the matter receives" is a true and proper causal locution.[3] By contrast, it will not be proper to say that the agent acts because the matter receives. So it is in this sense that in comparison to the matter the efficient cause is said to be first in the nature of causing.

Second, one may reply that the matter is excluded by the term 'whence', since, strictly speaking, this term signifies a relation to an extrinsic principle. For the matter is a cause of the change by virtue of the fact that it receives that change intrinsically within itself and sustains it within itself, whereas the agent is a principle of the action or change solely by virtue of the fact that the action or change emanates from the agent /581b/ and bears an essential relation to the agent as to an extrinsic principle on which it depends. And it is this proper concept and relation that is made manifest by the term 'whence' (a term equivalent to the phrase 'from which'), which is properly attributed to the efficient cause. For the material principle is, by way of contrast, that 'out of which'. Hence, for the sake of greater clarity, the efficient cause could be said to be a *per se* extrinsic principle from which a change first exists.

2. Suarez has the action of creation *ex nihilo* in mind here.

3. The term 'passion' (*passio*) is being used here in the sense in which it corresponds to the Aristotelian category of *being acted upon*. In every instance of efficient causality that involves a subject or patient being acted upon, there is an accidental entity, viz., a passion, which exists in the patient for the duration of the agent's action. Suarez himself claims that in such a case the very same accidental entity, *A*, existing in the patient, is both (i) the action, insofar as *A* is emanating from the agent, and (ii) the passion, insofar as *A* is being received in the patient. Suarez insists that this accidental entity is distinct from all the following: the agent itself, the power being exercised by the agent, the patient itself, and the effect being produced in the patient. See *DM* 49. 1.

3. *How the end is excluded by the definition.* But then a third difficulty occurs, since the definition thus clarified applies to the final cause rather than to the efficient cause. For the end is a *per se* and extrinsic principle, and it is prior to the efficient cause in causing, inasmuch as the efficient cause does not act unless it is moved by the end. This is why the final cause is commonly said to be the first among all the causes.

However, because the influence of the final cause is exceedingly obscure, especially with respect to physical and real change, one may reply succinctly that even if the final cause is prior in the order of intention, the efficient cause is nonetheless first in execution. Indeed, it is the efficient cause alone that really has an influence—that is, effects motion—*per se* and extrinsically. And it is in this way that the aforementioned definition should be understood—a point which the term 'whence' or '*from* which' makes sufficiently clear. For the end is a principle or cause '*for the sake of* which' a change comes to exist or '*toward* which' it tends. But it is not properly called a principle '*from* which' or 'whence' an action first emanates; instead, this is said most properly of the efficient cause.

4. *Whether this definition applies to both the First Cause and secondary causes.* But a fourth difficulty occurs immediately, since the definition does not embrace every efficient cause:

(i) For, from what has been said, the definition seems to apply only to the First Cause, since the First Cause alone is that whence every change first begins; or else it applies at most to a principal cause but not to an instrumental cause or to a faculty that is a proximate principle of acting. For an instrument does not act unless it is moved; that is, it does not act except in the power of a prior agent; and so one cannot claim that an instrument is that whence a motion first exists.

(ii) What's more, from another perspective, the definition does not seem to apply to the First Efficient Cause as regards his first and most powerful type of efficient causality, which is through creation. For creation is not a change.

As for the first point, one should reply that the phrase 'whence a motion first begins' should not be taken to mean a first principle absolutely speaking—that is, a principle that is altogether independent and has no prior cause. Otherwise, as the argument concludes, the definition would apply only to the First Mover—that is, to the First Efficient Cause. Instead, the phrase in question should be taken to mean the first principle within a given order of causing /582a/ or within a given genus of causing. Hence, a secondary cause is called a first principle whence a motion exists by reason of the fact that a motion arises from it first within the genus of proximate causes; and thus it is that Aristotle posits the example of a father with respect to his son. Now some think, along with Alexander of Aphrodisias, that instrumental causes are excluded by the phrase "whence the motion first begins," because they are not causes properly speaking. But since Aristotle gives the example of an advising cause, which seems to be even more improper, and concludes in general that the definition applies to every efficient or transmuting cause, one should, it seems, say instead that he meant *every* mode of efficient cause, as Scotus observed, and that each cause has within its own order the nature of a principle from which an action first exists—either as from a principal principle or as from an instrumental principle or as from a perfecting and executing principle or as from an advising or expediting principle.[4] Therefore, the term 'first' is added only in order to exclude completely *per accidens* causes, which do not in any way have a proper influence on the action, or in order to indicate the efficient cause's proper mode of causing and to distinguish the efficient cause from the material and formal causes, which are not first causes in the way that the efficient cause is, as was explained above.[5]

As for the second point, if we examine Aristotle's intentions, it does indeed seem that he defined only the natural efficient cause, which always acts through motion or change. For in *Physics* 2 Aristotle was discussing only natural causes, and yet in *Metaphysics* 5 he did not add anything at all either to the definition or to his doctrine concerning the efficient cause. Nonetheless, in both places he did suggest that, *mutatis mutandis*, the definition can be extended to every efficient cause. This is why, in giving examples, he said: "For example, one who advises, and a father with respect to his son, and, in a word, that which effects with respect to that which comes to exist, and that which produces change with respect to that which is changed" [1013a29–32]. Therefore, if we replace the words 'change or rest' with the word 'action', the definition will encompass every efficient cause, even the First Efficient Cause insofar as he creates. For, as we will see below,[6] creation, too, is an action, even though it is not a change.

5. *How it is not the case that what is being defined is itself contained in the definition.* But from this another difficulty springs up, since it seems that what is

---

4. An advising cause of an effect E is, roughly, a rational agent who, by means of counsel, inducement, provocation, request, persuasion, threat, command, prohibition, etc., influences another agent to contribute freely to E. An advising cause of E "seems to be [an] even more improper" cause of E than an instrumental cause, because its efficacy with respect to E is mediated by a distinct action on the part of a free agent—whereas, according to Suarez's argument below in section 2, an instrumental cause attains directly to its effect.

5. See §2.

6. See *DM* 20. 1.

defined in this way is somehow being posited in the definition. For according to the explication just given, an efficient cause will be a *per se* principle from which an action first exists. But it is equally unclear what an action is. Indeed, an action is almost the same [as an efficient cause] and stands in need of the same sort of explication, since an action and an effecting are the same thing. Thus, it is because of an action that something is called an efficient or agent cause. Therefore, to define the efficient cause /582b/ in terms of the action is to define the same thing by means of itself or to explain the obscure by means of the more obscure.

What's more, the cause has to be defined in terms of the effect, since they are correlatives. But the action is not the efficient cause's effect; instead, it is the very nature of the causing, as I will explain below.[7]

Nonetheless, one should reply that since the action is related to the agent in the manner of a form, there is nothing wrong with explaining the nature of an agent in terms of its relation to an action.[8] Aristotle, for his part, used the noun 'change' because it is better known to us, inasmuch as through this noun we understand, in the case of each thing, its emanation from or dependence on that principle from which it receives *esse*.[9] Hence, even though, as we will see below,[10] an action's proper nature and its distinctness from the agent and from the effect are rather obscure, nonetheless, in the present context it is sufficient to understand by the term 'action' the effect's emanation from and dependence on that extrinsic cause from which it is receiving *esse*. For in this sense, speaking vaguely and generally, it is utterly obvious that there is in the effect a dependence on or emanation from its principle, whatever that dependence or emanation might be.

6. Therefore, even though the action is not the agent's effect, still, because the action is a path to the effect—that is, the effect's dependence on the agent—the effect is sufficiently included or indicated within the action itself. For

7. See *DM* 18. 10.

8. To say that the action is related to the agent in the manner of a form is to say that it is by virtue of the action that the relevant substance is constituted as an agent or efficient cause—in a manner analogous to that in which a given entity is constituted as, say, an aardvark by a substantial form of the appropriate type.

9. Suarez takes the core notion of efficient causality to involve the communication of some sort of being (*esse*) to a substance by an agent via an action. He speaks of the communication of *esse* rather than of the communication of form (or formal perfection) in part because this leaves conceptual space for a sort of efficient causality—viz., creation *ex nihilo*—in which the effect is not just a formal perfection inhering in a preexistent subject but is instead the being of *all* the constituents, material as well as formal, of a given substance.

10. See *DM* 18. 10; and 48. 1–5.

to say that an efficient cause is a first principle whence an action exists is the same as saying that it is that whence the effect exists by means of an action; that is, the same as saying that it is a principle from which the effect flows forth, or on which it depends, through an action.

The difference between the efficient cause and the other causes is also correctly expressed in this locution. For the matter and the form, speaking *per se*, do not cause by means of an action; instead, they cause by means of a formal and intrinsic union. The end, on the other hand, causes only by means of a metaphorical motion insofar as it is an end.

The efficient cause, by contrast, causes by means of a proper action that flows from it. And in this it is also included that the efficient cause does not give its own proper and formal *esse* to the effect, but instead gives another *esse* that emanates from it by means of an action. In this the efficient cause differs from the formal and material causes, because the latter cause their effect by giving to it their own proper being, and this is why they are called intrinsic causes. The efficient cause, on the other hand, is an extrinsic cause, that is, a cause that does not communicate its own proper and (as I will put it) individual *esse* to the effect but instead communicates to it a different *esse*, which really flows forth and emanates from such a cause by means of an action.

From these considerations, then, both Aristotle's definition and the thing itself—namely, what an efficient cause is—are sufficiently clear, as is the way in which the efficient cause differs from the other genera of causes. All this will be grasped more precisely when we explain each of the particular things that come together for this sort of causality and are required for it. /583a/

Section 2

The Types of Efficient Causes

1. Since the term 'efficient cause' extends very broadly and is attributed to many things quite loosely and by a sort of imperfect analogy, whereas, even though it is attributed to other things properly, it is nonetheless attributed to them according to various modes of causing, it follows that before we proceed any further, we must first lay out the various divisions of this cause, an understanding of which requires that we keep before our eyes the definition already given. For there will be differences among the causes corresponding to the diverse ways of participating in that definition.

PER SE CAUSE AND *PER ACCIDENS* CAUSE

2. *The various modes of* per accidens *causes*. A first division of efficient causes can be made into *per se* causes and *per accidens* causes; this division is proposed by Aristotle in the places cited above. A *per se* cause is a cause on which the effect directly depends for the proper *esse* that it has insofar as it is an effect, in the way in which (says Aristotle) a sculptor is a cause of a statue. And because only this sort of cause is a cause properly and absolutely speaking, almost the whole of the next disputation will be concerned with it alone. On the other hand, since a *per accidens* cause is not a true cause but is instead called a cause because of some relation or similarity to a cause or because it is conjoined with a cause, it cannot be appropriately defined by a single general description; rather, a cause is called *per accidens* in various senses. For a cause is called *per accidens* sometimes on the side of the cause and sometimes on the side of the effect.

That which is said to cause *per accidens* on the side of the cause is something that is accidentally conjoined to a *per se* principle of causing. Sometimes this is the subject itself of the form that is the principle of acting.[1] It is in this sense that water is said to produce heat *per accidens*, since it is accidental to water that it should be hot and thus accidental to it that it should produce

---

1. In §6 below, Suarez draws a distinction between the principle *quod*, which is the substance or suppositum that acts, and the principle *quo*, which is the power by which the substance acts. A cause is *per accidens* on the side of the cause to the extent that its connection with the relevant power is accidental rather than essential.

heat.[2] "And it is in this sense," Aristotle says, "that Polycletus is a cause of a statue" [*Metaphysics* 5.2.1013b34–1014a4]. In some cases, however, the thing in question is a second form that is accidentally conjoined to the first form in the same subject—I mean that it is accidental that it should be related to the power of effecting, regardless of whether the two forms are conjoined necessarily in some other sense. This is the sense in which a singer writes *per accidens* and in which what is white produces heat *per accidens*, and so on. However, Aristotle adds that this latter sense is looser or more remote than the former, since a concomitant form contributes nothing at all to the effect of another form, whereas the subject of a form, given that it at least sustains that form within itself, does seem to contribute something. He adds further that these *per accidens* causes /583b/ can be designated both particularly and generally (that is, as in a species or genus)—as, for example, in '*This* white thing is producing heat' or '*Some* white thing is producing heat'. Likewise, they can be expressed either simply or compositely—as, for example, in 'The *singer* is building' or 'The *singer Polycletus* is building'. But these points pertain more to modes of predicating than to modes of causing, and since they are *per accidens*, they can be multiplied ad infinitum according to the various modes of conceiving and of speaking.

3. *A problem is resolved.* The only thing that one can have doubts about is why, given that actions belong *per se* to supposita, Aristotle says that an action is attributed *per accidens* to the suppositum of the [relevant] form.[3]

I reply, first of all, that an action is *per se* from the suppositum as affected by a given form but not necessarily from the suppositum taken in itself; and this is why what is hot produces heat *per se*, whereas water does not. I then add, however, that an action is attributed accidentally to the suppositum when, in addition, the power of acting is in it accidentally, as in the example just given. For in such a case the power of acting is in no way contained in the suppositum taken just by itself, and so the action is conjoined to it accidentally in every way. On the other hand, if the power of acting is in the suppositum *per se*, then even if the suppositum is mentioned just by itself, it

2. To understand this example and others that appear later, one should note that the characteristic primary qualities of the four elements are as follows: water—coldness and moistness; fire—heat and dryness; air—heat and moistness; earth—coldness and dryness. Hence, apropos the present example, water is naturally apt to be cold, and so it is accidental to it that it should be hot.

3. A suppositum is an ultimate bearer or subject of characteristics. Even though there are theological cases in which it is important to distinguish between suppositum and substance, in almost all the cases with which Suarez is concerned here, the acting suppositum is simply the substance that is exercising a power inherent in it.

will not be called a *per accidens* cause of the action but will instead be called a *per se* cause of it. And this is why I insist that the propositions 'The sun gives light' and 'Fire produces heat' are *per se* in the fourth mode of *per se* predication found in *Posterior Analytics* 1.4 [73b10–15]. For 'fire' fundamentally and implicitly includes the proper notion of producing heat.[4]

You will object: "In that case the proposition 'A human being is making a statue' is *per se*—which is contrary to what Aristotle says." Some will reply that this proposition is not *per se* because it is contingent and not necessary. But this is irrelevant to *per se* causality or (what amounts to the same thing) to the fourth mode of *per se* predication. For it is also the case that the propositions 'The singer is singing' and 'The fire is producing heat' are not necessary, and yet they are *per se* in the fourth mode. Hence, as far as causality is concerned, I insist that the following are *per se*: 'An animal is moving itself', 'A human being is thinking', 'A human being is talking', and so on. On the other hand, 'A human being is making a statue' is instead *per accidens*, because even if the craft in question cannot exist except in a human being (I exclude the intelligences[5]), nonetheless that craft is absolutely accidental to a human being. Hence, 'human being', uttered by itself, does not include that craft except in potentiality—a very remote potentiality.

4. *Causes that are* per accidens *on the side of the effect.* It is also customary in some cases for a cause to be designated as *per accidens* on the side of the effect, i.e., with respect to that which is accidental to the *per se* effect. And in this sense a *per se* cause of a given effect is itself a *per accidens* cause of that which is conjoined to the *per se* effect—in the way in which a motion is a cause of heat /584a/ or in which a hot thing is a cause of something black. This is also the sense in which things that happen by chance or by fortune are said to have a *per accidens* cause—as, for example, that someone who is digging should discover a treasure.

However, as regards this genus of *per accidens* causes one should note, first, that in some cases the effect is called *per accidens* with respect to the confluence of certain causes even though, given that confluence, the effect in question emanates *per se* from such a cause. For example, it is accidental that while the rock is falling, Peter happens to be moving in just that direction; yet, given this confluence, the rock's striking him with its force and producing such and such a wound is an effect that proceeds *per se* from the active force of the rock. And so in such a case the rock will not be called a *per accidens* cause of the effect except with respect to the confluence in question

4. The fourth mode of *per se* predication occurs when a natural or essential connection is asserted to obtain between a substance and some effect brought about by that substance.

5. The intelligences are purely spiritual creatures—i.e., angels.

or, again, except with respect to the intention of the one who is moving. But we will have more to say below about effects that are *per accidens* in this sense when we discuss chance and fortune.[6]

Again, one should note that when an effect is called *per accidens* by reason of the fact that it is conjoined to a *per se* effect, there are two possible ways in which it can be called *per accidens:* in one way, with respect to the agent's intention alone; in another way, with respect to the action itself as well and with respect to the connection of the one effect with the other. For it is possible for an effect not only to fall outside the agent's intention but also not to be connected in any way with the agent's action—as, for example, that one who is digging in the ground should discover a treasure. And in such a case the cause and the effect are *per accidens* in the most proper sense.

In some cases, however, the one effect is connected by its nature with the other effect, even though it falls outside the agent's intention. For example, the corruption of one thing is necessarily conjoined by its nature with the generation of another; yet it falls outside the natural agent's intention, and for this reason it, too, is commonly called a *per accidens* effect—though not in as proper and absolute a sense as in the previous case. For to the extent that [the corruption] is connected necessarily [with the generation], it is in some sense *per se*. An indication of this is that there can be scientific knowledge and demonstration with respect to it. Indeed, since within the genus of a given disposition the privation of the contrary form is, as it were, a necessary means for the introduction of the relevant form, one can claim that the effect in question does not fall altogether outside the agent's intention. For even though this effect is not intended for its own sake, it is nonetheless in some sense intended for the sake of the principal end, and so, as far as the present discussion is concerned, we are not counting effects of this sort among those that emanate from a *per accidens* cause. Hence, all such effects either (i) have more to do with the type of predication than with causality, as when one says 'The doctor is curing the singer' /584b/ (and almost all the examples adduced above are of this sort), or else, to be sure, (ii) are traced back to chance and fortune, which we will discuss below.[7]

5. *Whether the conditions required for acting are* per accidens *causes.* In addition to the above two senses, it is also common to number among the *per accidens* causes certain conditions, necessary for acting, which do not have a *per se* influence on the effect or the action: for example, the proximity of the agent to the patient, the removal of an impediment, and any other similar condition that is customarily called a *sine qua non* condition. However, even

6. See DM 19. 12.
7. Ibid.

though such a condition is *per accidens* with respect to proper and direct causality, it is nonetheless in some sense *per se* with respect to physical necessity
and insofar as it falls under scientific knowledge. And so these necessarily
required conditions will have to be treated below in their own right.[8]

I note only that because a *sine qua non* condition of this sort agrees with
a *per se* principle of action in being necessarily required, in some cases it is
not easy to discern in which of these two ways a given disposition or property of a thing concurs with respect to an action, that is, whether it concurs
as a *per se* principle or only as a *sine qua non* condition. Sometimes this can
be known on the basis of the general nature or mode of the property in
question. For instance, we readily discern that proximity is only a condition,
since it is only either a relation or a mode of presence, which by their very
genus are nonactive. And in the same way we infer that shape and density
are not *per se* principles of actions but are at most conditions required for
certain actions or for the rapidity and manner of such actions. Sometimes,
on the other hand, this is less clear and has to be ferreted out on the basis
of some argument that is peculiar to the thing under discussion—as is the
case with the familiar question of whether the cognition of an object is only
a necessary condition for the appetitive faculty's effecting its own motion or
whether it is also a *per se* coefficient principle. For neither of the two positions can be established by a definitive [general] argument, and so one must
appeal to special considerations derived from the particular subject matter.

However, two general points should be noted here. One is that whenever
(i) it is obvious from experience that a given property is necessary for an
action and (ii) a sufficient reason for that necessity can be given only by
appeal to proper and *per se* causality, then one should not take refuge in a
sine qua non condition; instead, this is a sufficient indication of some sort
of *per se* efficient causality. A very good example of this has to do with the
necessity of an impressed species for an act of seeing. For no such species
can be understood to be sufficient unless one posits /585a/ a *per se* efficient
causality, and so it will be incorrect to say that this species is a *sine qua non*
condition.[9] By contrast, when a sufficient reason for the necessity of such a

8. See *DM* 18. 7–9.

9. An act of seeing is the act of a passive or receptive material power—viz., the faculty
of sight—and occurs by a necessity of nature in the appropriate circumstances. Suarez's
point here is that the impressed sensory species that results from the modification of the
optical faculty by the object cannot be thought of as a mere occasion for an act of seeing
that object but must instead be thought of as making a genuinely causal contribution to
that act. More specifically, the species itself actuates the power of seeing. In the next example, by contrast, the relation between a cognitive act with respect to a given object and

condition can indeed be given without appealing to *per se* efficient causality, then it will be readily discernible that the condition in question is only a *sine qua non* condition—especially if some other cause has a power that is suitable enough to be seen as sufficient for effecting the action. Perhaps this is the way it is with the aforementioned example that had to do with a cognition's being required for eliciting an appetitive act—this is discussed elsewhere.[10] So much for the first division of efficient causes.

PHYSICAL CAUSE AND MORAL CAUSE

6. *What is meant here by the term 'physical cause'; the sense of 'moral cause' that is relevant here; the two ways of acting associated with physical causes.* Second, efficient causes can be divided into physical causes and moral causes. In this context 'physical cause' does not mean a corporeal or natural cause that acts by means of corporeal and material motion; instead, it is being taken more generally for a cause that has a true and real influence on the effect. For just as we claimed above that in some cases the term 'nature' signifies any essence whatsoever, so, too, sometimes the term 'physical influence' is used for that which is effected through true, real, proper, and *per se* causality. And in this sense God is a physical cause when he creates, and an angel is a physical cause when he effects a motion in the heavens or even within himself, and the intellect is a physical cause when it effects an act of understanding, and the will is a physical cause when it effects a volition, and so on.

On the other hand, there are two senses in which a cause can be called a morally efficient cause. For sometimes a cause is called a moral cause solely because it acts freely, and in this sense a moral cause is not altogether distinct from a physical cause when the latter is taken in the general sense that we have explicated; instead, a moral cause will be distinguished from a physical cause that acts naturally and necessarily. For in this sense the will, when it loves freely, is a true and physical cause of its own love, which it nonetheless effects morally—that is, freely.

However, 'moral cause' is taken in another sense according to which a moral cause is altogether distinct from a physical cause, and it is predicated

---

a consequent appetitive act with respect to that same object is more obscure, especially where these are acts of the rational soul. The difference is that the appetitive power is not merely a passive or receptive power but is instead capable of moving itself. Hence, it is not outlandish to claim in this case that the cognition of the object is merely an occasion for, rather than a cause of, the object's being desired or willed.

10. See *DM* 18. 8. 40.

of a cause that does not truly effect anything *per se* but that behaves morally in such a way that the effect is imputed to it. This is the sense in which an advising cause or an imploring cause or a cause that does not prevent something when it can and should prevent it is called a moral cause. And it is in this second sense that we are now taking 'moral cause', so that a cause that truly effects something is being called a physical cause, whereas a cause that effects something only by imputation is being called a moral cause. It follows that if we consider these things from a physical or metaphysical point of view, then this division is reduced to the previous division into *per se* causes and *per accidens* causes. For 'cause which truly effects something physically' is predicated only of a *per se* cause, whereas a cause which causes only morally or by imputation is, when considered from a physical point of view, /585b/ only a *per accidens* cause, since it does not have a real and *per se* influence. Thus a moral cause is always either (i) a cause that does not prevent something when it can and should prevent it or else (ii) a cause that applies or induces a *per se* cause, whether by means of advice or entreaties or payment or sometimes even by means of local motion, as when someone applies fire to a house. For even though the individual in question is a *per se* physical cause of the motion itself, he is nonetheless only a *per accidens* cause of the burning.[11] But this latter causality, which is *per accidens* from a physical point of view, is regarded as *per se* from a moral point of view and by imputation. Therefore, we do not have to say any more about the moral cause taken in this sense. For to the extent that it is *per accidens* from a physical point of view, it does not fall under scientific knowledge, whereas to the extent that it is *per se* within the genus of morals, the treatment of it pertains to moral science and not to metaphysics.

Now a physical and true cause can act in one of two ways, either naturally or freely—that is, either necessarily or contingently. We will discuss these two modes of acting below, since they are especially relevant to explicating (i) the perfections and natures of diverse causes, (ii) the sequence of and connections among the effects in the universe, and (iii) the First Cause's mode of influencing—that is, concurring with—secondary causes.[12] On the other hand, the treatment of morality, which deals with free acts insofar as they are free, belongs not to the present science but rather to moral philosophy or, better, to divine theology.

11. In such a case the arsonist does not have any intrinsic power to incinerate the house but instead uses or applies something—viz., the fire—that does have this power. Nonetheless, the arsonist is *per se* or directly responsible, morally speaking, for the house's destruction.

12. See esp. *DM* 19. 1–4.

PRINCIPAL CAUSE AND INSTRUMENTAL CAUSE

First Explanation

7. Third, true and proper efficient causes are divided into principal causes and instrumental causes. The use of these terms is usually very ambiguous and equivocal. For this reason, their signification has to be explained carefully.

A principal cause is commonly said to be a cause to which an action is attributed properly and without qualification. However, this description does not sufficiently clarify the matter. For, first of all, a thing's form—for example, a soul—is in some sense a cause, and, as is obvious, it is not an instrumental cause. Therefore, if the division in question is adequate, then a soul is classified as a principal cause. And yet action is not properly attributed to it, since a soul, as Aristotle said, does not properly act'.[13] Therefore, the description in question does not apply to every principal cause. For, as the argument just given makes clear, there is one sort of principal cause which operates and another sort which is a principal principle of operating—they are commonly called, [respectively], a principal cause *quod* and a principal cause *quo*.[14] But the description given above applies at most to the former of these causes and not to the latter.

Indeed, /586a/ one could object further that this description does not apply to every cause *quod* but applies instead only to a proximate and particular cause and not to a universal and first cause. For as will become clear below, principal efficient causes are divided into first causes and secondary causes: that is, into universal causes and proximate causes; and both of these are principal causes. Indeed, the first cause is a more principal cause than the secondary cause, and yet the effect is attributed properly and without qualification not to the first cause but to the secondary cause. For when a human being walks or sees or understands, it is not the case that God is said to walk or see or understand, even though he effects those motions more principally than the human being does.

However, this objection is not very persuasive, since the effects of secondary causes can in fact be properly and truly attributed to the First Cause. For "it is neither he who plants nor he who waters that matters; rather, it is God who gives the increase" [1 Corinthians 3:7]. Thus, even though the earth brings forth verdant vegetation, it is nonetheless attributed to God that he "produces grass for the cattle and vegetation for the use of men" [Psalm

---

13. Suarez may have in mind here *On the Soul* 1.4.408b1–18.

14. As noted above, a principal cause *quod* is the suppositum that acts, whereas a principal cause *quo* is the power by which the suppositum acts.

104:14], and that he forms the fetus in the womb, and, in short, that he effects all our works, as we will explain in more detail below.[15] Now the reason why denominations such as 'sees' and so on are not attributed to God is that they are not derived from efficient causality as such but are instead derived from a thing's being informed by and receiving the motion or act that belongs to the effect. For not just anyone who brings about an act of seeing in any way whatsoever is said to see; rather, it is the one who acts in such a way that he is informed by the act of seeing. Indeed, it is from this latter relation that the denomination 'sees' is mainly derived—so much so that if this relation were able to perdure in the absence of efficient causality (or at least in the absence of a principal efficient causality), it would be sufficient for that denomination. Therefore, there is no doubt that, as far as efficient causality as such is concerned, the effect can be truly and properly attributed to every principal cause that operates as a principle *quod*.

8. *Whether the agent's absolute denomination is attributed to an instrument.* This leads to a more serious problem, since [the description in question] does not seem peculiar to the principal cause.[16] For in some cases [the effect] is attributed [properly and absolutely] to the instrumental cause, as is evident from theological examples. For a man is said to consecrate, to absolve, and so forth, even though he does these things only as an instrument.[17] Among natural things, moreover, the semen is properly said to dispose the matter and to effect the generation by means of that disposing.[18] And the reason seems to be that the denomination in question is properly attributed to a suppositum that operates, and so if an instrument happens to be a suppositum that is in some way operating *per se*, then the action can be attributed to it, too. For if water, even though it is only a *per accidens* cause, is properly and without qualification said to produce heat merely because it is a suppositum that sustains the principle of producing heat, then is it any wonder that /586b/ an action is attributed to a human being (or other suppositum) even if the latter has only an instrumental power of operating?

But to this argument one can reply that the denomination in question is never attributed to a cause except by reason of some sort of principalness (as I will put it) which it has in the given operation. For example, it is attributed

15. This is the topic of *DM* 22.

16. The "description in question" is that a principal cause is a cause to which the effect is attributed properly and without qualification.

17. The man in question being the priest who administers the sacraments of the Holy Eucharist, confession, etc.

18. The shared assumption here is that the semen is the instrument of the agent that generates a member of the same natural kind.

to a man that he consecrates or absolves and so on because (i) in performing the external actions whereby the effects in question come to exist, he is
operating as a principal cause, and because (ii) this same cause operates as
one who has dominion over his own actions. The semen, on the other hand,
is not properly said to generate; nor is it even properly said to organize or
dispose the matter, except to the extent that by its own power it is able to
effect some antecedent thing—and in this it behaves as a principal agent.
Finally, the water is said to produce heat not *per se* but *per accidens*, and so
this example is beside the point, since we are talking here about *per se* attribution. What's more, this *per accidens* denomination itself has a basis in
the fact that the water, insofar as it subsists and insofar as it sustains the
principle of producing heat, behaves as a principal operator.

So, then, absolutely speaking, it is peculiar to a principal cause that the
action and effect should be attributed to it. And this point could be proportionately accommodated to both an agent *quod* and to a principle of acting
quo—to the former insofar as it operates and to the latter insofar as it is a
principal principle of operating.

One can also add that 'principal cause' is predicated without qualification
of a cause that operates as a principle *quod*, whereas it is predicated of a
principle [of operating] only by reduction and *secundum quid*. And so it is
sufficient for the description [of a principal cause] to be accommodated to a
principle in the same way. Therefore, the definition in question can be sustained in this manner, though it does not make clear the precise reason why
the effect is attributed without qualification to the principal cause—despite
the fact that it is just this that the proper notion of a principal cause would
seem to consist in.

Second Explanation

9. Alternatively, a principal cause is commonly said to be a cause that influences the effect by its own power or else a cause that influences the effect by
a sufficient power; that is, a cause which, given the concurrence owed to it,
is sufficient to produce the effect.

However, the proper and adequate nature of a principal cause does not
seem to be made sufficiently clear by any of these ways of talking. For to
influence the effect by one's own power belongs not only to a principal cause
but also to an instrumental cause—especially among natural instruments,
whatever the case might be with other instruments. For natural heat, which
is an instrument for converting food into the substance of the one who is
nourished, has a natural and innate power with respect to that action; and,
similarly, if the heat of a fire is an instrument for introducing /587a/ the
substantial form of fire, it has a proper and intrinsic power with respect to

that instrumental action. For it is not able to act without a proportionate power, and it does not have that power as an extrinsic or adventitious power. Therefore, it has it as an innate and proper power.

And if someone claims that [the heat] has this power, to be sure, but that it has it [only] as an instrumental power, [our reply is that] this is just what we are asking about: namely, what the heat lacks, as far as the notion of a principal principle is concerned, given that it has been shown to operate by its own power.

Nor does what was added in the second formulation about a sufficient power seem necessary. For, first of all, just as the heat is not sufficient by itself to introduce the form of fire, so neither is the fire's form sufficient by itself in the absence of the heat; therefore, by the same argument the form will not be a sufficient principle. Second, principal causes have to be divided further into total causes and partial causes, and both of these are distinguished from instrumental causes. But a partial cause does not operate by a sufficient power; therefore, it is not in this that it is correctly distinguished from an instrumental cause. Further, when it is said that the power of a principal cause has to be sufficient, this may mean that it has to be sufficient within every genus or order of sufficient causes. But this is false; otherwise, no secondary cause would be a principal cause, since no secondary cause is absolutely sufficient. Indeed, even the First Cause would not be a principal cause in those cases in which it concurs with a secondary cause, since in such cases it does not operate by itself as a sufficient *per se* cause.[19] On the other hand, if what is meant is that the power is sufficient within its own genus, then even an instrumental cause is sufficient within its own order. Therefore, the proper notion of a principal cause is not made adequately clear in this way.

Finally, that which is added concerning the concurrence owed to a principal cause does nothing to clarify the matter any further, both because (i) the need for concurrence does not apply to every principal cause but applies only to every secondary cause and also because (ii) such concurrence is owed not only to a principal cause but also to an instrumental cause. For concurrence is owed to heat both for producing heat and for producing fire, if it is

---

19. The topic of God's general concurrence with secondary causes is treated in *DM* 22. The point is that when God operates as a general concurring cause, his causal contribution to the effect is not sufficient by itself to produce the effect, since this would render the secondary cause's contribution superfluous. Note that this claim is compatible with the thesis that any entity produced by God in cooperation with a secondary cause could have been produced by God alone without any secondary cause. However, when God produces an entity by himself, he acts as a particular—rather than a general—cause.

a sufficient heat. Therefore, none of these ways of speaking seems either to clarify adequately the notion of a principal cause or to distinguish a principal cause from an instrumental cause.

Third Explanation

10. In light of these considerations, there is another possible way of speaking, according to which a principal cause is a cause that influences the effect (or the form that constitutes the effect) proximately and by its own proper influence. This position becomes clearer if we immediately add the definition of an instrumental cause and the difference between the two. An instrumental cause will be a cause which does not immediately attain to the effect (or form) by its own action but instead /587b/ attains to some antecedent thing from which the form in question results, a form that the instrument does not attain to proximately and in itself. From this it follows that every instrumental cause is a principal cause with respect to some effect—namely, that effect which it attains to proximately and *per se*—whereas it is an instrumental cause with respect to another effect which results therefrom.

This is clarified by examples. First, among artifacts: A saw, for instance, is an instrument for making a given artifact. By striking the middle parts [of the wood] and moving them locally, this instrument proximately effects only a division [of the wood] and is related to this effect more as a principal cause. But what results from this is the form of the artifact, to which the saw is related as an instrumental cause. For it does not attain to this form immediately by its own action; rather, the form merely results from the prior effect.

Next, among natural things: A fire's heat is an instrument for [producing] the [substantial] form of fire, since it immediately attains to the heat, which it is related to as a principal cause. But what results from this is the substantial form [of fire], which, according to the plausible opinion of Scotus and others, the heat does not attain to immediately.

Finally, among supernatural things: According to the opinion of Paludanus, Capreolus, and others, the sacraments are called instruments of grace because they do not attain to the grace itself but instead attain to something antecedent to it. Hence, this way of speaking can be justifiably attributed to these authors with regard to the first˙ and second˙ examples cited above— examples which St. Thomas seems rather well-disposed toward in *Summa Theologiae* 1, q. 45, a. 5, when he says that a secondary instrumental cause does not participate in the action of a higher cause except to the extent that, by means of something proper to itself, it operates dispositively with respect to the principal agent's effect. And the reason that can be given is that an instrument's concurrence is always imperfect, and so it does not pertain to an instrument that it should itself immediately attain to the induction of the form with respect to which it is an instrument; rather, what pertains to it is only that it should, by acting, prepare the way for that form. Thus, conversely, every cause that immediately attains to the form will be a principal cause and not an instrumental cause.

11. *Instruments attain to the form intended by the principal agent.* However, this position cannot be proved. For, first of all, it is false that an instrumental cause as instrumental never attains immediately and in itself to the form intended by the principal agent.

This is clear, first of all, from an induction contrary [to the one given above]. For, among supernatural things, the sacraments are instruments for effecting grace by virtue of their attaining in themselves to the grace. And, similarly, through the actions of his human nature, Christ immediately attained to the supernatural works that we discussed at length /588a/ in *Summa Theologiae* 3, vols. 1 and 3.[20]

Again, among natural things, it is more plausible to claim that accidents, as the instruments of substances, immediately attain to the eduction of a substantial form. It is also a plausible opinion that a phantasm instrumentally attains to the production of an intelligible species, and yet it does not attain to anything antecedent [to the species]; instead, it immediately attains in itself to the very species.

Finally, among the instruments of a craft, it seems that in some cases the form of the effect is proximately attained to through the form of the instrument, as, for example, when a similar shape is imprinted by means of a seal on wax or on a coin—although even in such a case what is really effected *per se* is not the shape but a "where," whatever Scotus means by this in the text cited below. Thus, one may claim more generally that even though it is true that such instruments do not attain *per se* to the shape or form of the artifact, still, this is not because they concur instrumentally but rather because that sort of form is not producible *per se* in any other way. Hence, not even the principal agent itself induces it in any other way. For it effects *per se* only the motion's local terminus, which is a "where," and it effects the motion in a manner and sequence which is such that the relevant shape results from it. Therefore, in this sort of action the principal and instrumental agents cannot be distinguished from one another by whether they attain to the effect mediately or immediately. In fact, if we consider the terminus that

---

20. Here and below, any reference to the *Summa Theologiae* which is attributed to an author other than St. Thomas, including Suarez himself, should be taken as a reference to that author's commentary on the *Summa Theologiae*. A similar point holds for St. Thomas's *Summa Contra Gentes* (or *Contra Gentiles*).

is produced *per se*, which is a "where," then it is the instrument that seems to attain to it more immediately. For a painter does not effect a color except by means of a brush, and so on for the other cases. But the ultimate form or shape is not attained *per se* by any other action; instead, it results from the prior terminus.[21]

12. This point is further clarified by an argument. There are three modes in which an instrument can be thought of as concurring with respect to the principal agent's effect: either (i) merely remotely—namely, by attaining to something antecedent to the effect—or (ii) merely proximately—namely, by attaining immediately to the form intended by the principal agent—or (iii) in both these modes at once. But the notion of an instrument is not limited to the first mode, even if an instrument can sometimes concur in that mode. Therefore, an instrument is not correctly distinguished from a principal agent by appeal to that mode of attaining to the effect.

The minor premise of this argument is sufficiently clear from the examples adduced above. Also, one can argue that even if an instrument's concurrence is of a lower type, nonetheless, because an instrument attains *per se* to the effect not by itself alone but rather insofar as it is aided and strengthened by the principal agent, there is nothing absurd in the claim that an instrument immediately attains to the principal agent's effect. Hence, in *Summa Theologiae* 3, q. 77, a. 3, ad 3, and q. 79, a. 2, ad 3, St. Thomas says: "Nothing prevents an instrumental cause from producing an effect which is higher and goes beyond its own species." /588b/ The foundation for the contrary position is destroyed by this argument.

Nor does St. Thomas disagree with us in the other place cited above;[22] it is rather this very position that he is endorsing. For he does not claim that an instrument concurs only dispositively with respect to the principal agent's effect; instead, he claims that an instrument participates in the principal agent's action only by means of its own action. The Thomists infer from this that every instrument has two actions: (i) one action by which it does something proper to itself, an action in which it does not fully play the role of an instrument, and (ii) a second, properly instrumental action by which it immediately influences the principal agent's effect. In *Contra Gentes* 2, chap. 21, Ferrariensis contends that these actions are always really distinct from one

21. The general point here is that the form of an artifact results from various instances of local motion, where each such motion involves the instrument's occupying a series of particular places. Hence, the motion of the saw (or the seal) has a series of places as its immediate *per se* effects, and the new shape taken on by the wood (or wax) is a concomitant effect resulting from that motion.

22. The reference here is to *Summa Theologiae* 1, q. 45, a. 5.

another. However, in *Summa Theologiae* 1, q. 45, a. 5, Cajetan claims more correctly that this is not necessary, since in some cases there is only a single action within which we distinguish conceptually or for the sake of convenience between something that the instrument can attain to in its own right and something that it attains to as an instrument. Still, both authors agree that, as far as the present topic is concerned, an instrument, insofar as it is an instrument and through the action that it exercises as an instrument, attains immediately and *per se* to the principal agent's effect to the extent that this effect is attainable or producible *per se*. And, indeed, there is hardly any other way to preserve the notion of a natural instrument—except improperly and by extrinsic denomination, as I will explain below.[23] Scotus also inclines toward this position in *Sentences* 4, dist. 1, q. 1.

Fourth Explanation

13. There is a fourth possible way of speaking, according to which an instrumental cause is a cause that acts only insofar as it is moved by another, whereas, by contrast, a principal cause is a cause that has the power to operate through itself and without the motion of another. This explanation seems to be derived from the things we know by experience in the case of the instruments of a craft. For these things are better known to us, and in their case there is no other mode of operating.

Hence, in *Contra Gentes* 2, chap. 21, arg. 4, St. Thomas claims that an instrument is never used to cause anything except by way of motion, since it is part of the notion of an instrument that it should be a moved mover. And in argument 5 he claims that an instrument lies between the principal cause and the effect in such a way that the principal agent's efficacy reaches the effect by means of the instrument's motion. There are those who, dissenting sharply from the third way of speaking discussed above, infer from this that when the principal cause and the instrumental cause concur simultaneously, /589a/ (i) the effect is attained to more immediately by the instrumental cause than by the principal cause—more immediately, I mean, by an *immediacy of suppositum* (as they put it), since the principal agent does not act except through the instrument—whereas (ii) the principal agent is said to act more immediately by an *immediacy of power*, since the instrument does not act except in the power of the principal agent.

And on this basis the present position is confirmed by the following argument: An instrument as such does not act except in the power of the principal agent. But an instrument cannot in its operating depend on the power of the principal agent except by virtue of the fact that it is moved by the principal

23. See *DM* 18. 2.

agent. Therefore, the notion of an instrumental cause is correctly explicated by appeal to the fact that an instrumental cause acts insofar as it is moved by another, and, consequently, a principal cause will be a cause that does not need the motion of another in order to act.

14. *Whether an instrument takes any motion from the principal cause.* However, this position, too, fails to clarify the matter fully; nor is it satisfactory. For when it is said that an instrument acts insofar as it is moved by another, there are two senses in which this can be understood. In one sense, it is taken to refer to a real motion or change that is received in the instrument itself and is antecedent to its action. And this is how the proposition in question is understood by Ferrariensis in *Contra Gentes* 2, chap. 21.

However, taken in this sense, the proposition cannot be universally true—indeed, it is hardly true except in the case of the instruments of a craft, which are applied to their operations by means of local motion. By contrast, among natural instruments the proposition is not true at all. For if a phantasm is an instrument, then what action does it antecedently receive within itself in order that it might act? Does it receive within itself some spiritual light? But this is spurious and plainly repugnant to a material subject. Likewise, a fire's heat is its instrument for generating fire, and a vital heat (that is, a nutritive power) is an instrument for producing flesh; yet in these instruments no real antecedent motion is conceivable. Likewise, semen is called an instrument of the one that generates; but once it is separated, it receives no new motion from the principal agent. (I leave aside supernatural instruments, which I have discussed at length in *Summa Theologiae* 3, q. 13 and q. 62.)

Next, I add that not all things that are moved movers act as instruments in the proper and strict sense; rather, some of them act as principal agents, at least as partial principal agents. For certain things do not produce alterations unless they themselves are altered. For example, a pepper does not produce heat unless it is heated, and yet it produces heat not only through the power it receives but also through its own proper and innate power, which is an eminent power with respect to producing heat.[24] Hence, in this it behaves as a principal agent. Likewise, a man does not move a staff except by moving his hand; but even though the hand is for this reason commonly said to be an instrument—or, rather, an instrument for instruments, that is, an instrument antecedent to instruments, /589b/ as Aristotle says in *On the Parts of Animals* 4.10 [687a20]—nonetheless, it is in fact a partial principal mover, since it has within itself a partial power of pulling or pushing or

24. The pepper is not itself hot but nonetheless is capable of producing heat under certain circumstances. Because of this, it is said to have an eminent (as opposed to formal) power for producing heat.

elevating. Hence, in such cases the one thing's motion is oftentimes only a necessary condition for the pulling or pushing of some other thing—which is not enough to revoke the notion of a principal agent and induce the proper notion of an instrument. Indeed, even a celestial body (as many claim) does not effect motion unless it is moved, and yet it does not effect motion as an instrument—more on this below.

And so it is incorrect to distinguish an instrumental cause from a principal cause by appeal to the notion or status of being a mover that is moved through a real change received within itself. For not all instruments are moved in this way to act, and it happens that some principal causes are moved in almost the same way in which some instruments happen to be moved. An indication of this is that the instruments of a craft require some motion even in order to do what they are capable of doing by their own power, and the only thing that happens because of the craft is that the motion in question is effected in an orderly fashion.

15. *Whether creatures should be called God's instruments.* To resume, there is a second sense in which an instrument can be said to act as moved by another: namely, insofar as it is subordinated to that other or insofar as it takes the place of that other or, again, insofar as it is aided by the principal agent in ways corresponding to the various types of instruments that will be explained below.

And, to be sure, it is true in this sense that every instrument acts insofar as it is moved by another (if it is still permissible to speak in this way). However, this feature is not peculiar to an instrument taken in the strict sense, in the way that we are now talking about an instrument and distinguishing it from a principal cause; to the contrary, this feature is common to every lower principle of acting and to every cause except the First Cause.

For, first of all, all secondary agents act as moved by the First Cause— that is, act with the concurrence and assistance of the first cause, as we will explain below[25]—and yet they are not, properly speaking, instruments but are instead principal causes within their own genus. I realize that a few of the older authors sometimes call secondary causes the instruments of the First Cause, as is clear from St. Thomas, *De Potentia*, q. 3, a. 7, where he concludes in this way: "So, therefore, God is a cause of every action insofar as every agent is an instrument of the divine power operating." The same thing is found in *Summa Theologiae* 1, q. 105, a. 5. And in his own *Physics*, chap. 9, Damascene speaks in the same way when he says that this is the teaching of Plato, whom he insists should be preferred on this point to Aristotle. In *Physics* 1, text 29, Simplicius says the same thing.

25. See *DM* 22.

This is why in *Sentences* 4, dist. 1, q. 1, reply to the question, Scotus says that there are two ways in which a cause may be said to operate principally. /590a/ First, it may operate principally in the sense that it operates independently, and in this sense secondary causes are not principal causes but instrumental causes. Second, it may operate principally in the sense that it operates through a proper and intrinsic form; and he claims that in this sense secondary causes are principal causes. Even though, in saying this, he does not adequately explicate the notion of a principal cause, he is nonetheless correct in claiming that secondary causes are principal causes. And within Aristotle's doctrine it is certain that they should be called principal causes, as is seen in the places already cited from *Physics* 2 and *Metaphysics* 5. What's more, it is clear from the very meaning of the terms that operating principally and operating independently are not the same thing.

Therefore, in order for a cause to be a principal cause, it is not necessary that it be altogether independent. And, conversely, the fact that a cause is dependent and requires the assistance of another higher cause is not sufficient for its being an instrumental cause. Further, the intellect is commonly thought of not as an instrument but as a principal principle of its own natural acts, and so too with the will and other similar faculties, even though in acting they are subordinated to their forms. It is true that all these faculties (indeed, all accidents as well) are called instruments by some—and correctly so, if by the term 'instrument' they mean any principle of operating *quo* that exists not for its own sake but insofar as some suppositum makes use of it. But this is not correct if we are speaking in a strict sense about instrumental causes and actions. For heat is not, properly speaking, an instrument for producing heat, since the effect does not exceed the perfection of the principle or cause.

The Correct Explanation

16. *Various acceptations of the term 'instrument'.* Therefore, since the difficulty with this topic seems to depend in large part on the use of the terms, it follows that in order not to be laboring under equivocation, we must distinguish the significations of those terms. And to begin with 'instrument' or 'instrumental cause', an instrumental cause can in one sense be distinguished from a cause that is principal antonomastically: that is, from a cause that operates altogether independently, as Scotus said.[26] And in this sense

---

26. Antonomasia is a figure of speech in which an individual is designated by invoking a paradigm instance of a relevant class, as in "The speaker, Jones, was a veritable Cicero." So, too, a cause that acts altogether independently is a cause *par excellence.*

the general distinction between the two components [of the division in question] is an easy one. However, I am not now speaking in this way, since I take this manner of speech to be improper.

Second, an instrumental cause can be said to be any cause or power that is given to a thing in order that the thing might operate through it. In this sense even the [substantial] form can be called the suppositum's instrument—though, by reason of the fact that the form essentially constitutes the suppositum itself, this instrument is not 'used' by the suppositum. Still, 'instrument' so taken is predicated of every other power that is added to a suppositum; indeed, it is sometimes predicated even of integral parts, /590b/ especially organic parts such as a hand or an arm. It is in this sense that theologians call Christ's human nature the Word's conjoined instrument—though this is said more properly in relation to his miraculous and supernatural actions than in relation to the actions that are connatural to his human nature. And every power or principal of acting that is given to an operating suppositum in order that the latter might act through it is called an instrument in this second sense, even if the power in question is sufficient for and just as perfect as, or even more noble than, the effect. By contrast, a principal cause, in the sense opposed to an instrumental cause so taken, will be the very suppositum which operates insofar as it has the power to operate through itself (that is, through its own substance) or through its own form.

Again, in a third sense an instrument is said to be that which takes the place of another in order to execute an action—even if it should happen that such an instrument is more noble than the action or effect toward which it is aimed. In this sense gravity is commonly called an instrument of that which generates, and impetus is called an instrument of the thrower. And thus a principal cause, in the sense correspondingly opposed to this sort of instrument, will be the cause that the instrument takes the place of. It is in moral matters that this sort of instrumental cause—that is, ministerial cause—is most frequently invoked.

17. Lastly, and in the most proper sense, an instrumental cause is said to be a cause that concurs in, or is elevated to, the production of something more noble than itself; that is, something beyond the measure of its own proper perfection and action—for example, heat insofar as it concurs in producing flesh and, in general, an accident insofar as it concurs in producing a substance.

There are many who have doubts about this sort of instrument—not only among natural things but also among supernatural things—when they speak, as we are now speaking, about instruments that are truly effective and that physically attain to the higher effects themselves. One can see this in Scotus and others, *Sentences* 4, dist. 1. We will deal with this matter at greater length in the next disputation, when we discuss the efficient cause of substances.[27]

We ourselves, however, assume that there can be instruments of this sort within every order of things: (i) with regard to natural things, we will show this in the place just cited; (ii) with regard to supernatural things, we discussed it in *Summa Theologiae* 3; and (iii) with regard to artifacts, everyone admits it—even though in such cases, as I have explained, the form that is principally intended by the craftsman is not attained to *per se* and immediately by the instrument but instead [merely] results [from the instrument's action]. Still, the form, in whatever way it might come to exist, in some sense exceeds the power of the instrument considered in itself and is effected by the instrument insofar as the latter is directed and moved by the craft.

Thus, it is in this proper and strict sense that we are understanding an instrument when we distinguish it from a principal cause. /591a/

18. And so a principal cause will be a cause which through a principal power—that is, a power that is more noble than, or at least as noble as, the effect—influences the action whereby such an effect is produced. And it is not only the First Cause but also secondary causes, both univocal and equivocal, that are included under the name and notion of a principal cause in this sense. Further, this notion applies not only to a total cause but also to a partial cause, as long as the latter is operating by a similar power. For 'partial cause', properly speaking, expresses a relation to a co-partial cause of the same type and order—a relation such that neither of them is subordinated to the other, but instead the two coalesce into a single total principal cause of that same order which is composed of those causes as parts. And so each of the two is a principal cause, albeit a partial principal cause.

. Further, a principal cause in this sense is correctly said to operate by its own power, not only because it has an intrinsic and innate power to act but also because it has a power that is *per se* proportionate to the effect and does not stand in need of any elevation. And even though a cause of this sort sometimes requires the concurrence of a superior cause, this is because of the general nature of a participated being and not because of any special lack of proportionateness vis-à-vis the effect. Hence such a cause needs only the concurrence that is owed to it by reason of its own perfection.

19. *The sense in which an instrument is said to operate in the power of the principal agent.* On the other hand, an instrumental cause, in the sense corresponding to a principal cause so taken, is a cause that influences the effect through a power of a lower nature or perfection, as was made clear by the argument

---

27. See *DM* 18. 2.

and the examples above. This sort of cause is said to operate "in the power" of the principal agent, though not because it does not require any intrinsic power (that is, power existing within it) for its instrumental action—whether this power be innate or else added to the thing or whether it be permanent and such that it endures when the action ceases or else is fluid (as they put it) and such that it exists [just] in the motion. For such power can be found in various modes in the various sorts of instruments, and yet some such instrumental power is necessary. Otherwise, no action at all could proceed from the thing in question, as Scotus correctly noted in the place cited above and as I explained at length in *Summa Theologiae* 3, vol. 1, disp. 31, q. 6. Rather, the reason why these instruments are said to operate in the power of the principal agent is that the power that exists within them is not proportionate or sufficient, and the instrument has the ability to operate only according to the measure of the principal agent's power and elevation. Hence, the concurrence or elevation in question is not owed to the instrument properly or because of itself; rather, it is owed only to the principal agent or only by reason of the principal agent.

And on this interpretation all the difficulties mentioned in the other explanations disappear. /591b/ Indeed, many of the things asserted in those explanations, with the exception of the third explanation, are restored to a coherent sense.

FIRST CAUSE AND SECONDARY CAUSE

20. On this basis it is easy to grasp the other divisions among efficient causes, which are subdivisions of the aforementioned types. For, fourth, the efficient cause is divided into first cause and secondary cause.[28] Now if we speak loosely, then it is efficient causes in general that can be divided here, since every cause that depends on another—be it a principal cause or an instrumental cause—can be called a secondary cause. However, if we speak more strictly, then it is principal causes that are being divided here. For there is one sort of cause that operates altogether independently, and this is called a first cause, and there is another sort of cause that is dependent, even if it operates by means of a power that is principal and proportionate, and this is called a secondary cause.

Now it is absolutely evident that both types of causes exist in reality. For if one grants that among real things there are principal causes that depend

28. On Suarez's view, even though it is true that there can only be one First Cause, this truth requires an argument and is not built explicitly into the very definition of a first cause.

on another in operating, then from this component of the division the other
component is necessarily inferred. For one cannot proceed to infinity among
dependent causes, and thus we must stop at some independent cause. We
will pursue this in more detail below, when we demonstrate that God exists.[29]
On the other hand, if one admits an independent cause, then once again the
other component of the division is necessarily inferred, since it cannot be the
case that all causes are independent; indeed, there can be only a single such
cause, as we will demonstrate at length below when we treat the actions of
the First Cause and when, further on, we discuss God's uniqueness.[30]

We will say nothing further about this division here, since almost the
whole of our discussion of the efficient cause will be devoted to its two
components.

UNIVOCAL CAUSE AND EQUIVOCAL CAUSE

21. *Instrumental causes are not equivocal causes.* Fifth, causes can be divided
into univocal causes and equivocal causes. This, too, can be a partition of
causes in general if we call instrumental causes equivocal causes. However,
this manner of speaking is improper and goes beyond common usage, as
St. Thomas noted in *Sentences* 4, dist. 1, q. 1, a. 4, q. 1, ad 4, drawing from
Alexander and from the Commentator in *Metaphysics* 11, comment 24. Therefore, it is principal causes that are being divided here, and they can, to be
sure, be divided in general, since the First Cause is also an equivocal cause.
However, since the First Cause is assumed to be not only an equivocal cause
but also a cause of an altogether different order, it follows that the division
in question is more appropriately applied to proximate principal causes.

Now there are some causes that produce an effect of the same type, and
these are called univocal causes: for example, fire when /592a/ it generates
fire. And, in general, a cause which, operating through the power of its own
form, produces a similar effect is a univocal cause as well as a principal cause
within its own order, as St. Thomas correctly notes in *Summa Theologiae* 3,
q. 62, a. 4. On the other hand, there is another sort of cause that produces
an effect of a different type. This sort of cause has to be more noble than
the effect—otherwise, it would not be a principal cause but an instrumental
cause—and it is called an equivocal cause, since it does not formally agree
with the effect in the same form but instead contains that form eminently.

29. See *DM* 29.

30. God's actions are treated in *DM* 20–22, while his uniqueness is argued for in *DM*
30. 10.

Again, principal causes can also be divided into causes that act˙ by a necessity of nature and causes that act with freedom. Likewise, they can be divided into those that act through motion or change in a presupposed subject and those that act without motion or change and in the absence of a subject. However, these divisions are contained in the above divisions, and they merely clarify the aforementioned causes' determinate actions or modes of operating—all of which will have to be discussed in detail below.

CONJOINED INSTRUMENT AND SEPARATED INSTRUMENT

22. Sixth, one should also take note of the division of instrumental causes or instruments into conjoined instruments and separated instruments. There is commonly a great deal of equivocation in these terms, and so one should pay careful attention to the fact that there are two possible ways of understanding what it is for an instrument to be conjoined to a principal agent (for it is with respect to the principal agent that an instrument is said to be conjoined or separated): namely, either *secundum esse* or *secundum causalitatem*.

What I am calling a conjoined instrument *secundum esse* is an instrument that is united to the principal agent in some way or other, whether through contact or through some sort of presence or through some real union—in the way that a writing pen, say, is a conjoined instrument. By contrast, the opposed separated instrument will be an instrument that is not conjoined to the principal agent in any way—as, for example, semen after it has been separated. And corresponding to the various modes of conjunction and separation there can be some latitude and variation in these terms.

What I am calling a conjoined instrument *secundum causalitatem* is an instrument that requires the principal agent's actual and proper influence and causality in order to cause—in the way that, once again, a writing pen is a conjoined instrument. Hence, the corresponding separated instrument will be an instrument that in its action does not require the principal agent's special influence and causality. And in this sense, if heat is called a fire's instrument for producing heat, then even though it is conjoined to the fire *secundum esse*, it can be called a separated instrument *secundum causalitatem*, since in order to produce heat, it does not require an influence over and beyond its own proper power. /592b/

It follows that sometimes an instrument can be conjoined in the first sense but separated in the second, as is clear from the example just given. And, conversely, the sacraments are called separated instruments—*secundum esse*, of course—of Christ's human nature as it exists in heaven, and yet they are probably conjoined instruments *secundum causalitatem,* since they cannot effect anything unless Christ has an actual influence along with them through his human nature. Sometimes an instrument can be conjoined in both senses—for example, an act of seeing or an impressed species; sometimes an instrument can be separated in both senses—for example, the gravity of what is generated with respect to that which generates. All these things are obvious as long as the terms are understood.

The only remaining substantive difficulty is how there can be such a thing as a separated instrument *secundum causalitatem,* speaking now of an instrument properly and strictly in accord with the last sense of 'instrument' explained above. For the answer is clear if 'instrument' is taken broadly for a power that is *per se* sufficient for the effect and that takes the place of the cause that impresses it on the instrument—for example, the impetus of projectiles, gravity, and so on. However, in a proper instrument, which has to be elevated in order to produce a higher effect—for example, semen—this is extremely difficult to understand. But a treatment of this matter presupposes many points that have to be explained beforehand—points that will be dealt with in the following disputations.

Disputation 18

*On the Proximate Efficient
Cause and on Its Causality
and on All the Things That It
Requires in Order to Cause*

Virtually the only thing we explicated in the preceding disputation was the nominal definition of an efficient cause and of its various species and modes. Now we have to discuss in a precise way all the things that pertain to this sort of cause under the headings or questions we touched upon with the other causes: What is it that causes? What does it cause? By means of what— that is, by what principle—does it cause? What conditions does it require in order to cause? Lastly, what does the actual causality of this cause consist in?

Now all these questions could be discussed with reference to efficient causes in general. However, it seemed to us to be in the interests of greater clarity to investigate all of them first with reference to created causes, which are better known to us, and only afterwards to treat the First and Uncreated Cause and then the dependence of the other causes on it. Still, we are not separating the discussion of the efficient cause of substances from that of the efficient cause of accidents, since, as we will see, they are connected in such a way that the production of substances /593a/ is effected only by means of accidents. And for the same reason we are not separating the treatment of principal causes from that of instrumental causes, since when we discuss the proximate efficient cause, to which an action is attributed *per se* and properly, we must ascertain at the same time which principles or which instruments it uses in producing the effect.

Section 1

Whether Created Things Really Effect Anything

1. *Various opinions; D'Ailly a stranger to the first opinion.* In this matter there was an old position which asserted that (i) created things do nothing but that instead God effects all things in their presence, whereas (ii) action is attributed to fire, water, and so on because of the appearances and because God has resolved, as it were, to produce certain effects only in the presence of such things.

This opinion is mentioned by Averroës in *Metaphysics* 9, comment 7, and *Metaphysics* 12, comment 18; by Albert in *Physics* 2, tract 2, chap. 3; and by St. Thomas in *Contra Gentes* 3, chap. 69, in *Summa Theologiae* 1, q. 105, a. 5, and in *Sentences* 2, dist. 1, q. 1, a. 4—though there is no particular author whom they cite on its behalf. However, Philo seems to lean toward it in *Allegoriae* 2 when he says, "God is the only efficient cause," and in *De Cherubim et Flammeo Gladio* when he says, "Acting is proper to God, whereas being acted upon is proper to a creature." But these words could easily be understood as antonomasia,[1] as could the other passages concerning God's action that we will cite below from the philosophers.

The opinion in question is also commonly attributed to Peter D'Ailly in *Sentences* 4, dist. 1, a. 1, at the end. However, in that place he says explicitly that secondary causes truly and properly act by their own power and in reality, and not just by God's will. To be sure, he adds that it is also true that a creature effects nothing unless by God's will and unless God himself effects it as well—indeed, unless God also brings it about that the creature itself acts and, consequently, unless God does more than he would if he were acting by himself. These claims have to do with the necessity for God's concurrence and can have a true as well as a false sense, as we will see below in a special disputation.[2]

It is instead Gabriel who is well-disposed toward this opinion in *Sentences* 4, dist. 1, q. 1, a. 3, dub. 3, where he judges this position to be plausible. And in support of it he adduces these words from 1 Corinthians 13: "God does all in all," as well as these from 2 Corinthians 3: "Not that we are sufficient to think anything on our own, as if it were from ourselves; rather, our sufficiency is from God." Nonetheless, he does not venture to assert this position himself.

1. For an explanation of antonomasia, see DM 17. 2, n. 26.
2. See DM 22.

2. *Arguments for the preceding position.* I do not see a foundation for this position that carries any weight. /593b/ Yet its principal foundation seems to have been that to whatever extent efficient causality is attributed to the creature, to that extent the divine power of the creator is diminished. For either God does everything, or he does not do everything. The latter detracts from the divine efficacy, and for this reason we will show below that it is altogether false and erroneous, since it implies that something exists without depending on God. But if God does everything, then I ask again whether he does it immediately and by means of a sufficient power or only mediately and by means of a power that is not sufficient. The latter detracts from the divine perfection. But if the former is true, then any other efficient causality is superfluous, since one sufficient and efficacious cause is enough to produce the effect. Thus, since "nature does nothing in vain,"[3] it has not conferred on created things any power to operate.

And I confirm this as follows. Anything that God might be assumed to bring about along with a secondary cause, he is able to bring about by himself alone (for at least this much pertains to his infinite power, as will become clear below[4]); therefore, he in fact brings it about by himself alone. The consequence is evident both from the fact that (i) this is more becoming to the divine power and efficacy and especially from the fact that (ii) this seems necessary in order for a creature to come to exist.

I prove this last point as follows. A creature has an essential dependence on God alone, since it cannot come to exist without him, and it can come to exist without anything else. Therefore, a creature cannot exist without this essential dependence that it has on God alone, since it cannot exist without those things that are essential to it. Therefore, every creature exists through a dependence on God alone. Therefore, it exists through the efficient causality of God alone, since efficient causality and dependence are either the same thing or correlatives. Therefore, no creature has efficient causality with respect to another creature, and, consequently, no creature is a secondary cause that effects anything.

3. *The second position.* The second position denies that corporeal creatures can effect anything but concedes that spiritual creatures can. St. Thomas refers to this position in the places cited above, drawing from Avicebron in *Fons Vitae*, where the latter claimed that no bodies are active but that a certain power belonging to a spiritual substance and existing deep within the bodies effects all the actions which appear to be effected by the bodies.

His argument seems to have been that the agent has to be intimately

---

3. See Aristotle, *Physics* 2.8.

4. See *DM* 30. 17.

present to the patient but that bodies cannot be present to one another in this way because quantity impedes the sort of intimate penetration of one thing by another that an action requires. Hence, he claimed that quantity is not only nonactive but that it even impedes action.[5]

And this is confirmed by the fact that a corporeal substance is the lowest of all things and the most dissimilar to the First Agent. And so it has no lower substance subject to it on which /594a/ it might be able to act, and it cannot have any likeness to God in acting. This is why in *De Civitate Dei* 5, chap. 9, Augustine says explicitly, "Corporeal causes are not to be numbered among the efficient causes."

4. *The third position.* The third position was that corporeal things are able to effect accidents but not substances, whereas created spiritual substances are able to effect certain lower substances. St. Thomas alludes to this position in the same places, drawing from Avicenna's *Sufficientia* 1, chap. 10, and his *Metaphysics* 9, chaps. 4 and 5.

Avicenna seems to have espoused two errors regarding this matter. The first is that one created spiritual substance is able to create another; for the uncreated First Cause immediately effects just a single intelligence, the most perfect one, whereas that one creates the second intelligence, and the second creates the third, and so on down to the lowest. The second error asserts that this lowest spiritual substance infuses substantial forms into matter that has been disposed by proximate corporeal agents, which are not themselves sufficient to effect the substantial forms.

His argument for the first error was that only one thing proceeds proximately and immediately from one thing. As for the second error, which is more pertinent to the present discussion, his argument was that the corporeal agents in question do nothing except through the mediation of accidents, which are themselves insufficient principles for effecting substantial forms. And he confirms this as follows. It is obvious from experience that many substances which do not have proximate causes sufficient to introduce the relevant forms are generated because of accidental dispositions that come together fortuitously or by chance—as when animals are generated from putrefaction. This, then, is an indication that there is some higher spiritual power which is prepared, as it were, to induce substantial forms as often as such accidental dispositions come together in a sufficient manner. Therefore, it is by this power that *all* substantial generations are effected.

---

5. Quantity is being thought of here as an accidental entity that inheres in a material substance and gives it determinate extension in three dimensions. On the most common scholastic theories, a substance's quantity is the immediate subject of its material qualities.

FIRST ASSERTION

5. Nonetheless, one should claim, first, that created agents truly and properly bring about effects that are connatural to them and proportioned to them. I take this truth to be not only absolutely evident to the senses and to reason but also absolutely certain according to Catholic doctrine. Thus, just as St. Thomas called the opposite opinion stupid on the former ground, so too we can call it temerarious and erroneous on the latter ground.[6] And so it is justifiably rejected by all philosophers and theologians.

For even though Aristotle never explicitly alluded to or refuted the opposite position, /594b/ he nonetheless everywhere assumes, as absolutely evident, that natural causes effect something. Indeed, all the ancient philosophers whose opinions he refers to in *Physics* 1, *Metaphysics* 1, and elsewhere often assume that natural causes effect something; and this is why they take pains to explain what these causes are able to effect and out of what they are able to effect it—since nothing is effected out of nothing. In addition, Plato, whom I cited in the preceding disputation, drawing from Damascene, calls natural causes the instruments of the First Cause in the sense that they have a power to act which is derived from and depends upon the First Cause.[7] It is also in this sense that Trismegistus claimed that the world is God's instrument and that it received seeds from him in order that it might produce all things. And in the same way Philo, in *De Congressu Quaerendae Eruditionis Causa*, said that God has permitted this lowest genus of things to sow and to bear fruit. The Commentator and other later thinkers followed these philosophers.

Among the Fathers, Augustine, in *De Trinitate* 3, chaps. 7–9, seems to imitate the aforementioned philosophers' manner of speaking when he says, "God put the seminal reasons of things into the elements and other created causes." These seminal reasons are nothing other than those active and passive principles of natural generations and motions that God placed in created things—as is elegantly explained by St. Thomas in *Summa Theologiae* 1, q. 115, a. 2, and in *Sentences* 2, dist. 18, q. 1, a. 2 (see Durandus, Hervaeus,

---

6. The terms 'erroneous' and 'temerarious' are here used as technical terms of theological censure, stronger than 'false' and weaker than 'heretical' or 'proximate to heresy'. However, the precise meaning and ordering of such terms of theological epistemic appraisal is itself a subject of theological inquiry. For an interesting treatment of some of the issues involved, especially as they affected the post-Tridentine period, see John Cahill, O.P., *The Development of the Theological Censures after the Council of Trent (1563–1709)* (Fribourg: University Press, 1955).

7. See *DM* 17. 2. 15.

Giles, and others in the same place); and by Capreolus in *Sentences* 1, dist. 42, a. 3. Again, the selfsame Augustine, talking about God in *De Civitate Dei* 7, chap. 30, says, "All the things which He has created He administers in such a way that He also allows them to exercise and effect their own proper motions." This position is confirmed and proclaimed by all the scholastics whenever they discuss either efficient causality or human freedom—which one can see them doing in the places already cited and also in *Sentences* 2, dist. 1, especially Durandus in q. 5.

6. *The assertion is proved from experience; absurdities follow from the opposite conclusion.* And this is proved, first, from experience. For what is better known to the senses than that the sun gives light, fire produces heat, water cools? And if they reply that we do, to be sure, experience that these effects are brought about when the things in question are present but that we do not experience that the effects are brought about *by* those things, then they are clearly destroying the whole force of philosophical argumentation. For there is no other way in which we can experience the emanation of effects from causes or in which we can infer causes from effects. And this experience is attested to by the common consensus and voice of all people, who hold the same view about the things in question.

Second, I argue from absurdities. For, given the opposite position, living things cannot be distinguished from nonliving things, /595a/ since it would not be the case that some things possess the principle of their own actions to a greater degree than do other things. Next, nature would have uselessly given different things the various qualities and powers which we experience in them. Indeed, neither would we be able, on the basis of action, to infer the variety of such qualities in the elements or, consequently, in other things either. For if it is not fire that produces heat but rather God who produces it in the presence of fire, then he could produce heat just as naturally in the presence of water; therefore, from that action we are no more able to infer that fire is hot than that water is. For if, equally in keeping with the natures of things, God could have stipulated that heat should be produced in the presence of water, then suppose he had done this. In that case it would not be permissible to infer from the production of heat that water is hot; therefore, neither can we now infer that it is cold or that fire is hot.

7. Someone might reply that [God's actual] stipulation was not altogether arbitrary but was based in some way on the natures of things—not in the sense that those things are active but rather in the sense that they have qualities similar to the qualities which are to be produced. And so we infer that fire is hot from the fact that God produces heat in its presence, since the stipulation in question was based on such a quality's belonging to fire.

However, this reply cannot be maintained philosophically, since, first of all, for the same reason God should have, in accord with the natures of things, produced whiteness in the presence of whiteness. For if heat is of itself no more active a quality than whiteness is, then the stipulation in question is in reality no more fitting in the case of heat than in the case of whiteness, and the same argument can be made with respect to any other quality and, indeed, with respect to quantity or substance or any entity whatsoever. Second, this reply is irrelevant in the case of equivocal causes, which do not have a similar form or quality; nor is it necessary that a more eminent form or quality should exist in them if such forms and qualities are not going to effect anything. What's more, given this position, the preparation of the earth, the rain, the plowing, the motions of the heavens, and so on are superfluous if none of them effects anything. Instead, the fact that wheat is present would be sufficient for God's generating wheat in its presence— and so on for other things. Moreover, there is an analogous argument based on the various organs and instruments by means of which God composed bodies, especially living ones. For just as in virtue of that preparation certain things appear apt to be acted upon, so too other things are apt to act—all of which would be superfluous if these things did not effect anything.

Finally, in *On the Heavens* 2.3 [286a9–10] and *Ethics* 1.7 [1097b22–32] Aristotle asserted altogether correctly that "all things exist for the sake of their own operation," which is why nothing is more repugnant to the establishment of things and to their purpose than for them to lack all efficient causality. /595b/ What's more, if created things did not effect anything among themselves, then all of them would in reality be equally incorruptible, since they would be unable to be acted upon at all by a created agent. Therefore, it was useless for God to have ordained so many celestial motions and such a great multitude of causes in order that these species of lower things might be conserved for a long time through the succession of generations and corruptions. For the very same things that were created at the beginning would just as easily have endured forever as long as God himself did not corrupt anything, since those things would not have struggled among themselves or corrupted one another.

It is easy to think of many similar absurdities, from which one sees that the whole order of nature militates against the position in question.

8. *An a priori argument for the conclusion.* Third, there is an a priori argument. Having the power to act is not repugnant to created things but is instead absolutely consonant with their perfection; therefore, since God has established each thing as complete within its own nature, one should not deny that he has created such things as have a connatural power to act.

The antecedent is proved from the fact that not every power to act requires an infinite perfection; therefore, the finite power of a creature will suffice for its being able to have some sort of efficaciousness. The antecedent [of this proof] is evident from the fact that there is no plausible argument that establishes the necessity of an infinite perfection for every action. To the contrary, as we will see below, theologians have worked very hard to discover an argument that proves that an infinite power is required in order to create [*ex nihilo*].[8] Therefore, such a power is not required for other actions and changes, especially among those agents that do not act without a dependence on a higher agent.

9. *An objection arises.* You will object that on this very point there is a contradiction: namely, that something might be an agent and yet depend in its acting on a higher agent. And so an infinite power is indeed required in every agent, since if it acts, it acts by its own power alone and without depending on another agent.

This objection touches upon the foundation for the contrary position, a foundation that will have to be treated at length below when we discuss the necessity for divine concurrence.[9] For the present, I will reply briefly by denying what is assumed. For just as it is not contradictory for a thing to exist and yet to exist with dependence on another, so too it is not contradictory for a thing to act and yet to act with dependence on another. For why should it be contradictory? Because it is contradictory for the same action to proceed simultaneously from more than one total cause? But this is false if the causes in question belong to different orders and are essentially ordered to one another. Thus, it is so far from being the case that this efficient causality on the part of secondary causes detracts from the divine efficacy or authority /596a/ that it rather acclaims and enhances that power to the highest degree. For, as St. Thomas argues in the places cited above, God communicated his goodness to created things in such a way that he also gave them the inclination and power to communicate to others what they share of the goodness of God himself by imparting it, according to their own capacity, to each individual thing. For as Plato said on this point in the dialogue *De Natura* [*Timaeus* 29e], "God is good, and he is not touched by malice, nor is he envious of anything." And so he made all things good and similar to himself in their desire to communicate themselves according to their capacity. Hence, some things communicate themselves as material causes; others communicate themselves as formal causes. Therefore, it is not contradictory that they should also communicate themselves as efficient causes.

10. *Whether God does more when he acts with secondary causes than he would if he acted alone.* Thus, what D'Ailly said above—namely, that God does more

8. See *DM* 20. 2.
9. See *DM* 22. 1.

when he acts with secondary causes than he would if he were to effect everything by himself alone—is presuppositionally true (as I will put it) but formally false. That is, if a secondary cause effects something, God is presupposed to have effected the secondary cause itself and to have communicated an active perfection to it (in this he better displays his own power); and afterwards he effects along with the secondary cause whatever it itself effects. And it is in this sense that he does more presuppositionally. However, in the very action by which he acts along with the secondary cause he does not do more than, or even as much as, he would do if he were acting by himself alone, since he does not apply the total efficacy required in order for him to act by himself alone. Thus, even though in such a mode of acting he acts by a sufficient power within the genus of a first cause, nonetheless, he does not act with sufficient power within every genus of cause. Nor does this bespeak any imperfection on God's part, since it happens not because of a lack or impotence on his part but because of a voluntary and eminently prudent application of his power.

It is in this sense that something else D'Ailly said is also true: namely, that secondary causes effect nothing except because of God's will. For, as we will explain below, they require God's concurrence, which God grants not by necessity but by his volition.[10] Yet that volition is not purely absolute (excepting miracles) but is instead accommodated to the natures of things and arises from a certain requirement, as it were, of just distribution. And so this voluntariness does not prevent efficient causality of the sort in question from being unqualifiedly natural to created things. Likewise, it is also the case that things have the very power to act because of God's volition—and yet not because of a volition which is entirely extraneous to and, as it were, only gratuitously grafted onto the volition by which he wills that such creatures should exist. Rather, these [two] volitions are conjoined in accordance with a natural requirement of, and connection with, the things themselves. Hence, God's having willed that fire should produce heat /596b/ and that water should produce coldness is not purely arbitrary but is in its own way something required on the supposition that he has willed to create such things. (We are speaking here of the connatural power to act, since in the case of a supernatural and infused power to act there is a different explanation, which does not concern us here.[11]) And so at one and the same time the proposed conclusion has been proved, and the foundation for the first position has been refuted.

10. See *DM* 22. 1 and 4.

11. Here Suarez has in mind powers that are bestowed on natural things to render them fit to be sacramental instruments of grace, as well as those supernatural and infused virtues which make free creatures capable of performing meritorious actions.

11. What was adumbrated in the confirming argument about essential dependence will have to be discussed explicitly below in the disputation on creation.[12] For the present, I will simply assert that an equivocation is perpetrated in the proposition 'A creature depends essentially on God alone.' For this proposition can be understood both positively and negatively.

If understood positively, it has the following sense: 'A creature essentially requires that it should depend on God alone.' And this is not true, generally speaking, even if it could perhaps be verified for a given action or entity because of some special feature. (This has to do with special questions concerning creation or grace and so forth.)

On the other hand, if the proposition is understood negatively, its meaning is that the nature of a creature does not as such essentially require any dependence except on God. And this is true, since its import does not rule out a creature's being able to have a dependence, whether de facto or according to a given mode of production, on both God and some creature—as is self-evident.

THE FIRST ASSERTION IS DISCUSSED ON SUPERNATURAL PRINCIPLES

12. Up to this point the proposed thesis has been discussed philosophically. But because we also claimed that it has certitude according to the teaching of the Faith, it is necessary to add a few things from that side.

This certitude is inferred, first of all, from divine Scripture's manner of speaking in Genesis 1: "Let the earth bring forth verdant vegetation" and "Let the earth bring forth living things." In homily 9 Basil observes on the basis of these and similar passages that natural things have received an efficacy for continuously effecting the generations and corruptions of things. Ambrose pursues this more extensively in *Hexameron* 3 (from chap. 8 on) and *Hexameron* 4 and 5 (almost the whole books). Further, in Mark 4 Christ says, "The other seed fell upon good ground and yielded fruit," and later, "Of itself the earth bears the crop, first the blade, then the ear, then the full grain," and in Luke 21, "When the trees are already producing fruit from themselves," and so on. And in Wisdom 16 it is deemed a miracle that the fire, forgetful of its own power, did not consume the just men and their garments.[13] And in the same place it is said of water that it extinguishes all things and of serpents that they have poisonous fangs /597a/ for killing. And

12. See *DM* 20. 1.

13. This is a reference to the story of the three young men in the fiery furnace from Dan. 3.

if such things are sometimes impeded from these actions, this is attributed to God's power.

What's more, there are other truths of the Faith that cannot stand without this principle. The first and most important of these is the truth of free choice, which cannot consist in anything but a power and manner of acting, as we will show below.[14] This is why the Council of Trent, session 6, canon 4, condemns those who claim that created free choice "does nothing at all and is purely passive."[15] By this decree it plainly condemns the first position referred to above and establishes our thesis. In addition (and this proves the point a fortiori), it is not only in natural operations but also in supernatural operations—that is, in the free works of grace—that the Council asserts that the human will has efficient causality.

It is on this basis, by the way, that we are to understand the passages that Gabriel adduced for the contrary position, passages having to do specifically with works of grace, which are attributed to God as a first cause in such a way that our cooperation is not excluded. For in the same place Paul says both that we are not sufficient of ourselves and also that our sufficiency is from God. And he who says in one place that God operates in us says in other places that he cooperates with us and that we are cooperators with God's grace.

13. No less efficacious is the argument derived from the effecting of a sinful act. For if it is not the secondary causes that act but rather God who acts in their presence, then it is not we who effect evil volitions but rather God alone who infuses them into us in the presence of the objects—which is blasphemous and erroneous, not only because in that case we would not sin freely but also because in that case our sins would come not from ourselves but from God.

Moreover, there is an excellent theological argument derived from the decrees of the Councils concerning the mystery of the Incarnation, decrees whereby they teach us that in Christ there are two operations and two principles of operating—that is, two operational powers—concerning which one can read Damascene, De Fide Orthodoxa 3, chap. 15. None of these things or similar things can be true if in a created nature there is no power to act.

Lastly, there is an excellent argument based on the creation of the rational soul. For, given the contrary opinion, it is no less true that a human being who generates creates a rational soul than that fire generates fire. For just as

14. See DM 19. 2. 18–21.

15. The passage cited from Trent appears in session 6, Decretum de Iustificatione, in H. Denzinger and A. Schonmetzer, Enchiridion Symbolorum (hereafter Denzinger) 32d ed. (Freiburg, 1963), #1554 (new numbering), p. 378.

God effects fire in the presence of fire and the action is attributed to the fire only because it is a *sine qua non* condition and is such that when it is posited, God acts infallibly, so too God infallibly creates the soul in the presence of human semen and not in the absence of that condition. But the consequent is an error from the point of view of the Faith.[16] /597b/

SECOND ASSERTION

14. *The sort of efficient causality that Augustine denies to bodies.* Second, I claim that not only incorporeal substances but also corporeal substances can have real and physical efficient causality. This assertion follows from the preceding one, by almost the same demonstration and with almost the same certitude. For the experiences, arguments, and authorities adduced above hold for natural and material causes as well as for immaterial causes. Indeed, if we are speaking of efficient causality through *transeunt* action, then it is better known and more evident to us that bodies act than that incorporeal substances do.[17] Therefore, it is unnecessary to add anything by way of confirmation for this [second] thesis.

Nor does the foundation for the contrary position carry any weight, since in order for one body to act on another, it is not necessary that it exist intimately together with it in the same place; rather, it is enough that the bodies be sufficiently proximate to one another, as experience itself testifies and as will be explained more fully below.[18] Therefore, even though the quantity is nonactive, it nonetheless does not entirely impede the action—just as matter, too, is nonactive and yet does not impede the action of the form. For the quantity seems to be related to the qualities in the same way that the matter is related to the form. Hence, neither of them impedes the action, but instead each contributes to the action in its own way—if not by acting, then at least by sustaining the principle of action and applying it in a connatural manner.

As for the confirmation, one should reply that a corporeal substance belongs to the lowest order [of things], or is maximally distant from God, not according to itself as a whole but only according to its primary matter. And

16. According to Catholic doctrine, the human soul, unlike the souls of other animals, is an immaterial form and thus cannot be generated; instead, it must be created *ex nihilo*.

17. A *transeunt* action is one whose effect is outside the agent. It is contrasted with an *immanent* action—e.g., an intellectual or volitional act—whose effect remains within the agent *quo* and is a modification of the agent.

18. See *DM* 18. 8.

so we admit, with respect to the primary matter, that it has no proper power to act. However, bodies have a greater perfection and a greater likeness to God according to their form, and so it is according to their form that they can have the power to act.

Moreover, in the cited passage Augustine is speaking of efficient causes which in some way act on their own—that is, which have control over their own actions and can apply themselves to acting. For this is what he says: "Corporeal causes, which, rather than act, are acted upon, are not to be numbered among the efficient causes, since they are capable of doing only what the wills of spirits do by means of them."

THIRD ASSERTION

15. Third, I claim that (i) created causes cannot effect a substance according to itself as a whole—that is, *per se* and primarily—but that (ii) they are none-theless able to generate a substance from presupposed substantival matter by educing a substantial form; /598a/ however, (iii) this sort of efficacy should be attributed to corporeal causes rather than to created spirits.

The first part of this assertion is absolutely certain, since created causes are not able to create anything, as we will show when we discuss creation. But a substance cannot come to exist *per se* and primarily and according to itself as a whole except through creation. For it cannot come to exist [as a whole] from a presupposed subject, because no subject is presupposed for the substance taken as a whole, since it is an entity that is *per se* complete. Therefore, it must necessarily come to exist *ex nihilo* and thus through creation. And from this it follows that a created spiritual substance cannot procreate another substance that is similar to itself in species or in grade [of being], since a spiritual substance, given that it is simple in essence, cannot come to exist except through creation. And for the same reason a material substance, as far as its matter is concerned, cannot be effected by a created cause, whether that cause be incorporeal or corporeal. And it is in this sense that we are claiming that a substance cannot be effected by a created cause according to itself as a whole and *per se* and primarily—that is, as regards its whole being and without presupposing anything that belongs to the substance. But more will have to be said about this in what follows.[19]

16. *Substantial forms come from presupposed bodies.* The second part of the [third] thesis, which has to do with the educing of the substantial form through the proper efficient causality of secondary causes, is not as evident

19. See *DM* 20. 1.

or certain as the previous theses regarding efficient causality taken absolutely. This is because the effecting of a substantial form is less able to be sensed and is thus less evident to us than is the effecting of accidents, and also because there is no little difficulty involved in explaining this sort of efficient causality, as we will see in the next section.

Nonetheless, this part of the assertion is rather plausible, especially when we take it absolutely and do not descend to the particular ways of explaining the sort of efficient causality in question. And it is proved, first, by the fact that just as we see that fire produces heat, so too we see that it generates fire and that the sun produces minerals and that the earth brings forth vegetation by the action of the sun as well, and so forth. Second, since these things come to exist not through creation but rather through generation, it is not the case, either because of the thing produced or because of the way in which it is produced, that an infinite power is required in order to effect them. Therefore, the relevant power does not exceed the capacity of the created causes; therefore, it is communicated to them by the First Cause and is connatural to them. However, there are several things in the next section that pertain to this part of the assertion, since this part cannot be proved and defended with precision unless the relevant mode of efficient causality is first explained.

17. *Spiritual substances are unable to effect substantial forms.* The third part of the [third] thesis—namely, that this sort of efficient causality /598b/ should not be attributed to created spirits—is evident from the fact that they are not proportioned to the type of action in question, whereas corporeal causes are more proportioned to it and accommodated to it. Now among created things, a given thing's being more perfect is not sufficient for its being able to effect a less perfect thing unless the former is known on other grounds to contain the latter eminently. But even though created spirits are more perfect than bodies, still, because they are limited to their own grade [of being] and because each of them is limited to its own specific˙ perfections, they do not contain corporeal things eminently. And because they are not forms in matter but are instead altogether separate [from matter], they are not proportioned to introducing forms into matter.

On this topic we will likewise have more to say below in the discussion of created intelligences, where we will show that they are unable to effect either substantial forms or qualities in bodies.[20] For they are unable so much as to alter bodies at the command of their own will; but if they are unable to do this, then they are all the less able to induce a substantial form in matter, since anything that does not have the power to dispose matter is all the less

20. See *DM* 35. 6.

able to have the power to inform matter. By contrast, since corporeal* agents are able to alter and dispose matter, they are more proportioned to being able to inform it, either by educing a substantial form from it or by introducing a substantial form into it, depending on the capacity and quality of the form.

18. Therefore, as far as Avicenna's foundation for the first error is concerned, we deny that only a single intelligence or a single effect was able to have proceeded from the First Cause. For it is not the case that the First Cause acts by a necessity of nature, so that it is determined to a single effect. Rather, the First Cause is an intellectual agent who has within himself the exemplars of infinitely many things, the effecting of which he decrees by his own volition and choice.

The foundation for [Avicenna's] second error, on the other hand, poses a problem that pertains to the next section.

Section 2

The Principle by Which One Created Substance Produces Another

1. *Matter is not the principle of any action.* We are investigating at one and the same time both the principal principle and the proximate—that is, instrumental—principle, since the one cannot be adequately explained without the other. Now from what has been said, it is clear, first of all, that the discussion concerns only corporeal causes, since created spirits are unable to effect any substance, as has been explained.[1]

Moreover, given that in a created substance there are matter, form, and accidents, it is clear to everyone, second, that the matter is not a principle of the sort of /599a/ efficient causality in question—I mean a principle *quo*, or formal principle. For the principle *quod* is the suppositum, just as in other actions. However, even though a material substance consists of matter, form, and subsistence, and even though it has accidents as well, it nonetheless does not have its power to act from the matter, which is nonactive, as we have said repeatedly. Moreover, we are not going to discuss subsistence here, since subsistence is only a certain mode of, and terminus of, the nature—a mode and terminus which, to be sure, naturally precedes every action but which does not *per se* confer the power to act, as we will explain in more

---

1. See *DM* 18. 1. 17. To better understand the discussions that follow, one should keep in mind that when speaking of generation, Suarez has in mind (i) the generation of the *elements*, his favorite example being the generation of one fire by another through the instrumentality of the latter's heat; (ii) the generation of the *minerals* from the elements, where each kind of mineral has its own peculiar proportion of the four elemental qualities of heat, coldness, dryness, and moistness; (iii) the generation of *plants*, which have sentient souls as their substantial forms; and (iv) the generation of *animals*, both *imperfect* animals—that is, animals of a lower type such as worms, insects, and so on, which do not exhibit the full array of possible animal powers—and *perfect*—that is, higher—animals such as mammals. Each of these classes of generated things is associated with problem cases. E.g., a red-hot piece of iron generates fire in a combustible thing even though it itself does not seem to be on fire. Again, minerals seem to be generated in part by the sun through the heat it produces "deep in the bowels of the earth"; and yet it is difficult to see how the sun can act through a dense medium like earth. Certain imperfect animals appear to be generated "from putrefaction" and not from other animals like them in species. Again, it is not clear how the semen which plays a role in the generation of higher animals can be capable of educing the substantial form of an animal whose perfection far exceeds that of the semen itself. All these cases are discussed in some detail below.

detail below when we treat subsistence.[2] Therefore, the whole controversy centers around the substantial form and its accidents—that is, its natural properties.

2. *No accident is a principal cause of a substance.* As for the latter, it is clear, third, that an accidental form cannot be a principal principle for producing a substance. On this almost everyone agrees. For even though John Major, *Sentences* 4, dist. 12, is commonly cited in favor of the contrary opinion, he does not deny this point; nor does anyone else I have looked at.

Nor can there be any reason for doubt here, since, as we have shown, a principal cause must be either more noble than, or at least no less noble than, the effect.[3] For since no one gives what he does not have, how can an imperfect form have within itself or communicate to its suppositum a principal power for effecting a more perfect form, a form which it is unable to contain either formally or eminently? But an accidental form is more imperfect than a substantial form. Therefore, an accidental form cannot be a principal principle for educing a substantial form. And this will become even more evident from what will be said below in both the discussion of the first position and also the confirmation of our own last assertion.[4]

3. *The substantial form is the principal principle by which the efficient cause acts.* From this it follows further that if in a material substance there is some principal principle *quo* for effecting a substance, then that principle can only be the substantial form. For once an enumerative induction has been made, nothing else remains.[5]

What's more, this claim also seems to be accepted by the common consensus of everyone. For since the substantial form is the principal act of the suppositum and that which principally gives it *esse*, it must also be the principal principle of operating. For the operation follows upon the *esse*.[6]

---

2. See *DM* 34. 7. On Suarez's view, subsistence is a mode (or inseparable accident) that belongs to a substance and formally constitutes that substance as a suppositum or ultimate subject of characteristics. Not every substance is a suppositum. E.g., some parts of substances count as substances but not as supposita; and in the case of the mystery of the Incarnation, Catholic doctrine has it that Christ's human nature is a substance but not a suppositum, because it has a dependence on the Second Person of the Blessed Trinity, who is the ultimate subject of the characteristics belonging to Christ's human nature.

3. See *DM* 17. 2. 17–18.

4. See §§5–8 and 28–42 below.

5. So in the sort of case Suarez has in mind here, (i) the substance itself will be the principal principle *quod*, (ii) the substance's substantial form will be the principal principle *quo*, and (iii) the active powers or accidents by which the substance acts will be the instrumental principles *quo*.

6. Suarez here invokes the scholastic adage '*agere [operatio] sequitur esse*'—roughly, the way a thing acts and the effects it produces are a function of the sort of being it is.

Finally, the substantial form cannot be an instrumental principle; therefore, it will be a principal principle. The consequence is evident from the
fact that there is no third alternative and from the fact that the form cannot
be totally excluded from being a principle, given that it is the source of the
entire *esse* and of all the properties. The antecedent, on the other hand, is
evident from the fact that the substantial form does not presuppose /599b/
any other form whose instrument it could be. For the substantial form is the
primary and principal form of all the forms—I mean of all the forms *within
the same suppositum*, since if a lower form is ordered to a higher form, it can
be called an instrument of that higher form, as was adumbrated above and
as will be explained below.[7]

And on this basis almost everyone takes it for granted that the accidents
are the substantial form's instruments for producing a substance. For the
substantial form does not produce a similar substance immediately and by
itself alone but instead makes use of the accidents, as seems obvious from
experience and as is proved by the argument made on Avicenna's behalf in
the last section.[8]

4. Therefore, granted all this, two points remain to be explained. The first
is the way in which an accident is an instrument for producing a substance;
the second is the way in which the substantial form is a principal principle
for educing a similar form. Hence, there are two main problems. The first
is whether an accident is an instrument in such a way that it immediately
attains to the eduction of the [new] substantial form itself or whether instead
it is called an instrument only because it operates dispositively for the induction of the substantial form that is the effect primarily intended by the
principal agent.[9] The second problem is whether, assuming that an accident
does indeed attain immediately to this eduction, the substantial form, too,
has a proximate influence along with it or whether the substantial form has
only a remote and, as it were, originating influence.

THE EFFICIENT CAUSALITY OF ACCIDENTS WITH
RESPECT TO A SUBSTANCE

First Position

5. As for the first problem, the first position is that the accidents are instruments only in the second way: that is, only by concurring dispositively.

7. See *DM* 17. 2. 15–19, as well as the discussion of the fourth assertion, beginning with
§28 below.

8. See *DM* 18. 1. 4.

9. A cause acts dispositively (i.e., acts as a disposing cause) when it prepares the patient
to receive a given form but does not actually effect that form.

This could be interpreted as applying to the very accidents that are received within the patient and that are themselves formal dispositions of the matter. Philoponus seems to have understood it this way in *Physics* 2, text 27, and he accordingly traces these instruments back to the material cause. In this he speaks in opposition both to Aristotle and to reason. For Aristotle traces semen and similar instruments back to the efficient cause—and justifiably so, since nothing is called an instrument unless it has an influence on the effect by means of some action. And so no cause other than the efficient cause is properly said to have instruments.

Therefore, the position in question must be understood in an alternative sense to apply to the accidents that exist in the agent itself and are the powers through which the agent proximately acts and through which it effectively induces in the patient those dispositions by which it gradually prepares the matter until the matter becomes proximately fit for the substantial form. And it is in this way that the accidents are instruments for inducing /600a/ the [new] substantial form—not because they immediately *attain to* it or *effect* it (for their action ceases and is terminated in the effecting of accidents that are perfectly similar to themselves) but rather because, insofar as they are subordinated to their own substantial form, their action *tends toward* the production of a similar substantial form.

Scotus held this opinion in *Sentences* 1, dist. 37, in *Sentences* 2, dist. 17, and more extensively in *Sentences* 4, dist. 12, q. 3; and Ockham adopts it in *Sentences* 2, q. 23. The principal argument for it is that an accident, since it is a more imperfect being than a substantial form, cannot in any way effect the latter.

Some reply that even though an accident is less perfect as a being, it can nonetheless be more suitable as an active principle, and in this sense it can be said to be more perfect in acting.

However, this claim is incorrect. For the power to act, especially in an accident, is nothing other than its being—or if it is in some way (at least conceptually) distinct from the accident's being, it still follows from that being and is commensurate with it. Therefore, an accident cannot be more noble in acting than it is in being. Otherwise, given the same distinction, someone could claim that an accident is a *principal* principle for producing a substance by reason of the fact that even though it is not more noble [than a substance] in being, it can be more noble [than a substance] in action—which is absurd. What's more, we would never be able to infer an efficient cause's nobility with respect to being from the nobility of its action. And (as Scotus argues) someone would be able to claim of God himself that he is more noble in action even though he is not more noble in being.

6. *The more frequent reply of the Thomists is examined.* For this reason, a more

frequent reply [to Scotus] is that even if an accident is less noble and so cannot attain to the production of a substance by its own power, it can nonetheless attain immediately to the eduction of the [new] substantial form in the power of its own substantial form, whose property and power of acting it is.[10]

Scotus, however, counters by asking what this power is in whose force and efficacy the accident is said to attain to the eduction of the substantial form. For either it is something distinct from the accident, or it is not. If it is not distinct from the accident, then a substance can no more come to exist in its power than it can come to exist in the power of the accident. If, on the other hand, it is distinct from the accident, then it is itself either an accident or a substance. If it is an accident, then the same argument goes through, regardless of whether it is an absolute accident or a relative accident; indeed, it will be all the less active if it is a relative rather than an absolute accident.[11] But if it is a substance, then it will be nothing other than the substantial form. And so the substantial form itself will be a power of acting and the principle by which the accident attains to the eduction of an accidental form rather than vice versa.[12]

The Thomists, drawing from Cajetan, *Summa Theologiae* 1, q. 53, a. 3, and q. 77, a. 1, /600b/ commonly reply that when one says that an accident produces a [new] substance in the power of the substance, the phrase 'in the power of' should be taken not *transitively* but rather *intransitively*. For the meaning is not that there is some power added to the accident by means of which it produces a [new] substance; rather, the meaning is that the accident is able to attain to a [new] substance through its own being because that being is itself a certain power of the substance [in which the accident exists].

However, this reply does not seem to weaken the force of [Scotus's] objection. For given that heat is by its nature a power and faculty of a substance, when it is said to act in the power of the substance, all that is being said is that the heat has the sort of activity in question by its nature. But this seems to be naturally impossible, since a less noble form cannot be a natural power sufficient for producing a more excellent form.

7. Lest we seem to be getting bogged down in words, and in order to clarify the problem that exists in the thing itself, I ask whether (i) the action by

10. See the parallel discussion in *DM* 17. 2. 13–15.

11. It is a scholastic adage that a relative accident, or relation, is not of itself active and hence cannot be an efficient cause.

12. This last part of the argument is a *reductio ad absurdum*, since it is taken to be an obvious absurdity that an accident should use a substance or substantial form as an instrument.

which a substantial form is educed from the potency of the matter proceeds immediately from, say, the heat alone and only remotely and originatively from the substantial form insofar as the heat emanates from it or whether instead (ii) the action proceeds immediately from both forms, from the one as from a principal cause and from the other as from an instrumental cause.

If this second interpretation is affirmed, then, to be sure, the problem touched upon in the argument disappears, since in this sense there is nothing absurd about a more imperfect form's concurring instrumentally with respect to a more perfect effect. And it is in this sense that the phrase 'in the power of' is best explained; for it signifies, namely, that the thing in question has an actual influence insofar as it is aided by a higher power.

But then other, no less serious, problems arise. First, the experiences that seem to prove that accidents attain to the effecting of a substance prove that the accidents do this by themselves alone. For either (i) there is no substance [in which they exist], as when the accidents of the consecrated wine generate wine (and the same argument, though less effective, is commonly made in the case of a red-hot piece of iron that generates fire);[13] or else (ii) the substance [in which they exist] is not applied, as when the sun induces the substantial forms of minerals in the bowels of the earth, from which it is very far distant.

Second, on the interpretation in question the substantial form is now being posited as an immediate principle of some action. But this surpasses its perfection. For it is because the substantial form is not proportioned to this that it received from nature the accidental forms through which it acts.

This gives rise to a third argument, which Scotus and Ockham suggested. If this immediate influence must necessarily be granted to the substantial form, then the immediate influence of the accidental form is superfluous. For if the generation in question is univocal, then the substantial form, which is assumed /601a/ to have an immediate influence, has the perfection and proportionateness required in order for it to be a proximate principle that is sufficient for producing a form similar to itself. For if heat is sufficient in this

---

13. In the Sacrament of the Altar, according to Catholic doctrine, the substance of the bread and wine no longer underlie the sensible accidents (or species) of the bread and wine. The question then arises: What if some water were added to the consecrated wine? Under ordinary circumstances this water is mixed with (unconsecrated) wine and thus itself become wine. However, if this generation of new wine is, in the normal case, attributed to the substantial form of the preexistent wine, what should it be attributed to in the case of consecrated wine, given that the substantial form of wine is no longer present? Are the remaining accidents of the wine sufficient by themselves to generate wine? See St. Thomas's discussion of this and related questions in *Summa Theologiae* 3, q. 77, a. 8.

way for effecting a similar heat, why won't a substantial form be sufficient for effecting a similar form, since it is now being assumed that an immediate influence is not repugnant to it? On the other hand, if the generation in question is equivocal, then since the form of that which generates is more eminent [than the form of that which is generated], it will be all the more sufficient for the corresponding action.

8. However, if because of these problems the first interpretation is chosen (and it does indeed seem to be espoused more frequently),[14] then the problem mentioned in the first place remains in all its force, since it is impossible to see how a less noble instrument can produce a more noble effect by itself alone and through a power connatural to itself without any participation on the part of a more noble agent. For what does it matter that this instrument is the power of another thing? For from this either (i) it follows only that the instrument is separated from the other, in the way that the semen is separated from the animal, and on this score there is no increase in [the instrument's] power, which is only as great as the perfection it receives within itself and not as great as the perfection of that from which it receives it; or else (ii) it follows at most that [the instrument] takes the place of the other in acting, in the way that gravity takes the place of the generating thing[15]— and it is this that seems astonishing and contradictory: namely, that nature should substitute an imperfect power in order that the latter, by itself alone and without the actual aid of a higher power, might produce a more noble effect in place of the principal agent.

What's more, there are other problems with this way of talking. The main problem is that it follows that substantial forms have no proper activity but that instead they concur only *per accidens*, as it were, in every action. For if, by way of example, God merely produced and conserved the heat and did not afterwards have an immediate influence on the action that proceeds from the heat, he would be a *per accidens* cause and not a *per se* cause of that action.[16] Therefore, similarly, if the substantial form is related in this same way to all the heat's action, it cannot be truly called a *per se* efficient principle of the action but instead will be called at most a remote principal

14. See §7 above. The first interpretation was this: "The action by which a substantial form is educed from the potency of the matter proceeds immediately from, say, the heat alone and only remotely and originatively from the substantial form insofar as the heat emanates from it."

15. In *DM* 18. 7. 21–28, Suarez takes up the natural motion of heavy and light bodies and discusses the view that such motion is to be attributed to the cause that generated these bodies.

16. For more on this claim, see *DM* 22. 1.

principle and a principle by extrinsic denomination, in virtue of the fact that
a proximate principle of acting is taking its place or (to put it more correctly)
making up for its lack of power. For in reality the form itself would have no
per se activity. But this seems absurd, since if it were so, then a substance
would never be *per se* active or generative of what is similar to itself; nor
would any action proceed from a created substantival suppositum except
by reason of its accidents. But this is incompatible with the perfection of a
substance. For, as /601b/ Scotus argues in *Sentences* 2, dist. 16, if an accidental form is immediately productive of something similar to itself, then why
won't this be true of a substantial form as well?

The position in question also seems to go against Aristotle in *Physics* 2.7
[198a22–27], where he attributes three kinds of causality to the [substantial]
form, namely, formal causality, final causality, and efficient causality. Therefore, just as the first and second of these belong properly and *per se* to the
form, so also does the third.

Second Position

9. The second position affirms that the accidents are a substance's instruments for producing a [new] substance in the sense that they proximately
and *per se* attain to the production of the substantial form in the power of the
other forms whose instruments they are.

This position is held by St. Thomas, *Summa Theologiae* 1, q. 45, a. 8, ad 2
and 3, and q. 77, a. 1, ad 3 and 4, and q. 115, a. 1, ad 5, and *Summa Theologiae* 3, q. 77, a. 3; by Cajetan, in the places cited above; by Ferrariensis,
Contra Gentes 4, chap. 66; by Capreolus, *Sentences* 1, dist. 3, q. 3, a. 2, and
Sentences 4, dist. 12, q. 1, a. 3; by Giles, *Quodlibeta* 3, q. 1, ad 2, and *Hexameron* 2, chap. 11; by Henry, *Quodlibeta* 14, q. 1; and by Hervaeus, *Quodlibeta* 3,
q. 12.

It also seems to be the common position of the Peripatetics. For Aristotle
indicates everywhere that natural action and generation are brought about
by means of accidents. Thus, in *On Generation and Corruption* 1.7 [323b30–
324a9], he says that action, especially corruptive action, takes place only
between contraries; but contrariety is properly found only among qualities.
And in *Sense and Sensibilia* [4.441b12–14] he says that nothing acts or is acted
upon insofar as it is fire or water or even insofar as it is similar but only
"insofar as it is subject to contrariety"—that is, insofar as it is affected by
contrary qualities. In the same place Alexander [of Aphrodisias] notes that,
according to the Peripatetic position, fire emits an action not insofar as it is
fire but insofar as it is hot—that is, not through the form of fire but through
heat. Likewise, in *On the Soul* 2, text 10 [4.416b15–16], and *Metaphysics* 7, text
3 [9.1034a35–1034b4], and *On the Generation of Animals* 3 [1.749a15], Aristotle

teaches that semen is the instrument whereby one animal generates another as an efficient cause. In addition, in *Metaphysics* 7, comments 22 and 31, and *Metaphysics* 12, comment 18, the Commentator says that it belongs to the same power to prepare the matter and to induce the form. Therefore, since it is obvious that the substance uses the accidents in order to prepare the matter, one must say that it is through those same accidents that it induces the form.

10. *Arguments for the second position.* The arguments by which this position is confirmed are mainly these.

First, a substantial form is not *per se* immediately active but is instead active through a power, which is a quality distinct from it; therefore, it does not induce a substantial form except /602a/ by the mediation of an accidental power.

The antecedent is evident, first, by induction. For we see that any substance whatsoever uses accidents for all its other actions—this is true not only of material substances but also of created spiritual substances. Therefore, this is an indication that it exceeds the perfection and limitation of a created substance for it to be simultaneously a principal principle and a proximate principle of its own actions.

Likewise, a substantial form is of itself determined only to giving *esse* as a formal cause, whereas with respect to its actions it is an indeterminate principle, since it is almost always able to effect several actions to which it is determined by its accidents. And so it is a proximate principle of an action not through itself but rather through its accidents. Therefore, the same thing should be said of the action by which it produces a substance.

11. The second argument, which confirms the last inference of the preceding argument, is this. The action through which a substantial form is educed is not properly an action distinct from the motion of alteration that is ordered toward and tends toward that [substantial form] but is instead the terminus, as it were, of that motion; and so they are not counted as two actions but as one and the same action. But the entire alteration that tends toward the generation is effected by means of the accidents, as is obvious *per se*. Therefore, the substantival generation itself is effected by means of the accidents.

The major premise is evident from the fact that the substantial form, which is educed from the potency of the matter by the mediation of the motion, comes to exist in the matter as a result of that motion. Therefore, it is effected by the same action, physically speaking, and by means of the same instrument. And this is confirmed by the fact that the accidents are instruments for expelling the substantial form of the thing that is corrupted. Therefore, they are instruments for effecting the form of the thing that is generated.

12. The third argument is this. A proper action comes to exist only between

contraries. Therefore, only that which properly has contraries is a proper principle of such an action. But it is a quality, and not a substantial form, that is of this sort. Therefore, etc.

13. *Various experiences that tell in favor of the second position.* Fourth, and most important, this position is based on certain experiences. For substances are often generated by means of accidents when there is no substantial form from which the action could proceed, either because the form is too far distant or because there is no such form at all.

Scotus replies that in some cases the fact that a form is distant does not prevent it from having an influence on the eduction of the [new] form, since by its force and efficacy it is able to attain to distant places. And he believes that this is how the forms of the minerals are educed immediately by the form of the sun. On the other hand, when there is no form that is proportionate or that is applied within /602b/ the sphere of its own activity, he claims that the eduction of the form is effected immediately by the First Cause, whose role it is to supply what is lacking in the lower agents. And he claims that this is how animals are very often generated—not only those animals that come to exist from putrefaction but also those that come to exist from semen whose power is imperfect and insufficient for educing a soul from the potency of the matter.

However, the first part of this reply contradicts the Aristotelian principle that the agent and the patient have to be in the same place—I will discuss this in a little while.[17] The second part, on the other hand, savors of the opinion of Plato, who claims that substantial forms are induced by the separated Ideas. For if it is true that Plato posited the Ideas only in the divine mind, then this was the same as claiming that substantial forms are effected by the First Cause. Philoponus, too, teaches this in *Physics* 1, at the end, where he says that substantial forms come from the Universal Craftsman of nature. However, in his own book *On the Soul* 1, chap. 24, and 3, chap. 52, Themistius claims that they come from the world soul, whereas Avicenna, as cited above, says that they come from the lowest intelligence.

Scotus differs from these authors in his claim that not all forms but only many forms and the more perfect forms (even material ones) are effected by a separated agent—which seems even more problematic. For given that all these forms are educed from the potency of matter, it is not the case that an infinite power is required for their production. Why is it, then, that certain forms have the power to effect forms similar to themselves, and others, especially those that are more perfect, do not?

Thus, it is experiences of the sort in question that seem especially to con-

17. See *DM* 18. 8.

firm this [second] position. For, as we will soon see, the [three] arguments are not as a matter of fact effective in this regard.

14. But before we settle this point, we must broach a second point which we touched upon in the argument made above in favor of the first position and which is especially relevant for understanding and correctly defending the second position, even though it seems to have been almost entirely overlooked by the authors of that position. Given that the accidents are instruments that immediately and *per se* attain to the eduction of a [new] substantial form, the question is (i) whether they are instruments that are separated *secundum causalitatem* from the substantial forms themselves or whether they are conjoined instruments and, consequently, (ii) whether the substantial form should be called a principal principle of this action only remotely and originatively or whether it also has a proximate and *per se* actual influence.[18]

To be sure, almost all the authors of the second position seem to think that the accidents are separated instruments. For if the arguments and experiences adduced above prove anything at all, they especially establish this point, since /603a/ accidents seem to generate a substance even when there is no substance that concurs with them. And this opinion is held not only by the cited authors but also by Paludanus in *Sentences* 4, dist. 12, q. 4, a. 1, concl. 3; and in the same place by Richard, a. 3, q. 2; by Thomas of Argentina, q. 1; by John Major, q. 1; by Hispalensis, q. 1, a. 3, notabile 3; and by Albert, a. 16. All the latter are talking about the sacramental species, which remain in the absence of a substance, and they claim that these species have the same sort of efficient causality in the power of the substance that they can have when they are conjoined to the substance. Giles, too, explains this in detail in *De Eucharistia*, theorem 48. In addition, Zimara, in theorem 114, while discussing at length Averroës's claim that "it is the same agent that disposes the matter and introduces the form," claims that the whole action is immediately from the qualities whereas it is from the [substantial] form only insofar as the form communicates its own power of acting to the quality. In *Summa Theologiae* 1, q. 53, a. 3, Cajetan discusses this same point in detail.

Nonetheless, this position still encounters the problems that were touched upon in the middle of the confirmation of Scotus's opinion on the first point above.[19] For it is not clear how the substantial form can transfer (as I will put it) its whole power of acting to an accidental form in such a way that even when (should this be necessary) the substantial form perishes and only the

18. For an account of the distinction between conjoined and separated instruments, see *DM* 17. 2. 22.

19. See §13 above.

accidental form is conserved, the latter can by itself effect a substantial form more perfect than itself—even though it does not actually have as perfect an *esse* and even though it is not actually being aided by a higher form.

15. Because of these problems, I believe that it is difficult to pass judgment on the positions in question; nevertheless, I will briefly say what I think. I claim, first, that one should not deny that the accidents are instruments for producing a substance in such a way that they attain proximately and *per se* to the eduction of the substantial form.

This is proved, first, from the position common to so many philosophers, a position that is not to be casually rejected when there is no evident argument to the contrary.

Second, experience, which philosophy especially depends upon, confirms this claim to a very high degree; and there is nothing that contradicts it, as will become evident when we refute the objections to the contrary.

Third, if this is not so, then it will be necessary in many cases to attribute the entire effecting of a substance to universal causes or even to the First Cause—something that ought to be avoided in philosophy as far as possible. For the proper management of the universe demands that whatever can be brought about appropriately and connaturally by secondary causes should be brought about by them.

And finally, fourth, this mode of efficient causality is consonant with the nature of an accidental form, which /603b/ is given to a substance not only for its embellishment and beautification but also for the exercise of its actions—as is obvious from an induction with regard to actions other [than the production of a substance].

16. You will object that there is a disparity between the action in question and the other actions. For the other actions are accidental—for example, intellection, seeing, producing heat, and so forth—whereas the action in question is substantival—that is, it is terminated *per se* and primarily in a substantival terminus. And so even though accidents are apt instruments for the other actions, they are not apt instruments for the action in question, since the proximate principle of an action must be proportioned to the action; and so if the action is of a higher order, then the principle must also be of a higher order. For example, since intellection is a spiritual action, nature would not have provided an apt instrument for it if it had furnished a material power or instrument—even if the soul, which is the principal prin-

ciple [of intellection], were itself spiritual.[20] In the same way, therefore, an accident will not be an appropriate instrument for a substantival action even if the form is itself a substantial form.

To this objection one could reply, drawing from Cajetan, *Summa Theologiae* 1, q. 54, a. 3, that a substantival generation is not an operation or action in its own right but is instead the terminus of the previous motion or alteration, and so the principle of the alteration is an altogether apt instrument for, or principle of, the generation.

Some moderns embrace this response to such an extent that they base almost the whole plausibility of St. Thomas's position concerning the efficient causality of accidents upon it, and they maintain that prior to Scotus no one had ever claimed that the action in question is distinct from the alteration.

However, I am astonished that they could have been drawn into this position, which seems to me contrary to Aristotle's doctrine, to their own principles, and to the evident deliverances of reason. For in the whole of *Physics* 1 and *On Generation and Corruption* 1 Aristotle is mainly concerned to distinguish substantival generation from alteration. And in *Physics* 5.1–2 [225a1–226a35], where he claims that there is *per se* motion, properly speaking, with respect to three of the categories,[21] he says that with respect to substance there is no motion (*motus*) but rather change (*mutatio*), since change with respect to substance is not a change in the subject with respect to the subject but is instead a change from a being-in-potency to a being *simpliciter*.[22] That is why in the same places he distinguishes the principles of generation from the principles of other motions, where the principles of generation are (i) the proper matter insofar as it is pure potency, (ii) the substantial form, and (iii) the privation.

17. *Whether and how a generation is the terminus of an alteration.* Hence, the authors in question are using words equivocally when they claim that a generation is the terminus of a motion or alteration.

20. The soul's intellective power is the faculty of intellect, which, according to the scholastics, is an immaterial power—i.e., a power whose exercise cannot be attributed to a corporeal organ. Note that sentient and vegetative souls are called "material" souls, since they and all their powers are essentially dependent on matter.

21. These three categories are (i) *quality*, with respect to which there is alteration; (ii) *quantity*, with respect to which there is augmentation and diminution; and (iii) *place*, with respect to which there is local motion. Changes in accidents belonging to any of the other categories are always reducible to one or more of these three basic types of change.

22. By a change "in the subject with respect to the subject" (*ex subjecto in subjectum*) Suarez means a change which is such that numerically the same subject of accidents perdures.

For something can be called a terminus *intrinsically* and properly, and in this sense /604a/ the claim in question is plainly false. For in this sense the terminus of an alteration is none other than the quality that comes to exist through the alteration; indeed, it is impossible in general for an action to be the terminus of any motion, since by its instrinsic nature an action is a *path* [to the terminus], and it comes to exist not through another action but through itself.

In a second sense, something can be called the terminus of a successive motion insofar as it is an instantaneous change that *extrinsically* terminates the motion. This can be understood in two ways.

First, it can mean that the terminus is a certain indivisible change—that is, a certain changed *esse*—which is related by reduction to that same motion and which in reality is of the same nature as the changed *esses* that were [previously] maintaining the motion. 'Terminus' cannot be predicated in this sense of a generation with respect to a prior alteration, since a generation is not of the same order as an alteration and cannot in any way be reduced to an alteration. What's more, a change that terminates a motion within the nature or scope of the motion contributes something toward bringing to completion the terminus of the motion within its own proper nature and being; for example, a changed *esse* in which local motion does not primarily exist brings to completion that "where" which comes to exist through such a motion and which begins to exist at the instant in question after not having yet existed prior to that instant.[23] And the same thing holds analogously for an alteration, since at the instant in question a qualitative terminus comes to exist which did not exist beforehand. By contrast, through a generation no qualitative terminus comes to exist which pertains intrinsically and within its proper genus to the completion of the generation; rather, a new form of a higher nature comes to exist. Therefore, a generation cannot in this sense be called an [extrinsic] terminus of a motion or alteration.

Something can be called an extrinsic terminus in the second sense merely because of an immediate consecutiveness or concomitance. And this interpretation [of the claim that a generation is the terminus of an alteration] is true; yet it does not prevent the generation from being a distinct action. For in this sense an act of illuminating is both the terminus of a motion and also a proper action. Likewise, in this sense the creation of the rational soul, which no one will deny is a distinct action, can be called the terminus of a generation with respect to a previous alteration; and, a fortiori, the same is

---

23. The "where" or place that terminates a local motion (i) is of the same nature as the continuous path of places that served as the material basis for the motion, (ii) lies outside that motion or path, and yet (iii) is the goal toward which the motion was tending *per se*.

true of the uniting of that soul with the body, since this uniting is an action posterior to the creation of the soul.[24]

Therefore, if the generation of a human being is an action distinct from an alteration even though it is in this last sense the terminus [of an alteration], then, a fortiori, the same will be true for other instances of generation. And this is necessary especially if we assume (as the aforementioned authors assume) that at the instant of generation the whole preceding alteration and its intrinsic terminus cease to exist.[25] For the generation cannot in the present sense be called a terminus [of the alteration] except because it immediately succeeds that alteration. Therefore, it is impossible for the generation not to be a new action; /604b/ for the fact that the one thing follows immediately upon the other does not destroy the newness or the distinctness of the action.

18. Thus, finally, I argue a priori: A generation is really and essentially distinct from the whole preceding alteration; therefore, it is *per se* a proper and new action.

The antecedent is evident from the fact that a generation is the eduction of a new form, really distinct from the preceding form, and that it comes to exist in a distinct subject; namely, it comes to exist immediately in the primary matter, whereas the alteration comes to exist in the whole [previous] composite or at least in the matter [of that composite] by the mediation of the quantity. Again, the entire alteration precedes the generation in duration, and according to a plausible opinion the alteration's intrinsic terminus does not even remain.

The consequence, on the other hand, is proved from the fact that the action in question is the eduction of a new form which tends *per se* and primarily toward a new composite that is *per se* one; therefore, it is *per se* a new action.

Perhaps they will reply that it is not an action in its own right but instead something that results from the prior alteration.

But this reply cannot be maintained, especially if we assume that the acci-

24. When Suarez claims that the creation of the rational soul is an action that is prior to the uniting of the rational soul to the body, he is talking about natural priority rather than temporal priority.

25. This assumption is based on the view that accidents cannot migrate from one substance to another. If this view is correct, then in a substantial change, where a new substance comes into existence, the accidents of the new substance cannot be numerically identical with the accidents that were present, even just before the moment of generation, in the corrupted substance—and this is so even if there are scientifically ascertainable laws of regular succession governing the accidents of the two substances. For more on this debate as it redounds on the question of individuation, see *DM* 5. 3.

dents which previously existed in the corrupted thing do not remain in the generated thing. For a form is said to 'result from' an action only to the extent that it results from the terminus of that action, since each action comes to rest proximately in its own terminus. Hence, nothing results mediately from an action except insofar as it results from the terminus of that action. Therefore, if at the instant of generation neither the alteration nor its terminus remains, then how can the substantial form result from that alteration?

Perhaps they will answer: "Because the substantial form naturally follows upon the alteration." But this is not the same as its *resulting from* the alteration. For resulting bespeaks a certain mode of efficient causality through natural emanation, but such an emanation cannot exist between things that follow upon one another proximately when the one follows upon the other as the latter perishes.[26] Otherwise, it could even be claimed that the form of the generated thing "results from" the form of the corrupted thing. For this reason the sort of succession in question does not remove the need for a new action. Instead, it absolutely requires a new action, so that by dint of this action a form can be introduced which expels the other [previous] form and, consequently, expels the accidents (if they depended on that other form).

19. Hence, an even less coherent claim is made by those who, because they are otherwise convinced that the accidents that existed in the corrupted˙ thing do not remain in the generated˙ thing, assert that the substantial form results within the matter by the instrumental power of the accidents that are introduced by the motion, as soon as those accidents reach their fixed terminus. For if those accidents no longer exist, then how can they constitute an instrumental power? Again, the accidents that do reach the fixed intrinsic terminus are not the same ones that existed beforehand, /605a/ and, as regards that terminus, they follow upon the [substantial] form according to the position in question; therefore, they cannot be instruments with respect to that form. Further, as we adumbrated above in discussing the material cause of accidents,[27] even if the very same accidents do remain, they cannot be instruments with respect to the [new] substantial form, since they have no preceding action of their own by means of which they might be elevated to the principal agent's effect.

For this reason, the instrumental causality in question should be attributed not to the accidents that come to exist within the patient and that dispose the matter but rather to the accidents that exist in the agent and from which those other accidents proceed. From this it also follows that the substantial form cannot truly be said to result from the accidents that dispose the matter.

---

26. See the discussion of natural emanation in *DM* 18. 3.

27. See *DM* 14. 3.

And, finally, whatever the term 'result from' means and whatever the truth might be about whether the accidents of the patient also have an efficient causality in the eduction of a [substantial] form, it cannot be denied that this eduction is a new action and that it is altogether intended *per se*, since it is a proper action that is brought about in the power of the substance. For the alteration is a proper action of the accident itself according to its own nature, and it is, as it were, a means that is ordered toward the generation, which is itself the action that is intended primarily and *per se*. It is in this way, too, as Aristotle testifies, that nutrition is an action properly and *per se*, and augmentation as well, even though neither of them is effected except by means of a previous alteration and by means of the dispositions in connection with which a part of a substance can be produced.

20. Therefore, one should reply in a different way to the proposed objection:[28] namely, by conceding that the action by which the substantial form is educed is a substantival action as regards its terminus and is more noble than any action or alteration that an accident is able to execute by its own power. It is not only Scotus who lighted upon this position; rather, before him it was taught by Aristotle, *Physics* 2, text 14 [1.193b12–18] and *Physics* 8, text 62 [8.265a3–5]; by Averroës, *Physics* 4, comment 129; and by Simplicius, *Physics* 5, text 8. And many Thomists after Scotus adopted the same claim, as one can see in Capreolus, *Sentences* 1, dist. 13, a. 3, reply to the argument against concl. 1; Soncinas, *Metaphysics* 7, q. 22; and Ferrariensis, *Contra Gentes* 2, chap. 17.

And yet these authors assert, and rightly so, that an accident proportioned to a substantial form can by its nature be a fitting instrument for such an action. For even if within the realm of being an accidental form is of a lower order as compared to a substantial form, nonetheless in their modes of being they are proportioned to one another if both of them are dependent upon matter. And, similarly, they are commensurate with one another in the way that a disposition and a form are, and for that same reason they can be

---

28. It might be helpful to reset the context here. The objection Suarez alludes to, found in §16, went as follows: "You will object that there is a disparity between the action in question and the other actions. For the other actions are accidental—e.g., intellection, seeing, producing heat, etc.—whereas the action in question is substantival—i.e., it is terminated *per se* and primarily in a substantival terminus. And so even though accidents are apt instruments for the other actions, they are not apt instruments for the action in question, since the proximate principle of an action must be proportioned to the action; and so if the action is of a higher order, then the principle must also be of a higher order." In §16–19 Suarez has discussed and rejected the common Thomistic reply to this objection: viz., that the eduction of the substantial form is not an action distinct from the alteration that precedes it. Now he will give his own reply.

proportioned to one another in the way that an instrumental power and an action /605b/ —that is, a terminus—are. For just as it is connatural to a substance that it should operate through accidents proportioned to it, so too it is connatural to a substance that it should come to exist, as through a fitting instrument, through accidental dispositions that are proportioned to it. For this reason, there is no parallel with the objection that was made about a material power vis-à-vis a spiritual intellection,[29] since in the latter case there is no proportionateness, either in the nature of the subject or in the nature of the disposition or in any other way; and so a material power would not be an appropriate instrument—especially in view of the fact that the intellect is not only an instrument but also in its own way a principal principle of an intellection that is connatural to it, as I will explain in the next section.[30]

21. *Whether accidents attain to the generation of a human being as efficient causes.* But someone can object that at least in the generation of a human being the accidents are not apt instruments in the sense of being able to attain immediately to the action by which a human being is generated. For the action in question is the uniting of a rational soul to matter, a uniting through which that same soul's mode of union immediately comes to exist. But this mode is immaterial, since it is identical in reality with the soul.[31] Therefore, the unitive action is itself also spiritual, since it is identical with its proximate and formal terminus. Therefore, a material accident cannot be an instrument for such an action.

One might reply, first of all, by conceding the whole objection, since in [our first] thesis we did not assert that accidents are instruments for *uniting* any substantial form with matter; instead, we asserted that they are instruments for *educing* a form (an educible form, of course).[32] Now in order to unite a *rational* form [with matter], it is sufficient that the accidents of the semen concur as efficient causes in disposing and organizing the body. However, the dispositions themselves are only material causes and stand in need of the union in question. This is enough for a human being to be said to generate a human being, even though it is God alone, the creator of the soul, who also unites it as an efficient cause. Scotus held this in *Sentences* 4, dist. 43,

29. See §16 above.

30. See *DM* 18. 3. 21.

31. The mode is "identical in reality" with the soul in the sense that it depends on the soul for its existence and, unlike a full-fledged accident, cannot exist in separation from the soul, even by the power of God. So it is only 'modally', and not 'really', distinct from the soul. For more on the types of identity and distinction, see *DM* 7. 1.

32. The rational soul is not "educible" from the relevant matter, since, unlike the souls of plants and irrational animals, it is immaterial. Thus, it cannot be said to exist 'in potency' in the matter which it comes to inform.

q. 3, a. 3, and the same thing is deemed probable by Richard in *Sentences* 4, dist. 43, a. 3, q. 2. In addition, Henry, *Quodlibeta* 11, q. 14, presupposes the same thing when he says that the rational soul, which is created by God alone in a body disposed by a natural agent, unites itself without any new efficient causality on the part of an extrinsic agent but instead, as it were, through the union's resulting naturally from the soul itself. For it follows from this position, too, that the proximate agent in human generation does not by its efficient causality attain immediately to the union of the soul with the body but instead attains to it only remotely by way of the dispositions. This opinion is also held /606a/ by the Conimbricenses, *Physics* 1, q. 11, a. 3.

Second, if someone wanted to defend the claim that the accidents attain to this union instrumentally—a position held by Capreolus, *Sentences* 2, dist. 15, q. unica, a. 3, and more clearly in *Sentences* 4, dist. 43, a. 3, reply to the arguments of Henry and Aureoli against concl. 2—then he could reply that even if this union is in itself immaterial, it can still participate in certain of the properties of a material thing, especially given the fact that, because of its essential and actual relation to matter, it depends on matter both in its coming to exist and in its existing. For this reason the union also has a kind of branching out from the side of the matter. And because of this it can happen that the material accidents are elevated as instruments for effecting this union—a claim that will not seem troublesome to those who believe that a material phantasm is an instrument for effecting a spiritual species.[33]

SECOND ASSERTION

22. *An instrumental form is not a sufficient principle for acting unless a form that is a principal principle is adjoined to it.* I claim, second, that one should not deny that a substantial form has its own proper and principal efficient causality with respect to the eduction of a similar form from the potency of the matter, and this because the substantial form has through itself an immediate influence along with the accidental and instrumental principle, as long as it is conjoined to the latter in reality and is sufficiently proximate to it, with the result that in this sort of efficient causality the accident behaves as a conjoined instrument of the form and not as an instrument that is altogether separated *secundum causalitatem.*

33. The philosophers in question claim that the sensory image (or phantasm) produced by the material process of sensation is an instrumental cause, and not just an occasion, of the corresponding intelligible species that is abstracted by the intellect in the process of forming a general concept.

This entire thesis, along with its intent and meaning, were, I believe, adequately explained above. And they are more fully clarified as follows. When a fire, say, is generated out of nearby flax, we claim that it is not only instrumentally through its heat but also principally through its own substantial form that the generating fire has an influence on the action, which is intrinsically terminated in the eduction of the substantial form. And we claim that the fire has this influence not only mediately and remotely—that is, by virtue of giving *esse* to its own heat along with the power through which the heat is a cause—but also because within its own genus it has a proximate influence along with its heat. And we claim that this very feature is preserved in *every* eduction of a substantial form, as long as there is no impediment on the part of the agent from any other source, either because of a lack of existence or because of spatial distance.

The foundation for this assertion, thus explained, was also suggested above, and it consists in two principles.

The first is that an instrumental form, taken by itself alone and deprived, as it were, of the actual influence of the principal agent, cannot be /606b/ sufficient, within the genus of a proximate cause, for effecting a form more noble than itself. This principle seems to me to be almost known on the basis of the terms themselves. For if in a given case the form in question is not being actually aided by a higher form, then it has an influence only through that which it actually has within itself. Therefore, since the latter is something imperfect, the form cannot by itself alone effect anything more perfect. Likewise, it is impossible for heat to effect a substantial form by its own power alone; rather, when it operates by itself alone without the influence of a higher form, it operates only by its own power, since the only power it has is that which is connatural to its being—that is, that which it has by dint of its own proper *esse*. On the other hand, the fact that it has this *esse* from the fire's [substantial] form or that by its nature it is a faculty of the fire or that it takes the fire's place so as to act in its name, as it were—all these things, I repeat, since they only add certain relations or denominations to the heat, cannot be sufficient for its being the case that the heat by itself, deprived (as I will put it) of all higher assistance, should be a sufficient proximate and immediate principle of the sort of action in question.

Likewise, if this were not so, then the heat would be a power for producing a substance in the same way that it is a power for producing heat—which, as is obvious from the very fact that a substance exceeds [an accident], is utterly absurd. The inference is evident from the fact that the heat has both these actions insofar as it is a certain power of the substance's and takes its own *esse* from the substance.

Finally, since the heat's power to act in any way at all is nothing other than its own being and perfection, and since this being and perfection are far less than those which exist in a substantial form, it is not readily conceivable how a total power, sufficient by itself alone for educing a substantial form, might be transmitted to the heat. Therefore, the heat by itself cannot take the place of an entire principal principle.

23. *A material substantial form constitutes a suppositum that is able to be an efficient cause.* The second principle on which the posited assertion depends is that the mode of activity in question can, speaking *per se*, belong to a material substantial form, as long as the general conditions required for acting are not absent for some other reason.

This principle seems to be adequately proved by the arguments given at the end on behalf of Scotus's position[34]—arguments that Aristotle confirms to no small degree in *On Generation and Corruption* 2, texts 54 and 55 [9.336a2–4], where, rebuking those who denied that forms have efficient causality, he says: "Thus it is that in various ways they attribute to bodies the instrumental faculties through which things are generated, and in the meantime they remove the cause which pertains to the form."

Nor is it sufficient to reply that efficient causality is attributed to [substantial] forms because the qualities through which alone they exercise /607a/ all their actions emanate from them. For, as we explained above, this is not proper and *per se* efficient causality but rather only remote and originating efficient causality, since an action that arises immediately from an accidental form alone likewise depends *per se* and essentially on it alone as on a proximate principle. (I am here leaving to one side the concurrence of a universal cause.) An indication of this is that if God conserves, say, the heat [without the fire], then every action that proceeds proximately just from the heat can be conserved, too—as the authors of the contrary position also acknowledge. Therefore, this is an indication that the substantial form is not a *per se* principle of any such action. Therefore, if the [substantial] form is never able to have an actual influence along with the accidental power, then it will never have a true and proper efficient causality—the very claim that Aristotle reproved above and that detracts in no small way from the perfection of the substantial form.

Further, it cannot be proved that there is anything contradictory in this mode of efficient causality; therefore, there is no reason why it should be denied. For by a similar line of reasoning we proved above that secondary causes have the power to be efficient causes from the fact that it pertains to a creature's perfection and to the Creator's efficacy that they should have the power to communicate themselves to the extent that this is consonant with

34. See §8 above.

their natures.[35] Therefore, one should say the same thing about substantial forms vis-à-vis the present sort of efficient causality, as long as such causality is not repugnant to them for some other reason. But, speaking *per se*, no such repugnance can be proved, either on the part of the form that is educed or on the part of the form that educes it. The first point is evident from the fact that the educed form is finite and is effected in (as I will put it) a finite mode—that is, through eduction with no trace of creation. The second point is evident from the fact that the [educing] form is not less perfect [than the educed form] or disproportionate to it, since it is of the same order. For it is a more noble or an equally noble act of matter, and by its nature it has been instituted for, and is especially inclined toward, generating that which is similar to itself.

24. *The arguments for the second position are answered; the first argument.* Finally, the arguments for the second position either do not attack or else are not at all convincing against the sort of activity in question.[36]

For the first argument[37] proves at most that the instrumental activity of the accidents should not be excluded. But it does not prove that the relevant influence of the [substantial] form is impossible or that it is unnecessary.

And so there are two ways to understand the claim that a substantial form is a proximate principle of a given action. In one way, it means that [the substantial form] is a proximate principle in an exclusive manner (as I will put it)—that is, without the aid of any other proximate and instrumental principle. And, given this way of understanding the claim, it does not follow that a substantial form is a proximate principle of any proper action. /607b/ This is at most what the considerations proposed in that [first] argument prove.

As for the second way, the claim can mean that the substantial form is a proximate principle in the sense that through its substance it has an immediate influence on the action or effect—yet not by itself alone but insofar as it elevates or aids an instrumental power and insofar as it is channeled by that power to a given action. And, given this way of understanding the claim, we deny that it exceeds the perfection of a substantial form to be a proximate

35. See *DM* 18. 1. 8–9.

36. Once again, it may be helpful to remember the context. Suarez agrees with the second position (see §9 above) that the accidents do, as instrumental causes, attain to the eduction of substantial forms. However, he also wants to insist, against some proponents of the second position, that, in addition, the agent's substantial form has an immediate influence in the action of generation.

37. See §10 above. The argument goes as follows: "A substantial form is not *per se* immediately active but is instead active through a power, which is a quality distinct from it; therefore, it does not induce a substantial form except by the mediation of an accidental power."

principal principle for effecting a given action. In the next section we will
show that this is true not only for substantival generation, which is what we
are now talking about, but also for certain accidental operations. And the
reasons adumbrated in that [first] argument do not count against this, since
the relevant mode of efficient causality does not exclude an accidental power
or instrument.

25. *The second argument; the third argument.* As is obvious from what has
been said, the second argument[38] proceeds from a false foundation: namely,
that the generation is not properly an action distinct from the alteration.

The third argument,[39] on the other hand, carries little weight, both because (i) a privative contrariety or opposition suffices for efficient causality
in the strict sense, especially when the effecting occurs not through a proper
successive motion but through an instantaneous change, as in substantival
generation;[40] and also because (ii) even though a formal contrariety may obtain between qualities, there is nonetheless a *root* contrariety (as I will call it)
among substantial forms. And so it is not always the case that a quality is by
itself the principle of an action; rather, in some cases the [substantial] form
is a principle as well, especially when what is to be introduced through the
action is not only a contrary quality but a [substantial] form repugnant to the
other [previous] form.

Finally, even though a corruptive action does not occur except between
contraries, nonetheless, the qualities themselves effect not only the formally
contrary qualities but also the [substantial] forms, in which one finds the
root of the contrariety and repugnance. An indication of this is that even
though the action begins from a proper contrariety, it nonetheless does not
come to rest in it but extends to its root. Is it any wonder, then, that the
[substantial] form itself can also be, within its own genus, a principle of such

---

38. See §11 above. The argument is this: "The action through which a substantial form
is educed is not properly an action distinct from the motion of alteration that is ordered
toward and tends toward that [substantial form] but is instead the terminus, as it were, of
that motion; and so they are not counted as two actions but as one and the same action. But
the entire alteration that tends toward the generation is effected by means of the accidents,
as is obvious *per se*. Therefore, the substantival generation itself is effected by means of the
accidents."

39. See §12 above. Here is the argument: "A proper action comes to exist only between
contraries. Therefore, only that which properly has contraries is a proper principle of such
an action. But it is a quality, and not a substantial form, that is of this sort. Therefore, etc."

40. A change must involve the transition from one contrary to another. Suarez's point
here is that the contrariety required may simply be an opposition between *having* and *lacking* a given characteristic F, rather than an opposition between having F and having some
other positive characteristic F* that is incompatible with F.

efficient causality, at least to the extent that it attains to a substantial form and [thus] to the root of the contrariety?

On the other hand, the experiences that were brought to bear at the end[41] do not tell against this conclusion, which was posited solely on the hypothesis that the form is sufficiently present. But what one should say about these experiences will be obvious from the assertions that follow.

26. *The first assertion is shown not to be opposed to the second.* The only thing that can be brought to bear against these two theses is Scotus's objection.[42] /608a/ The second conclusion seems to contradict the first, since if the substantial form has through itself a proximate influence for effecting a similar form, then the immediate activity of the accidents is superfluous. For if the heat is by itself sufficient within the genus of a proximate principle for effecting a similar heat, then why won't the fire's [substantial] form be sufficient by itself for educing a similar form, given that we are now assuming that it can have an immediate influence on that form? But if it is indeed sufficient, then any other principle is unnecessary.

One may reply, first of all, that it was necessary for the accidents to have an instrumental activity because, as we will explain in a moment, the accidents were conferred not only to act in the presence of the form but also to act in its absence. For this is often necessary in the case of natural generations.

Next, from this we infer that (i) the proper power to dispose and prepare the matter and (ii) the instrumental power to educe a [substantial] form when the relevant form is educible are conjoined by the nature of things. And so even if we grant that another active power is not absolutely required by the [substantial] form when it is sufficiently present, nonetheless, because the [instrumental] power in question is *per se* necessary and connatural for another reason, it concurs in the case at hand as well and provides great assistance in the action.

Finally, one can add that perhaps it is also because the substantial form is never by itself a sufficient principle of acting that this [instrumental] power is necessary in the circumstances in question—both (i) by virtue of the fact that the substantial form is of itself an indifferent and, as it were, general principle of action, and also (ii) because just as, in order to be educed from the potency of matter, a substantial form requires accidental dispositions on the part of the matter even though an accidental form does not require them, so too, in order to be educed from the potency of matter, it requires, on the part of the principle, the cooperation of an accidental instrument.

41. See §13 above.
42. See §7 above.

THIRD ASSERTION

27. I claim, third, that the accidents are not the substance's conjoined instruments for educing a substantial form in a sense that rules out their being able to exercise their entire activity with respect to a substance even if they are separated from or distant from the substantial form.[43] This is the clear position of St. Thomas, a position embraced by all the authors cited above in the second position on the first point above, as well as those cited in the second point.[44]

This position is proved by the natural experiences adduced above and also by that experience which, given the mystery of the Eucharist, is based on the action of the species of the wine.

Moreover, there is an a priori argument. Regardless of how the being of these accidents is conserved when they are separated from their proper substantial form, the entire power of acting that is connatural to them remains in them, /608b/ since this power is not distinct in reality from their being. Therefore, if they are applied to a patient in the appropriate way, they will have the action that is connatural to them with respect to that patient, an action whereby they dispose its matter for a form proportioned to themselves. But if this action attains to its required terminus, then by the nature of things it has conjoined with it an instrumental action whereby the substantial form is educed, since this latter action cannot naturally be separated from the last disposition [of the matter]. Therefore, accidents of this sort are able to have this latter action too, even if they are distant from their proper [substantial] form, as long as they retain the entire intrinsic perfection or intensity required for acting and for sufficiently disposing the matter.

FOURTH ASSERTION

28. I claim, fourth, that (i) when accidents that are separated from their own [substantial] form produce a substantial form in such a way that they cannot be aided by their own form, it is necessary for their own form's influence, which is absent in this case, to be supplied by the concurrence of some higher cause; and that (ii) this cause cannot be a created intelligence but must instead be a corporeal cause, such as the sun or other similar cause, or else, if this latter sort of cause is also absent or found to be insufficient, then

43. For a description of conjoined instruments, see *DM* 17. 2. 22.
44. This includes all the authors cited above in §§13 and 14 with the exception of Scotus.

the deficiency in question must be made up for by the concurrence of the
First Cause.

The first part of this thesis follows by a necessary implication from what
has preceded. For, as was proved in the second assertion, an accidental
form is not, taken by itself and deprived of the substantial form's aid, a
sufficient principle, as a proximate cause, of a substantial form. Therefore,
when it lacks the substantial form's influence, it cannot bring the principal
agent's effect to completion unless the influence in question is supplied from
some other source. For an effect can never be produced in the absence of
a sufficient cause. Nonetheless, it often happens that in the absence of the
influence of their proper [substantial] form, accidents are able by their action
to attain to a substantival effect. Therefore, in such cases this influence is
supplied by the concurrence of some higher cause, since there is no other
principle that such an action could be traced back to. For no lower cause is
sufficient (due to the argument that has been repeated again and again), and
no same-level cause intervenes.

The present assertion is proved, next, by a certain opinion that is common
to all philosophers. For they all think that, because of a deficiency in the particular or univocal cause, certain substantival effects must be attributed to a
higher or celestial cause as a proximate principal cause. Thus, they claim that
animals generated from putrefaction are produced by the power of a celestial body; /609a/ likewise, many believe the same thing about minerals and
about the form of a cadaver.[45] But if accidents were sufficient by themselves
to produce a substantial form without the assistance of a higher cause, then
it would never be necessary to have recourse to a higher cause in the case
of these effects. Instead, one would always have to claim that each thing is
produced by a thing that is similar to it, either formally similar or similar by
a power that exists in its accidents, without any influence on the part of a
celestial body and without any influence on the part of the other Universal
Cause over and beyond that which it has with all other causes.

For example, if it were true that in a red-hot piece of iron there is no formal
fire but only a heat intense enough to dispose the matter of the flax for the
substantial form of fire, then even if such a piece of iron generated a fire
[in the flax], neither the celestial bodies nor God would be concurring with

45. Minerals are problematic because great heat is necessary for their generation, and
yet there seems to be no appropriate medium through which the sun's heat could be transmitted to the bowels of the earth. The case of a cadaver is problematic because the normal
causes of an animal's death seem insufficient or inappropriate for generating the form of
the dead body.

a greater concurrence than if a fire were generating the fire. And, as a result, this generating of fire would be attributed to a universal cause to no greater degree than if a fire were doing the generating. Therefore, by parity of reasoning, when gold is generated in the bowels of the earth, the sun does not concur there by any special influence in producing the substantial form of gold; instead, the accidents that sufficiently dispose the matter for the form of gold (for they are always necessary for educing any form whatsoever) will, in the power of the form of gold, induce a similar form. Therefore, gold is generated not by the celestial bodies but by gold, and a cadaver is generated by a cadaver, and so on for all other things. But this is contrary to the opinion of all those philosophers who claim that in such cases a universal cause makes up for the deficiency of the particular cause. Therefore, one should say the same thing whenever a similar deficiency occurs. This will be explicated further when we discuss a few of these effects in detail.

29. *The various ways in which accidents can be separated from their connatural or principal substances.* There are various ways in which it can happen that accidents are separated from their substantial form.

In the first way, the accidents are conserved by God's power outside of every substance, as happens in the mystery of the Eucharist. And in such a case the separated accidents—for example, the species of the wine—by their own proper power and God's general concurrence dispose, say, a drop of water that is mixed with them in order that they might convert it into wine.[46] Now even though, when they arrive at the instant of the substantival transmutation, these same accidents do, to be sure, apply all the instrumental efficient causality that by their nature they are able to apply for the eduction of the form, nonetheless, because the substantial form's influence is absent, God must apply, in addition to his general concurrence, a greater efficient causality by which /609b/ he supplies the influence of the [substantial] form in question. I explained this point in *Summa Theologiae* 3, vol. 3, disp. 57, sec. 1, where I alluded to those authors who philosophize in this way and yet call that action "natural" because the entire concurrence in question is owed [to the accidents] once the prior miracle has been posited. Still, in all other respects the action is brought about by a natural power and in a natural manner.

30. *Whether a red-hot piece of iron really has fire in some part of itself.* The second way in which an accident can be separated from its proper substantial form is by existing in an extraneous subject, in the way that intense heat exists in water or in iron or in the way that light exists in the air. For we are calling

46. See n. 13 above.

"extraneous" not only a subject that is repugnant [to a given accident] but also a subject that, by virtue of its own form, lacks such an accident unless it receives it from an extrinsic agent.

Now if an accident that exists in this way in an extraneous subject is of the same species as the dispositions required for introducing a given form, it is rarely capable of producing a sufficient disposition for the form that is connatural to it. So either (i) it has to have the form conjoined to it as an active principle or else (ii) the generation will follow entirely *per accidens* from the disposition of the matter, and in that case the power of a higher cause will be all the more necessary. And the reason is that, for example, heat that is separated from fire or from an animal is not sufficient, speaking *per se*, to dispose the matter sufficiently for the form of fire. For when it exists in an extraneous subject, it never has the intensity necessary for the form of fire; nor is it sufficient to generate flesh or to introduce a soul, since in an extraneous subject it is not moderated in the way that the disposition for a soul requires.

This argument goes through in general for any similar accident, since in an extraneous subject either the accident does not reach the degree [of intensity] required by the other form or else it does not have conjoined to it the other qualities required for the constitution of such a form. And so, speaking *per se*, it cannot sufficiently dispose the matter for the [substantial] form in question, and, consequently, it cannot introduce the relevant form into the primary matter as an instrumental cause. Hence, in the common example of a red-hot piece of iron, the heat that inheres in the iron is in fact not sufficient to generate fire (though it does have a conjoined real fire, instilled inside the pores of the iron, by which the [new] fire is generated). Nonetheless, the iron's heat does contribute to the quickness and intensity of the action.

Also, in some cases, because of the patient's disposition, it happens that even though the proximate agent introduces only heat of a certain degree, a disposition for an entirely different [substantial] form results *per accidens*. For example, if /610a/ the matter is moist and is heated by a fire, then a mixture of the hot and the moist readily results, along with the [substantial] form of some mixed body that requires that disposition.[47] And it is in this way that many mixed bodies, especially imperfect ones, are generated. Perhaps minerals, too, are often produced in this way. (For it is probable that [this production] is *sometimes* brought about *per se* through the action of something similar to the minerals, and this by means of a sort of accretion and augmentation—not, to be sure, by means of a *vital* accretion or augmentation but

47. A mixed body (*mistum*) is a body compounded from the four elements.

rather by means of a juxtaposition.[48]) Likewise, animals that are generated from putrefaction or from rain falling on hot earth seem to be produced *per accidens* in this way.

In the case of *per accidens* generations of this sort it is not difficult to believe that what is required is the power of a higher agent whereby such forms might be introduced. For the proximate agent not only lacks a similar or same-level substantial form, it does not even have a quality or constitution that is *per se* sufficient for disposing and preparing the matter or, consequently, for an adequate instrumental action. Moreover, as I have repeatedly explained, the dispositions received in the patient do not concur actively, even as instruments, in introducing their own form. For either (i) they no longer exist at the instant [of generation], but instead there are different dispositions that result from that form, or (ii) if they are the same dispositions, they do not have any proper action there and so cannot have any instrumental action. Therefore, in all these generations that are brought about, as it were, *per accidens*, some higher cause, which introduces the form, is properly required.

And almost the same argument applies to the introduction of the form of a cadaver, which (i) is produced *per accidens*, as it were, in order that the matter not remain without a form, and which (ii) is produced not so much by the action of the agent that, say, kills the animal (such an action often consists merely in the division of a continuum) but is instead produced by the material disposition that remains or preexisted in the patient.

The same is true when, because of the vehement motion of a collision or banging together of bodies, a fire is sparked by the vehement heat that the motion causes in some particle of the matter that is well-disposed for that fire.

And, finally, the same argument applies to all generations that can be brought about *per accidens*.

31. However, if an accident existing in an extraneous subject is of a *higher* species than, rather than of the same species as, the dispositions by which the lower matter is prepared for the form of the thing to be generated, then it can happen that the generation of a lower substance is brought about by that accident not only *per accidens* by reason of the dispositions of the matter but also *per se* in accord with the intention of a higher agent. This occurs when /610b/ the principal agent, because it is distant in place, diffuses a certain power through the medium by the mediation (as they put it) of a supposi-

---

48. Suarez may have in mind here certain processes involving bonding or perhaps crystallization.

tum, so that through this power it is joined to the patient by an immediacy of power—in the way that a celestial body acts on the lower things here below by means of light or other influences that are qualities of an order and type higher than the elementary qualities by which the matter is proximately disposed.[49] And with regard to this sort of action one can claim that even though the principal agent seems to be distant in place, it nonetheless does not stop having an actual influence. For the principal agent exists within its sphere of activity and has contact with the patient by means of the diffused power. And in this way one can see that the action proceeds not from the accident alone as from an altogether separated instrument, but that instead it proceeds from the accident as from an instrument that is conjoined to its principal agent under the notion of causality. However, this claim is contingent upon a difficulty, to be discussed below, concerning the required proximity of the agent to the patient, and so it will be deferred to that place.[50]

32. Lastly, even if an accident does not exist in an extraneous subject, it can be separated from the principal generating thing by reason of the fact that both the accident and its subject are cut off from the generating thing and are set up to take the latter's place in acting. And this occurs especially in the generation of animals by means of semen, which is a separated instrument in the most proper sense—separated not only with respect to subject but also with respect to place and in some cases even with respect to time. For it can happen that the semen effects a generation when the generating thing no longer exists.

From this it is also patently obvious that such an instrument is separated in causality from the animal from which it is cut off, and so in the case of this sort of instrument the necessity for some influence on the part of a higher cause is more clearly seen; otherwise, given that the semen is a very imperfect entity, it is not apparent how it could by itself alone, as a sufficient proximate cause, produce a thing that is far more perfect. For even if the fact that it is a power cut off from a more perfect thing and left in its place is sufficient for some sort of instrumental action (as Aristotle, too, claims in *On the Generation of Animals* 2.1 [733b24–735a28]), nonetheless, this cannot be sufficient for its being an absolutely total proximate agent.

Nor is it enough to claim that the semen is an instrument not only by reason of its accidents but also by reason of the substantial form that exists in the spirits included in the dense part of the semen, spirits in which the seminal and instrumental power resides. For even though this is plausible,

---

49. By "elementary qualities" Suarez means the qualities of the elements: viz., heat, coldness, dryness, and moistness.

50. See *DM* 18. 8.

it is nonetheless not sufficient, since the whole substance in question, /611a/ along with its form, is much less perfect than the soul that is introduced through the action. Therefore, it needs a greater concurrence and assistance on the part of a higher cause, especially in the generation of perfect animals and living things.[51]

33. *How the organization of a fetus is effected.* Indeed, some authors—especially Scotus, *Sentences* 2, dist. 18—add that the semen's power is insufficient even for the accidental arrangement of an organic body, since this action is so varied and complex that it is in no way clear how it could be brought to completion by a power that is simple and imperfect and that acts only naturally. This is why the Commentator, whom Scotus also cites, says in *On the Heavens* 2, comments 69ff., that the semen acts and organizes by means of a divine power. And in *Metaphysics* 7, text 31 [9.1034a30–1034b6], he says that the semen's power is divine, artistic, and similar to an intellectual power. "And this is why," he continues, "Galen wondered whether or not that power is a creator." Galen discusses this in *On the Formation of the Fetus,* where he honestly and freely confesses that even though he has worked hard on this problem, he has found no solution that satisfies him. Nonetheless, he concludes that the semen's wondrous operation is not devoid of explanation or beyond understanding.

And the action in question is indeed so marvelous that it can hardly be comprehended at all. Therefore, if even the action of organizing the body can scarcely be attributed to the semen without some special concurrence and assistance on the part of a higher cause, then what wonder is it that the semen should need more aid and assistance for educing the substantial form from the matter which is the subject of that form? For it is beyond doubt that there is a big difference and a sharp distinction between these two actions.

For given that the organization of the body is accidental rather than substantival, one can correctly see that with respect to this entire organizing action there is, as it were, an eminent and universal power in the semen— whether by reason of the semen's substantial form or by reason of some accidental faculty. For both of these can be understood to be instruments of the soul sufficient for effecting that mixture of the primary qualities that is appropriate for and connatural to the members of an organic body. All that seems to be required is a certain diversified application in order that this same power on the part of the semen might be able to arrange the various members in diverse ways and bring about by its own power the marvelous ordering that is apparent in the appropriate arrangement of the members.

51. By "perfect animal" Suarez means higher animals, such as mammals, as opposed to lower life forms such as worms.

And perhaps the semen is assisted in this by some natural power of the mother's womb or by some celestial influence or at least (if this be necessary) by some motion or direction on the part of the author of nature. This is so especially because the semen does not, by its own power alone, perfect from the beginning /611b/ the whole organization of the body. Instead, it perfects the organization of some principal part into which the sentient soul is introduced, and it is the sentient soul that, a little while later, perfects the organization of its body—as St. Thomas explains at length in *Summa Theologiae* 1, q. 118, a. 1, ad 4.

However, as far as the production of the sentient soul itself is concerned, the semen's power is deficient not only as regards its mode of action but also as regards the substance of the action (as I will put it), and so with respect to that action it stands in much more need of the actual help, influence, and concurrence of a higher cause, as will be manifestly obvious to one who ponders the matter carefully.

34. *An objection to the claims made above.* The only possible objection is that it seems to be contrary both to the appropriate order of nature and to the perfection of the agents in question that in the generation of these things a higher cause (or the First Cause) always has to make up for the proximate cause's deficiency. For when it happens, *per accidens* and by a fortuitous conjunction of causes, that a generation is brought about in the absence of a sufficient proximate cause—that is, when a generation is brought about by the necessity of matter rather than by the intention of a natural agent—it is no surprise that a universal cause has to make up for the deficiency of the particular cause in introducing the form.[52] But the idea that in the very mode of *per se* generation instituted by nature the proximate cause is always so imperfect or always applies its power in so imperfect a way that it is never sufficient to produce the effect, seems to bespeak both a disordered arrangement on the part of nature and a great imperfection on the part of the particular causes that generate in this way.

And this is confirmed by the fact that inanimate corporeal agents have, speaking *per se*, a power sufficient for producing things similar to themselves. Therefore, animate agents, since they are far more perfect than inanimate things, should also have this power.

It is confirmed, second, by the fact that otherwise one could just as easily claim that a secondary cause of the sort in question contributes nothing at all to the eduction of the substantial form, but that instead the *whole* effect is brought about by the First Cause, which makes up for the deficiency of

---

52. Suarez has in mind here the generation of lower animals from putrefaction.

the particular cause. But if this latter claim seems absurd because it is not consonant with the natures of things, then the claim in question should also seem absurd.[53]

35. *A subordinate question in preparation for a reply to the objection.* Before I reply fully to this objection, I must first explain which universal cause it is that makes up for this deficiency in the particular cause—that is, that assists its instrument—the point that we proposed in the second part of the above assertion.[54]

In that part of the assertion we claimed, first of all, that the efficient causality in question cannot be attributed to the created intelligences, since we judged that they do not have the power to produce /612a/ anything in bodies other than local motion, as will be explained below when we discuss the intelligences in their own right.[55] Hence, natural agents do not depend *per se* on the concurrence of the created intelligences for their actions, just as they do not depend on the created intelligences for their *esse* either. And so when natural agents require more aid and concurrence, it is not the intelligences they look to for that concurrence and assistance but rather some other cause to which they are subordinated *per se*. Nonetheless, there is no shortage of authors who claim that even though the intelligences cannot of themselves have an influence on bodies in the way in question, they nonetheless can have such an influence through the celestial bodies as through their instruments. But I will explain in a moment how difficult it is to understand and believe this claim.

Therefore, what remains is that a universal cause of the sort in question is either a celestial body or the very author of nature himself; for apart from these, there is no other conceivable higher cause. And, to be sure, a celestial body does of itself seem to be a proportionate agent. For since it is a body, and since it is otherwise of a higher order and perfection, it has a more eminent power to alter lower bodies, as experience itself also makes sufficiently clear to us. And so it is not surprising that a celestial body should also have the power to generate substances and thus to assist accidents in the generation of substances.

---

53. Suarez's final answer to the objection comes only in §41 below.

54. See §28 above. The second part of the assertion goes like this: "This [higher] cause cannot be a created intelligence but must instead be a corporeal cause, such as the sun or other similar cause, or else, if this latter sort of cause is also absent or found to be insufficient, then the deficiency in question must be made up for by the concurrence of the First Cause."

55. See *DM* 35. 6.

36. Still, there are two intervening obstacles, not to be taken lightly, that seem to render problematic this influence of celestial bodies on the substantial forms of the things to be generated.[56]

The first obstacle is a general one that applies to all the things, animate or inanimate, that are generated in the element earth or in the other elements. A celestial body acts for the eduction of substantial forms either (i) through its accidents alone or (ii) immediately through its substantial form as well. If the first answer is given, then the same difficulty with which we are presently occupied arises again: namely, how these accidents are sufficient by themselves, without the actual influence of either their own substantial form or some other substantial form, for educing a substantial form. Perhaps one might reply that celestial accidents are more perfect beings than the material forms of generable things, especially inanimate things. But this is absolutely false, since, as I will show below, a substantial form is a more perfect being than any accident, not only in general but without exception and in each particular case.[57] Also, in certain cases, as with the forms of gold, silver, diamonds, and so on, the claim in question is *per se* incredible. This is so especially in light of the fact that the celestial bodies proximately produce these effects by means of qualities—for example, light and perhaps other nonsensible qualities (if there be such) that they impress on the air and on other intervening bodies—qualities that are no more perfect /612b/ than even the form of air, not to mention all the other forms.

If for this reason the proper and actual efficient causality of the sun's form itself or the forms of other stars is necessary, then the very great spatial distance seems to pose an obstacle. For how can the sun's form immediately through itself produce the form of gold in the bowels of the earth, which are so far distant and remote from it? It was because of this problem that Scotus claimed that it is possible for a form to act immediately on a distant thing—a claim that other philosophers can scarcely listen to or tolerate, since this *dictum* of Scotus's conflicts with an Aristotelian doctrine accepted by all philosophers.

Nor will one resolve the present difficulty by claiming that just as the efficient causality of the sun's accidents penetrates into the inner parts of the earth, so too does the efficient causality of the sun's form. For there is no similar rationale that applies to both cases, since the accidents diffuse their power by means of other accidents that are produced by them, whereas the substantial form cannot diffuse its power by means of [other] substantial forms, as is patently obvious *per se*. For the substantial form does not cor-

---

56. The first of these obstacles is discussed in §§36–37 and the second in §§38–40.
57. See *DM* 32. 2.

rupt the intervening bodies; nor is it able to add substantial forms to the forms of those bodies in the way that accidents [add accidental forms]. But if the sun's form diffuses its power solely by means of accidents, then we fall back into the original problem, since the sun's form still does not itself have an immediate influence in the eduction of another form; instead, it has an influence only through the accidents.

37. There are two possible ways of replying to this difficulty. The first is to claim that through its own substantial form together with its accidental power the sun or celestial body has an immediate influence on lower bodies by an immediacy of power, even though it is not immediately conjoined to them by an immediacy of suppositum. However, this way of replying involves no little difficulty, and a plausible way of defending it cannot be explicated until section 8*,[58] in which we will explain the sense in which an agent has to be conjoined to a patient in order to act on it; and so the matter will be deferred to that place.

The second way of replying is to claim that (i) the substantial forms in question are not effected solely by the principal power of the celestial influence, but that instead it is necessary for the author of nature to apply a greater concurrence whereby he brings the proximate cause's effect to completion, whereas (ii) the effects in question are attributed to the celestial body either in the general sense in which the sun and a human being are said to generate a human being (which we will explain below in discussing causes that are essentially ordered to one another) or else, in some cases, in the more specific sense that the celestial body takes the place of the proximate cause and applies the entire efficient causality that the particular causes normally apply, through their instrumental powers, to disposing the matter /613a/ or to educing the form through the instrumental action of their qualities, even if those particular causes are unable to have an immediate influence through their own proper [substantial] forms. And perhaps this is the way in which the sun produces gold or other minerals.

38. *Whether a celestial body is able to produce living things.* A second, less general, obstacle has to do with the forms of living things. Since a celestial body is not animate, even if its spatial distance did not prevent it from being able to have an influence through its own form, its less perfect grade [of being] would still seem to prevent it from being able to have an influence with respect to the forms of living things.

Some authors reply that even though a celestial body is not alive, its form—by reason of its specific difference—is nonetheless more perfect, absolutely speaking, than the living forms that are generated by the celes-

58. See *DM* 18. 8. 24.

tial body. This reply can be gleaned from St. Thomas, *Summa Theologiae* 1, q. 115, a. 3, ad 3, where he says that celestial bodies, because of their universal power, contain within themselves whatever is generated among inferior things; and in *Summa Theologiae* 1, q. 105, a. 1, ad 1, he says that the effect is similar to the agent either according to species or according to virtual containment. "And it is in the latter way," he says, "that animals generated from putrefaction, along with plants and mineral bodies, are similar to the sun and the stars, by whose power they are generated."

First of all, however, even if what is assumed in this reply is plausible with respect to imperfect living things or animals, it does not seem probable with respect to perfect animals, since in both their operations and their mode of operating the latter far exceed the perfection of a celestial body. Second, since the grade of life is as such more perfect than the grade of nonliving things, it seems impossible that a form which is not a soul should eminently contain a soul, so that it might be able to be a principal principle for causing it. For a form that eminently contains a soul also contains the grade of life— not, indeed, according to its whole potentiality but according to its actual and precise perfection. But it is inconceivable that a form contained under a lower grade should contain eminently the perfection of a higher grade.

39. *A celestial body together with an intelligence is unable to generate a living thing.* For this reason there is a second reply: namely, that a celestial body is not by its own power able to produce the forms of living things, but that because it does not act unless it is moved by an intelligence, it is able to produce forms of this sort in the power of the intelligence whose instrument it is. This is the way St. Thomas replies in *Summa Theologiae* 1, q. 70, a. 5, ad 3; hence, in the places cited earlier it seems that he is talking about a celestial body insofar as it is conjoined to an intelligence or insofar as it includes an intelligence. /613b/

However, to my mind this reply is also difficult to understand. For I do not think that an intelligence impresses on a celestial body anything other than local motion, which does not make for an increase of active power but instead serves only to apply that power in various ways—as Aristotle explained sufficiently in *On Generation and Corruption* 2. 10, text 55 [336b4]: "For the impulse gives rise to continuous generation because it makes the sun, which is the author of the things to be produced, approach and retreat."

And this is evident from the following argument. What is it that an angel impresses on a heavenly body other than motion, given that he is not able to impress any qualities on it? For corporeal matter is obedient to angels only with respect to local motion, as the selfsame St. Thomas teaches in *Summa Theologiae* 1, q. 110, a. 2–3. But if an intelligence impresses nothing other than a mode on a celestial body, then how can it augment the body's power in order that it might effect something beyond its own proper perfection?[59] For local motion is not of itself active; neither does it bestow a power to act.

And in this respect physical agents, such as celestial bodies, are not comparable to the instruments of a craft, whose motion is subservient to the form [effected by] the craft, since this form is nothing other than a mode that results from the various positions or places of the body and of those parts of it that are changed by the motion. Physical agents, by contrast, induce proper and perfect forms that result from the motion not *per se* but only *per accidens*, to the extent that the power of acting is applied through the motion. Further, a celestial body is not by its nature the instrument of an intelligence, since it does not have a natural relation to an intelligence. Nor is any intelligence by its nature conjoined to a celestial body or ordered toward its motion; instead, an intelligence is conjoined to a celestial body only because of the choice of, and only at the pleasure of, the author of nature.

Again, it is not by reason of local motion alone that something is an instrument; otherwise, whoever applied a fire or any other agent cause would be using it as a physical instrument, and for this reason an applied fire would be capable of doing something more in the power of the one who applied it [than it could otherwise do]—which is plainly false. The inference is obvious from the fact that a celestial body gets nothing from an intelligence other than the application [of its power]. And as long as a celestial body is receiving a uniform motion, it is not the case that it has something more or something less by reason of the fact that it is being moved by a more perfect or less perfect intelligence or by any other thing.

And, finally, when it is claimed that a celestial body produces living things in the power of a living intelligence, I ask whether (i) the intelligence taken together with the celestial body influences and produces the souls of the living things through itself actually and immediately or whether (ii) it does this only through the celestial body in such a way that the intelligence's action consists in the motion of the celestial body, from which the remainder of the efficient causality arises immediately. The first answer /614a/ is false and contrary to St. Thomas, as we have repeatedly stressed, and it coincides in large measure with Avicenna's opinion. On the other hand, if the second answer is given, it does not solve the problem of how an instrument that does not in itself have a sufficient form can produce the effect without the actual assistance of a higher and more principal cause.

Therefore, it is better, and closer to the truth, to claim, as is assumed in

---

59. See n. 2 above. Suarez says that an intelligence impresses "nothing other than a mode" on a celestial body in causing its motion, because he regards places as mere modes of the bodies that have them rather than as full-fledged separable accidents.

the second reply above, that a celestial body is not by its own power able to produce souls, but that it is able to produce them in the power of God, the author and general overseer of nature who supplies by a greater concurrence whatever power is lacking in the proximate causes.

40. *The reply to the subordinate question; God influences the effects in question as a particular cause*. Therefore, one should claim that whenever it is the case among lower things that the substantial form's influence is insufficient to educe a similar form, then that influence is supplied by the power of celestial causes in those effects that do not exceed their perfection and power. However, in those effects that do surpass their perfection and power, the influence in question is supplied by the efficient causality of the First Cause, whose role it is to supply the necessary general concurrence to lower causes according to their natural capacity and need. Hence, not only in the case of events or effects which occur *per accidens* but also in the case of those which are connected to the natures of given things *per se*, as it were, and which follow upon their natural mode of acting, it is God's role as the author and overseer of nature to concur in this way with secondary causes for acting.

In some cases this concurrence of God's is owed for a general reason that applies to all of nature: namely, lest the order of the universe be perverted or lest matter remain without form or pass into nothingness. For instance, water's moving upward to fill a vacuum proceeds solely for the sake of nature as a whole and so is believed to be brought about by the command and impulse of the author of nature alone—unless perhaps God has assigned this role to some intelligence, given that local motion does not exceed its activity and ministry. (More on this elsewhere.[60])

In other cases, by contrast, such concurrence is owed because of the peculiar nature and condition of some particular agent that is not able to communicate or propagate its own nature in any other way—as we believe happens in the generation of perfect animals and as most certainly happens in the generation of a human being, though for a far deeper and more noble reason. For since the human soul is not only more perfect than, but also of a higher and more elevated order than, all other souls, it follows that what is required for the generation of a human being is not only a greater concurrence /614b/ on the part of the author of nature but also a higher mode of producing the soul: namely, through creation. It follows from this that human semen cannot even act instrumentally to produce that soul but is instead able only to organize the body. However, in the generation of other animals, even perfect ones, since the souls are material, they are educed from the potency of the matter, and so the semen is able to concur at least

60. See *DM* 35. 6.

instrumentally in their production, though not without the aid of a higher cause that supplies the principal form's assistance (as I will put it) and actual influence.

41. *The original objection is answered.* Nor is there any imperfection or disorder in nature because of this, as was objected above. Rather, this is a natural condition or requirement that accompanies the mode of generation and propagation that such a species demands by its nature. Just as the fact that the infusion of the soul by creation is required for the generation of a human being bespeaks not an imperfection or disorder in nature but rather a condition that is naturally consequent upon the nature of a human being (and so, given the institution of such a nature, the action in question is not out of the ordinary but is instead in keeping with a general law), so too one should deal with the present case by an analogous, though not altogether identical, argument. Thus, just as in the case of a human being it is not because of an imperfection that a human being is not able, as either a principal or an instrumental cause, to produce a soul similar to his own, so too in the case of other animals it is not because of an imperfection that they are unable to apply the entire principal power that is necessary for educing their forms but instead are able to apply only an instrumental power. For they occupy, as it were, an intermediate position. From the fact that by comparison with the rational soul they have less perfect—that is, material—souls, it follows that they can apply at least an instrumental power for producing those souls, something a human being cannot do. On the other hand, from the fact that by comparison with the forms of inanimate things the forms of living things are far more perfect, it follows that more is required for their production, along with an excellent and peculiar mode of generation. And from this it follows that the particular causes cannot apply the entire principal power for producing those forms but are instead able to apply only an instrumental power.

However, from the fact that the principal power in them is not sufficient, it does not follow that an instrumental action should also be denied to them. For they are sufficiently proportioned to this latter action and not to the former. Moreover, nature gave to each corruptible species the power and action to propagate its own nature, /615a/ and it gave this power and action to the extent that it was able to, given the species' capability and manner of acting. Thus, nature gave to a human being the power to act at least by disposing; it gave to other things the power to act instrumentally; and it gave to still other things the power to act as principal causes. Therefore, the manner of speaking according to which, as we saw above, St. Thomas and the others call secondary causes the instruments of the First Cause is in a sense more properly true in the case of living things, especially perfect living things.

42. I realize that other explanations are conceivable. For since in the case of the more perfect animals the semen does not perfect the generation unless it is conjoined to a female, some have thought that the soul of the female herself has a distinctive principal influence in the substantival formation of the fetus. On the other hand, in the case of imperfect living things, especially plants, some claim that the form of the thing that is substantivally generated does not exceed the form of the seed itself, as seems to be the case with wheat and other such things.

However, these and similar claims encounter many problems that cannot be pursued here, since they depend in large measure on the science of the soul. And so the position that we have expounded seems more plausible than all of them, and experience itself teaches that living things are *per se* less sufficient and stand in need of greater assistance, not only with respect to inducing the substantial form but even with respect to disposing and organizing the matter, as is evident in the case of plants. Indeed, even among inanimate things, simple bodies are generated more easily than compound bodies are. Therefore, there is nothing problematic about admitting that living things require a higher concurrence in order to generate things similar to themselves, even though they do not lack a certain power and action that is proportionate to and connatural to themselves.

And in this way we believe that the arguments for the first position have been amply dealt with. For those arguments establish the second and fourth of our assertions but do not count at all against the first and third assertions, as we made sufficiently clear in our discussion of the latter. Moreover, we do not believe that the second position is contrary to the doctrine we have handed down. Nor can the arguments for that position pose any obstacles, as has been shown.

Section 3

The Principle by Which Created Substances Produce Accidents

1. *The reasons on both sides for perplexity.* The reason for perplexity is this: A substance produces an accident either (i) by means of an accident or (ii) by itself alone and through itself.

If the first answer is given, then an infinite regress follows. /615b/ For if one accident is produced by means of another, then I ask concerning that other accident by what principle it is produced. If it is produced by means of still another accident, then the same question reappears. On the other hand, if we stop the regress at some accident that is produced proximately by the substance, then the same thing should have been said about the first accident, since there is no stronger argument in the one case than in the other.

However, if for this reason one claims instead that a substance produces an accident through itself, then it follows, first of all, that no accident is a principle for producing another accident. It follows, second, that the powers and faculties for acting that exist in created substances are none other than their [substantial] forms. Or, at the very least, if, in order to avoid these problematic claims, one asserts that some accidents are produced immediately by a substance through itself whereas other accidents are produced by means of accidents, then it will be necessary to provide some explanation for this difference and distinction and to make clear which accidents are produced in the one way and which in the other.

In addition, it will be necessary to explain in cases where one accident is a principle *quo* for producing another whether it is a principal principle or an instrumental principle. For it seems clear that an accident can act at most as the instrument of a substance, given the fact that an accident is a being of a being (as philosophers put it) and that it has its entire *esse* both from the substance and also for the sake of the substance as an end. From another perspective, however, it seems that an accident should be a principal principle [for producing an accident], since the effect does not exceed its perfection.

2. In order to explicate this matter, I assume that there are two ways in which accidents can be produced. In one way, an accident is produced through a proper action, as when light is produced through illumination or when a "where" is produced through proper local motion. In the second way, an accident is produced through a natural resulting, as when a relation results from its foundation once its terminus is posited (if a relation is a

mode distinct from its foundation) or when a shape results from a division or from a motion or a terminus of a local motion.[1] The proper attributes of things are also thought to be produced in this way.

Now there is a third way in which accidents could be understood to be produced: namely, concomitantly with a substance but without resulting from it—in the way, for example, that quantity comes to exist with primary matter. However, I will ignore this third way for now, since (i) if it is a real mode of production, then it can be assimilated to one or the other of the preceding modes, as we will explain below, and since (ii) in this mode of production the principle that produced the substance will also be the principle that produces the accident that comes to exist along with that substance.

FIRST ASSERTION: ON NATURAL EMANATION

3. Therefore, I assert, first, that when an accident is produced through a natural emanation, its proximate principle in such a mode of efficient causality (whatever that mode might be) can be /616a/ the substance if the accident in question is immediately connected with that substance; in some cases, however, an accident can result by means of [another] accident if it has a closer connection with that accident.

This thesis is commonly accepted in its entirety, and it can be proved, first, by induction. For the intellect, for example, emanates proximately from the substance of the soul, and quantity emanates proximately from the matter or from the form. Hence, with respect to these properties one cannot designate any intrinsic accidental principle; therefore, the principle is substantival.[2] By contrast, a shape or a "where," for example, results by the mediation of the quantity, and whiteness results from a given mixture of the primary qualities.

The thesis is also proved by the reason for perplexity stated at the beginning. For if an accident belongs to a substance intrinsically, then it cannot in all cases belong to it by the mediation of an accident as its intrinsic principle. Instead, it must necessarily be the case that some accident is immediately connected with the substance, though it does not have to be the case that *all* intrinsic accidents are like this. And the reason for this difference among

1. Suarez discusses the hotly disputed question of the ontological status of relations in *DM* 47. See also the discussion of the shape of an artifact at *DM* 17. 2. 11.

2. Suarez is here using the term 'property' (or 'proper accident') in a technical sense, for an accident that is apt to flow or emanate from a substance's essence. Thus, not every characteristic or accident a substance has counts as a property.

the accidents is simple: namely, that some of them have a more immediate relation to the substance than others do.

4. I realize that one could reply that even if an accident is intimately and immediately connected with a substance, it is still not necessary that it be connected by means of an *efficient emanation* of the accident from the substance. Instead, it might be connected solely by virtue of a natural aptness and inseparability—in the way that, as we claimed above, we can plausibly think about quantity and [primary] matter.[3] And on this view it will be necessary not that some accident should emanate immediately from the substance but rather that some accident should be received immediately in the substance from the same agent by which the substance is produced.

Still, the thesis posited above assumes as more probable the contrary position: namely, that the accidental properties, especially those that follow upon or are owed [to a substance] by reason of its form, are caused by the substance not only as a material cause and a final cause but also as an efficient cause through a natural resulting—either immediately, if the property in question is a primary property, or mediately, if it is a secondary property.

St. Thomas holds this view in *Summa Theologiae* 1, q. 77, a. 6, where he is talking about the powers of the soul, but the same argument applies to any [substantial] form whatsoever and to the properties that follow upon it or are owed to it by reason of itself. And this view is highly probable. For since a substantial form exists as a first act, whereas an accidental form exists as a second act, it is probable that the substantial form has a certain power for having its proper accidents emanate from it.[4] Likewise, in this way one discerns more clearly /616b/ the natural connection between a [substantial] form and its properties, as well as the *per se* ordering that obtains between them.

This is strongly confirmed by the sensory example of water reducing itself to its pristine coldness. For this reduction can be brought about only by the [substantial] form through a natural resulting, as was shown above.[5] For the same reason, therefore, one should say the same thing about any property that is naturally connected with the form, especially if there is neither a contradiction on other grounds nor a dependence on anything extrinsic.

3. See *DM* 14. 3. The question, then, is whether the relation of a proper accident to its substance is properly a causal relation.

4. The 'first act' of a given entity involves its existing and having its characteristic causal power, whereas its 'second act' consists in the exercise of that causal power.

5. See *DM* 15. 1. As for the example, water has coldness as one of its natural properties. So when, after being heated, a quantity of water becomes cold again, this reversion to its natural state must be attributed to its own nature or form as a principle *quo* and not to any extrinsic principle *quo*.

And in this example of the water it is manifestly obvious that the posited thesis is true: namely, that some accident can result immediately, via efficient causality, from a substantival principle. For the degree of coldness in question can have no more proximate principle from which it results than the substantial form of the water.

5. *The notion of natural resulting is clarified; Cajetan's opinion.* But before we proceed further, we must first explain what this natural resulting is and, more specifically, whether it is true efficient and active causality.

For if it is true efficient causality, then a proper accidental action will occur here, since efficient causality consists in an action, as we will see below.[6] And so in that case the substantial form will be the immediate and unique principle of some accidental action, and actions will be multiplied in the production of the form and its properties, and there will be a *per se* action with respect to each of the entities co-produced or co-created with the others— all of which seems contrary to the common teaching of philosophers.

On the other hand, if it is not true efficient causality, then it cannot be called efficient causality, since what is not true gold is not gold at all and cannot be called such except by virtue of some similarity or analogy. But no such similarity or analogy is evident in the present case; indeed, it is impossible to imagine what this resulting might be if it is not efficient causality.

On this point, Cajetan, in *Summa Theologiae* 1, q. 54, a. 3, suggests that the emanation in question is a natural consequence without any mediating operation. However, he does not explain what this 'natural consequence' is or how it might occur in the absence of a mediating action or operation. And in *Summa Theologiae* 1, q. 77, a. 6, ad 2 and 3, he says explicitly that this resulting occurs through efficient causality in the absence of any mediating action, and he claims that this is St. Thomas's opinion in the same article, ad 3. However, in that place St. Thomas does not say that the emanation of the accidents from the subject occurs without an action; rather, he says, "It occurs not through any transmutation, but through a natural resulting."

6. Therefore, if we are to speak precisely, I take it to be closer to the truth that this resulting does not occur without a real action, even though it is not always /617a/ counted either as a distinct action *per se* or as a proper change.

As I see it, this claim is sufficiently proved by the argument given above. For either this resulting is true efficient causality or it is not, since there can be nothing in between. Thus, if it is true efficient causality, then an action occurs. If it is not efficient causality, then neither is it a resulting or a natural

---

6. See *DM* 18. 10. By calling an action a 'proper accidental action' Suarez means to designate its ontological status as an entity in the accidental category of action. This category is discussed at length in *DM* 48.

causal consequence; instead, it is merely a *logical* consequence by reason of the fact that when the one is posited, the other is posited because of a natural appropriateness—in the way that there is a natural connection between the matter and the form of a celestial body, but no emanation of the one from the other.[7]

Some authors seem to posit something in between these two [sorts of consequence], claiming that the resulting in question is not efficient causality but a quasi-efficient causality that consists solely in the fact that the cause that produces the substance is determined, by reason of the substance, to give it the properties that are appropriate to it.

In the first place, however, this is no true efficient causality but merely a connaturality of the sort that also exists between a natural passive power and its act. Second, the example of the reduction of water [to coldness] forces us to countenance a more robust and more genuine efficient causality. Finally, even given the claim made [by these authors], it is necessary to maintain that, as far as the point in question is concerned, even if the cause that produces the substance also concomitantly produces a distinct property, it nonetheless does not do so in the absence of a concomitant action. For it is contradictory for a distinct thing to be produced without a distinct action if that thing is not included in the primary terminus itself of some other action. For an action is just a certain mode of the formal and *per se* terminus itself, as I will show below.[8] I will explain this argument more fully in a moment.

7. *The two modes of natural emanation.* I argue further as follows. The natural resulting in question occurs in some cases by itself alone and separately from the production of the entity from which it results. However, in other cases it is conjoined with that production in such a way that it is never posterior to it but is altogether simultaneous with it. For example, when water reduces itself to its pristine coldness, this is a natural emanation, as Cajetan admits in the aforementioned q. 54, a. 3, at the end, where he also says the same thing about the motion of a heavy thing that has been generated in a higher place, a motion which, when the impediment is removed, naturally results from its gravity. Now whenever a resulting occurs in this way, it is absolutely evident that it does not occur without efficient causality or without a true action and change, as is manifestly obvious from the examples just given. The reason is that in such a case something that did not exist beforehand begins to exist in the subject, and it begins to exist *per se*, without the *de novo*

---

7. In *DM* 13. 11, Suarez argues at length that celestial bodies are neither generable nor corruptible. Hence, their forms can in no way be thought to be educed from—or in that sense to emanate from—the potency of matter.

8. See *DM* 48. 2.

production of any other thing. Therefore, it begins to exist through some efficient cause and through a proper action and change. Hence, that action is a proper cooling [in the one case] and a local motion [in the other]. And the same argument applies whenever an accident /617b/ comes *de novo* to a preexisting subject by itself alone—that is, in the absence of any other prior accident. (For if several accidents that are connected to one another come to a subject simultaneously, then the one that is the first and the source of the others is judged to come by itself, whereas the others are judged to come concomitantly.)

You will object: In that case, when a relation comes to a foundation because of the positing of its terminus, a new *per se* action occurs there, since this relative accident comes *de novo* to the subject by itself at that time.

Some reply by conceding the inference. Others deny it on the ground that it suffices that the relation should [merely] result from the positing of the terminus. Still others claim that no action occurs at all, since a relation of this sort is not an entity or a mode that is distinct in reality from the foundation. We will investigate this question in its proper place.[9]

8. Now it is on the basis of the latter sort of resulting, which is separated in time from the production [of the substance], that one should judge concerning every other sort of resulting, even if it is conjoined at the same instant. For simultaneity in duration does not destroy the distinction [between the production of the substance and the emanation of the accident], especially given the fact that even though they are naturally simultaneous, they can be separated supernaturally—which is a sufficient ground for a distinction.

The assumption is confirmed as follows. When God creates the substance of the soul, he could [at first] suspend the emanation of the powers from it and after a while permit that emanation—that is, give his concurrence for such an emanation. And in that case, by the very same argument that was adduced above concerning the cooling of water that reduces itself to its natural state, this later emanation would be an instance of proper efficient causality and a true action. Therefore, even when the emanation occurs simultaneously [with the production of the substance], it is a proper and distinct action.

Further, there is an a priori argument that was touched upon above. Accidental forms of the sort in question—that is, properties—are entities distinct from the substance; therefore, even if they are produced along with the substance or result from it, it is necessary that they be produced through a distinct action, whether this action is concomitant with the other action or subsequent to it.

The consequence is evident from the fact that the two entities in ques-

9. See *DM* 47.

tion—namely, the substance and the property—are not produced equally primarily as two parts of one composite terminus. Instead, the substance is, absolutely speaking, produced prior in nature, and then the proper accident results from it or is added to it. For example, when the soul is created, the creative action terminates *per se* in the substance alone. For the substance alone is produced *ex nihilo* and terminates that action *per se*. Therefore, in order for some distinct entity to be added to it, another instance of efficient causality, and hence a new action, is required, even if this new action necessarily accompanies the other action because of a natural connection. Moreover, the proximate principle of this latter instance of efficient causality is also, according to our position, a distinct principle, since this principle is the inward substance itself, /618a/ which is the terminus of the prior action. Likewise, it is often the case that the material principles are diverse. For instance, in the aforementioned example of the creation of the soul there is no material principle, whereas the substance of the soul is itself the material principle of its own powers.[10] Also, the proper termini, we are assuming, are distinct in reality. Therefore, an action that is distinct in reality occurs there—even though physically and in the common manner of speaking they are counted as one action by reason of the fact that they have an intrinsic connection and consecutiveness.

9. *A noteworthy difference between the aforementioned modes of natural emanation.* In this regard one should note a difference between the two modes of natural resulting that we distinguished above. When an emanation is such that it can never occur by itself, separately, but instead can occur only insofar as it is connected to a prior action and to the terminus of that action, then that emanation is judged not to be a proper and *per se* action, even less a change, but is instead judged to be a sort of accidental completion of the prior action. And this is why it is said that there is no *per se* action or motion with respect to accidents or properties of this sort. By contrast, when such an instance of resulting occurs by itself and separately, as in the reduction of water [to its pristine coldness], then the resulting is judged to be a *per se* action and a proper change that tends *per se* toward an accidental terminus of the sort in question. This difference is not so much a difference in reality as a difference in the denominations that are derived from the separation of the actions in the one case or from their concomitance in the other.

Three Corollaries of the Above Doctrine
10. From the arguments just adduced one may infer, first, that the resulting in question occurs with real efficient causality and real action only when that

10. The intellect is the 'material' principle of its powers in the sense that it is the subject 'from which' the powers flow.

which results is distinct in reality from that from which it results. For if it is only conceptually distinct, then even if it might be said to follow 'metaphysically' from the other, there cannot in such a case be any real efficient causality or physical emanation. Instead, there is only a metaphysical consequence—in the way that we say that a form's being a principal principle of acting 'results from' its being a formal principle of *esse*. And the same thing holds for all the similar attributes that, given our manner of conceptualization, are attributed to a thing as its properties despite the fact that they are not actually distinct from it within the thing itself. For in none of these cases can there be any real efficient causality, since real efficient causality exists not among concepts but among things themselves; hence, it necessarily requires a distinction in reality between the principle and the terminus.

11. *Which accidents result from a substantival principle.* Second, on these same grounds one may infer that /618b/ this natural resulting from a substantival principle occurs only with respect to those accidents that are connatural to such an extent that they absolutely presuppose [the existence of] the very substance whose properties they are. The reason I draw attention to this is that according to a probable opinion which asserts that (i) the dispositions that temporally precede the [substantial] form are at the instant of generation intrinsically terminated in the grade [of being] required by such a form and that (ii) numerically the same dispositions remain [after the generation]— according to this opinion, I repeat, these accidents do not emanate from the [substantial] form at the instant of generation even if they are properties that are maximally connatural to it, as in the case, say, of heat with respect to fire or of coldness with respect to water.[11] This is so not because such a [substantial] form would not be sufficient for effecting [the quality in question] by means of resulting, but because the quality is presupposed as already having been produced *per se* by the agent via the whole of the transmutation that temporally precedes [the generation] and is terminated at the instant of generation, naturally prior to the [substantial] form's being introduced.

12. *A subordinate question is resolved.* But, you will ask, even if this resulting does not occur at the instant of generation, does it not occur immediately afterwards in the mode of conservation?

I reply that this question is not peculiar to those qualities that exist beforehand in the order of nature. Rather, with respect to *all* the properties that result from [substantial] forms at the very beginning one can similarly ask whether the resulting in question occurs only in the mode of *production* at

---

11. The discussion that follows is predicated, then, on the disputed assumption that the accidents of the matter prior to the generation are numerically identical with those that inform the newly generated substance. For more on this, see *DM* 18. 2, n. 25.

the first instant or time at which the thing is produced or co-produced or whether instead it perdures in the mode of *conservation* for the whole time during which the property itself perdures, with the result that just as, in the case of illumination, it is not just the light but also the action of illuminating that perdures, so too, in a soul that has an intellect, it is not only the intellect but also the emanation of the intellect from the soul that perdures—and similarly, in the case of fire or water, it is not only the heat or coldness that perdures but also their actual emanation from their forms.

As I see it, on this question nothing can be established by a conclusive argument; instead, each of the two positions can be rendered probable on the basis of reasonable conjectures. For once the property in question has been effected by a natural emanation, there is no reason why it should need continuous conservation, since it already has perfect *esse* and exists in its connatural subject. On other grounds, however, it seems probable that this actual emanation does not cease, since its principle remains present and conjoined to it to the highest degree, and it always retains the same power to sustain the emanation. Likewise, it is necessary that the property in question be actually conserved by God; therefore, since there is in this case an intrinsic and proximate principle by which /619a/ it could be conserved, it is more natural for it to be conserved by the mediation of that principle.[12] Further, one can better explain in this way why, other things being equal, it is possible for there to be greater resistance in the expulsion of a property from its proper subject than there is in its expulsion from some other subject.[13]

Hence, the second position seems more probable. And if this position is presupposed, then one must as a result claim that (i) at the first instant of the generation of water, for example, the coldness does not emanate from the form of the water, since the water at that moment acquires a coldness that has already been produced by the generating thing, but that, nonetheless, (ii) once the action of the generating thing ceases, the coldness is conserved by the intrinsic form [of the water] by means of a natural emanation, in just the way it would have been conserved if it had emanated from the form of the water from the very first instant.[14]

---

12. Just as there can be secondary causes of a thing's production, so too there can be secondary causes of its conservation. An interesting further question is whether there can be secondary causes of creation as well. For Suarez's treatment of this question, see *DM* 20. 2.

13. A standard scholastic example is that it is easier to heat air (which is naturally disposed to be hot and moist) than water (which is naturally disposed to be cold and moist).

14. As should be clear, this argument presupposes that the disposition in question— viz., coldness—existed prior to its inhering in the generated substance.

13. *The distinctness of the natural resulting*. Third, one may infer from what was said above that the emanation or natural resulting in question is something distinct in reality (i) from the form that results, (ii) from the [substantial] form from which it results, and (iii) from the actual informing [by which the resulting accidental form informs the substance from which it results]. For these latter can all exist in the absence of a natural resulting; therefore, the natural resulting is something distinct from them.

The antecedent is evident from the fact that coldness exists in air as actually informing it and is accidentally conjoined to the form of air, and yet it does not emanate from the form of air. By contrast, heat, too, is conjoined to and informs air, and, in addition, it emanates from the form of air.[15] Therefore, emanation adds something.

You will object that even though this appears to be the case when one compares a proper accident with an extrinsic accident, nonetheless, in the case of a proper accident itself the resulting or emanation does not seem to be something distinct from the accident itself as actually informing [the substance].

But against this I reply, first, that it is one thing to inform and another to emanate; the former falls under the notion of a cause, the latter under the notion of an effect.

Second, in the example posited above concerning a last disposition,[16] which does not emanate from the [substantial] form at the first instant [of the generation], one finds a proper accident which [at the instant of generation] actually informs and is conjoined to its proper form and does not result from it, yet which, in the time following [the generation], does result—that is, is conserved. Therefore, the resulting in question is distinct from the proper accident as [actually] informing [the substance].

Third, this is proved as follows. Because the resulting in question is a certain kind of efficient causality, it does not occur without the concurrence of the First Cause. Therefore, it is possible for God at first to suspend this concurrence and prevent, say, the intellect from emanating from the soul and afterwards to posit the intellect in the soul through his own efficient causality alone. For if one considers just the concept of efficient causality, there is nothing contradictory in his doing by himself alone that which can be done by the mediation of the soul. Therefore, in such a case we have the substance and being of the soul, along with the actual inherence of the intellect [in the soul], /619b/ without the actual emanation of the intellect from the

---

15. Once again, according to the background theory being presupposed here, air is apt by nature to be hot and moist.

16. See §12 above.

soul (which is instead from God alone). This, therefore, is an indication that the emanation in question is something distinct, since whatever is separable in reality must also be distinct.

And on this basis the claim we made above is confirmed: namely, that the natural resulting in question does not occur without an action. For what the resulting adds, over and beyond the being of an inhering accidental form, is just the intrinsic property's mode of dependence on its [substantial] form as on an active principle. But, as we will see below, dependence on an active principle is the same thing as action.[17]

14. *An objection arises.* But you will object: It follows that *every* action that is effected naturally and without freedom is a sort of natural resulting. For just as, once the form of water is posited, a given property results through a real action and dependence, and later on another property results from that one (as St. Thomas teaches in *Summa Theologiae* 1, q. 77, a. 7), so too, once the sun, say, is posited, light naturally results in the air by means of an act of illumination.

I reply that on this point there is indeed some similarity. But there is a difference as well, since a natural resulting is wholly intrinsic and in a certain sense has to do with the completed production of a thing, since it tends solely toward constituting the thing in the connatural state which is *per se* owed to it by dint of its generation. By contrast, an action, speaking properly and in the sense in which an action is normally distinguished from a natural resulting, is instead extrinsic; and, speaking *per se*, it presupposes that the thing has already been constituted in its complete and natural state. That is also why it is commonly claimed that a natural resulting is attributed to the generating thing and that it does not proceed from the [substantial] form or from an intrinsic property except to the extent that the [form or property] takes the place of the generating thing and is, as it were, its instrument. From this we have the axiom, "That which gives the form gives whatever follows from the form." For it is the role of the generating thing to constitute the generated thing along with the properties owed to it, whereas in other, proper actions the thing is already operating by its own power, and an action is attributed to it as to a principal agent within its own genus. This is the source of another difference that we will touch upon in a moment; for we believe that enough has been said [for now] about natural resulting.

17. See *DM* 18. 10.

SECOND ASSERTION: ON THE PROPER EFFICIENT
CAUSALITY OF ACCIDENTS

15. *The thesis is proved for the actions of bodies.* The second assertion is this: When an accident is effected by a proper action that is distinct from a natural resulting, then the proximate principle for effecting that accident is always some [other] accident.

This assertion /620a/ raises the familiar question about the distinction, among created things, of an active power from a substance, a question that is usually discussed with respect to (i) an angel's substance and his powers, (ii) the soul and its powers, and (iii) other forms and their active powers. And the thesis just posited is consonant with the teaching of St. Thomas, who everywhere draws the distinction, within all creatures, between a prox- imate faculty of acting and the substantial form, as one can see in *Summa Theologiae* 1, q. 54, a. 3, and q. 77, a. 1. This distinction is defended by Caje- tan in the places just cited; by Capreolus in *Sentences* 1, dist. 3, q. 4; by Soto in *Logica,* chap. entitled 'On Properties,' q. 2; by Giles in *Quodlibeta* 3, q. 10; and by Hervaeus in *Quodlibeta* 1, q. 9.

The assertion is proved, first, by an induction made over all the effects that we experience. For, in the first place, we see that the elements exercise effi- cient causality only by means of the primary qualities, which, it is obvious, are true˙ and proper accidents. Next, the elements do not have even natural local motion except by the mediation of the qualities. For even though such motion pertains to natural resulting, an a fortiori argument can nonetheless be derived from it.

Further, as far as we can tell from experience, a celestial body acts through qualities that are distinct from its substance—namely, through light or brightness—and from this we derive the argument that other, more hid- den influences are brought about proximately by the mediation of accidental qualities. For if the influence that is seen to be the greatest and most perfect of all is brought about in this way, then other influences will, a fortiori, be brought about in this way.

Again, when inanimate compound bodies (for example, metals, precious stones, and others of this type) have actions of the sort in question, they seem clearly to exercise those actions through accidental powers. One indication of this, among others, is that these powers can be intensified, weakened, or destroyed, and in this they depend on the disposition of the primary qualities.

The same argument can also be made in the case of herbs and plants, which have powers directed toward various remarkable actions of attracting and expelling. In addition, some of them have heat-related powers, others have cold-related powers, and these powers are weakened in them by the passage of time or by changes in their disposition, despite the fact that the substance remains the same. This, then, is an indication that the powers in question are accidents.

The mystery of the Eucharist has also confirmed this same point for us. For we see that even after the substance [of the bread and wine] has been removed, the whole power of acting that previously existed in the accidents is conserved.

16. *The thesis is proved for the actions of spirits.* From here we ascend further to the actions of the soul in each of its grades. As far as we can tell from sensory experience, the principles of the accidental operations /620b/ are themselves accidents. This is evident in the case of vital or nutritional heat and in the case of the absorption or expulsion of excrement and similar things. For, first of all, the very diversity of such actions seems to be a sufficient ground for a distinction among the powers. And, further, there is also room here for the argument adduced above—namely, that these powers are intensified and weakened.

Next, the same point seems obvious in the operations of the senses. For over and above the diversity of the operations, the diversity of the organs is itself a sufficient indication that the proximate powers for these actions are *per se* distinct from one another and are thus accidental powers. And in the case of a human being these [sensory] powers must surely be necessarily distinct from the soul. Otherwise, they would be spiritual entities—which seems implausible, as will be proved at more length in its own place.[18]

Now as regards spiritual actions themselves and their principles, we cannot have as clear an experience. Nonetheless, since we can philosophize about them only on the basis, *mutatis mutandis,* of the things we do experience, we may justifiably infer that the same judgment should be made concerning them.

17. *Every active power is really distinct from the substance.* Therefore, from this induction St. Thomas infers with sufficient probability that in every created suppositum a proximate power of acting and operating is distinct from its substance and is consequently an accident.

It should also be added that in cases other than that of substantival generation, every instance of a substance's efficient causality is an instance of some accident's efficient causality. For a substance can effect a substance only through generation. And so if a substance effects anything other than a generation, that whole thing is an accident. Therefore, the proximate principle for effecting an accident is always another accident.

18. See §20 below.

This is confirmed by the fact that an accident is the proximate principle for effecting even a substantival generation, and this in a twofold manner: first, by preparing the way for the substantival generation by means of some previous accidental action, and, second, by cooperating instrumentally with the substance itself in the eduction of the [new] substantial form—as we saw in the preceding section. Therefore, an accident will, a fortiori, be the proximate principle for effecting every accidental action, either as a principal principle or as an instrumental principle—as we will see in a moment.

The consequence is evident from the fact that a substance is less proportioned to an accidental action than it is to a substantival generation; and, conversely, an accident is a more proportionate principle for an accidental action than it is for a substantival generation.

18. *Arguments in support of the foregoing line of reasoning.* However, an a priori proof /621a/ is difficult here, even though in the places cited above St. Thomas adduces several probable arguments—arguments that Scotus and others impugn with many arguments. Now subsequent to Capreolus, Cajetan defends these arguments rather extensively and copiously; but I take this defense to be both arduous and useless, since the arguments in question are not in fact demonstrations, and there is no reason why, on such an obscure matter, they should be welcomed by a prudent philosopher. For unless one proves that it exceeds the perfection of a created substance to be the proximate and sole principle of an accidental action, we cannot give an a priori proof for the claim that the creatures that now exist and are now operating always require an accidental principle for operations of the sort in question. For we do not grasp the proper natures of these creatures in such a way that we might derive from those natures the specific reasons for this requirement or necessity. Therefore, if we proceed a priori, we will necessarily have to base our argument on the general concept of a creature, as St. Thomas astutely observed. But if the foundation for the argument is taken from the general concept of a created substance, then one will necessarily have to claim that it is impossible for God to create a substance that acts immediately through itself alone. However, this may be difficult to prove or to argue for persuasively, since the relevant mode of operating does not seem to require an infinite perfection in the genus of being or substance. But every perfection that does not require a lack of limitation seems to be communicable to a creature. And if it is indeed communicable, then on what basis is it clear that it has not in fact been communicated? Or how can the aforementioned requirement be proved from the general concept of a creature?

19. *An induction over actions ordered toward substantival generation.* Nonetheless, one should claim that even though the point in question cannot be demonstrated, it may be inferred with sufficient probability, on the basis of

the induction made above, that a created substance is such that because of its own limitations it cannot by itself be the total and proximate principle of an accidental action or form.

The ostensible reason for this is the disproportionateness and distance that lie between such a principle and such an action, with the result that they cannot be conjoined except by the mediation of some proportionate means such as an accidental faculty or power. And so only an infinite substance, which surpasses every proportion and is able to overcome every disproportion, is sufficient by itself for all effects or actions of the sort in question.

And we can confirm this as follows. Every operation of a substance other than a substantival generation is such that either it tends toward effecting a substantival generation or it does not. It is fitting that an action /621b/ of the first type should require a proximate accidental principle, since it is an accidental disposition ordered toward a substance. For if the substance that is generated is such that it cannot be effected in the absence of antecedent accidental dispositions, then what wonder is it that the substance that generates it should also require accidental dispositions that are at the same time powers of acting and of disposing with respect to the generation of a similar substance?

You will object that this argument is straightforwardly successful for the case of an agent that is univocal and of the same type but not for the case of an equivocal agent, whose power can be of a higher type.

One may reply that if an equivocal agent is finite (and this is the sort of agent we are now discussing), then one should think about it by analogy with a univocal agent. For if an equivocal agent, through its own substantial form, contains eminently the substantial form of the thing that is going to be generated, then it will also contain eminently, through its own more noble accidental dispositions or properties, the accidental dispositions for that form. For since a substantial form is limited and fixed within its own genus, it cannot by itself alone contain eminently the perfections of diverse genera, and it cannot *per se* be capable of both the [substantival and the accidental] actions. This is sufficiently clear from the mode of acting that belongs to all bodies, both lower bodies and celestial bodies, as was shown by the induction made above. For just as there is no substantial form, of whatever order or perfection, which does not have within its own matter dispositions or properties that are proportioned to itself, so too there is no form which, in disposing another matter toward some substantial form, does not use its own accidental dispositions or properties as proper principles of acting—regardless of whether [this new form] is equal to or lower than it.

20. *An induction over operations that are not ordered toward substantival generation.* On the other hand, to the extent that we can tell from our experience

of things, all operations that are not ordered toward a substantival generation are either operations of sentient and intellective life or else various and
diverse local motions.

I am leaving to one side acts of illumination, as well as the intentional actions of sensible species, since in their case it is sufficiently clear that they are
effected by sensible accidents. Nor am I taking into account the operations of
vegetative life, since they all tend *per se* toward a certain substantival regeneration. The same argument holds for this regeneration as for the original
generation, since regeneration is likewise effected by means of an antecedent accidental alteration and disposition, as well as by certain intervening
local motions—namely, motions of attraction and /622a/ expulsion.

On the other hand, other *transeunt* actions and operations, even if they are
effected by means of eminent powers, are always either such that (i) they
are effected by means of an alteration that is *per se* and primarily terminated
in one or another of the primary qualities, whose proximate principles have
already been shown to be certain accidents, or else such that (ii) they consist
solely in a local motion of attracting or repelling, and so forth.

Now an argument for the claim that accidental faculties are required for
the operations of cognizing and loving in the sentient grade [of soul] can be
derived, first of all, from the very diversity of the operations and from the
various dispositions that those operations require in their organs.

Likewise, an argument can be derived from the fact that immanent actions
of this sort exist in the proximate principles themselves by which they are
elicited. Hence, if those powers [that is, principles] were nothing other than
the substantial forms themselves, then all the operations in question would
remain in the substantial forms alone. From this it would follow further that
[sentient] operations of this sort in a human being are spiritual operations,
in the same way that the [substantial] form itself is spiritual. In fact, it would
also follow that such operations have to be spiritual without exception and
in all [subjects], since every form that has an operation that is both proper
to it and independent of matter as a subject must be *per se* subsistent as
well as independent, in its own *esse,* of matter as a subject. For an independence in operation indicates what sort of independence there is in *esse.*
This is the most powerful premise from which to infer the subsistence and
immateriality of the human soul: namely, that its intellectual operation does
not depend on the body as on a subject, even though it does depend on the
body to supply the [sensible] species. Therefore, if the sentient operations
[of the human soul] were independent of matter in the same way, then it
would also be the case that *every* sentient soul is independent, and so both
[the rational soul and the sentient soul] would be immaterial and spiritual.
Therefore, it is from the mode of such material operations that one may best

infer that a substantial form is not *per se* capable of exercising a [sentient] operation without a mediating faculty that must itself also be material and that must be present to the matter as soon as the latter has been informed by a substantial form of the sort in question.

21. *An induction over intellectual operations.* Now this last argument, which is taken from the materiality of the relevant action, does not go through in the case of intellectual operations. However, the other argument, the one from the diversity of the operations, does go through.

Also, in the case of the rational soul there is another, distinctive argument: that the rational soul informs the body through its substantival being but does not inform the body through its intellect or will, since these powers are nonorganic precisely because they do not inform matter.

This argument does not apply to angels, and so, as Durandus claimed and as we will see in the proper place below, the matter is more doubtful in the case of angels.[19] /622b/ Nonetheless, the general argument taken from the diversity of the operations is sufficiently effective even in the case of angels. For wherever an intellectual operation is accidental, there is a great diversity in the operations of the relevant grade [of being], especially in acts of understanding and affection. Therefore, since a created substance is of itself indifferent with respect to eliciting and receiving operations of this sort, it is very likely determined to and, as it were, accommodated to those operations through their own proper faculties and powers.

Likewise, every intellectual substance, by the very fact that it is created, necessarily has an accidental intellectual operation—as is obvious in the case of human beings and as we will show below in the proper place for angels. Such a substance also requires other accidental principles: for example, intentional species and habits. What wonder is it, then, that it should require an accidental power that is proportioned to its operation? This is so especially in view of the fact that every intellectual nature must have within itself a power that is *per se* and primarily ordered toward the operation of understanding or the operation of loving. For since an intellectual nature is instituted for the sake of these operations, it ought not to be instituted without a power that is *per se* and primarily ordered toward them. But since a power that is *per se* and primarily ordered toward an accidental operation takes its own species from that operation, it, too, is accidental.

And this seems to be the thrust of St. Thomas's argument that (i) the *essence* of a created substance is, as such, ordered only toward its own *esse*, whereas its *power* is ordered toward an accidental operation, and thus that (ii) [the essence and the power] are distinguished from one another in the

19. See *DM* 35. 4.

way that powers are normally distinguished from one another, by reference to their diverse acts. For even though this argument seems to presuppose that a created essence is distinct from its *esse* and is related to its *esse* in the way that an active or passive power is related to its act, nonetheless, if one abstracts from this question, the argument can be accommodated in the way just explained.

22. *Powers with respect to local motion are really distinct from the substance.* And on this basis, finally, one can be readily persuaded that the powers that exist in created things for effecting various local motions are accidental.

For, first of all, if the most important operations and the operations that are more intrinsic and vital require faculties of this sort, then, a fortiori, local motions require them.

Second, we know from experience that in natural things local motion, especially natural local motion, is effected by the mediation of an accidental faculty—for example, gravity or lightness. Therefore, a fortiori, when a magnet attracts iron to itself or when rhubarb expels bile, they do so by means of accidental faculties. Therefore, the same thing will hold for all similar cases.

Third, even though local motion is more perfect than other motions /623a/ in the sense that it changes the substance or subject less, it nonetheless seems distant from the substance, especially by virtue of the fact that it is not ordered *per se* toward the substance and that it has almost no agreement with or similarity to it. And so it is no wonder that a substantial form is not by itself capable of effecting this sort of motion without an accidental faculty.

Therefore, it is clear in general that created agents effect accidents through proximate accidental principles.

23. *Authors who have contested the aforementioned line of reasoning, and their arguments.* There has been no shortage of philosophers and theologians who have at least in part contradicted this thesis in their discussions of either the powers of the soul or the powers of angels. This is evident from Gregory, *Sentences* 2, dist. 16, q. 3; Scotus, *Sentences* 2, dist. 16, q. unica, and *Sentences* 4, dist. 45, q. 3; Durandus, *Sentences* 1, dist. 2, q. 2, and *Sentences* 2, dist. 3, q. 5; Marsilius [of Inghen], *Sentences* 1, q. 7, a. 7, and *Sentences* 2, q. 17, a. 2; and from other philosophers in [their commentaries on] *On the Soul* 2. These last will be dealt with [in our commentary on *On the Soul* 2], and we will say a few things below about angels.[20]

For now I only want to call attention to the fact that there is a difference between Scotus on the one hand and Gregory and his followers on the other. For Gregory does not posit any distinction at all in reality between forms and their faculties. From this it follows that he grants that it is through one

---

20. ibid.

and the same principle that the soul understands, wills, sees, hears, and so forth—which is quite absurd.

By contrast, Scotus, in order to avoid this absurdity, posits a formal distinction between the powers and the forms. However, if by a formal distinction Scotus means a distinction that does not actually exist in reality but that at most exists virtually and "foundationally" and is brought to completion by the mind, then he differs from Gregory and the others only in his manner of speaking. On the other hand, if he means a true and actual distinction—at least a modal distinction—that exists in reality, then, first of all, he does not contradict the thesis posited above. For the mode in question will be a certain sort of accident—which is sufficient for the truth of the aforementioned assertion. Second, he is incorrect to deny that there is a real distinction in the most proper sense. For, as I will explain in a moment, a proximate faculty of operating is not a mode but a proper entity and real form. And so if the faculty of operating is distinct in reality from the substantial form, then it is distinct not as a mode but as an entity, and so it is really distinct in the proper sense. This is so especially in light of the fact that if there are any arguments that prove that there is a distinction in reality, then they prove a real distinction no less than a modal distinction; and, conversely, if the arguments adduced by [Scotus] and the others against St. Thomas's position carried any weight at all, they would work just as well against a modal distinction. /623b/

24. However, I do not consider it expeditious at this point to lay out the relevant arguments one by one—because (i) they do not seem troublesome to me, because (ii) they are sufficiently answered by Cajetan and others, and, finally, because (iii) almost all of them are aimed at showing that entities should not be multiplied without necessity but that in this case there is no sufficient necessity—a claim they [try to] prove either by replying to St. Thomas's arguments or by arguing that because a substance is more noble [than an accident], it is fully capable of causing anything such that an accident might be added in order to cause it.

And, in particular, an argument taken from the first assertion above can be urged against us. If the powers flow from the essence by means of a true efficient causality, then the essence contains those powers eminently; therefore, the essence will be sufficient to effect through itself whatever it is able to effect through the powers.

However, one may reply that there is a sufficient necessity for a created substance to have principles accommodated to accidental actions, a necessity that is sufficiently proved by the inductions and arguments adduced above. For it is not the case that there can be demonstrations with respect to everything. Nor does it matter that a substance is more perfect [than an accident], both because (i) it is not always the case that what is more perfect is able to effect anything that a less perfect thing is able to effect and also because (ii) from [the greater perfection of a substance] one may infer at most that the substance is a principal or root principle, but not that it is also a proximate principle. But to be a principle in both these ways is something more than to be a principle in just one of them. In this sense we can even claim that what is more perfect is the substance together with its powers rather than the substance by itself. And, finally, it is also the case that a hand is more perfect than a pen, and yet one cannot write without a pen.

To the last objection one can reply, in the first place, by appealing to a sensory example. For water is sufficient through its own form for coldness to result from it, and yet in the absence of the coldness it is not sufficient to make other things cold. Therefore, the consequence should be denied. The first reason that can be given is that it is possible for the power of a [substantial] form or principle to be limited both to perfecting its own suppositum and to a given mode of action or emanation. For instance, gravity moves the heavy body in which it exists but no other body. Second, in some cases a formal power or faculty is accommodated to an action in such a way that no virtual power suffices. For example, the agent intellect, either by itself or together with the phantasm, virtually contains the intelligible species. And yet [the intellect and the phantasm] cannot concur by themselves alone for an intellective act; rather, they can do so only by means of the species that they effect. Third, and most important, I do not think that an essence contains its properties eminently; rather, it is only /624a/ insofar as it is an instrument that it contains them. This is why, as I explained before, the effect is attributed to the generating thing.[21] But it is possible for something to be an appropriate instrument for effecting another thing—that is, another faculty—and yet not be an appropriate instrument for immediately effecting the action of that faculty—as is manifestly clear in the case of the instruments of a craft.

21. See §14 above.

Section 4

Which Accidents Are Capable of Being Principles of Acting

1. *The nature of the difficulty.* With respect to the doctrine laid down in the preceding sections, a few minor perplexities remain to be explicated. The first is the one posed in the title of this section. This perplexity can be taken to apply generally, both to the activity of accidents with respect to substances and to the activity of accidents with respect to other accidents. However, since, as has been explained,[1] an accident does not effect a substance except by means of the antecedent effecting of some accident, it follows that the whole question can be directed to the proper efficient causality that accidents have with respect to other accidents.

And this gives rise to a reason for puzzlement. An accident is said to be a proximate principle for producing [another] accident insofar as it is proportioned to the latter. Therefore, the accident that is the principle of the action will have to be of the same type as the accident that is the terminus of the action. Therefore, a quantity will be a proximate principle for effecting a quantity, and one "where" will be a proximate principle of another "where," and so on. However, just the opposite is true, since, according to the common position of philosophers, qualities alone are proximate principles of action—and not all qualities, but only some—the reason for which must also be investigated.

2. *An accident can naturally emanate from another accident.* On this question we must first draw the distinction, posited above, between an activity that occurs through a natural resulting and one that occurs through a proper action. One should assume that we are talking only about the latter—a point which, having once been made, applies to the whole discussion. For natural resulting is being counted as one with the production of a thing.

However, if along the way something peculiar to natural resulting can be noted, we will not omit it. Thus, in the present context, just as we said above that an accident can result from a substance, so too from any accident there can result another accident that is either really or at least modally ˙ distinct from it, as long as the former has the capacity for such a property. For it is in this way that a shape or a relation of equality (if the latter is a distinct mode) results from a quantity; and it is in this way that, according to many authors, one relation can result from another—for example, a similarity from

1. See *DM* 18. 2. 16–21.

111

a paternity, and so forth.[2] And the reason is that every essence, of whatever kind, can be a principle of its own intrinsic properties through the natural resulting of those properties. /624b/

3. *Among accidents, only qualities are principles of true efficient causality; and, first, on quantity.* Therefore, as regards proper accidental efficient causality, one should claim, first, that only a quality can be a proximate principle of it.[3]

This assertion can be proved, first of all, from experience. For all the actions that tend toward [the production of] a substance are normally effected by means of qualities—either the primary qualities or qualities that eminently contain the primary qualities. Vital actions are also effected by means of qualities. Likewise, a faculty for producing local motion is always some power that belongs to the category of quality, so much so that even in the case of the motion of projectiles philosophers deem it necessary that there should be an impressed impetus, which is a quality that effects motion.

Second, the assertion can be proved by briefly running through the other categories. For, as experience shows, a quantity does not produce another quantity. And the reason is, first of all, that the quantity follows upon the matter and so imitates the matter's nature, which is to receive and not to act. Second, it is not the case that a quantity can of itself be produced *de novo*. Indeed, according to our position, it cannot even be produced concomitantly, that is, in such a way that a quantity that did not exist beforehand now begins to exist through the actions of natural agents. For we maintain that quantity is coeval with matter.[4] Instead, all that happens is that a quantity which, along with the matter, previously belonged to one thing begins to

2. The example is explained as follows. In becoming a father for the first time, Jones becomes similar to Smith in being a father. Hence, Jones's paternity or fatherhood is the foundation in Jones for his being similar to Smith in the relevant respect.

3. Here Suarez begins an induction over all the categories of accidents or accidental beings: quality, quantity, relation, action, passion, place ("where"), time (duration or "when"), position, and having. It should be noted that he does not believe that all the entities falling under these categories are on a par ontologically. On his view, only the categories of quality and quantity contain accidents in the strictest sense—i.e., entities that (i) are apt by nature to inhere in a subject, (ii) are really distinct from the subjects in which they inhere, and, consequently, (iii) are separable (at least by God's power) from those subjects. Other entities designated as accidents are modes, which (i) are likewise apt by nature to inhere in a subject but (ii) are only modally, and not really, distinct from their subjects and, consequently, (iii) are absolutely inseparable from their subjects. In addition, according to Suarez, the category of position contains only modes that are also contained in the category of "where." Suarez discusses accidents in general in *DM* 37–39 and each of the accidental categories in particular in *DM* 40–53.

4. See *DM* 5. 3 and *DM* 13. 14. 15–16.

belong to another thing. Hence, if quantity is added to a preexisting thing, then an augmentation occurs—either a proper augmentation or an improper augmentation, in accord with the diverse modes of that sort of change.[5] However, such a change or addition is always effected by means of an antecedent alteration and generation (or regeneration), the proximate principle of which is a quality. And so a quantity does not have an action of which it can be the proximate principle. For the termini of quantity, which in some cases result from the division of a continuum, and so on, come to exist through natural resulting rather than through proper efficient causality of the sort we are talking about.

4. *On relation.* Again, according to the position held by everyone, a relation is not active. And the reason usually given is that a relation has the least being.

And this is confirmed by an a fortiori argument taken from the divine relations,[6] which, given just what is proper to them, are nonactive—as theologians teach on the basis of the firm principle that the Trinity's actions with respect to external things are undivided.

But even if we leave aside the divine relations (concerning which I take the appropriate argument to be that they are directed only toward subsistence and that subsistence as such is not a principle of acting but only a terminus of the nature, which is itself the principle of operation, as is argued at length in the material on the Incarnation and the Trinity[7]), an argument can be made in the case of created relations by appeal to the plausible /625a/ opinion that a relation adds no [new] entity to its foundation. It follows that they are not active except by reason of their foundation. But if that foundation is not active, then the relations do not have efficient causality from it, and the foundation is never active except when it is a quality.

In addition, a relation *qua* relation cannot be a principle for effecting an absolute thing, because (i) [relative things and absolute things] belong to

5. A proper augmentation involves the growth of a living organism through the assimilation of food to its substance. Improper augmentation involves an increase in the size of a thing by its juxtaposition with other things.

6. According to scholastic Trinitarian theology there are four relations which constitute the three Persons of the Blessed Trinity: *active generation* (Father), *passive generation* (Son), *active spiration* (Father and Son), and *passive spiration* (Holy Spirit). Further, it is the divine nature itself, rather than the Persons as such, which is the principle *quo* of action or operation.

7. For more on subsistence, see *DM* 18. 2, n. 2. In the Trinity each of the Persons is a suppositum subsisting in the divine nature. So the Persons are the ultimate subjects of divine action, even though, as noted above, the divine nature which they share in common is the sole principle *quo* of operation.

different orders [of being], and because (ii) it is exactly backwards that an absolute thing should follow upon a relative thing.

Again, it is not possible for a relation to produce a relation, since a proper relation is not produced *per se* but is instead produced only insofar as it results once the foundation and terminus have been posited.

5. *On action; whether immanent actions are true efficient principles.* Further, an action is not truly and properly a principle of acting. For, as we will show below,[8] an action is an agent's very causality, and it is in this that the nature of causality consists. But the causality is not a principle of acting. Rather, the causality proceeds from the principle, which it presupposes.

Likewise, if an action is compared to its terminus, it is not a principle for effecting that thing but is instead a *path* to that thing; that is, the action is the dependence of that thing on its principle. On the other hand, if an action is compared to other entities, it cannot through itself be a principle of any of them, since it cannot even be a principle of another action. For, speaking naturally, an action does not follow immediately from another action; at most it follows by the mediation of the terminus [of another action]. Nor can an action be a principle of a terminus other than its own. For no principle attains to its terminus except by the mediation of an action, and it is impossible for any action to go beyond its own intrinsic terminus—that is, to attain through itself to another terminus. For it is identified with its own terminus and is merely a certain mode of that terminus.[9]

But someone will raise an objection concerning immanent actions, which are sometimes principles for effecting something. For many claim that an act of understanding effects a [mental] word that is really distinct from it; others hold that an act of cognizing is an efficient cause of an act of love or of delight. And there are more authentic examples: that is, that immanent acts are efficient causes of habits, and that sometimes one act causes another act that belongs to the same faculty—for example, an assent to the principles causes an assent to the conclusion, and the intending of an end causes the choosing of the means. Moreover, it is silly to hold that in this sort of efficient causation an immanent act does not behave as a principle for producing something else but is instead identical with the very production of that thing. For it is a contradiction for an actual production to be an entity distinct from the thing produced, whereas a habit is a thing distinct from the act by which it is produced. Likewise, if the one act is compared to the other act, the one that proceeds from the other is intrinsically an immanent action;

8. See *DM* 18. 10.

9. For more on this claim, see *DM* 48. 2.

therefore, it is intrinsically and of its very self a certain /625b/ production; therefore, the other act is not the production of it.

There are others who, because of this objection, restrict the present assertion, so that it holds true [only] for actions other than immanent actions. But this restriction is unnecessary, and no plausible argument can be adduced for it. For why won't an act of illuminating also be an active cause? Again, why won't the effects that proceed from the light be attributed to the act of illuminating itself as to a principle of acting?

Therefore, it is closer to the truth to claim that just as an act of illuminating has its own proper intrinsic terminus in which it itself is terminated, whereas it is this terminus that is the principle of all further actions (if there be any) that follow from the illuminated thing, so, too, immanent actions, insofar as they are actions, have their own intrinsic termini, which are qualities, and it is these qualities that are the proximate principles of any further action when a further action happens to follow.

However, that this is so will have to proved at more length below when we discuss action.[10] For the present, it is adequately confirmed just by the argument adduced above. For how would an immanent act be a principle for producing a habit, which is a true quality, unless it itself were a quality? Again, given that the habit and the act are analogues of one another, why do we distinguish, within the habit itself, the nature of a quality from the intrinsic production or dependence through which the quality is effected by the act itself, if we are not going to distinguish, within that same act, the nature of a quality from the intrinsic dependence or action through which it is effected by its faculty?[11]

6. *On passion.* As far as the category of passion is concerned, it is almost unnecessary to add anything, since, as I will show below, an action and a passion are not actually distinguished in reality but are distinguished only "foundationally" in cases where an action has a passion adjoined to it.[12] Hence, if an action is not a principle of acting, then, a fortiori, a passion is not, and the arguments already adduced can be equally applied to both.

10. See ibid.

11. Suarez's point is that the effect of an exercise of, say, the intellect is a modification (or quality) of the intellect itself. This quality, effected by an action on the part of the intellect, is itself called an "act" because it is the actualization of a certain cognitive potentiality. So within this act (call it A), as within any other quality effected by an efficient cause, we can distinguish the action, which is A's dependence on its efficient cause, from that which terminates the action, viz., the quality which is A itself.

12. See *DM* 49. 1.

The only possible objection has to do with local motion, which is a sort of change and hence a passion. For a change, taken broadly, and a passion are the same thing. But a local motion is a cause of heat. Hence, it seems to be a principle of heat.

However, one may reply that a local motion does not effect anything by itself but is instead only a path to a "where"—even though it does contribute to actions as a necessary or enabling condition either for applying the principle of acting or for removing impediments. And it is in this way that a local motion is sometimes a *per accidens* cause of heat and also sometimes a *per accidens* cause of coldness. This will be discussed in another place.

7. On place, [position], duration, and having; why it is that a quality originates this activity before the others. Further, as regards place—that is, a "where" as such—it is clear that it is not a principle of acting. For if a place is taken to be the containing surface, then it is not a principle of acting, for the same reason that /626a/ a quantity, too, is not a principle of acting. For a place in this sense is nothing in reality other than a surface, though it does add a certain relation to, or denomination with respect to, an extrinsic thing— none of which has anything to do with the notion of acting. (I said, however, that I was talking about a place as such—that is, just insofar as it is a place— since, insofar as it is either a natural place or a violent place, it can have some action on the located thing. But it does not have this action except by the mediation of certain qualities, as is obvious from philosophy.)

On the other hand, if we are speaking of a "where" insofar as it is an intrinsic presence—that is, a mode of the located thing—then it is immediately obvious that it is not a principle of any action. To be sure, it is sometimes a [necessary] condition of acting because of proximity, as we will explain later; it is not, however, a ground or principle of acting, as experience itself makes sufficiently clear. Now there seems to be no reason for this other than that a "where" is merely a certain mode of the thing that is present, but does not of itself have its own proper being. Thus, it does not of itself confer activity either. Likewise, it is impossible to see what a "where" might bring about *per se*. It cannot produce another "where" in a different body. For a "where" is not effected *per se* except by means of a local motion. But one thing moves another locally not by means of its own "where" but rather by impelling it or attracting it or in some similar way.

From this it is clear a fortiori, that neither a position nor a time (that is, a duration or "when") nor a having (that is, being adorned) is a principle of acting according to just the notions by reason of which these things constitute categories. For a position is not really distinct from a "where"; it is distinct from it only by virtue of some denomination, either a relation or a shape.[13] A having, on the other hand, adds only a certain extrinsic denomination, whereas a time, and in general a duration, is not something distinct from the entity that endures or else is at most a mode. Therefore, all these things, taken formally and as such, are nonactive; instead, it is the entities with which they are identified that are able to be active. For instance, if the entity that endures is a quality or an article of clothing, it can be active by reason of certain qualities.

What remains, therefore, is that among accidents only qualities are *per se* principles of acting. And one can argue, first of all, that, apart from quantities, only qualities have a proper being that is really distinct from the substance, and so they are accidental forms and proper acts in the strictest sense—which is what is required for the notion of a principle of acting and in order for something to have its own activity.

Second, a quality is the sort of entity that follows upon a [substantial] form and thus imitates the nature of the form. And it is attributed to a quality that it should be the form's instrument or proximate power for acting, especially given that a substantial form /626b/ is not by itself a sufficient proximate principle of actions of the sort in question.

8. *Which species of quality are active; shape is not.* You will object: If this argument is sound, then it proves that *every* quality is a principle of some action or other, since every quality follows upon the [substantial] form and must consequently imitate the nature of the form. This is so especially because just as the substantial form is a certain act, so too a quality is an act; but just as every act gives *esse*, so too it gives operation.[14] And this can be confirmed by the fact that each thing exists for the sake of its own operation; otherwise, it would exist in vain, as is claimed in *On the Heavens* 2.3 [286a8] and *Ethics* 1.7 [1097b22–1098a19].

Nonetheless, one should reply that it is not the case either that all the

13. See *DM* 52. 1. 9: "The form . . . of a position, which gives the denomination of this category, is the very 'where' itself conceived of under a different concept . . . The distinction consists in the fact that a 'where' as such bespeaks the mode in question only insofar as it constitutes the thing as present to a given location, and this is why we always explain the 'where' itself through relations of distance or proximity or close presence, since we conceive of it as the foundation for those things. Position as such, by contrast, expresses that same mode to the extent that it denominates the thing as disposed within itself by a certain disposition resulting from the local arrangement of its parts."

14. In this context, the claim that the substantial form is an act is just the claim that the substantial form actualizes the matter's potentiality to be a substance of a certain sort. Likewise, to call a quality an act is just to say that the quality actualizes the substance's potentiality to be qualified (or perfected or completed) in a certain way.

species of quality enumerated by Aristotle are active or that all the qualities subsumed under the individual species are active. Instead, [being active] applies just to the first three species with regard to *some* of the qualities subsumed under them. I will now explain the individual cases.[15]

First of all, starting with the last [species], shape is not *per se* a principle of any action. This is affirmed by the common position, which is taken from St. Thomas, *Summa Theologiae* 2-2, q. 96, a. 2, ad 2, and *Contra Gentes* 2, chap. 76, and *Contra Gentes* 3, chap. 105; and from Cajetan and Ferrariensis in those same places. Scotus holds the same position in *Sentences* 4, dist. 1, q. 4, as does Cajetan of Thiene in *On the Heavens* 4, last chapter. The claim in question is also based on Aristotle, *Metaphysics* 12.3, text 14 [1070a4–8], and *Ethics* 6.4 [1140a1–24], and *Physics* 2, text 2 [1.192b24–33]; in these places he claims that artifacts do not as such have a principle of motion or of action. There is no reason for this other than that a form effected by a craft is only a shape, which is not a principle of acting. This is also the basis on which Augustine, *De Civitate Dei* 10, chaps. 9 and 11, refutes the error of those who think that some power of acting resides in astronomical shapes and images. He then demonstrates that all the things in question are effected at the stipulation of, and by the power of, demons.

Now the explanation, which is also based on Aristotle, *Physics* 1.5, text 46 [188b9–20], is that shape adds nothing to a thing except a certain arrangement or ordering of the parts, which gives rise to that mode of quantity which is the shape. And so shape cannot be a *per se* principle of acting, both because it is only a certain mode and because it is a mode of quantity and a property that follows upon quantity. Hence, since quantity is not active *per se*, neither can shape be active *per se*.

And the assertion in question is confirmed, finally, by the fact that there is nothing that a shape might effect *per se*, since one shape cannot effect another similar shape. For it will neither effect a statue nor be able to effect a quality or any similar thing.

9. *An objection and reply.* You will object: Shape /627a/ contributes greatly at least to local motion; a sharp shape contributes greatly to a cutting motion, and a circular shape to a circular motion. For this reason, in *On the Heavens* 4, at the end, Albert suggests that a sharp shape is a power for effecting a motion, or at least that it constitutes such a power along with other conditions—that is, weight and hardness. Durandus is of the same opinion in

---

15. The four species of quality are (1) habit or disposition, (2) causal power, (3) proper sensible (i.e., sensory qualities that are the proper objects of a single sensory faculty), and (4) shape or figure. Suarez discusses this division of the category of quality in *DM* 42. 4.

Sentences 1, dist. 45, q. 2, n. 8, where he adds that the shape of a seal is a *per se* principle of the similar shape that is impressed upon the wax.

However, one may reply that shapes of this sort are merely dispositions on the part of an instrument or body for its moving or being moved more easily in a given way, either because it puts up less resistance when it is moved by the craftsman, as in the case of the motion of a sphere, or else because it meets with less resistance, as in the case of a cutting motion. For the sharper the instrument is, the fewer parts it touches, and so the less resistance it meets with. Conversely, when the cutting is effected because of the motion of the other thing without a motion on the part of the cutting body, as in the case of flowing water, the reason that a sharp shape is well-disposed for that cutting is that it contributes to the flowing water's being resisted more easily, because the water directly touches the sharp object with fewer of its parts and so impresses less force on it. And so it is in the case of the seal as well. Since some of its parts are sharper than others, and since some stick out while others are, as it were, hollow, it follows that they cut, or press down upon, some parts of the wax more easily than others. And this is how the [new] shape comes to exist [in the wax]—not because the one shape is a *per se* principle of the other but rather because, given the local motion of certain of the parts, a given shape comes to exist. An indication of this is that the shape comes to exist in the wax in just the opposite way from how it existed in the seal. For the parts that stuck out in the seal are, as it were, hollow in the [wax] that is sealed, and vice versa.

10. *In the first three species of quality, some qualities are active, and some are not.* It is in the other three species of quality that some active qualities are found. For the habits of [various] faculties are principles for eliciting acts, and, conversely, acts (which are also classified under the first species and are dispositions) sometimes effect habits. Powers effect both acts and habits. Sensible qualities are also active, as is obvious in the case of heat.

However, in each of these species one finds some qualities that are not principles of acting. For example, in the species of habit there are qualities that are proximately ordered toward some sort of *esse* and not toward acting. Health is usually classified in this group, though it is called a habit somewhat improperly—and so perhaps there is no example among natural things. (It is incorrect to use intelligible species as an example, as some do; for /627b/ they are in fact principles of acting.) Among supernatural things, on the other hand, a common example is the grace that exists in the essence of the soul.[16]

---

16. The sort of grace in question here is *sanctifying* (or *habitual*) grace, whereby, according to Catholic doctrine, we share in the life of God. This grace is distinct from *actual* grace,

However, a more certain example is a [sacramental] character, which I will deal with elsewhere.[17]

Likewise, in the species of disposition there are many acts that do not effect anything: namely, when the faculty in question does not require a habit, as in the case of vision, or when it does not require a habit that can be effected by an act, as in the case of supernatural acts. Also, there are many acts that do not produce either other acts or habits, as is evident in the case of each of the senses, in the case of the enjoyment of God, and in similar cases.

Likewise, powers are usually divided into active powers and passive powers, among which passive powers as such are not principles of acting, even though it is uncertain whether there is any quality that is a purely passive power—as we will see in the proper place below, where we will also discuss the question of whether the power of resistance is an active power or a passive power.[18]

Again, among sensible qualities there are many—for example, whiteness and the other colors—that do not effect qualities similar to themselves, even if they do effect intentional species. There are other sensible qualities, however, that are active in both these ways: for example, light, heat, and so forth.

Now it is difficult to give a reason for this variety. The general reason seems to be that a substance requires all this variety for its own complete perfection, and so it receives from nature diverse qualities which, in accord with their diversity, are ordered toward diverse effects. Hence, certain qualities have been instituted for acting, while others have been instituted for informing or embellishing the substance and, as it were, filling out its capacity to the limit—all of which pertain to the role of a form. So qualities that are nonactive are not otiose, and so do not lack participation in or agreement with [the notion of] a form.

And this is the way in which the reason for perplexity [proposed at the beginning of this section] is resolved. However, the task of explaining which qualities in particular are of the one type or the other lies beyond the scope of the present discussion.[19]

which is directed toward specific actions.

17. See *Summa Theologiae* 3, q. 63, disp. 11.

18. See *DM* 43. 2.

19. See *DM* 42.

Section 5

Whether Accidents Effect Other Accidents by Themselves
without the Concurrence of Substantial Forms

1. As for this question, the common way of replying is to say that the accidental form is a proximate principle but that the substantial form is the principal principle of all the suppositum's actions, even of its accidental actions. However, the doctors do not explain what this notion of a principal principle consists in or what the influence of a principal principle is—or, if they do say something in passing, they suggest that this influence consists solely in the fact that the [substantial] form is the source and origin of the accidental power that is given to it by nature in order to serve as its proximate principle for eliciting an action. /628a/ However, the substantial form is not thought to have a proximate and actual influence in the very exercise of an accidental action.

And an argument for this position can be adduced both from the axiom that a created substance cannot be a proximate principle of an accident and also by appeal to the claim that a sufficient principle for effecting an accident is another accident.

2. *In vital functions it is not just the accident, but the substance as well, that has a proximate influence.* Nonetheless, my own view is that we must invoke a distinction. For among the actions in question, some are vital actions, while others are not.

Concerning the first group, one should claim, it seems, that it is not only an accidental power but also the soul itself, through its own substance, that has within its own order a proximate influence on these actions.

Experience seems to support this thesis. For these vital actions are effected in so intimate a way that they seem to proceed in actuality from the first principle of life itself: namely, the soul. Thus it happens that even if the eye has an image present to itself and receives a [sensible] species from it, it does not see unless the soul is attentive.

It makes no difference if someone objects that this occurs because the imagination or the common sense is distracted, since I can make exactly the same argument in the case of both the imagination and the common sense.[1]

---

1. The common (or internal) sense is the faculty or power whereby all the sensory information about a given object is brought together in a unified sensible likeness (or species) of the object.

And if someone claims that in the case in question the sensible species does not proceed beyond the external sense, then from this we can adduce the following argument against the first attempt to evade [our thesis]. If the species of a sensible object that is present to, and alters, an external sense does not reach the internal sense when the soul is not attentive, then this is because a species belonging to an external sense is not communicated to the internal sense except through the mediation of the external sense's act. From this it follows that the external sense's sensing takes place prior in nature to the internal sense's cooperating with it, since this cooperation seems to follow upon the external sense's operation. Therefore, the reason why the external sense does not sense in the aforementioned case has nothing to do with the internal sense; rather, the reason why the internal sense is not affected by the species of the object in question is that the external sense does not perceive that object. Therefore, one must seek another explanation for why in such a case the external sense does not effect its own act, and this explanation seems to be none other than that in such a case the soul is not influencing or cooperating with the external sense.

You will object that the explanation is not that the soul is not cooperating with the external sense through its own substance but rather that it is not cooperating with it through the animal spirits that are necessary for sensation and motion.

However, even if it is true that these spirits are necessary, this very fact only serves to confirm the argument as well as the experience appealed to above. For what is required for these vital acts is not only the proximate faculty but also the concurrence of the spirits, /628b/ which have an influence on the act not by chance but by virtue of some faculty that directs those spirits to that act. Therefore, there must be some common principle which actually uses the two faculties in question and which, because of a natural inclination or sympathy, orders the action of the first faculty toward the act of the second faculty.

3. Further, the thesis in question is confirmed by that other sort of experience through which we proved above that there is only one soul in a human being.[2] For it is indisputable that excessive attentiveness to the work of one faculty impedes the work of another. For example, if a man is looking at something very intently, he will not hear someone who is speaking to him. And lest this be attributed to a defect in the [animal] spirits, it is also the case that the intellect's attentiveness impedes the operation of the senses, and that the more profound and perfect that attentiveness is, the more it diminishes the imagination's motion or representation as well—and (what

2. See DM 15. 10.

is more) it even impedes or suspends the works of the nutritive part of the soul. But if each faculty had its own operation through itself alone, then there would be no explanation for why the operation of one faculty should impede the operation of another. For, given the multiplicity of the powers, if the one did not depend on the other, and if both did not depend on a third faculty whose power, when applied to both, is diminished in each of them, then there would be no explanation for why their operations could not be multiplied simultaneously and exercised in an equally perfect way.

Further, the best argument from the contrary assumption is taken from the connectedness of the operations, since as long as the intellect is understanding, the will is excited toward loving, and so on. However, this is because the selfsame soul is actually operating through both these powers. For a sort of habitual rootedness—that is, a remote emanation from the same soul— would not by itself be sufficient for this actual causality (that is, motion and excitation) if each of the operations proceeded in actuality from its own faculty alone, without being connected in some common principle. And it is this that also gives rise to the dependence between cognition and the vital appetite, a dependence that is such that nothing can be loved unless it is antecedently cognized.

Moreover, an a priori argument can be adduced from the proper mode of a vital operation, which requires this sort of intimate connection with its principal formal principle, in order to be able to be effected in a way consonant with its nature and also in order to be able to affect its own principle or suppositum in the vital mode. For as far as we can ascertain from experience, this is what actual life consists in, and this is the primary difference between living and nonliving things.

And the argument is confirmed by the fact that it is for the reason in question that everyone believes that a faculty of sight which is separated [from the soul] is unable to see—that is, to elicit an act of seeing—and that an intellect which is separated [from the soul] is unable to understand.

There are a few objections that can be raised against this position, /629a/ but I will deliberately pass over them, since either they are not troublesome or else they necessarily touch on many points that pertain to the science of the soul. Moreover, if someone should ask why in the world accidental and vital faculties are necessary, given that the [substantial] form itself also has an actual influence, he will get a sufficient reply from what was said in section 3˙.[3] For the [substantial] form is, as it were, a universal principle, whereas the [accidental] faculty is required as a particular principle and as a principle that is more accommodated [to the act] and proper to it, as was

3. See *DM* 18. 3. 16–18 and 20–21, as well as *DM* 18. 2. 26.

explained at length there. Moreover, in a moment we will refute some other, less serious objections.

4. *A nonvital accident does not necessarily proceed proximately from the substance.* Now as regards accidental actions that are nonvital, one should claim that it is possible for them to be effected by accidents alone. This is evident in the case of heat, which, when it exists in water or in any subject other [than fire], produces heat in the absence of the form of fire. Likewise, a whiteness does not require a higher concurrence in order to produce an intentional species of itself.

Again, this is the reason why an entity that has two active qualities is just as capable of exercising the action of both of them at once as it is of exercising the action of just one of them. For example, water produces coldness and moisture simultaneously, to the extent to which it is capable, and so forth.

Finally, the thesis is proved by appeal to the reason for perplexity that was proposed above. For if the perfection of the effect is considered, then the power and perfection of a similar or more eminent accidental form are sufficient to communicate that perfection. Moreover, the mode of [a nonvital] action does not require as intimate a dependence as [in the case of a vital action]. So there is no reason why such a dependence should be necessary.

This, incidentally, is the way to deflect the present argument insofar as it might be turned against the first assertion above. For though one can have doubts about whether a vital operation is more perfect in its being than the power from which it proceeds, nonetheless, even if we assume for a moment that the power is more perfect [than the operation], our claim is that the principal principle's actual and immediate influence is still required because of the special mode of such an operation. Nor is it repugnant to this mode [of operation] that the substantial form should have an influence on the action— as long as it has an accidental principle by which it is proximately channeled to that action. For it is not always the case that an accidental form is called a proximate principle by virtue of the fact that it *alone* has an immediate influence; rather, sometimes it is called a proximate principle by virtue of the fact that it is a principle that channels the substantial form to a given action. In the same way, the reason why a particular cause is called a proximate cause vis-à-vis the First Cause is not that the First Cause does not have an immediate influence but rather that the particular cause is within its own genus that which channels the action.[4]

5. *The substance does not concur immediately in the production of any nonvital*

---

4. Suarez did not discuss the proximate/remote and immediate/mediate distinctions in *DM* 17. 2. As he points out here, 'proximate cause' and 'remote cause' are used somewhat loosely, and so it is always important to disambiguate them within the given context.

action; whether the organizing of the body is a vital action. But regarding this last thesis, /629b/ someone might ask whether, even if the influence of the [substantial] form is not necessary for these [nonvital] actions, it is nonetheless possible and useful—whether, for example, heat which exists in a fire might be aided by the form [of the fire] in producing heat and, consequently, whether, other things being equal, the heat in question might produce heat more readily than does heat that exists in some other type of subject.

Also, against the first thesis someone might object that a vital action sometimes seems to be exercised by a power that is separated from the soul—for example, in the case of semen.

To the first part of this objection I reply that one finds no sufficient indication of the sort of influence in question, and so it should not be posited capriciously and without any basis. This is also confirmed by the mystery of the Eucharist, where the accidents of the wine act equally well in the absence of their [substantial] form's influence. I realize that it can be claimed that God supplies this efficient causality in order to promote faith in the mystery. But where there is no compelling necessity, one should not resort to divine causality.

As for the second part of the objection, it is probable that, as regards the spirits implanted in it, the semen has a vegetative life—the sort of life which corresponds to the vital mode that seems to exist in the generation of a living thing. This is what Aristotle seems to say about semen in *On the Generation of Animals* 2.1 [716a2–17], since the semen has the power to organize and generate the body, a work that seems to belong to the vegetative soul. Nor, it seems, does St. Thomas disagree with this position in *Summa Theologiae* 1, q. 118, a. 1, ad 1.

Second, whatever the truth might be with regard to this last point, one may reply that the vegetative soul's actions with respect to [an animal's] substance are of the same type as actions effected by an extrinsic principle. For they are all either local motions, alterations, or the eduction of the substantial form—and so these actions have the nature of vital actions only because of the special relation they bear to the soul as a principle that is conjoined to them in the same self-moving suppositum. In the same way, human speech is a vital action, whereas an angel's speaking in an assumed body is not a vital action, even though the two sorts of speaking are similar in outward appearance.[5] Therefore, the semen's action, just insofar as it proceeds from

5. Suarez has in mind here a story like that narrated in the book of Tobit, where the angel Raphael assumes a human body and assists Tobiah. Suarez's point is that a human or rational soul is the form of a human being's body and hence that intelligent actions that proceed from the soul through the body—e.g., speaking—are rightly counted as vital or

the semen, is not a vital action but merely a natural action. On the other hand, the fact that in its craft (as I will put it) or manner of acting the semen contributes to a mode of life must be traced back to another, higher principle, as was adumbrated above.

---

life-related actions. By contrast, an angel's relation to an assumed body is such that he is not the subject of the body's actions; i.e., the angel brings it about that the body emits certain sounds which imitate human speech, but these sounds are not the angel's own.

Section 6

Whether an Accident Is Merely an Instrument in the Production of Another Accident

1. There are those who contend that an accident should be called merely an instrumental principle. /630a/ This opinion is commonly attributed to St. Thomas, who suggests it in *Sentences* 1, dist. 3, q. 4, a. 3, ad 2, and that is why his followers very often adopt it. They support it with the following arguments.

First, an accident is essentially subordinated to a substance in *esse*, and consequently it is subordinated to it in action as well.

Second, it is from the substance that an accident receives its whole power of acting. And it does not matter that a principal proximate cause likewise receives the power of acting from the First Cause. For the secondary cause and the First Cause belong to diverse orders [of causes], and it is not contradictory for a lower principal cause to receive its power from a cause of a higher order. By contrast, an accident, in acting, belongs to the same order as its substance, and together with the substance it constitutes a single complete proximate agent and receives its power of acting from the substance. But it is proper to an instrumental cause to receive its power from another agent of the same order in this way: namely, by constituting with the latter a single proximate agent.

Third, acting is analogous to *esse*. But an accident's *esse* belongs to its substance, since an accident is a being of a being. Therefore, an accident's acting belongs principally to its substance. Therefore, the acting belongs only instrumentally to the accident.

And this is confirmed by the manner of speaking used by all philosophers, since they attribute all the actions in question to substances as the primary agents of those actions.

2. Other doctors often hold the contrary position, as one can see in Scotus, *Sentences* 4, dist. 13, q. 3; Paludanus, *Sentences* 4, dist. 13, q. 4, concl. 1; John Major, *Sentences* 4, dist. 13, q. 1; and Giles, *Quodlibeta* 3, q. 4, and *Theoremata de Esse et Essentia*, theorem 43.

Now in order to explain the foundation for this position, one must presuppose that the question here has to do not with a principal cause *quod*—that is, with that which operates—but rather with the principal principle *quo*.[1]

1. For more on the distinction between a principle *quod* and a principle *quo*, see DM 17. 2. 7.

For if we are talking about the former, then it is obvious that the suppositum is that which operates. Now if the suppositum is being taken formally—that is, as a *per se* cause of the accidental action—then it has to be thought of as being the subject of the accidental form that is the principle of such an action. This is why Aristotle claimed that Polycletus is a *per accidens* cause of the statue whereas the sculptor is a *per se* cause. This, then, is the sense in which the accident is called the principal cause as a principle *quo*, whereas the substance, insofar as it is the subject of the accident, is called the principal cause as a principle *quod*.

And the opinion in question is proved as follows. An accidental form effects another accident by its own proper power. But a principal cause is a cause that operates by its own proper power. Therefore, etc.

The major premise is evident whenever heat effects heat and, in general, whenever one accident effects another similar accident or whenever a more noble accident effects a less noble accident, as when light effects heat. For in such cases the perfection of the effect does not exceed the perfection of the accident that is the principle of acting. /630b/ Therefore, the effect does not exceed the latter's power either. Therefore, in such cases an accident is the principle of the action by its own proper power.

Given this argument, the position in question must be understood to apply to an accident [only] when it operates in the way in question. For if a lower accident is elevated so as to effect an accident of a higher type, then it will not be denied that it is an instrument.

The second argument is this. A principal principle of acting is that to which the effect is similar. But it is through the act of heating as such that the effect is made similar to the cause as regards heat. Therefore, the heat is the principal principle of that action.

Third, a heat that exists on its own, separated from a substance, exercises its own action with the same power and efficacy, and so it does not need the influence of the substance or of any other cause that might supply that influence. Everyone admits this in the case of the Eucharistic accidents with respect to their accidental actions.

Fourth, whiteness, for example, does not effect intentional species as an instrument of the substance, since the substance seems to be related altogether accidentally to that action.

3. Given what was said above [in section 5] concerning the second problem,[2] it seems that the present disagreement can only be about ways of talking. For as far as the reality is concerned, the only question is what sort

---

2. See *DM* 18. 5. 4. Suarez refers here to the second of the three problems that constitute the topics for secs. 4, 5, and 6, respectively.

of influence an accident requires from its substance in order to bring its own proper action to completion. And if, after this has been established and explained, someone asks whether the accident is an instrument or a principal principle, the only possible disagreement has to do with the meaning of the terms.

Accordingly, the soul's powers with respect to vital actions can rightly be called conjoined instruments of the soul, since they are subordinated to the soul as a principal form in such a way that they cannot effect their own operations without the actual influence and, as it were, motion of the soul— even though in another sense they can be called principal principles, at least partial ones, given that the power which they have within themselves and by means of which they cooperate to bring about the effect is of itself proportionate to and commensurate with the relevant effect, since the effect does not exceed the perfection of the power itself. (For I am speaking here about connatural actions.) Thus, an [accidental] power and its [substantial] form can also be likened to a proximate principle and a universal principle, since each is within its own order a principal and sufficient and total principle. However, because, of the two of them, the form to which the power is subordinated is the more principal principle, this subordination and dependence can be [appropriately] signified by the term 'instrument'.

4. However, in the case of other accidents that are not dependent in this way on the substantial form in their actions, the nature of an instrument is found to a far lesser degree in the case of such actions.

Hence, as far as the reality is concerned, [these accidents] are most accurately thought of as /631a/ principal principles of such actions, in just the way that the arguments adduced above for the second position urged. For they elicit these actions just by dint of the perfection they have from their species or being. Likewise, an [accidental] form of this sort is *per se* sufficient by itself to furnish the suppositum with the [sort of] *esse* that is required *per se* and formally for such an action. For example, in the case of hot water the only sort of *esse* that is *per se* required for producing heat is 'heat-*esse*'.[3] Therefore, just as heat is a form that *per se* and by its very nature gives 'heat-*esse*', so, too, it is really a principal principle for producing heat.

And it is neither relevant nor problematic that an accident has its existence in the substance, for the sake of the substance, and from the substance. For we are not discussing how, or by virtue of which causes, the accident has its power of acting. We admit that it has its power (i) from the substance as from a *material* cause, (ii) for the sake of the substance as for the sake of a *final* cause, and perhaps even (iii) from the substance as from a mediate or

---

3. Literally, 'being hot' or 'hot-*esse*' (*esse calidum*).

immediate *efficient* cause via a natural emanation. Rather, we are discussing the question of whether the accident has formally within itself the whole power that is sufficient and necessary for the action in question. And we claim that it does indeed have this power, and we maintain that it is this alone that is signified when the accident is called a principal cause—not a principal cause *quod* but a principal cause *quo*. And the fact that an accident is a being of a being—that is, a being that belongs to a substance—and that its whole *esse* is "of another" is in no way opposed to this claim. To the contrary, the particle *quo* seems to suggest and to signify all these things. Hence, even the substantial form itself—since it, too, is a principle *quo* with respect to its own suppositum—is in its own way a being of a being.

However, lest there be a dispute over the term, we will also concede to the first position that if the term 'instrument' or 'instrumental cause' signifies (as in fact it sometimes does) just the relation that an accident bears to its substance by virtue of the fact that (i) it is given to the substance in order that the substance might operate through it as through its own instrument and by virtue of the fact that (ii) it is for this purpose that the accident receives its power from the substance, is sustained in *esse* by the substance, and depends in its *esse* on that same substance, then in this sense an accident can be called an instrument. However, it is more properly called a power or faculty of the substance.

Section 7

Whether, in Order to Act, an Efficient Cause Must Be Distinct in Reality from the Recipient of the Action

1. *Which conditions must obtain between the agent and the patient in order for there to be an action.* We have explicated the *per se* principles of acting among created causes; it remains for us to discuss the conditions required for acting. Even though various such conditions are customarily enumerated, still, there are three that seem more important as well as more troublesome, /631b/ and it is to these three that all the others are traced.

Now it should be taken for granted that every created agent requires a patient in order to act, since, as was claimed above and will also be shown below, a created agent brings about effects not by creating but from presupposed matter.[1] Thus the conditions required for acting are not conditions that must obtain between the cause and the *effect*. For if they were, then they would not be prerequisites for acting but would instead follow upon the action. Therefore, they are conditions that must preexist between the agent and the *patient*—that is, between the efficient cause and the material cause.

The first condition, then, is the necessary distinction between the agent and the patient. Given this distinction, the second condition is the necessary proximity [of the agent and patient to one another]. The third condition is the dissimilarity and proportionality [between the agent and the patient]—although, as we will see below, this third condition seems in some sense to pertain to the very nature of acting.[2]

2. I am passing over the condition of existence, since, as I have said repeatedly, I do not regard this as a condition that is distinct in reality from the agent or from the principle of acting. Hence, in *Metaphysics* 4.4, text 16 [1008a23], Aristotle justifiably asked, "How will things that do not exist either speak or walk?"

Further, this condition is included in all the others. For if it is necessary that the agent and the patient be proximate to one another, then it will be all the more necessary that they exist. For how will places that do not really exist be proximate to one another?

---

1. For the distinction between creation and other types of efficient causality, see *DM* 13. 4 and 20. 2.

2. I.e., the condition in question is part of the very nature of acting instead of being just a necessary condition for acting. For a discussion of this condition, see *DM* 18. 9.

Likewise, we proved above that in order to act, even by means of a resulting, it is not enough that [the agent] should have existed immediately beforehand.[3] Therefore, it is all the more evident that existence is necessary for proper efficient causality.

Now no one will deny this in the case of natural efficient causality. This is sufficient for our present purposes, but the point must be understood to apply analogically as follows. That which acts through itself exists in itself, whereas that which acts only through a separated instrument exists only virtually in the instrument, since it is said to act only by an extrinsic denomination that is taken from the instrument; but this virtual existence consists in nothing other than the fact that the instrument itself exists.[4] We will show elsewhere that this sort of existence is also necessary in the case of God's instruments.[5]

3. I am also passing over another condition that is normally required in a material agent: namely, that it be extended and that it exist in a quantitative mode. For this condition is necessary in order for such things to act, only to the extent that it pertains intrinsically to their natural mode of being. Whether they would be able to act naturally if by God's power that mode of existing were taken away from them is not so much a metaphysical question as a theological question—one that we have dealt with sufficiently in *Summa Theologiae* 3, vol. 3, disp. 49, sec. 1. /632a/

THE DIFFICULTY POSED BY THE PRESENT QUESTION, ALONG WITH VARIOUS POSITIONS

4. Given these presuppositions, the first [of the three] conditions will be discussed in this section. As regards this condition, the problem arises primarily from the many examples that seem to prove that it is unnecessary for there to be a distinction in reality between the agent and the patient: first, because of *natural emanations* (for the intellect emanates from, and is received

3. See *DM* 18. 1. 6.

4. Suarez makes this point because he has claimed above, and continues to claim below, that certain acts (e.g., the motion of heavy and light things toward their natural places, the emanation of primary properties from their substance, and the emanation of the powers of the soul from the soul itself) are to be attributed to the generating thing as the principal principle *quod*. But the generating thing may no longer exist when the action in question occurs.

5. See *DM* 20. 3. In *DM* 18. 8. 20 Suarez alludes to a discussion of divine instruments in vol. 3, disp. 31, sec. 7, of his commentary on *Summa Theologiae* 3.

into, one and the same soul); second, in the *immanent actions* of cognizing and especially of loving (for the same soul, by means of the same will, both elicits and receives an act of loving); third, in *physical motions* (for heavy and light things move themselves, and living things do so more properly, and water cools itself, and so on).

Finally, the following argument poses an objection [to the condition in question]. Even though this condition is often present in things that act by a *transeunt* action (since it is natural for them to act upon other things), nonetheless, there is no argument that necessarily prescribes this condition.[6] For if there were such an argument, it would certainly be the common argument that the same thing cannot simultaneously be both in potency with respect to receiving and in act with respect to acting. But this argument does not seem persuasive, since, as Scotus proves, it is possible to be both in virtual or eminent act and also in formal potency—that is, to have both the eminent power to effect a given form and also the capacity to receive that form formally.[7] For there is no contradiction involved in this.

However, in support of the contrary position there is the axiom handed down by Aristotle in *Physics* 7 and 8: namely, "Whatever is moved is moved by another"—an axiom that is accepted to such a degree that it serves as the foundation and principle of a demonstration by which it is proved that God exists.

5. *The opinions held by some.* On this matter there are some who maintain that the condition in question is not necessary for all agents, even though it is present in many of them. This is the opinion held by Scotus in *Sentences* 1,

6. For an explanation of the distinction between *transeunt* and immanent actions, see *DM* 18. 1, n. 17.

7. This distinction plays a prominent role in what follows. To say that an entity is in *virtual act* with respect to a given form (or perfection) is to say that it has an active power to effect that form. If the form is one that the entity itself lacks (i.e., does not have formally), then the entity is also in *eminent act* with respect to it. If, in addition, the entity, though lacking the form, has the potentiality to receive it, then it is in *formal potency* with respect to that form—i.e., it has the potential of being the subject of that form. Finally, to have the form is to be in *formal act* with respect to it.

Suarez will later discuss the Aristotelian principle that nothing can be simultaneously both in act and in potency with respect to the same thing. He will interpret the principle to mean that nothing can be simultaneously in both *formal act* and *formal potency* with respect to the same form. The truth of the principle so interpreted follows straightforwardly from the above characterization. For if something actually possesses a given form (to a given degree), then it is not in potentiality with respect to that form (to that degree). However, Suarez will accept Scotus's claim that it is perfectly possible for a thing to be simultaneously in both *virtual act* and *formal potency* with respect to the same form.

dist. 3, q. 7, and *Sentences* 2, dist. 2, q. 10, and *Metaphysics* 9, q. 14. And it is supported with the arguments adduced above by Antoine André, *Metaphysics* 9, q. 1; by Gregory, *Sentences* 2, dist. 6, q. 3, a. 3; and by Jandun, *Physics* 8, q. 12. The Commentator is well-disposed toward these arguments in *On the Heavens* 3, comment 28, where he says that the same thing can be acted upon by itself via an equivocal action.

Others, by contrast, more often accept Aristotle's axiom without qualification; and they require the condition in question as altogether necessary for every agent, not only with respect to *transeunt* actions but also with respect to immanent actions. This position is asserted explicitly by Capreolus, *Sentences* 1, dist. 3, q. 3; by Giles, *Quodlibeta* 3, q. 16, and *Quodlibeta* 5, q. 15; and by Ferrariensis, *Contra Gentes* 1, chap. 23, where, however, he makes an exception for efficient causality through natural resulting—an exception which, if he were speaking consistently, would perhaps /632b/ not be necessary.

Still other authors, on the other hand, make various qualifications, as we will explain in the course of our discussion.

A FEW PRESUPPOSITIONS FOR THE RESOLUTION OF THIS QUESTION

6. *The agent is not necessarily distinct in suppositum from the patient.* First of all, then, one should claim that it is not necessary for the agent to be distinct *in suppositum* from the receiving patient. This is sufficiently obvious from the induction made above and is explicitly asserted by Aristotle in *Physics* 8, at the beginning [2.253a7–20], and in *Physics* 8.4 [254b12–32]. From this he infers that the same thing can move itself as long it is differentiated into a part that produces the motion *per se* and a part that is moved *per se*—in the way, he says, that animals move themselves by local motion and in almost the same way as living things move themselves by a motion of augmentation. (For the latter act directly on the food, which they convert into and unite with themselves, and it is in this way that they grow.) So, too, it is not absurd for the same thing to move itself *per accidens*, in the way that the soul is moved when the body is moved.[8]

7. *There are various ways in which the agent is distinct from the patient within the same suppositum.* Second, one should assume that there are various ways

8. When the body is moved locally by the power of the soul, the soul is moved *per accidens*, because it is present to the body even though it is not the immediate subject of the motion. So in this sense the soul moves itself.

in which the agent can be differentiated from the patient within the same suppositum that acts upon itself. First, they may be differentiated as diverse integral parts. Second, they may be differentiated as diverse substantial and essential parts—if, for instance, [a suppositum] acts through its form and receives through its matter.[9] These first two modes [of differentiation] can apply to bodies but not universally to all agents (and we are now discussing agents *in general*); for spiritual entities also act upon themselves. Third, they may be differentiated at least in the sense that there is the faculty of acting and another faculty of receiving. This distinction can be either a total and real distinction or at least a distinction between that which includes and that which is included.[10] We will give examples of all these modes below.

8. *The various actions to which the question applies.* Third, we must distinguish various actions and go through them one by one, so that we can formulate a general rule based on all of them. Thus, among the relevant actions we can first enumerate natural emanation or resulting; next, physical and material motions, which by their genus are effected by means of *transeunt* action and which can, for the sake of clarity, be distinguished into their species: namely, alteration, augmentation, and local motion. (I pass over substantival generation, since it is evident *per se* that the same thing cannot generate itself.) To these one can add the local motion of spiritual entities that move themselves; for this sort of motion is in part similar to the motions of bodies (since it constitutes a *transeunt* action) and in part dissimilar to the motions of bodies (since it is not a physical motion /633a/—that is, it is not extended on the part of the subject).[11] And, finally, besides all of these, there is efficient causality through the immanent actions of the senses or the [sentient] appetite and of the intellect or the will.

FIRST ASSERTION: ON NATURAL RESULTING

9. Therefore, I assert, first, that in the case of natural resulting, even though (i) it is possible for the *proximate* efficient cause not to be distinct from the recipient, nonetheless, (ii) the effect is traced back, absolutely speaking, to an efficient cause that is distinct from the patient.

The first part of this assertion is evident from the argument adduced above

9. The form and matter of a composite substance are called its *essential* or *substantial* parts. By contrast, the *integral* parts of such a substance are its limbs, organs, etc.

10. For an example of this latter sort of distinction, see §47 below.

11. For more on the motion of spiritual beings, see §41 below, as well as *DM* 35. 3. 46–50, and 51. 3.

concerning the powers of the soul, which flow from that same soul.[12] For even though, as Ferrariensis notes in the place cited above, it is possible to distinguish within the soul the character of effecting those powers from the character of receiving them, still, since this distinction is only a distinction of reason, it is irrelevant in the present context—especially with respect to a primary property that results immediately from the substance alone. (For a secondary property may emanate by the mediation of a primary property, even though it is proximately received in the substance alone, as St. Thomas asserts in *Summa Theologiae* 1, q. 77, a. 8.) And the same holds for the substance of angels and their powers.

In material things, by contrast, it is almost always possible for the efficient principle of such an emanation (at least the principle *quo*) to be distinguished in reality from the character of receiving the emanating property. For the property emanates from the form but is not received in the form, since it is not a subsistent form; rather, it is received in the matter or else in the composite by reason of the matter. The only possible exception has to do with quantity. For it may be that the quantity emanates from the being of the matter and is also received in it; but this is uncertain.

10. The second part of the assertion is obvious from section 3*.[13] For we claimed that a property emanates from the substance or essence not as from a principal agent but rather as from an instrument of the generating thing. Therefore, the effect in question has to be attributed to the generating thing as to a more principal cause. But the generating thing is obviously distinct from the thing generated and from the latter's powers.

You will object as follows: To trace this effect back to the generating thing is to trace it back only to a remote and *per accidens* cause that bestows the form from which the other faculties emanate. But (as I myself pointed out above) here we are looking not for a *per accidens* reduction but instead for a *per se* reduction and a reduction to a proximate cause. Otherwise, it would be easy for us to claim that everything that comes to be comes to be from another thing that is distinct from it even in suppositum—from another thing, I repeat, that either acts proximately or else has remotely bestowed the power to act.

The reply is that this reduction is not a reduction to a *per accidens* cause but is instead a reduction to a cause that is principal and *per se*. This is so, first of all, because of the intention and order of nature, since the power in question is bestowed in order that it might operate as the instrument /633b/ of another thing whose place it is taking in some way. For example, projectiles

12. See the discussion of natural emanation in *DM* 18. 3. 3–14.
13. See *DM* 18. 3. 14.

are said to be moved *per se*, not *per accidens*, by the projector that impresses the impetus—not only because the projector bestows the power of acting but also because it bestows that power in conjunction with the condition that the power should be an instrument that operates in place of the projector.

Second, when the essence does not contain the relevant faculties eminently but only instrumentally, it is likely that a greater influence is required from the generating thing or from the author of the nature in question than would be required if the [proximate] cause in question were a proper and principal cause to which the effect must be wholly attributed.[14] For from the very fact that the proximate principle does not contain the effect either formally or eminently, it follows that it cannot be a proper and adequate cause of that effect, even within the genus of proximate and principal causes. Therefore, if, within an entire species, one does not find this eminent power with respect to the properties that naturally follow upon that species, then necessarily, the property that is in the generated thing either (i) is effected by a similar property that is in the generating thing or else (ii) emanates from the form along with a reduction to the author of the whole species as that which principally effects it.

SECOND ASSERTION:
ON PHYSICAL MOTION AND ACTION

11. Second, I assert that every cause that effects something through physical motion and *transeunt* action is in some way distinct in reality from the material cause that receives the effect. This thesis is consonant with the intention of Aristotle, who may have meant nothing other than this in the place cited above. For there he talks about the physical motion of corporeal things, makes an induction only over physical motions, and in his arguments

14. One might wonder why, e.g., in the case of the soul, Suarez believes that the soul does not contain its own powers or faculties eminently prior to their emanation. Why does he instead claim that the soul must be thought of as the generator's *instrument* and so in need of 'elevation' in order to give rise to its own faculties? The reason seems to be that these powers or faculties are themselves included in the terminus of generation itself; i.e., to have such faculties is part of the very notion of being an animal of a given sort, as opposed to being included under the notion of the animal's development. In technical terminology, the having of such faculties is included in the *first act* of the given species, while the proper use of those faculties falls under *second act*. Given this claim, it makes good sense to attribute the emanation of the faculties to whatever generated the animal in the first place.

invariably presupposes that the motion under discussion has parts on the side of the thing moved.

Because there is less of a problem regarding the motions of alteration and augmentation, the thesis will first be briefly explicated with respect to those motions. For when an induction is made, one finds no proper alteration which is enacted *per se* and primarily by any agent on itself—that is, according to the same part [of itself]. To be sure, it is possible that the same thing should, through one part, alter itself in another part, if the parts are disposed in dissimilar ways. However, this cannot happen with respect to one and the same part, as is clear from an induction over all cases.

The only objection is the common one concerning the reduction of water to its pristine coldness, and the same goes for any similar reversion. For we showed above that such an action comes not from an extrinsic agent but from an intrinsic agent.

The reply, however, is that the action in question has to do with natural resulting, which we have already dealt with in the first assertion, and so this action is customarily /634a/ attributed to the generating thing, as was noted by Capreolus, *Sentences* 2, dist. 6, q. 1, a. 3; by Giles, *Quodlibeta* 2, q. 16; and by Henry, *Quodlibeta* 11, q. 6.

12. From this it is patently evident that in a motion of augmentation it is likewise the case that the same thing does not act *per se* on itself. For such a motion is effected only by means of a previous alteration. But an alteration is not enacted by the same thing on itself with respect to the same part. Therefore, neither is an augmentation.

Now there seems to be no a priori argument for this part of the assertion other than the one Aristotle touched upon: namely, that the same thing cannot simultaneously be both in act and in potency with respect to the same thing.

To this argument there is, of course, the objection made above: namely, that the argument goes through at most for a univocal alteration—that is, for an alteration that proceeds from a quality of the same type—but not for an equivocal alteration, which proceeds from a virtual quality—that is, a quality of a higher type. For in the latter case there would be no contradiction involved in the same part's having the virtual quality and lacking the formal quality and so acting on itself.[15]

For this reason Scotus and the others cited above maintain that Aristotle's argument is not a general one. This is to claim, in effect, that the argument is not efficacious, especially because, as we will see below,[16] Aristotle also

---

15. See n. 7 above. Here Suarez uses the term 'quality' instead of 'act'.
16. See §20 below.

uses that argument in the case of local motion, where the action is always equivocal. For a moving power is always of a different type from the form—that is, terminus—of the local motion.[17]

13. *By 'part that moves* per se' *and 'part that is moved* per se' *Aristotle does not mean form and matter.* Others use the following argument: A material alteration, which is effected by a material substance, proceeds actively from the form (since the matter is not a principle of acting), whereas it is received in the composite by reason of the matter, which is a principle of being acted upon. And so, even if it is possible for the same thing to act on itself with respect to the same integral part, the agent is nonetheless distinct from the patient as far as the principles of acting and being acted upon are concerned.

However, this argument is plainly contrary to the intention of Aristotle, who is not talking about the formal principle *quo*, since it was obvious enough that the matter and the form have diverse roles in corporeal things. Rather, he is talking about the principle *quod*—either the whole principle *quod* or at least a partial principle *quod*—as St. Thomas correctly noted in *De Veritate*, q. 22, a. 3, and as is clear from *Physics* 8.4 [254b11–255a19]. Otherwise, when he was discussing the motion of heavy and light things, he would not have had to resort to the generating thing but instead would have resorted to the form that effects the motion and to the matter that receives the motion. Nor would he have had to distinguish, within animals, the part that effects motion *per se* from the part that is moved *per se*—which Aristotle, in *Physics* 8, text 28 [4.254b732], clearly intends to be a distinction among integral parts. /634b/ And, finally, in moving up to the motion of a celestial body, one would not have to designate a separate mover for such a motion; instead, one would designate (i) the intrinsic form, which would be the active principle of the motion, and (ii) the matter, which would receive the motion.

14. *Aristotle's intention on this topic is explained.* Therefore, in keeping with Aristotle's intention, one should say that the same material composite cannot alter itself *per se*—that is, with respect to one and the same integral part. Now the reason for this can be rendered in such a way as to clarify or fill out Aristotle's first argument.[18] For if a substance has the formal quality but not the virtual quality in some part of itself, or if it has neither the virtual nor the formal quality, then it cannot move itself with respect to that same quality—

17. The terminus of a local motion is a place or a "where," and it is obvious that the power by which such a motion is effected is not itself a place.

18. See §4 above. Aristotle's first argument is that the same thing cannot be simultaneously both in act and in potency. His second argument is based on the axiom that whatever is moved is moved by another. This will be discussed below.

as the argument made above proves most elegantly. On the other hand, if the substance has the virtual quality in the part in question, then the formal quality is either (i) connatural to that same part or (ii) violent with respect to that part or (iii) neither.[19]

If the formal quality is natural, then that part will always have it, since a connatural property always belongs to it intrinsically. However, if the property is by chance such that it can be violently removed or diminished, then once the impediment is removed, the thing will return itself to its connatural state. But this will occur through the mode of natural resulting, and the action will be traced principally to an extrinsic principle, which is the generating thing.[20]

On the other hand, if the quality in question is violent, then it is impossible that the same thing should—through the virtual quality of, say, heat—produce heat formally within itself by means of a violent and preternatural act of heating. One can cite the example of a pepper, which has the power to produce heat in the tongue or in the belly and yet is unable to produce heat within itself, since such an act of heating would be violent to it. Now it is not easy to explain the reason for this. The claim made by some—namely, that the pepper is prevented by a law of nature from contributing to its own destruction or detriment—seems unsatisfactory. For one and the same living thing contributes to its own destruction when it is corrupted from within; and it seems to matter little whether this occurs according to diverse parts, with one part altering another, or through one and the same part according to diverse qualities. This is obvious from the following argument. The virtual quality is sufficient for effecting the formal quality in a suitable subject, and it acts naturally and necessarily. Therefore, if the subject in which the virtual quality exists is capable of receiving the formal quality and yet lacks it, then that subject will effect the formal quality within itself by a necessity of nature. Nor can it hold back its action, by virtue of the law of nature alluded to above, unless it is impeded from without; for it is not a free agent. /635a/

15. In addition, there are some who believe that within living things what is naturally hot desiccates itself and consumes what is naturally moist, not only according to diverse parts but even according to one and the same part. One can see this in Giles, *Quodlibeta* 2, q. 17, where he says that this con-

---

19. Alternative (i) is dealt with in the next paragraph, alternative (ii) in the rest of §14 and in §§15–17, and alternative (iii) in §18. The entire argument is then reviewed and summarized in §19.

20. As we saw above, in such a case the virtual quality will be an instrumental rather than a principal cause.

sumption of moisture comes about through a natural resulting of excessive dryness from innate heat.

I, however, judge this to be impossible. For since the action in question is violent, it cannot result naturally from within. For there is a contradiction in terms, since the violent is "that which is from without, with the patient contributing no power." Hence, I conclude that what Giles assumes is false and impossible: namely, that one and the same homogeneous part of an animal—that is, one and the same part disposed in the same way according to itself as a whole—should in a manner connatural to itself, through the heat that is innate to it (be it formal or virtual), diminish the moisture that is connatural to it by violently desiccating itself. For it is impossible that the same form in the same part of the matter should require dispositions that are either formally or eminently repugnant to one another; otherwise, there would be a repugnance within the thing itself and among its own inclinations.

16. *The reason why a virtual quality does not alter its own subject.* Therefore, if a substance—either as a whole or in some part—has, for example, virtual heat of a given intensity (say, of degree four), then either (i) it will at the same time necessarily have just as intense a formal heat connatural to itself or else (ii) it will have a temperature and natural disposition of such a kind that it resists and prevents the virtual quality from exercising its formal action on that very same part. And it is for this reason that nothing can, in one and the same part, alter itself from within by means of a violent alteration.

This is especially clear in the case of those mixed things that have active virtual qualities corresponding to their primary qualities. For virtual qualities of this sort presuppose a temperature appropriate to the primary qualities and to the other dispositions that follow upon the primary qualities. Therefore, it cannot happen that, within one and the same part, such a temperature should be subverted by the intrinsic action of the virtual faculty in question. This is confirmed by the example of the pepper. For the pepper is disposed and affected by other qualities and dispositions in such a way that its virtual heat does not have the power to heat the pepper itself to a degree beyond the connatural degree of heat that it requires insofar as it is a mixed thing of the sort in question.

There are others who contend that it is unnecessary to give any explanation other than that the quality is not active within the subject in which it exists, even if none of the other conditions [for acting] is absent. But I find this /635b/ claim unconvincing, since it obviously begs the question. For this is what we are seeking a cause of and explanation for.

17. *Another argument to prove the same claim.* However, another explanation can be adduced for why a pepper does not produce heat within itself:

namely, that it may not have the complete or total power to produce heat unless it is assisted from without. For it is obvious from experience that when a pepper is applied to the hand, it does not produce heat; instead, it requires some excitation or alteration and some commingling with the intrinsic heat of an animal. And the same can be said about wine and other similar things. Hence, even though none of these things is able, by itself alone, to alter itself by means of its own virtual quality, still, once it begins to be altered from without and to be conjoined with an extrinsic agent, there is nothing problematic about its afterward contributing to its own alteration and corruption. For the whole that does the altering in that case is sufficiently distinct from the patient. So, then, there can never be a violent alteration by one and the same thing with respect to itself by means of a virtual quality.

18. *An indifferent alteration is always from without.* Now an indifferent alteration—that is, one that is neither violent nor natural—cannot occur in a thing that has a virtual quality for effecting that sort of alteration. For such a quality acts naturally and necessarily as much as it can. Therefore, either (i) it finds within its own subject a natural disposition that is contrary to its action, in which case its action would be violent; or else (ii) it finds no contrary disposition, in which case the emanation will be natural, since it proceeds from an internal and innate quality and occurs by an intrinsic necessity of nature. Hence, if there is an indifferent alteration or action with respect to the quality (for example, illumination in the air), then it always and necessarily proceeds from an extrinsic agent. And the reason for this is clear. If the alteration or action proceeded from an intrinsic form—whether immediately or by the mediation of some quality connatural to that same form—then the quality in question would by that very fact not be indifferent but would instead be connatural.

19. *An adequate argument for the conclusion; the sense in which it is true that one and the same thing cannot be both in potency and in act, even virtual act.* Therefore, given all these considerations, the argument is summed up as follows. Every quality is either violent or natural or indifferent. If it is violent or indifferent, it obviously comes from an extrinsic agent. On the other hand, if it is natural, then it comes from the generating thing. (Alternatively, if one insists that it comes from within, then it exists through natural emanation; but we are not talking about natural emanation in the context of the present thesis.)

Now in order to accommodate this line of reasoning to Aristotle's argument, one should claim that the principle "The same thing cannot at the same time be both in act and in potency" is /636a/ true, even with respect to a virtual act, as long as two qualifications are added. One is that we are talking about an act that is a principle of physical and merely natural motion, so that we are excluding immaterial and vital actions, which we are not discussing at present. The other qualification is that the principle is meant to apply to a thing insofar as it exists in its natural state. For a thing in a preternatural state can indeed be both in virtual act and in formal potency—as happens, for example, in the case of hot water, which is virtually cold.[21] However, the action of this virtual quality is merely a natural resulting and is attributed to an extrinsic agent, as was explained above. Hence, if one wants to call this sort of containment [of the quality] an instrumental rather than a virtual containment, then the first qualification will be sufficient.

20. On this basis, the thesis in question can easily be proved for the case of local motion by bringing to bear the line of reasoning just adduced, along with the induction that, following Aristotle in the place cited above,[22] can be made as follows: A body moves either naturally or violently or by means of an indifferent motion. In the second and third of these modes, the motion always proceeds from an extrinsic cause, since under these two headings we include all the motions that Aristotle designated as "beyond the nature" of the thing in question, regardless of whether they are (i) contrary to the nature (these we call "violent") or (ii) wholly outside what is owed [to the nature]—that is, wholly outside the intrinsic principle of the nature itself; for example, the circular motion of fire in its own sphere and any similar motion, if there be such. On the other hand, natural motion belongs either to animals that are moving themselves or to inanimate things that are tending toward their proper places. But in both these cases the thing that effects the motion is distinct from the patient, since inanimate bodies are moved to their own natural places by the generating thing, whereas within animals the part that effects the motion *per se* is distinct from the part that is moved *per se*, and so an animal does not move itself as a whole except, as it were, *per accidens.*[23]

A Problem Concerning the Motion of Heavy and Light Things

21. As far as this induction is concerned, there are three principal problems. The first is the common problem concerning the motion of heavy and light things. However, since this is a purely physical problem, and since, although it is discussed with great contentiousness by those who hold differing opinions, there can hardly be any disagreement about it except over

21. I.e., water, which is apt by nature to be cold, is, when hot, such that it has both (i) the active power (virtual act) to cool and (ii) the potentiality (formal potency) to be cold.

22. *Physics* 8.4.

23. I.e., the animal moves not because it is, as a whole, the primary recipient of motion but rather because of its relation to the primary recipient of motion, which is some part of itself.

ways of speaking, I will indicate briefly, omitting the arguments, the core of the problem and how I believe one should think and speak about it.

There are many who claim without qualification that heavy and light things are moved by themselves to their proper places. See Scotus, *Sentences* 2, dist. 2, q. 10; Gregory, *Sentences* 2, dist. 6, q. 1; John Major, *Sentences* 2, dist. 14, q. 6; Abulensis, *Matthew* 22, q. 224; and Buridan, Jandun, Niphus, and Albert of Saxony, all in *Physics* 8.

Others contend /636b/ that these bodies are related merely passively to the motions in question, and that they are moved either by a celestial body or by being attracted by their natural places or by being expelled by the medium or by a contrary place. These and other possibilities, which I will ignore because of their implausibility, are mentioned by Richard, *Sentences* 2, dist. 14, a. 2, q. 4; by Zimara, *On the Soul* 2, text 54; and by Gregory, in the place cited above.

Now the common opinion is that the bodies in question are moved principally by the thing that generates them. This is taken from Aristotle in the places cited above, especially *Physics* 8, text 29 [4.254b32–255b19], and *On the Heavens* 4.3 [310a14–311a14]; and the Commentator says the same thing in the places cited, even though he sometimes seems to be undecided. The same opinion is held by St. Thomas in the same places, as well as in *Summa Theologiae* 1, q. 18, a. 1, and *Contra Gentes* 1, chap. 97; by Cajetan and Ferrariensis in these same places; by Capreolus, *Sentences* 2, dist. 6, a. 3; by Giles of Rome, *Quodlibeta* 5, q. 16; by Albert the Great, *Physics* 8, tract 2, chap. 4; and very often by expositors of *Physics* 8.

And this opinion, correctly explicated, is true—even though there are many, even Thomists, who go badly wrong in explicating it.

22. *Various ways of explicating the common and true opinion.* For there are those who contend that the motion in question is from the generating thing in such a way that within the moved thing itself there is no intrinsic and active moving power but only a natural passive power by reason of which such a motion is owed to that˙ thing˙. Opposed to this position are the evident arguments made by Scotus and others. For it is obvious that the generating thing cannot, by means of the form or qualities that it has within itself, immediately impress this motion in the absence of a quality imparted to the moving thing itself by virtue of which the motion might effectively perdure. For it can happen that the generating thing no longer exists or that it is so far away that it cannot produce the motion immediately.

However, there are others who draw a distinction. For (they claim) when a heavy body begins to move downward immediately after it has been generated, it is at that time being moved immediately by the generating thing and is itself only passively related [to the motion], since at that time the generating thing is able to impress the motion *per se*. By contrast, when a heavy thing is moved after an interval of time has elapsed following its generation, then at that time (they claim) it is not being moved by the generating thing but is instead being moved actively by itself. So says Soncinas, *Metaphysics* 9, q. 8; and in this he is followed by Cajetan of Thiene, *Physics* 8, and by Paul of Venice, *Summa de Caelo*, chap. 24.

But to my mind this is an implausible distinction, both because (i) the motion in question is always of the same type and always proceeds from the same natural principle and also because (ii) even if the heavy body begins to be moved immediately after the instant of its generation, it is not yet being moved intrinsically by the generating thing, since there is not yet a /637a/ motion, whereas immediately after that instant (or at least just a little bit later) it can happen that the generating thing no longer exists, even while the motion still perdures. And even if the generating thing does exist, nonetheless, immediately after the instant of generation it is already at a distance from the generated thing (I am assuming that the generating thing remains in its own place). Therefore, it cannot effect a motion *per se* and immediately in the generated thing. Thus, the generating thing is said to effect the motion only because at the instant of generation it impresses on the generated thing an impetus by means of which the latter is moved immediately afterward. But this impetus is nothing other than the body's heaviness, since anything else that might be postulated is pointless. For the generating thing impresses *per se* only that which follows *per se* upon the generation. But, relative to the present discussion, the heaviness is the only thing that follows *per se* upon the generation of a heavy thing. Therefore, at the time in question the motion is effected by the intrinsic heaviness of the heavy thing itself in the very same way that it is effected after any temporal interval whatever. And this is especially consonant with reason, since the heaviness is always the same and always has the same power; and the length of the temporal interval is irrelevant.

23. *The problem is resolved; Aristotle attributes the motion of heavy and light bodies to lightness or heaviness as to a proximate principle.* Therefore, one should say that whenever an inanimate thing tends toward its own natural place, the *proximate*—though not *principal*—efficient principle of that motion is its intrinsic heaviness or lightness. This is all but evident from experience and from the arguments adduced above against the preceding ways of explicating the common opinion.

Again, since these motions belong to the bodies in question *per se* and necessarily, one must designate some active principle of motion that likewise belongs to those bodies *per se* and necessarily. But there is no such principle other than the intrinsic form and the heaviness, since, as we were saying above, it can happen that the generating thing does not exist at all or is too far away and that all other causes are either absent or at least merely contingent.

There is no doubt that this is Aristotle's opinion. For in *Physics* 8.4, text 32, after having distinguished two sorts of potency—namely, remote and proximate—he adds: "What is cold is hot in potency. But when it is changed, it is fire; it now burns unless something prevents and hinders it" [255b5–7]. And he goes on: "Nor is it otherwise in the case of the heavy and the light. For the light comes to be from the heavy, for example, air comes to be from water, since the latter was first [light] in potency and is now [actually] light, and it will act immediately unless something impedes it" [255b7–10]. And later on: "But if what impedes it is removed, it will act" [255b20]. And in *On the Heavens* 4.1, text 2, he claims that heavy and light things have within themselves "some spark (read: stimulus) toward motion" [308a1]. /637b/ And, more explicitly, in *On the Heavens* 4.3, text 25 [310b15–20], he compares heavy and light things to a body that can be healed, claiming that just as the latter proceeds toward health, so too heavy and light things proceed toward their own places. But he adds a contrast, saying, "The only difference is this: These things, namely, the heavy and the light, seem to have the principle of change within themselves, whereas the subjects of healing and growth have the principle of change not within themselves but from without" [310b25–27]. He must be talking about the active principle here, since the passive principle is indeed within that which is subject to healing. That is why he adds, concerning things subject to healing and to growth: "though these things, too, sometimes seem to change by themselves, and the one attains health and the other growth with just a slight motion effected in the external things" [310b27–28]. Likewise, in *Physics* 4.9, text 85, he says: "The dense and the rare, insofar as they are endowed with heaviness and lightness, are productive of local motion" [217b24], whereas insofar as they are hard and soft, they have a principle not of moving but of either resisting alteration or undergoing alteration.

24. *Passages from Aristotle for the contrary position are examined and explained.* Nor does it constitute an objection that in *On Generation and Corruption* 2.2, text 8 [329b20], the selfsame Aristotle says that heaviness and lightness are not principles of acting. For in that same place he also says that they are not principles of being acted upon, since he is talking about a principle of acting upon or transmuting *another* or about a principle of being acted upon by *another* by means of an action or a passion that tends toward either generation or corruption—which is what he was dealing with in that place. Again, we could claim that he is talking about a proper and principal principle to which an action is attributed without qualification and that consequently he

is talking about efficient causality and action properly speaking. For the sort of efficient causality that belongs to heaviness and lightness is, by way of contrast, a certain natural resulting. In the sense in which this *is* a type of efficient causality, there is no doubt that heaviness is a principle of it.

This is also the opinion of St. Thomas in *Summa Theologiae* 1–2, q. 36, a. 2, in *Contra Gentes* 3, chap. 23, arg. 4, and in the other places cited by Capreolus above and by Peter of Bergamo in *Concordantia*, dub. 690 and 691. In addition, these authors reconcile the passages in question with other passages in which St. Thomas seems to deny that heavy and light bodies have an active principle of motion within themselves, by claiming that in these latter passages he has in mind a *principal* principle whereas in the former he has in mind an *instrumental* principle; that is, in the latter passages he is talking about a principle *quod*, whereas in the former passages he is talking about a principle *quo*.

25. *Whether the [substantial] form of a heavy or light thing has a natural influence on the motion of the thing.* But you will ask whether this internal principle is heaviness alone or whether it is also the substantial form. For the authors speak in various ways.

The reply is that if we are talking about a *per se* principle that has a proximate and actual influence, then that principle is the heaviness alone, since within the heaviness there is a sufficient power to effect the motion and its terminus—to no less a degree than there is within heat a /638a/ power to produce heat. This is made clear by the mystery of the Eucharist. For in the absence of the [substantial] form [of bread], the species of the bread have just as much heaviness and will move downward with just as much motion as would be the case if the substance of the bread were present there*. On the other hand, if we are talking instead about a remote intrinsic principle, then in this sense the substantial form is a principle, since it is from the substantial form that the heaviness, just like the other natural properties, naturally emanates and results.

26. *Motion of this sort should be attributed to the generating thing as a principal cause.* Nonetheless, one must add in the end that this natural motion should be attributed principally to the generating thing, which bestows the [substantial] form and through it the heaviness from which the motion results— just as the motion that emanates from an impetus is attributed to that which projects [the body] and impresses the impetus. For just as an impressed impetus, even though it is a true moving power and has within itself a sufficient power to produce that motion, nonetheless produces motion only as an instrument of the projector and in its stead, so, too, heaviness produces motion only as an instrument of the generating thing and in its stead.

This is the view of St. Thomas and of the other authors whom I cited above in discussing the last [of the three] positions.[24] And it is also, in the places cited above, the view of Aristotle, who in other places frequently claims, with this meaning in mind, that inanimate things do not have within themselves the principle from which their motion comes. And he always points to this as the difference between them and animate things—as one can see from *On the Heavens* 2.2, text 9 [284b31], *On the Soul* 1.2, text 19 [403b23–404b29], and *On the Soul* 2.2, text 13 [413a20–32]. And this difference between living and nonliving things has been accepted by the common consensus of everyone, as St. Thomas notes in *Contra Gentes* 1, chap. 97.

The reason for this attribution is that the perfection of these inanimate things consists not in their *moving toward* their own places but rather in their *being or remaining in* their own places—a status or perfection that is able to belong to such things at the very moment at which they begin to exist by virtue of their generation. And, just as the other properties and natural dispositions that belong *per se* to a generated thing by virtue of its generation are said to be bestowed by the generating thing, so too with its natural place. And from this it follows further that when, for whatever reason, the natural place is impeded or taken away, the journey or return to that place is always attributed to the selfsame generating thing. For this return is always effected by the same principle and by the same natural emanation*, and it belongs to the same thing to confer both the terminus and the journey or motion to that terminus.

This is the way St. Thomas explained the matter in *Contra Gentes* 3, chap. 23, where he said: "The form is the principle of local motion insofar as it is according to its form that a body is owed the place toward which it moves by virtue of its form's tending toward that place—and /638b/ because the generating thing bestows the form*, it is said to be the mover." So, too, we claimed above that the reduction of water [to its pristine coldness] is attributed to the generating thing because natural and perfect coldness is, speaking *per se*, owed to the water by virtue of its generation and its form. The only difference is that the water's motion of reduction to coldness proceeds immediately from the substantial form, whereas the reduction to a natural place occurs by the mediation of a moving power. But the reason for this is merely that coldness is a primary passion, whereas being in such and such a place is not a primary or immediate passion but rather belongs to the thing mediately by reason of something else: namely, its heaviness or lightness. However, this does not prevent both sorts of reduction from being natural emanations by virtue of the generation.

27. *Which actions of inanimate things are attributed to the generating thing, and*

24. See §21 above.

which are not. And from this argument one can infer the difference in light of which the actions of inanimate things on external matter are not attributed to the generating thing—as, for instance, when fire produces heat, and so on—even though they naturally follow upon a form and faculty bestowed by the generating thing. Likewise, one can infer the reason why the motion of growth whereby a generated thing tends toward its complete quantity is attributed not to the generating thing but to the generated thing itself. The reason is that these are not natural properties or perfections that are owed to the generated thing by virtue of its generation at the instant it is generated.

You will object: When hot water produces heat, it is not only fire but the water itself as well that is said to produce heat. So, too, if a rock, in falling, impels something else, then it is truly said to move that thing. Therefore, the rock will also be truly said to effect its own motion and so to move itself as a suppositum that sustains within itself a proper principle of that action. For this is the only reason why the action of producing heat is attributed to the hot water.

One may reply that there is a sense in which it is unproblematic to allow this way of talking, as was noted by Ferrariensis in *Contra Gentes* 1, chap. 97, and intimated by Capreolus in the place cited above: namely, because this way of talking denominates materially, as it were, a suppositum that has within itself a proximate principle of the sort of motion in question. However, because that principle takes the place of another whose instrument it is, it follows that, simply and absolutely speaking, the action is referred back to the latter, as is patently clear from the example concerning projectiles.

28. *An objection is answered.* Finally, you will object: Even though the harmonization just given makes sufficiently clear that this way of talking is philosophical and has some foundation in reality,[25] still, what does it have to do with real efficient causality or with the clarification of the conditions necessary for real efficient causality? For what was said above was sufficient for establishing that /639a/ a truly active power, in order to act upon some subject, does not necessarily have to be in a distinct subject or even in a distinct part of that subject.

One may reply that philosophers have wisely and justifiably considered and clarified this issue in order to show that things which lack life have not

25. The way of talking referred to here is that according to which the natural local motions of heavy and light things are attributed to the thing that generated them. The objection is that it has already been established that it is not a general rule that the agent must be distinct from the patient. Suarez's reply is an interesting one, since it gives a clear picture of the scholastic distinction between living and nonliving things, a distinction that proved to be difficult for Descartes and his followers to draw.

received from nature the power to perfect themselves, speaking *per se,* but that instead the nature of those things demands only that they be generated in their natural perfection. And on this basis philosophers have concluded that the difference between living and nonliving things—a difference that Plato also arrived at in the *Phaedrus* [245C–246D] and in book 10 of the *Laws* [893B–896A]—is that living things are instituted by nature in such a way that they are able to perfect or actualize themselves (it is properly about created things that we are speaking), whereas nonliving things have *per se* only a repose in the perfection that, unless they are impeded by some other source, they receive from the generating thing. However, since they have been instituted in the best possible way, they receive this perfection in conjunction with an appropriate connection between their essence and properties, the whole of which connection is justifiably attributed to the author or generator of such things. And so whenever things of this sort are kept by accident from their natural state and then later return to that state after the impediment has been removed, such a return is judged to occur not through their own action but instead through a natural resulting. And that is why it is attributed not so much to the things themselves as to the generating thing.

A Problem Concerning Animate Things That Move Themselves by Local Motion
29. The second problem concerning Aristotle's inductive argument has to do with the motion of animals when they move themselves, since within these animals the agent does not seem to be distinct from the patient. Aristotle solves this problem by claiming that an animal does not move itself *per se* and primarily—that is, in such a way that each part moves itself—but that instead, as seems to be shown by experience itself, through one part—namely, an integral and organic part—it moves another part, and so the agent and the patient are differentiated here at least as parts.

But one might press the following difficulty. This regress among moving and moved parts does not go on *ad infinitum,* since it is not a regress among parts of a given ratio[26] but a regress among equal parts—that is, among parts of some fixed magnitude; nor does [an infinite] regress occur among causes that are ordered *per se.*[27] Therefore, the regress must stop at some first mov-

26. 'Parts of a given ratio' are parts ordered in such a way that any given one bears the relevant ratio to the previous one. So, e.g., parts ordered according to the sequence 1/2, 1/4, 1/8, 1/16 . . . —i.e., in such a way that each is half of its predecessor—are 'parts of a given ratio' (or 'parts of the same ratio').

27. Causes that are ordered *per se* are such that each must have an immediate influence, within its own order, in order for the effect to be brought about.

ing part. But that part cannot effect motion unless it itself is moved. For that is what Aristotle himself teaches in *Physics* 7.1, text 3 [242a15–22], with respect to every corporeal motion, and it is especially true in the case of a body that moves another body by pushing it, as it were—which is the way that one part of an animal seems to move another. So I take the first part that effects motion /639b/ in an animal, and I ask what that part is moved by. It is not moved by another part, since it is the first mover within the relevant ordering. Therefore, it is moved by itself. For there is no other principle to which it might be traced back. Given that the motion in question is a vital motion, it cannot be attributed to the generating thing, and it does not occur through a natural emanation but instead occurs because of the animal's appetitive faculty. Nor will it be sufficient to reply that the motion of the part in question proceeds from the soul as informing that part and is received in that same part by reason of the matter. For, as I objected above, one could in this sense claim that every corporeal body moves itself by reason of its form and is moved by reason of its matter.

30. The same problem arises with regard to the heart's motion, which (i) is perpetual as long as the animal's life endures, (ii) oscillates between two termini, and (iii) is composed of a push and a pull. Hence, even though in this sense it always endures, it is nonetheless not a perfectly continuous motion, since a state of rest necessarily intervenes between an expansion and a contraction. Therefore, this motion has no efficient cause other than the heart itself, which, because it is homogeneous, cannot be separated into a part that effects motion *per se* and a part that is moved *per se*; rather, it moves itself as a whole *per se* and primarily. Nor can this motion be attributed to the generating thing, and this for the same reasons touched upon just a moment ago: namely, that it is a vital motion and that the perfection of a living thing consists in it; otherwise, the motion of augmentation would also have to be attributed to the generating thing.

31. *What the locomotive power of an animal is.* As for the first problem, the reply would be simple if it were true, as some think, that an animal's active moving power is none other than its appetitive faculty, which by its action immediately excites a nerve, which in turn is the first part that moves the others. For if this appetitive faculty is sentient, then it is in the heart, whereas if it is rational, it is in the soul itself; and through its act, which is formally immanent and virtually *transeunt*, it moves the first part of the animal. And in this way the agent is differentiated from the patient here, since the appetitive faculty either exists in a distinct part of the animal or at the very least is related to the animal as a sort of separated mover.

However, this reply presupposes a false opinion, since an animal's moving power, insofar as it is active, is in fact distinct from the appetitive faculty, as is proved at length in the science of the soul.[28]

Now˙ there are those who think that this moving power is the soul itself according to its own substance, or at least that it exists in the soul alone. And they claim as a result that it is the soul alone, as informing the nerve, which (i) through itself—that is, through /640a/ the power that is in it—moves the nerve, and which (ii) moves the next part through the nerve as through an instrument, and so forth. As for the objection raised above, one could, given this position, reply by conceding that in the first part of the animal's motion—that is, in the nerve—the integral part that effects the motion *per se* and the integral part that is moved *per se* are not distinct, but that instead it is only the essential parts that are distinct.[29] Nor is this problematic, since in such a case the soul, by the fact that it has the whole moving power within itself, behaves as if it were a mover *quod* and a separated mover. And so this view is not contrary to Aristotle's intention. Indeed, one could claim that it is sufficient that no corporeal movable thing should move itself primarily and *per se* as a whole and in its entirety—even if, with respect to the part that initiates the motion, it moves that part without any other instrument but only by reason of its form, as we will explain below in the case of the motion of the heart.[30] In this sense one could plausibly defend the present reply even if the moving power that is in the nerve exists not in the soul alone but instead in that very part insofar as it is composed of body and soul—which seems rather plausible, especially in the case of brute animals.

32. Further, we can add that the muscles, which are made out of flesh and nerves and certain ligaments, are the first instrument of an animal's motion, as Galen explains at length in *De Usu Partium*, chap. 3. But this instrument is not moved by itself in such a way that other things do not concur for its motion; and it is because of these other things that it can be said to be moved by another. For, first of all, this instrument is unable to initiate a motion unless some other part of the animal, on which it depends, remains unmoved; since in every motion of an animal it is clear from experience itself that the motion of one part can be effected only if some other part remains at rest. Therefore, the part that remains at rest also belongs to the instrument of the motion and is called an unmoved *per se* mover; and so by reason of this part the mover is differentiated from the first part of the animal that is simul-

---

28. This is in keeping with the general principle that the powers of the soul (be it vegetative, sentient or rational) are distinct from the soul itself and emanate from it.

29. I.e., the distinction is between the form and the matter of the first moved part.

30. See §§33–35 below.

taneously moved and moving. Albert noted this in *On the Soul* 3, tract 4, chap. 8.

Likewise, on the basis of St. Thomas, the Commentator, and others in *On the Soul* 3.10, we can add that the heart is in some sense the source of this motion, both because the nerves come from it and especially because it concurs by means of the animal spirits in moving the muscles.[31] For it is likewise evident from experience that this moving power cannot be exercised without the spirits, which the heart or the brain (according to the different opinions of philosophers) sends to the part by which the motion is to be initiated. Therefore, it is likely that these spirits also serve in some way as instruments of the motion. But these /640b/ spirits are themselves moved by being impelled or excited by the efficient causality of a power that exists in the heart or the brain—a power which, while itself remaining unmoved, impels the spirits when an appetitive act occurs, just as the power that expels excrement naturally expels it while remaining unmoved. Nor is it necessary that each body which effects motion should itself be actually moved; rather, it is enough that it should be movable at other times, or at least that it should be moved *per accidens* when the whole is moved. (This axiom will be discussed again below.[32])

33. *The motion of the heart is explained.* As for the second part of the problem, the reason why the motion of the heart has seemed remarkable to all philosophers is that this motion, even if it is a natural motion, appears to be composed of contraries. (For it consists in a continuous approach and withdrawal between the same termini, not in the manner of a circular motion but through expansion and contraction.)

That is why some have claimed that this motion proceeds not from the [animal's] particular and intrinsic nature but from nature in general and from an extrinsic mover. In *Opusculum* 15 St. Thomas calls this position ridiculous[33]—and justifiably so, since the purpose of the motion in question is not anything that pertains to nature in general but is instead something that

---

31. According to Galenic medical theory, there are seven so-called 'naturals': the elements, the mixtures, the humors, the members, the energies, the operations, and the spirits. The spirits include the natural spirit, which has its origin in the liver; the vital spirit, which has its origin in the heart; and the animal spirit, which has its origin in the brain. These spirits are diffused through the body.

32. See §37 below.

33. The opusculum referred to here and discussed in the next few paragraphs is *De Motu Cordis ad Magistrum Phillipum*. It can be found in R. Spiazzi, ed., *Divi Thomae Aquinatis: Opuscula Philosophica* (Rome: Marietti, 1954), §§452–463, pp. 165–168.

pertains to the particular nature of the animal itself: namely, cooling and the regulation of the heart's own vital heat by means of the air taken in through breathing. And so the motion is absolutely necessary for the conservation of life. Therefore, it occurs not because of nature in general but because of the particular nature of the animal itself. Hence, it must be the case that there is a proper principle of this motion within the animal's very nature. For those things that are intrinsically necessary and perpetual must have an internal principle within the very nature [of the thing].

34. Thus, in the opusculum just cited, St. Thomas claims that the motion in question proceeds effectively from the soul itself insofar as it is the natural form of the body. However, because the objection mentioned above came up immediately—namely, that this is not sufficient for there to be a distinction, in Aristotle's sense, between the part that effects motion and the part that is moved, from which it follows that the heart as a whole moves itself *per se* and primarily—St. Thomas adds that this motion must be attributed to the generating thing, since it results naturally in the manner of a proper passion from the form itself. This position is adopted by Capreolus and Ferrariensis in the places cited above.

But, of course, this position encounters no small difficulty in explaining, first of all, how so varied a motion can result from one and the same faculty acting naturally. For a naturally acting power is determined to one effect, whereas expansion /641a/ and contraction—that is, approach and withdrawal with respect to the same terminus—are contrary motions.

Nor is there a parallel among those animal motions that can likewise be called natural because they are brought about by a certain necessity of nature. For the latter proceed from an appetitive act that follows upon a cognitive act, and they can vary according to varying apprehensions, which themselves vary according to varying applications of the objects. By contrast, the heart's motion proceeds not from an appetitive act but from a merely natural property.

Again, there seems to be no parallel in the case adduced by St. Thomas—namely, the circular motion of a celestial body, which includes approach and withdrawal according to diverse parts with respect to a partial terminus—both because (i) in a circular motion this feature is found without any contrariety among the motions and with a genuine continuity among the parts of the motion, whereas in the case at hand there seems to be a genuine contrariety among the parts of the motion, and for this reason a genuine state of rest intervenes between them; and also because (ii) the circular motion in question proceeds not from an active internal principle but from an extrinsic mover.

However, the present problem arises with equal force regardless of

whether we claim that the [heart's] motion is effected by the generating thing
through a natural resulting, or whether we claim instead that it is effected by
the animal itself through a proper action. For in both cases it is effected by
a faculty that is acting naturally. And so there is nothing to say except that
the sentient soul, by reason of the fact that it is a more noble form, can have
natural faculties that surpass lower forms in their mode of operating. But
the moving faculty that exists in the heart is of this sort and so is not wholly
determined to one effect except, as it were, within its own sphere—that is,
within those termini which it approaches by expansion and withdraws from
by contraction. The motion as a whole, which is physically one even though
it is not mathematically continuous, is composed of these two parts.

35. However, once this is assumed, it is difficult to attribute that motion to
the generating thing.

For, first of all, the motion is a vital act. But an act of life proceeds from an
intrinsic principle and thus should not be traced back to an extrinsic principle. Perhaps someone will deny that this motion is a vital motion, since it
is not effected through an appetitive act and a cognitive act. However, this
claim is implausible and contrary to all the philosophers. For even though, as
Zimara explains at length in theorem 12, philosophers are in doubt about
whether this motion proceeds from the soul insofar as it is vegetative or
from the soul insofar as it is sentient, nonetheless, everyone agrees that it
proceeds from the soul insofar as it is a soul, since the soul is, as it were, the
source of life.

Second, it seems absurd to attribute my breathing to the thing that generates me and to claim that it is not I myself who breathe. But breathing, too,
is a natural action that is effected without the intervention of an appetitive
act. /641b/ Indeed, it is effected by the very motion of the heart and lungs.

Third, it is impossible to explain why nutrition should not also be attributed to the generating thing. For nutrition, too, is merely natural. It
originates from without only at the instant of generation, and then it perdures perpetually by itself. Moreover, insofar as it is nutrition—as opposed
to growth—it does not tend toward any perfection owed [to the animal] by
virtue of its generation. Instead, it tends toward conserving life by restor-
ing what has been lost. In the same way, the heart's motion originates from
without at the instant of generation, always perdures by itself, and does not
tend toward a place that is owed to the animal—that is, to the heart—by
virtue of its generation. Instead, it is effected by the living thing itself for the
purpose of conserving its life—a purpose that the motion in question contributes to, at least as a *per accidens* cause, either by removing and expelling
certain corrupting agents or else by taking in a cooling agent.

And so I do not consider it problematic to attribute this sort of operation to the animal itself and to assert that (i) it both produces the motion and is moved according to one and the same integral part and that (ii) it is sufficient that the characters of acting and receiving should be distinct from one another. For it was only with respect to the motion of the *whole* animal that Aristotle claimed that it is effected by the motion of one of the parts upon another. Consequently, according to this reply one should concede that the agent *quod* and the patient *quod* need not be distinct in this physical motion, since it is a vital and merely partial motion. There is nothing problematic about this, as will become clearer below from the third assertion.³⁴ And it seems to be fully consonant with Aristotle's intention at the end of *On the Movement of Animals* [11.703b2–704a1].

A Problem Concerning the Mover of a Celestial Body

36. The third problem is that Aristotle makes an induction only over sublunary bodies and overlooks celestial bodies or, better, argues from the former to the latter. But this does not seem effective, at least for inferring that a celestial body is moved by another mover *quod*; rather, it seems effective at most for inferring that a celestial body is moved by another mover *quo*— that is, by its own form. For what if someone claims that a celestial body's form is a special kind of soul which the given motion follows upon by natural necessity, not through one integral part [acting] on another but in each part through itself, by the mediation of the form and natural faculty alone— just as we claimed a moment ago in the case of the motion of the heart?

The reply is that it is true that Aristotle did not include the celestial bodies in his inductive argument but was instead arguing from lower bodies, which are known to us, to higher bodies, which are less known to us. Nonetheless, the argument will be quite effective once we assume that the motion of the celestial bodies is not natural to those bodies according to their proper and /642a/ particular natures in the way that the motion of the heart is or in the way that the motion of heavy and light bodies is, since the motion in question is ordered neither toward the conservation or perfection of those bodies nor toward a place that is naturally owed to them. In *Contra Gentes* 3, chap. 23, arg. 4, St. Thomas uses this line of reasoning to prove that a celestial body's motion does not proceed from an intrinsic form. For if it did, the motion would emanate naturally from the form, since the place conferred through such a motion would be owed to the movable thing, as is clear in the case of all natural bodies. But a place acquired by a celestial body through circular motion is not owed to it by reason of its form, since it is irrelevant to the perfection or inclination of its form that the body should have this "where"

---

34. See §41 below.

rather than another—that is, as far as its diverse parts are concerned. For example, it is irrelevant that it should have sunlight in this hemisphere rather than in the other.

What's more, one cannot claim, on the basis of local motion alone, that a celestial body's form is a soul—as was noted above and will also be explained below in our discussion of the intelligences.[35] Hence, even if someone contends that the motion in question is natural to a celestial body in the same way that the other motions of natural bodies are, he should nonetheless trace that motion back to the author of the heavenly body as the one who impressed the impetus for that motion—just as heavy and light bodies are said to be moved by the generating thing. However, if someone denies that a celestial body has an author and asserts that it exists of itself and has a natural inclination toward, and faculty for, the motion in question, then such an error would have to be refuted by appeal to other principles of metaphysics.[36] For, as we will explain at length below, this cannot be done on the basis of physical motion alone, even though it is utterly incredible that a thing that requires motion for its perfection or even for its action should have its *esse* of itself without communication—that is, production—on the part of another.

37. *A thesis is drawn from the foregoing problems and proved by an argument.* From these considerations it seems sufficiently clear by induction that every corporeal and physical local motion requires a mover or efficient cause distinct from the thing moved.

Now an argument for this necessity can be given, first, in terms of that principle of Aristotle's that nothing can simultaneously be both in potency and in act. However, this principle has to be modified and adapted in the way we explained above for the case of the motion of alteration[37]—though it may in fact have even less force in the case of local motion, given that local motion (or its terminus) is not, speaking *per se*, a principle—that is, either a power or an act—from which a similar motion proceeds; rather, the˙ relevant˙ power˙ is˙ a moving faculty of a sort higher /642b/ than the motion itself. Still, Aristotle's principle would be effective for the case of bodies if another axiom, which is pretty widely accepted and attributed to Aristotle, were true: namely, that a body does not effect local motion unless it, too, is moved locally. For regardless of whether this latter motion is required as part of the [very] notion of effecting motion or [merely] as a condition for effecting motion, the presupposition is that a body must already be actually moved in order for it to be able to effect motion. And from this one quite

35. See *DM* 35. 1.
36. See *DM* 29. 1.
37. See §19 above.

rightly infers that it cannot move itself, since it cannot simultaneously be both in act and in potency.[38]

On the other hand, the axiom in question is not accepted by everyone and appears to be subject to a few counterexamples. For instance, a magnet, while remaining unmoved, attracts iron, and so forth.

But one should reply that there are two ways in which one body can move another. First, it can move it *per se* and immediately by impressing nothing other than the motion; and in such a case it is indeed true that [a body] never effects motion unless it itself is moved locally. Second, [the moved body] can be moved locally by an antecedent alteration (it is in this way that a magnet attracts iron); and in such a case it is quite possible for one body, while remaining unmoved, to move another. But in this latter case, it will be necessary, at least by dint of the fact that the motion is effected by means of an alteration, for the mover to be distinct from the thing moved. And in this way the argument under discussion will be effective in the case of local motion—either immediately so by reason of the motion itself (as I will put it) or else mediately so by reason of the alteration, if the motion is effected by means of an alteration.

38. *Aristotle's other argument is examined.*[39] In *Physics* 7, text 2 [1.242a39–40], Aristotle adduced another argument in order to prove that a body cannot *per se* and primarily move itself locally. In summary form, the argument is this: Everything that is moved is divisible into parts; therefore, it cannot move itself *per se* and primarily.

The consequence is proved by the fact that if a thing moves itself *per se* and primarily, then its being at rest does not follow upon another thing's being at rest or ceasing to effect motion. For when it moves itself, it does not depend on another in its motion. But because a movable thing has parts, when a part of it is at rest, either (i) the whole is at rest, in which case the whole is not moved *per se* and primarily but is instead moved by that part which is such that when it is at rest, the whole ceases to be moved; or else (ii) the whole is still being moved, in which case it once again follows that the whole does not move itself *per se* and primarily but is instead moved by the part by which it is said to be moved when that other part is at rest.

Much has been written about this argument by the commentators, and many believe it to be a demonstration—for example, Alexander, Simplicius,

38. I.e., on the given assumption it could move itself only if it were already in motion— which is impossible, since if it already possesses a given motion actually and formally, then it cannot be in potency with respect to that very same motion.

39. In the end, Suarez rejects this second line of argument and falls back on the first argument.

Averroës, and St. Thomas—though they differ among themselves. For Averroës thinks that it is only an a posteriori demonstration, whereas St. Thomas
claims that it is an a priori demonstration which proves that the divisibility
of a movable thing is the reason why it cannot be moved *per se* and primarily.
However, there are others /643a/ to whom the argument appears sophistical
and inefficacious.

39. And, in fact, there does seem to be an equivocation on the phrase
'*per se* and primarily'. For there are two ways in which something can be
understood to be moved *per se* and primarily.

One way is this: The motion of the whole movable thing belongs to the
whole in such a way that it depends on nothing else, not even the parts.
Given this sense, the argument proves straightforwardly that it is impossible for a body to move itself *per se* and primarily. However, this does not
at all help one conclude that there is a necessary distinction between the
mover and the movable thing. For the dependence of a whole [body] on its
parts might be merely material and not efficient, except perhaps relatively
speaking—that is, insofar as each part moves itself, as will be explained in a
moment.

In a second way, something can be said to move itself *per se* and primarily
in the sense that it moves and is moved according to each part in such a
way that no part moves either another part or the whole as such, but instead
each part moves itself and so partially concurs in the motion of the whole, a
motion that itself results from the movements and motions of all the parts.
And indeed, if something moves itself in this manner, then it will be entirely proper to say that it moves itself *per se* and primarily in such a way
that within it the mover is not distinct from the thing moved. However, the
conclusion that it is impossible for a body to move itself in this way cannot
be effectively inferred from the argument adduced above, no matter which
of the two alternatives is granted.[40]

For, first of all, it could be the case that the reason why the whole is completely at rest according to each of its parts, given that a part is at rest, is
not that the whole is moved by just one part but instead that when one part
ceases to move itself and is at rest, it resists another part and prevents the
latter from moving itself—a point that one can see not only in the case of
different parts but also in the case of different movable things. For if two
rocks are moving downward, one right after the other, then if the first one is
detained, it will prevent the other one from descending not because it was

40. I.e., the argument can be refuted either (i) on the assumption that when a given part
is at rest, the whole is at rest, or (ii) on the assumption that when a given part is at rest,
the whole is in motion.

previously moving the other rock, but because it resists the motion by which that rock was moving itself.

Second, it is possible that when one part is at rest, the whole is at rest not according to each of its parts but only with respect to the one which is said to be at rest, whereas with respect to the other parts it is still being moved—as happens, for example, when, while the root of a tree is at rest, the other parts are excited. Once again, from this it does not follow that the whole was previously being moved only by the part that is still moving itself; instead, it follows only that this part had concurred in the entire motion of the whole along with the other parts.

40. *Aristotle's axiom is explained.* Thus, the axiom "If a thing moves itself *per se* and primarily, then its being at rest does not follow upon another thing's being at rest" has to be modified by a twofold distinction. For it is true that a movable thing is not at rest *per se* by virtue of the fact that /643b/ another thing by which it was not being moved is at rest; however, it is possible for it to be at rest *per accidens* and because an impediment is posited. Again, if that other thing that is at rest is not altogether extrinsic but is instead a part of the moving and movable thing, then it is straightforwardly possible that the reason why, given that that part is at rest, the whole ceases to be moved *per se* and primarily—that is, according to all its parts—is not that the whole does not move itself *per se* and primarily but instead that it was being moved partially by that part. For these two points are not contrary to one another, as is *per se* manifest. Therefore, the fact that the whole as a whole depends upon the parts does not prevent it from being the case that the motion of the whole proceeds *per se* and primarily from that same whole.

This is made manifestly clear by the fact that if it were not so, then one could prove in the same way that it is impossible for a body to be moved by another *per se* and primarily—which is obviously false, since a celestial body is moved *per se* and primarily by an intelligence, and [the element] earth is moved *per se* and primarily when it is borne downward, even if by the generating thing. And the inference is evident. For in these cases it is also true that if a part of the celestial body were at rest, then the whole would be at rest, or at least it would not be moved *per se* and primarily in the way it was before, since the *per se* and primary motion of the whole depends materially on the motion of a part as on an integral part [of that motion]. In the same way, contrariwise, a whole [elemental] earth is *per se* and primarily at rest at the center [of the earth], and yet the reason why the whole would no longer be *per se* and primarily at rest, if a part ceased to be at rest, is not that the whole was being made to rest effectively by that part but rather that the whole's being at rest resulted materially, as it were, from the part's being at rest. Again, as long as the whole of a volume of [elemental] water is cold, the whole can be said to be made cold *per se* and primarily; and yet the reason why, once a part begins to be heated, the whole is no longer cold *per se* and primarily, as it was before, is not that the whole was being actively made cold before by that part but rather that the coldness, insofar as it belonged to the whole *per se* and primarily, resulted materially, as it were, from the coldness of the parts.

Therefore, from the fact that the motion of the whole, insofar as it effects motion or is moved *per se* and primarily, depends on the motion or movement of each part, one can infer only that the whole is moved by the part partially and (as I put it) relatively—that is, insofar as each part moves itself—a sort of dependence that does not rule out the same thing's moving itself. Hence I do not see how the axiom under discussion is demonstrated by the line of argument in question. For this reason, the other proofs adduced above are more plausible.[41]

THIRD ASSERTION: CONCERNING THE MOTION OF SPIRITUAL THINGS

41. *A spirit is able to move itself locally.* I assert, third, that within a spiritual entity, a cause that acts through a motion or action that is in some sense *transeunt* is not always distinct in reality from the material cause or recipient of the motion except, /644a/ at most, with respect to the characters of acting and receiving.

This thesis is posited mainly because of the local motion of the angels, which I am calling 'in some sense *transeunt*' because (i) insofar as it falls under the notion of local motion, it can be effected by one thing acting on another suppositum[42] and because (ii) it is not in fact *per se* an immanent act within the faculty by which it is proximately effected. Hence, it is certain that by means of this motion an angel (that is, an intelligence) or separated soul is able to move itself by effecting motion within itself. For, as we will indicate in its own place below, the motion by which a spiritual substance is moved exists not in another distinct thing but within the very substance that is moved.[43] And this is all but evident from the meaning of the terms, since a thing is not said to be moved by extrinsic denomination but is instead said

41. Here Suarez is referring back to §§36–37 above.

42. I.e., local motion is the *sort* of motion that can be effected by one suppositum on another, even if in this particular case (i.e., when an angel moves himself locally) it is not so effected.

43. See *DM* 51. 3

to be moved by virtue of a true and real change that must necessarily have some efficient cause; and when it moves itself, there is no cause other than the very same spiritual substance that is being moved. It follows, then, that (i) the efficient cause cannot be distinct in suppositum from the recipient of the motion, since we are assuming that one and the same suppositum is moving itself, and also that (ii) [this suppositum] cannot be differentiated into a part that effects motion *per se* and a part that is moved *per se*, since it has no parts. Therefore, at most one can distinguish the *character* of effecting the motion from the *character* of receiving the motion or its terminus.

There are, to be sure, varying opinions [about the character of *receiving* the motion], but I take it to be most likely that the motion in question is received in the *substance* of the angel.[44] For in the same way that a body is present to a place through its quantity, so an angel is immediately present to a place through his substance; for he has no quantity, and there is no other imaginable accident in him by the mediation of which he might be capable of local presence. I am speaking here about the proximate and immediate subject of that presence, regardless of whether or not the action in question requires some action or contact of power with respect to a body.[45] This is irrelevant in the present context, since what is effected within the angel by virtue of a local motion is not an action on a body but instead the angel's real presence. But this presence immediately modifies the angel's substance. Therefore, that same substance has the character of receiving such a motion, since a motion and its formal terminus exist in the same proximate subject.

42. *What the proximate principle of local motion is in spirits.* Further, there are varying opinions concerning the character of *effecting* this motion.

For some claim that the motion is effected immediately by the will, from which it follows—assuming, as we ourselves assume, that the will is an entity distinct from the substance—that the proximate character of effecting the motion is distinct *in reality* from the character of receiving the motion.[46] (Those who deny that the faculty /644b/ of will is distinct in reality from the substance might perhaps claim that the actual volition to move oneself is the

44. So whereas it is plausible to believe that the quantity of a material substance is the immediate subject of a material substance's motion, this is implausible in the case of an immaterial substance, which has no quantity. Nor is there, among the accidents of the immaterial substance, any other plausible candidate for the immediate subject of local motion.

45. See *DM* 51. 3 and 4, for Suarez's discussion of the relation of angelic motion to bodies.

46. The claim here is that the distinction in question is a real distinction and not just a conceptual distinction.

proximate character of effecting the motion and that this volition is distinct from the substance.)

Others, however, think that the proximate and *per se* principle that effects the motion is not the will or the volition but rather a special moving power, whereas the volition is the application of—that is, the commanding of—that˙ moving power, a power which is such that, just as it is distinct from the appetitive faculty in us and in other animals, so, too, it is distinct from the will in angels.

Now there are some who think that this power is not distinct in reality from the substance; on their view it is also the case that the character of acting and the character of receiving the motion are distinct not in reality but only conceptually. We ourselves, by contrast, think it more probable that this moving power, even if it is believed to be distinct in reality from the will, is also distinct in reality from the angel's substance—and this because of the general principle, posited above,[47] that in a creature the proximate faculty for an accidental action is an accident distinct from the substance. And so we conclude that the proximate principle *quo* for effecting the motion in question is distinct in reality from the subject in which the motion is received. And the reason is that this principle is a purely active power that does not act except on a presupposed subject; therefore, it requires within that subject a passive power that is distinct from it.

And this is confirmed by Aristotle's definition in *Metaphysics* 9 [1.1046a9–11], where he says that an active power is a principle for transmuting another thing insofar as it is other; we will have more to say about this a little later.[48]

43. Neither Aristotle's principle, "Everything that is moved is moved by another," nor the arguments by which he confirms it stand opposed to this conclusion. For, as I noted above,[49] Aristotle was talking about physical and material motion. However, the motion of the intelligences is not of this sort; and it is a rather moot point whether Aristotle countenanced such motion or whether he believed instead that the intelligences are altogether unmovable. Hence, his inductive argument does not include the intelligences, as is evident *per se*; neither does the argument which presupposes that a movable thing is divisible into parts.

Now the other argument—namely, that a thing cannot simultaneously be both in potency and in act—is best answered here by appeal to the distinction between virtual act and formal potency. And the argument establishes at most the distinctness of the principle *quo* of acting from the receiving sub-

47. See *DM* 18. 3. 15–23.

48. See §§55–56 below.

49. See §19 above.

ject. For an angel who is in heaven is in formal potency to being on earth, whereas he has an actual power whereby he is able to move himself and to make himself present to the earth.

Nor is there a place here for the qualifications, posited above,[50] /645a/ whereby we claimed that the principle in question is true even with respect to a virtual act. For the one qualification was that the principle should be understood to apply to physical motion; however, the motion we are now discussing is not physical. And the other qualification—namely, that the thing must be in a preternatural state—is unnecessary here, since living things surpass nonliving things in that they are able to move themselves even when they exist in their natural state, and so in their natural state they are able to have simultaneously both a virtual act and a formal potency with respect to some motion.

44. *Three orders of things that move themselves locally from within.* Thus, from the line of reasoning adduced thus far one may infer that there are three orders of things that in some sense move themselves locally by means of an intrinsic principle.

The first is the order of things that move themselves in this way only when they are in a preternatural state; and in their case, even though the principle of motion exists in them, it nonetheless exists in them not as something proper to them but rather as the instrument or power of another. Inanimate things are of this sort.

There are other things that properly move themselves by an intrinsic principle as by something proper to themselves; however, they do not move themselves perfectly and *per se* and primarily but instead move themselves by moving one part through another and thus by moving the whole *per accidens*, as it were. And they are able to move at most one of their parts *per se* and primarily—namely, that part which is, as it were, the source of the motion of the other parts. Living bodies are of this sort.

Included in the third and highest order are those things that not only move themselves by an intrinsic principle as by something proper to themselves but also move themselves *per se* and primarily according to themselves as wholes, since they have no parts. And so in these things the principles *quod* of acting and receiving cannot be distinguished; at most, the principles *quo* can be distinguished. And this is consonant with the perfection of these things, since they occupy the most perfect level among living creatures.

50. See ibid.

FOURTH ASSERTION:
CONCERNING IMMANENT ACTIONS

45. I assert, fourth, that in a cause that effects an immanent action not only are the principles *quod* of acting and receiving not always distinct, but it is not even always necessary for the principles *quo* to be distinct in reality, though it often happens that they are.

The first part of this assertion is obvious and follows from the very notion of an immanent action. For an immanent action is received in the operating thing itself, and so it is not necessary that the suppositum that acts be distinct from the suppositum that receives or even that the suppositum should act and receive according to different parts. This is so both because the suppositum often has no parts and also because /645b/ an action of this sort is received in the same faculty by which it is elicited, with the result that even in a suppositum that does have parts the action is effected by and received in the same part.

And on this basis one can give a general argument for the second part of the thesis. For, given that an immanent action remains not only in the same suppositum but also in the same faculty that elicits it, nothing rules out its being the case that even within the proximate principle *quo*, which both effects the action and receives it, there is no distinction in reality.

46. But in order that this second part, as well as the whole thesis, might be further clarified and established, it will be necessary to differentiate these immanent actions more specifically and to explain how the assertion applies in each case.

All the actions in question pertain either to cognition or to appetition, and they can exist either in the rational part [of the soul] or in the sentient part. Again, in all these actions one can consider the principal (that is, substantival) principle *quo* or the proximate (that is, accidental) principle *quo*.[51]

Now to the extent that actions of this sort exist in the sentient part, the principal principles *quo* of acting and of receiving can easily be distinguished in them. The former is the soul, as is obvious from the definition of the soul, whereas the latter is the body. For according to the true doctrine, these sentient operations, because they are material, are received in the body or in the whole composite by reason of the matter.

On the other hand, to the extent that operations of the sort in question are found in the intellective part, the principal principle of acting and the prin-

---

51. In order to follow the argument, one must keep this distinction in mind. The principal or substantival principles *quo* (i.e., the soul and the body) are discussed in the remainder of §46, whereas the proximate or accidental principles *quo* are discussed in §§47–51.

cipal principle of receiving are only conceptually distinct in them, since the very same simple substance of an angel or of a soul plays both these roles. For the claim made by some—namely, that the two roles are differentiated within the substance itself by reason of the fact that the soul acts through its *esse* as through its act and receives through its essence as through its potency—falsely presupposes a distinction in reality between the *esse* and the actualized essence.[52] What's more, even if this distinction is granted, the claim in question does not follow. For given this opinion, the *esse* is not a principle of acting but is instead a condition in the absence of which the essence would not act. However, by the same token, the *esse* is also a condition in the absence of which the essence would not receive the operation, whereas the essence itself as existing—that is, as having such a condition—is the principle both of acting and of receiving an operation of the sort in question. Hence, in the case of Christ's soul, even if, in keeping with the position in question, that soul does not have a created *esse existentiae*,[53] nonetheless, the principal principle for eliciting a created act of understanding is not the uncreated *esse* itself but rather the substance of the soul itself according to its proper *esse essentiae*.

47. *Whether the character of acting is distinct from the character of receiving in cognitive operations; not only the [intelligible] species but the intellect as well effects a cognition.* /646a/ On the other hand, as far as the proximate and accidental principle is concerned, the explanation of cognitive actions seems different from the explanation of appetitive actions, both in the rational part [of the soul] and in the sentient part.

For in the case of cognitive actions, the proximate principle of acting is always (or almost always) distinct from the proximate principle of receiving. The reason for this is that in order to effect this sort of action, what is required, in addition to the vital faculty, is a species that takes the place of the object and concurs in its stead with respect to the act. And so the principle of acting is the faculty *as informed by the species*, whereas the principle of receiving is the faculty *by itself*, since the object—that is, its species—assists only in the acting and not in the receiving. Therefore, the proximate principle of acting is in some way distinct from the proximate principle of receiving.

---

52. For Suarez's own view of the distinction between *esse* and essence, see *DM* 31.

53. One Thomistic strategy for preserving the claim that Christ's individual human nature, while the same as ours in kind, is hypostatically united to a divine person was to deny that nature its own peculiar act of existing (*esse existentiae*). Christ would differ in this way from other human beings, but the difference would not be one that affects his essence as a human being. Suarez rejects this account and must thus come up with some other explanation for the difference between Christ's assumed nature and other, unassumed, human natures.

I say "in some way" because they are distinct only as that which includes and that which is included. For the opinion of those who think that the species constitutes the entire principle of acting and that the faculty is only the principle of receiving is implausible. Scotus correctly impugns this opinion in *Sentences* 2, dist. 3, q. 8, though he incorrectly attributes it to St. Thomas, who nowhere suggested it. And the reason why it is highly implausible is that a vital act must necessarily proceed actively from an intrinsic vital faculty. Therefore, it is certain that the same cognitive faculty in which a cognitive act is proximately received is simultaneously the proximate principle that effects that same act. The difference is that this faculty is [by itself] an adequate proximate principle of receiving the act but is not an adequate proximate principle of effecting the act unless it is taken together with the species—this according to the most plausible doctrine, concerning which one can consult Capreolus, *Sentences* 2, dist. 3, q. 2; Scotus, *Sentences* 1, dist. 3, q. 7; and Giles and Ferrariensis in the places that will be cited below.

48. *What the distinct principles of acting and receiving are in the act of understanding whereby an angel understands himself.* The only objection that can be made has to do with the act by which an angel sees himself through his own substance without the aid of a species. (This is so according to the most likely position, though others disagree, as we will see below when we discuss the intelligences.[54]) Therefore, this act of understanding has the same adequate principle of acting and of receiving: namely, the angel's substance and intellect.

Someone might reply that this act is attributed to the generating thing or author of the nature by reason of the fact that it is a merely natural act and is intrinsically necessary to the proper state of the [angelic] nature at the first instant of its creation. However, this type of attribution should not, it seems, be stretched to so great an extent in the case of proper vital acts—especially if one is talking strictly about physical causes. (For /646b/ it is more readily applied to moral causes, as I will explain shortly[55]).

And so, as I indicated in the assertion and will explain in a moment, I do not judge it problematic to concede the point for [immanent] acts if this is necessary. Still, in the case of the act in question there is no such absolute necessity; instead, some sort of distinction in reality can be discerned between the proximate principle of effecting that act and the proximate principle of receiving it. For while the angel's substance concurs in the case of other acts of understanding in just one way—namely, as a principal principle—it concurs in two ways, or two roles, with respect to the act under discussion:

54. See *DM* 35. 4.
55. See §50 below.

namely, (i) as a principal principle and (ii) as the object and, as it were, last form of its own intellect in intelligible *esse*. And so the proximate principle of this act is not the intellective faculty by itself but the intellective faculty as constituted in first act in its own way through its own substance insofar as the latter is conjoined to it in the manner of an actually intelligible object. By contrast, it is the intellect by itself that is the proximately receptive power and total principle of receiving that act; and, as far as this [receptive] principle is concerned, the substance has no greater concurrence with respect to this act than with respect to other acts. So it follows that in this case too the adequate principles of acting and receiving are differentiated as that which includes and that which is included.

49. *Whether the cognition of an object influences a volition as an efficient cause.* However, in the case of the actions of the [sentient] appetite and of the will there is a special problem, since these faculties do not require species, and so, it seems, it is through their being alone that they are principles of effecting and receiving those acts.

For this reason some claim that the cognition of the object concurs as an efficient cause in appetitive acts. This is what Soncinas asserts in *Metaphysics* 9, q. 10, 11, and 13. In addition, many theologians hold this position, as I recounted at length in *Summa Theologiae* 1–2.

However, this position does not seem convincing to me. I think that the cognition of the object concurs in an appetitive act merely as a necessary condition, in the sense that it applies the object. For the will is moved only by the goodness of an object. Therefore, if this latter movement, insofar as it comes from the object, is not an effecting movement (as in fact it is not), but instead a final and metaphorical movement (a point that even Soncinas concedes in *Metaphysics* 9, q. 12, as do the others), then there is no reason why it should be an effecting movement insofar as it comes from the cognition.[56] For once a good object has been presented, the appetitive faculty does not require an extrinsic agent in order to be moved toward that object; instead, it can be moved by a natural inclination or, better, by the soul insofar as [the appetitive faculty] has life through the soul.

50. *Whether the desire for an end should be attributed to the generating thing.* There are others who claim that (i) an appetitive act with respect to an *end*, even though it is effected by the will alone, must nonetheless be attributed to the generating thing or author of the nature, whereas (ii) an appetitive act with respect /647a/ to the *means* is not effected by the will alone but is instead

---

56. I.e., if the object's influence is as a final cause rather than as an efficient cause, then likewise the influence of the cognition of that object is in the order of final, rather than efficient, causality.

effected by the mediation of an appetitive act with respect to the end and is received in the will alone—and it is in this way that the principles of acting and receiving are distinct in it. For either the internal principles themselves are really distinct in some way, or else, if they are not distinct within the proximate agent itself, the action is attributed to an extrinsic agent. This is how the act of intending an end is thought of by the Thomists. See Cajetan, *Summa Theologiae* 1–2, q. 9, a. 4; Ferrariensis, *Contra Gentes* 3, chap. 89, where St. Thomas suggests this view; Capreolus, *Sentences* 2, dist. 25; and Giles, *Sentences* 2, dist. 25, q. 9.

However, even though this attribution [of the act to the generating thing] could be sustained if we were considering moral causes, since a human being does not move himself morally in intending the end as such in the way that he does in deliberating about and choosing the means (I deal with this elsewhere[57]), nonetheless, as far as real efficient causality is concerned, the attribution cannot be proved. Moreover, one should not deny that the human being himself effects the intending of an end by his own proper power and not as the instrument of another—especially in the case of those acts, included within the order of nature, that the will elicits by its own proper power with only [God's] general concurrence. Therefore, the action in question cannot be attributed to God to a greater degree than a fire's production of heat can be—especially because it is not only a vital action but also oftentimes a free action. Hence, it is in no way effected through a natural resulting, nor is it owed [to any entity] according to the connatural state which that entity requires at the instant of its generation.

51. For this reason, the claim that the act in question should be attributed to the generating thing is correctly denied by Scotus, *Sentences* 2, dist. 25; by Henry, *Quodlibeta* 9, q. 5; and by others. And the same thing should be said about the many other simple acts (for example, a desire for or delight in or simple love of some cognized good) that the will elicits from itself in the absence of any prior act.

What's more, this line of reasoning is out of place in the case of the sentient appetite, which does not operate formally for the sake of an end. Hence, in the sentient appetite there is, properly speaking, no choice that proceeds from the intending of the end as from a proximate reason for acting. Instead, all the appetitive acts proceed from the sentient appetite's natural inclination itself. Therefore, either one has to claim that all the acts of this appetitive faculty are attributed to the generating thing—which is ridiculous—or else one must grant that it is altogether the same power that through its very

---

57. For more discussion of acts of intending an end and choosing the means to that end, see *DM* 19. 8.

self is both the proximate principle of acting and the proximate principle of receiving such an act. And this is indeed granted by Scotus, Henry, and the others cited above, and at length by Antoine André in *Metaphysics* 9, q. 1.

Nor do I see anything following from this that is problematic to such a degree that, in order to avoid it, Soncinas, Javellus, and others should look so scrupulously, in the case of every acting and receiving faculty, /647b/ for something that is a co-principle of the acting and not of the receiving, with the result that they end up taking refuge in the efficient causality of a cognition with respect to an act of loving. If this causality is not shown to be necessary for other reasons, then it is unjustifiably invoked for the reason in question. For the problem they adduce is none other than this: that one and the same thing would, taken in the same respect, be both the agent and the patient and that, consequently, it would be both in potency and in act with respect to the same thing—which implies a contradiction. But this is no problem if the points explained above are taken into account and if the relevant terms are [correctly] understood. For there is no contradiction involved in the claim that one and the same faculty is both in first act and in potency with respect to an immanent second act.[58] For the first act does not formally include the second act but, rather, formally includes the *power to elicit* the second act—a power that can be had by the same faculty that is the receptive power with respect to that same act. And this is consonant with the nature of such an act, since it is an immanent act. And this is what the others claim: namely, that one and the same faculty can simultaneously be both in virtual act and in formal potency.

Hence, just as it is by one and the same act in reality that a thing is constituted as actually acting and as actually receiving, and just as one and the same thing is both an action and a passion according to diverse relations, so too it is by one and the same faculty in reality that a suppositum can be constituted in both the character of potentially acting and the character of potentially being acted upon. Therefore, in this sense there is nothing absurd in its being the case that the same thing should be constituted as both agent and patient with respect to the same thing—as long as this is taken proportionately; that is, as long as the thing is both agent and patient in potency or both agent and patient in actuality. What's more, the qualification "with respect to the same thing" merely reduplicates or designates one and the same entity but not one and the same relation—that is, not one and the same formal character as conceived of and separated off by an operation of the mind.

---

58. See *DM* 18. 3, n. 4, for more on the distinction between first and second act.

A COROLLARY TO THE FOREGOING DOCTRINE AND
THE FORMAL RESOLUTION OF THE QUESTION

52. Let us now reply formally and generally to the proposed question. From the things we have said so far it follows, first, that it is not part of the notion of an agent cause as such, or necessary for an agent cause as such, that it should be distinct in suppositum from the patient. This was already assumed and shown at the beginning, and it is even more patently evident from the whole discussion that has been presented. Hence, if this sort of distinctness [between agent and patient] is necessary in some cases, then that necessity derives not from the general notion of an efficient cause but from the notion of some particular type of efficient cause. For example, in the case of efficient causality through substantival generation, it is necessary that there be a supposital distinction (as I will call it) between the agent and the patient, since it is necessary that the agent and the patient differ absolutely in their *esse* and in their substantial /648a/ forms. And this same distinctness is necessary between any pair of generating and generated things. For one and the same suppositum cannot generate itself, since [its own existence] is necessarily presupposed in order for it to generate.

Now as far as nutrition (that is, substantival assimilation) is concerned, if the thing acted upon is thought of as at the beginning of the action or alteration, then it, too, must be a distinct suppositum, since it is necessary that it be a dissimilar substance. However, at the very instant of assimilation it is no longer a distinct suppositum but a new part of the same suppositum, since through that action it is converted into, and united to, a preexisting suppositum.

Again, a cause that acts by an accidental action or motion is normally, among inanimate things, distinct in suppositum [from the patient], especially when the patient is moved *per se* and primarily—that is, according to each of its parts. However, this derives not from a necessity on the part of an efficient cause as such but rather from the imperfection and characteristic condition of inanimate things, as has been explained.

Similarly, one should notice that the point in question must be understood to apply to a particular and *per se* cause. For if we are talking about the First and Universal Cause, then it is clear that such a cause must be distinct in suppositum from the effect as well as from the subject being acted upon (if the cause is acting via a change[59]). For the First and Universal Cause cannot act upon himself, since he is pure act. Again, if the cause under discussion is a *per accidens* and remote cause—that is, a cause that produced the proximate

59. I.e., if the action in question is not an instance of creation *ex nihilo*.

cause and gave it its power to act—then it, too, will be a distinct suppositum. (I am presupposing that it produced the proximate cause substantivally.)

Hence, even though Aristotle's axiom 'Whatever is moved is moved by another', when understood as applying to a proximate moving and *per se* cause, is not always rendered true by a distinct suppositum, nonetheless, when it is understood as applying indifferently to a moving cause—regardless of whether that cause is a proximate or remote cause, or a particular or universal cause—one will always find that every movable thing is moved by *some* distinct suppositum or other. That is, to use metaphysical terminology, every patient whatsoever is acted upon by *some* efficient cause that is distinct in suppositum from it.[60] However, this point cannot be demonstrated by means of a purely physical premise; rather, it can be demonstrated only by means of a metaphysical premise: namely, that every particular agent cause has its power to act not from itself but from another suppositum, and also that it is not able to act *per se* without the concurrence of a higher cause. This will become clear below from what we will say about God and about the First Cause.[61]

53. *An inference from what has been said.* Second, from what has been said it follows that it is not part of the notion of an efficient cause as such, or necessary for an efficient cause as such, that it should be distinct from the patient according to diverse substantival parts, /648b/ whether essential parts or integral parts; rather, in the case of agents in which this sort of necessity is found, the necessity derives from some particular notion and not from the notion of efficient causality as such. All this is obvious from what has been said. For the first part [of this claim] was established in the third and fourth assertions above, while the other parts were demonstrated in the preceding assertions.

For the fact that, within living material things, a distinctness among the integral parts is required in order for such things to move themselves by the first vital action, which occurs through nutrition, derives, first, from the nature of the material alteration which intervenes in such a case and with respect to which it is impossible for one and the same thing to act upon itself or for a similar thing to act upon a similar thing—as is explained in *On Generation and Corruption* 1, text 48 [5.322a16–27]. The reason for this was made clear in the first and second assertions. The fact in question derives, second, from substantival assimilation, since it is impossible for one and the same part to form itself substantivally—as is obvious. It derives, third, from

60. This follows directly from the thesis, defended by Suarez in *DM* 22. 1, that God acts immediately in every creaturely act.
61. See *DM* 20–22 and 30.

the fact that for genuine growth it is necessary that a new quantity be added to a preexisting quantity, since one and the same part cannot augment itself through its own quantity alone. Hence, to the extent that a sort of imperfect growth via juxtaposition can be found among inanimate things, it is necessary that the action be effected according to diverse parts. And the same holds true for alteration, if it is possible for an inanimate thing to alter itself in such a way that the action is attributed to it. For this can happen only according to diverse parts, when it is possible for the parts to be affected unequally—a condition that obtains *per accidens* in things of this sort.

Again, in the case of animals that move themselves locally, the fact that such a motion is effected through the distinctness of the integral part that produces the motion and the integral part that is moved derives not from the notion of an efficient or moving cause as such but from the fact that this sort of efficient cause, as well as this sort of living thing, is imperfect and thus does not partake of the intrinsic and natural power to move itself *per se* and primarily as a whole. Perhaps it also derives from the materiality of the body itself, which cannot be moved by the soul *per se* and primarily but can be moved [only] through its parts and through its diverse organs or instruments. To be sure, this renders it probable that it is not repugnant to this sort of living thing that it should be able to move *some* integral part of its body *per se* and primarily—that is, not through another prior integral part but through that part itself.[62] Still, within that very part (and, generally, within every material agent), the essential principles of acting and being acted upon are distinct—a fact that derives not from the precise notion of a particular efficient cause as such but rather from the imperfection peculiar to a material substance, which is active not according to itself as a whole but only by reason of its form. /649a/

54. Third, from what has been said it follows that it is not part of the notion of an efficient cause as such that the principles of acting and being acted upon should be really distinct in either their subject or their whole being or a part of their being. Rather, as often as this distinctness (which is frequent) is found, it derives from some special consideration.

All this is obvious from what has been said. For the condition in question is sometimes absent; therefore, it is not required *per se* and universally by the notion of efficient causality. Thus, the condition that the principle of acting and the principle of being acted upon should be distinct in subject is necessary only in those cases where the action has to be exercised either by a distinct suppositum or through really distinct parts—and this is where the necessity in question derives from.

---

62. See the discussion of the heart's motion in §§33–35 above.

This necessity is, to be sure, universal in the case of univocal actions, because of the principle that one and the same thing cannot simultaneously be both in act and in potency. However, in the case of equivocal actions that principle is not universally compelling in this way; nor is there any other such principle that is universal. And so the necessity derives from different principles in the case of different [efficient] causes, as has been explained.

Again, the condition that the principles of acting and being acted upon should be really distinct in their entire being, even if they happen to exist in the same subject and in the same integral part of that subject, derives either (i) from the fact that these principles are substantival and proper to material things—namely, the matter and the form—or else (ii), if they are accidental principles (especially the one that is the principle of acting), from the fact that the action is not an immanent action but is instead by its nature a *transeunt* action. This is clear in the case of the motion of a heavy thing to the extent that its heaviness is thought of as the active principle of that motion. And the same holds true, a fortiori, for the motion of the heart and, more clearly, for the motion of an angel who is moving himself [locally].

Further, in the case of certain things that act by immanent action, one finds the condition that the proximate principles of acting and being acted upon, even though they are distinct neither in subject nor in their whole being, differ at least in some entity that includes the principle of acting but not the principle of being acted upon as such. However, this condition derives neither (i) from the general notion of an agent as such, as is obvious from what has been said, nor even (ii) from the general notion of an immanent action as such, since there is no reason why an immanent action as such should require such distinctness. Indeed, an action will in a certain sense be all the more immanent if it remains in altogether the same principle by which it is proximately elicited. Therefore, the condition in question derives from the fact that an action of the type in question is effected through a sort of assimilation and so requires, over and above the intrinsic faculty, a proper principle of such assimilation.

And so it is that in the case of an immanent action that does not require this sort of assimilation and that does not, by virtue of any other special condition, require a principle that assists it in the manner /649b/ of an efficient cause, but instead requires only something that concurs within the genus of an end or within the genus of an extrinsic form—with respect to such an action, I repeat, it is not necessary for the principle of acting to be distinct even in a part of its being from the principle of receiving. And this, of course, is the mode of acting that fully befits the will, both because of the will's freedom and also because of the general notion of an appetitive faculty, according to which such a faculty can be moved toward an object proposed to it solely by means of its own inclination and efficacy.

Now at this point one could contemplate a certain distinctness in the principles of effecting and receiving an appetitive act. For, as I claimed above,[63] it is not only the faculty but also the substantial form that concurs for a vital act as an immediate efficient cause within its own order, whereas it is the faculty alone that seems to concur proximately and immediately in the receiving of the act. However, this sort of distinctness is in fact uncertain, since it may be the case that, by virtue of its inherence, the accident (especially a vital act) affects not only the accidental faculty but also the substance itself. And whatever one says about this on other grounds, the claim in question is not necessitated by the present reason, since in fact there is nothing problematic about its being the case that the same faculty that is the proximate principle of receiving an immanent act should also, through itself as sufficiently constituted in first act, be a sufficient proximate efficient principle of that same act.

55. *Two objections against what has been said.* However, there are certain objections to the last part of this resolution [of the question].

The first and main objection is taken from Aristotle, *Metaphysics* 9, text 2 [1.1046a9–11], where he says that an active power is a principle of transmuting another insofar as it is other; therefore, it is a contradiction that an active power should be an adequate principle of transmuting itself. This is why Aristotle immediately adds that the power to be acted upon is a principle of being passively changed by another insofar as it is other. And in *Metaphysics* 5.12, text 17 [1019a32–b3], he defines an active power and a receptive power in the same way. Therefore, it is by virtue of the precise notions of an agent and a patient that the distinctness between them is required, at least as far as the principles of acting and being acted upon are concerned. This is why, in *On Generation and Corruption* 1.7 [323b18–23], Aristotle deems it absurd that the same thing should be acted upon by itself. And in *Metaphysics* 1.3 [924a21–26] he posits the following principle: "That which is the subject does not effect change within itself." And he claims that it was this principle that prompted the discovery that the efficient cause is distinct from the material cause.

A second, commonplace objection is that one and the same thing cannot bear a real relation to itself, whereas an efficient cause bears a real relation to its effect; therefore, one and the same thing cannot in reality act /650a/ upon itself. This is confirmed as follows: If a thing is simultaneously both in

63. See *DM* 18. 5. 2–4.

active potency and in receptive potency according to the same thing, then why is it not *always* changing itself? It is confirmed, second, by the fact that the agent must be proximate to the patient, whereas one and the same thing cannot be proximate to its very self according to the same thing.

56. *The definitions of active and passive powers given by Aristotle are explicated; a relation founded in the action intercedes between the effect and the cause; why active powers sometimes refrain from actual operation.* To the passages from Aristotle[64] one can reply, first, that in those definitions he is talking about a *purely* active power and a *purely* passive power. But, in addition to these, there are certain powers that are simultaneously both active and passive, and the stated doctrine applies to them [only] when they are completely active with respect to their acts.[65]

Hence, second, one might claim that in *Metaphysics* 5 [12.1019a34–35] Aristotle was further clarifying the same point when he said that an active power is a principle of change in another or [in the same thing] insofar as it is other. And in this sense the will, to the extent that it effects its own act, can be said to be a principle of acting upon itself not insofar as it is active but [only] insofar as it is in potency.

However, I think that it is closer to the truth to say that Aristotle was talking about physical transmutations, which are effected through *transeunt* action, as I will show at length below when I talk about potency insofar as it is a species of quality.[66] And it is this same sort of change that Aristotle is talking about in *On Generation and Corruption* 1. For in that place he is discussing the sort of change that leads to generation and corruption. He is talking in the same vein in *Metaphysics* 1, where he explains in general terms how it is evident that in physical generations and changes the material and efficient causes do not merge into one and the same cause.

To the first argument[67] one may reply that a real relation obtains not between the agent and the thing acted upon but rather between the agent and the effect; and in this way, even if some faculty acts upon itself, it nonetheless produces an effect that is distinct from itself and that is such that there can be a real relation between it and the faculty.

To the first confirmation one may reply that if a faculty acts naturally, then the reason why it is not always acting is that it does not always have an

64. See §55 above.

65. I.e., the doctrine applies only when they have fully realized their potentiality with respect to the relevant forms.

66. See DM 43.

67. See the last paragraph of §55 above. There is actually just one argument, accompanied by two confirmations.

applied object, which is required not as a co-efficient cause but rather [as a cause] within another genus of cause—say, a final cause or an extrinsic formal cause. For example, the reason why a fire cannot act in the absence of a combustible thing is not that it requires the combustible thing as a co-efficient cause but rather that it requires it as a material cause. However, if the cause in question is a free cause, then even if all the other things are applied, it is able not to act—and this solely because of its natural perfection.[68]

To the second confirmation one may reply that identity is the highest or most eminent sort of proximity, as long as /650b/ the power to act and the capacity to receive are not absent for some other reason.

68. For more on the nature of a free cause, see *DM* 19. 2.

Section 8

Whether, in Order to Act, an Efficient Cause Must Be Conjoined with or Close to the Thing Acted Upon

1. Aristotle explicitly discusses this question in *Physics* 7.2 [243a31–245b2] with regard to physical motions. However, the question is more universal and indeed properly metaphysical, since it embraces every efficient cause. For this reason, theologians normally discuss it both with regard to God (in *Summa Theologiae* 1, q. 8, and *Sentences* 1, dist. 37) and with regard to angels (in *Summa Theologiae* 1, q. 52, *Sentences* 1, dist. 37, and *Sentences* 2, dist. 2). Here we are treating finite causes, since we will discuss God later on.

The question has to do with *transeunt* actions by which one thing acts upon another. For in the case of immanent actions and also whenever a thing acts on itself *per se* and primarily—that is, according to the same part—it is clear that the agent cannot be distant from the patient. However, when one suppositum acts upon another or when one and the same suppositum acts on one of its parts through another part, then it can be the case either that [the agent and the patient] are immediately next to one another or else that a body or a part of a body or a space is interposed between them.

Now there is no doubt among philosophers that an efficient cause can act on a distant thing through a nearby thing. Rather, the problem is this: When a cause acts proximately and immediately, through the power that it has within itself and not through another power that it diffuses, does it have to be in immediate contact, by its quantity or presence, with the thing on which it is acting, or is it instead able to act immediately on that thing even if it is spatially distant from it?

Conjoined with this problem is a second one: When a cause acts through a nearby thing that is not distant, how does it attain to a distant thing through the mediation of the nearby thing?

THE FIRST POSITION IS LAID OUT AND PROVIDED WITH A FOUNDATION

2. On this issue there are two prominent positions. The first is that (i) an efficient cause is able to act on a distant patient, and so its immediate proximity is not required, but that (ii) it can do this only within a set sphere of activity.

Now there is no doubt that a finite power has a set limit to the space or distance that it can attain to. For, as is clear from experience, a thing acts more forcefully on something nearby than on something distant. So a greater power is required for acting on a distant thing. Therefore, when a power is finite, it also has, by that very fact, a limited sphere [of activity]. On this point everyone agrees. However, the position in question asserts that within this sphere of activity the agent can act /651a/ *immediately* on a distant patient.

This is what Avicenna holds in his own *De Anima*, sec. 4, chap. 4, where he cites Hippocrates on behalf of this same position. So, too, with Alexander of Aphrodisias in *Metaphysics* 1, comment 18; Scotus in *Sentences* 1, dist. 37; and, in the same place, Ockham and Gabriel, as well as Bassolis, Major, and other Scotists. However, Scotus concedes, in the case of physical causes, that they never act on a distant thing by means of a given form or quality without effecting something in a nearby thing by means of another form or quality—though it is not necessary for them to attain to both the nearby thing and the remote thing by means of one and the same form. Later on we will see whether it is consistent for him to say this.[1]

3. *The position in question is given a foundation on the basis of various experiences.* One argues for this position by making an induction over all the types of actions.[2]

First, in the case of substantival generation, the sun generates on the earth various mixed things such as minerals or even those animals that are generated by putrefaction. But this action has to emanate immediately from the sun's substantial form, since the accidents that are diffused through the medium either do not attain to substantival generation or else are not sufficient for it.

4. Second, in the case of the motion of alteration, there seem to be certain things that alter a distant thing without altering any nearby thing.

The first example that is normally adduced has to do with the imagination, which is said to have the power to induce a new quality by altering a distant [bodily] member or other thing—as Avicenna, drawing from Hippocrates, teaches in the place cited above.

The second example has to do with the enchanting eye. For the eye sometimes does harm by altering a distant thing, as experience testifies in the case of the eyes of certain women, and as was also noted by Aristotle, *Problems* 20.34 [926b20–30]; by Alexander, *Problems* 2, no. 50; by Albert, *De Animalibus* 22, chap. 5; and by Marsilius Ficinus, *De Immortalitate Animae* 13, chap. 4. Further, in *Etymologiarum* 12, chap. 4, Isidore affirms that the basilisk kills

---

1. See §§17–19 below.

2. In §§24–48 below Suarez discusses each of the arguments and examples invoked on behalf of the first position from here through §8.

serpents with its breath, destroys human beings with its glance, and wounds flying birds even though they are far away. Quite similar things are recorded by Pliny in *Naturalis Historia* 8, chap. 31, where he attributes the same sort of power to the catoblepas—namely, that it kills a man who looks into its eyes—and, likewise, in chap. 22 he says that the glance of wolves is harmful and takes away a man's voice for a short time.

The third example that can be adduced has to do with the torpedo fish, which paralyzes the hands of fishermen from afar. Further, in *History of Animals* 9.37 [620b19–23], Aristotle says: "The torpedo affects the fishes that it craves with its paralyzing power and in this way captures and feeds on them, and for this purpose it hides itself in the sand and mud"—which is an indication that it does not act through a medium. And in the same place he alludes to /651b/ other similar experiences. Pliny relates the same thing in *Naturalis Historia* 32, chap. 1, where he explicitly says: "The torpedo brings this about at a distance and from afar, even if it is not touched by a staff or a stick."

The fourth example has to do with a certain herb called aproxis, whose root kindles fire from afar, as Pliny notes in *Naturalis Historia* 24, chap. 17, where he relates the same thing about naphtha, a certain kind of pitch (concerning which, see the same Pliny, *Naturalis Historia* 2, chap. 108).

Fifth, it often happens that a distant thing is altered more vehemently than a nearby thing is; therefore, this is an indication that the agent acts immediately on the distant thing through its own power. For it would not be able, by means of a quality that is weak in the medium, to effect a more intense quality in a far-off thing.

The antecedent is obvious from many experiences. For a fire heats the water in a kettle more intensely than it heats the bottom of the kettle; and it makes the oil poured on top of a sheet of papyrus heat up much more vehemently than the papyrus; and it heats a fiber of flax that is a little way off more intensely than it heats the air in between, so much so that it sometimes makes the fiber burst into flames. Again, the sun heats a mirror or the ground more intensely than it heats the air in between. Nor is it surprising that an agent should at times effect something greater in a distant thing than in a nearby thing, if the dispositions of the patients are unequal. This point is itself confirmed by other examples. For the sun illuminates those parts of the air that it reaches through a window or shines on directly more brightly than it illuminates those parts that lie off to the side—that is, along a bent line. Therefore, this is an indication that it illuminates the parts that lie along a direct path not just through the parts of the intervening air but immediately through itself.

The consequence is evident from the fact that in relation to the parts of the intervening air, the other parts of the air are equally close and equally applied, regardless of whether they lie along a direct path from the sun or are only off to the side. Therefore, if the illumination of the remote parts were effected only by the mediation of a nearby part, then remote parts that are equally close to a given nearer part would be illuminated equally, even if they had different exposures with respect to the sun. For that nearer part, taken by itself, acts equally on every part that is close to it.

A similar experience has to do with a hand or other thing that is exposed to the sun or exposed to a fire through, say, an oven door: namely, that it senses a stronger heat when directly exposed to the fire than when placed off to the side, even if it is equally close to the air in between. Therefore, this is an indication that the fire immediately attains to the distant hand if the hand is directly opposite to it and ˙ if ˙ the ˙ medium ˙ is ˙ nonimpeding ˙. Another sign of this is that if something is interposed between them or if the oven door is closed, then the strong sensation of heat that was coming from the fire's action immediately ceases, /652a/ and yet the medium still retains all the heat that it had absorbed. Therefore, this is an indication that the action in question was coming immediately from the fire and not just from the medium.

5. In the third principal category, the experiences adduced have to do with local motion effected by a corporeal mover (I will talk about incorporeal movers below[3]) in various ways: namely, by pushing, pulling, carrying, and twirling.[4]

In the case of pushing the experiences normally adduced have to do with projectiles and with heavy and light bodies, the motions of which are traced back to pushing, as St. Thomas notes in *Physics* 7.2. However, these examples carry no weight [here], since the proximate instrumental principle of such motions exists not only close to the movable thing but even within it, while the relevant sort of pushing either (i) is communicated through generation, concerning which we have already raised the question of whether it requires proximity, or else (ii) is impressed through some sort of quantitative contact.[5] For a corporeal mover cannot by itself immediately push a movable thing

3. See §7 below.

4. These are the four basic types of motion discussed by Aristotle in *Physics* 7.2.

5. Point (i) has to do with the natural motions of heavy and light things, motions that are attributed to the generating thing as to a principal cause, while point (ii) has to do with projectile motion, in which, according to Suarez, a quality (impetus) is imparted to the projectile by the thrower. So (i) raises no new issues not already mentioned in the paragraph on substantival generation in §3, and (ii) deals with a case which, according to everyone, requires quantitative contact.

except by being in contact with it. (This is not the place to explain what it is that is impressed through this contact or what pushing is; Aristotle discusses this in *Physics* 4.8 [215a14–19], in *Physics* 8, last chapter [10.266b27–267a20], and in *On the Heavens* 3.2 [301a1–301b30].)

And from this it is also clear that since twirling involves pushing, it requires the same sort of proximity that pushing requires. As far as carrying is concerned, moreover, it is *per se* evident that it requires contact, since that which is carried is moved *per accidens*, as it were, with the motion˙ of the one who carries it.

Therefore, it is only in the case of pulling that examples are adduced in favor of the position under discussion. The first example is that of the magnet, which pulls a distant piece of iron toward itself. A second possible example is that of amber, which raises chaff upward. A third example, of almost the same kind, that is commonly adduced has to do with the fish called 'the delayer' or 'the ship-holder', which detains a boat that passes by it, as is related by Aristotle in *History of Animals* 2.14 [505b18–22] and by Pliny in *Naturalis Historia* 9, chap. 25.

6. Fourth, an induction is made over the actions of the soul's faculties. For the faculty of imagination, which exists in the brain, immediately moves the appetitive faculty, which exists in the heart; and the appetitive faculty immediately moves the hands or the feet. Similarly, an external sensory faculty seems to impress a species on the imagination by its own act. For it seems improbable that it effects something throughout the entire medium. For example, it seems improbable that if the foot becomes warm, a species of heat ascends by a continuous path up to the head, where the imagination or common sensory faculty resides.

7. Fifth, the same sort of induction is made over the [*transeunt*] actions of the intelligences. Such actions can be of only two types: namely, (i) local motion, whether of a body /652b/ or of another spirit, or (ii) speech, which occurs only with respect to another intellectual thing.

Now this latter action can, according to everyone's opinion, be effected with respect to a distant thing, as is clear from St. Thomas in *Summa Theologiae* 1, q. 89, a. 7 and 8, and q. 107, a. 4, and in the disputed question *De Anima*, a. 18, ad 13. And it does not occur without efficient causality. For through this action the angel to whom the other is speaking receives the power to apprehend something that he was unable to apprehend beforehand: namely, the free thought of the other angel. But it seems that he cannot receive this new power without something new coming to exist in him—especially in light of the fact that he not only receives the power but is also stimulated to listen, and that he cannot be stimulated unless something is impressed on him. This is why, in *Summa Theologiae* 1, q. 107, a. 1, ad 3, St.

Thomas says: "Just as a sensory faculty is moved by what is sensible, so the intellect is moved by what is intelligible; therefore, just as a sensory faculty is stimulated by a sensible sign, so too it is through an intelligible power that the mind of an angel can be stimulated to pay attention." Therefore, just as a sensible sign does not stimulate a sensory faculty except by impressing something on it, so, too, angelic speech does not stimulate the hearer except by impressing something on him—for example, some intelligible species. Thus, in the disputed question *De Anima*, a. 20, ad 11, St. Thomas, in discussing the similar action by which intelligences effect species in a separated soul, says: "Since an action of this sort does not exist in a place, one need not in this case look for a medium that transmits [the action] spatially; rather, in this case the natural ordering [of intelligences] plays the same role that spatial˙ ordering˙ plays˙ among˙ corporeal˙ things˙"—thus indicating that the action in question requires subordination rather than proximity. For in *Summa Theologiae* 1 [q. 107, a. 4], he claimed, using similar words and a similar argument, that an angel's speech is not impeded by distance.

As for the other action of an intelligence—namely, local motion—the claim that it, too, can be effected with respect to a distant thing is made in *Sentences* 1, dist. 37, by Durandus, Gabriel, Ockham, Scotus, and Hervaeus Natalis. And this claim seems probable on the same basis: namely, that an angel does not of himself have a place and does not act in the manner of a corporeal thing but instead acts through intellect and will; therefore, his efficacy requires power on the part of the will rather than proximity of position. For, given that he effects the motion simply by willing it, why should he have to be substantivally present to the place where he wills to effect the motion?

8. *An argument for the position under discussion.* Sixth, one can formulate [an a priori] argument as follows.

A creature's active power has a certain quantity of perfection (as I will put it). Therefore, it is improbable that this power should be limited in such a way that it cannot act immediately through itself except on a point or on an indivisible surface. Therefore, it can act immediately within some quantified or quantifiable distance. /653a/ Therefore, it can attain immediately to even the distant parts of that sphere or space.

This argument is clarified and confirmed, first, as follows. When fire heats water by means of the air in between, it has only the last surface of the nearby air immediately proximate to itself. Therefore, according to the opposite position, it will act immediately through itself only on that surface, and, in fact, it will act on it immediately by means of just the heat that it has on its own last surface; and by the mediation of that surface it will act on the part that is immediately next [to the surface]; and by the mediation of a closer part it will act on a more remote part, by dividing the action, as it were, through all the proportional nearby and remote parts. But this manner of acting seems *per se* incredible and involves nontrivial difficulties.

The first difficulty stems from the [main] argument made above. For it seems unreasonable to restrict every power of acting, no matter how great it might be, to the precise spatial location at which it is acting, or at most to the last surface that touches it. For a power to act can be greater or smaller, and its efficacy consists not only in its effect but also in its manner of acting and in its having a greater sphere of activity.

Likewise, I take the surface of the air that is proximate to the fire, and I ask what it acts upon immediately. The reply will be that it acts immediately on the part next to it. Thus, since there is no part that is adequately next to it according to itself as a whole,[6] it will have to be granted that (i) [the surface in question] does not have an immediate subject—whether an indivisible one or one with a definite magnitude—on the whole of which it acts immediately, but that instead (ii) it acts immediately only on the 'next' thing, vaguely conceived, as it were. But this seems absurd: namely, that a determinate action, at the very instant at which it is effected by, say, the heat or light existing in the surface in question, does not have a determinate subject in which it is effected *per se* and immediately.

Likewise, this manner of acting—that is, acting on these parts through those parts, enumerating, as it were, all the parts of the same ratio[7]—seems scarcely intelligible, given that these parts are infinitely many, especially in the case of an action that does not spread successively through the subject but is instead effected, in the manner of a unit, all at once and in an instant.

9. Second, and lastly, the argument in question is confirmed by the fact that from the principle [asserted by the opposite position] it follows that, speaking *per se*, natural agents either do not have a sphere of activity or else they have no limit to their sphere of activity.

The inference is evident from the fact that if one considers what it is that such agents can act on immediately and *per se,* then they have no sphere [of activity] but only the surface that is next to them. On the other hand, if one considers everything that they can act on mediately—that is, by attaining

6. Even if one grants, as Suarez does, that there are indivisible entities such as surfaces, there will be no 'next' part of the air beyond its surface, because the air is infinitely divisible. Thus, for any extended part one designates as being next to the surface, a proper part of that part is still closer to the surface; and for any indivisible entity (i.e., internal surface) one designates as being next to the outermost surface, there will be another such indivisible entity that is still closer to that surface.

7. For an explanation of the phrase 'parts of the same ratio', see *DM* 18. 7, n. 26.

to a remote thing through a nearby thing—then there is no set sphere or limit /653b/ of that action, since for any designated limit to which the action might intrinsically attain, it will be possible for the action to proceed further through that limit, because some power to act exists in the limit. Therefore, that power will effect something in the thing next to it.

(I said "speaking *per se*", since it could happen that, because of the patient's resistance, the power reaches the limit in question so weakened that it is unable, either of itself or [insofar as it is acting] in the power of the most distant agent [in the series], to overcome the resistance of the next part. But this is something accidental that results from the resistance. Yet that point, too, is extremely difficult to explain: namely, how a quality received in the medium is able, in the power of a remote agent, to overcome the resistance of the part that is next to it—a resistance that the quality cannot overcome *per se* and by its own power—given the assumption that the remote agent effects nothing *per se* and immediately in that remote resisting part but instead acts on it only through the power received in the closer part. But more on this later.[8] For now the argument is being put forward on the assumption that we are speaking *per se* and prescinding from the medium's resistance.)

And so it follows [from the opposite position] that the sun is able in an instant to illuminate the air *ad infinitum*—which is plainly false, since it now illuminates a close part of the air more than a remote part, as is evident in the case of a lamp. Therefore, if the action spreads out too far, it will finally come to an end. What's more, one will not be able to give an explanation for this effect. For why does the lamp illuminate a remote part [of the air] less than a nearby part if it does not illuminate the remote part *per se* and immediately, in just the way that it illuminates the nearby part? By contrast, on the basis of the assumption [that it illuminates both of them *per se* and immediately] one can give an excellent explanation. For since the power is finite, it does not overcome a nearby thing and a distant thing equally, and so greater proximity makes for greater perfection in the action. On the other hand, if it acts on the remote part only through the nearby part, then it will communicate to the remote part the entire intensity of the quality that it communicates to the nearby part. For that quality effects what is similar to itself; and the remote part is capable of receiving the quality and is immediately next to the nearby part. Therefore, this is an indication that the action is not effected in the way in question, but that instead the agent attains to the whole sphere [of activity] immediately through itself.

8. See §23 below.

THE SECOND POSITION IS LAID
OUT AND EXPLAINED

10. The second main position is that in the case of every efficient cause it is a necessary condition for its acting that it be next to and nondistant from the thing that it primarily and immediately acts upon, so that if (i) both of them—namely, the agent and the patient—are quanta, then they are contiguous, and the action begins from the last surface at which they touch one another, and thus contact of power always presupposes quantitative contact; whereas if (ii) /654a/ the agent is spiritual, then it is proximate [to the patient] in an analogous way according to a substantival presence.

This is Aristotle's position in *Physics* 7.2 [243a31–245b2] and in *On Generation and Corruption* 1.6 [322b24–323a35]. And it is defended by St. Thomas in many places, especially *Summa Theologiae* 1, q. 8, a. 1, and *Contra Gentes* 3, chap. 68; by Cajetan, Ferrariensis, and other Thomists in those same places; by Capreolus in *Sentences* 1, dist. 37, and by Durandus in *Sentences* 1, dist. 37, q. 1. Richard suggests the same position in *Sentences* 1, dist. 37, a. 2, q. 1, while other authors presuppose it when they infer God's presence from his operation. The same position is held by Albert in *Physics* 7, tract 1, chap. 4, as well as by the Commentator, by Alexander of Aphrodisias, and, generally, by others in the same place. The holy Fathers—and, indeed, Sacred Scripture—endorse this position as well when they suggest that even in the case of God himself, his immediate presence is correctly inferred from his immediate operation. (We will discuss this argument at length later on when we deal with God's immensity.[9])

Aristotle proves this position not by any [a priori] argument but rather by induction alone and by appeal to experience of a sort that is fairly obvious to the senses—so far as such a proof is possible on the basis of frequent sensible effects. Still, the induction will be a complete one if we show that a natural action never happens to be effected in any other way, or at least that it cannot be proved by any experience that a natural action is effected in any other way. But this claim will become evident in the reply to the objections.[10] And so the argument reaches its conclusion as follows: The mode of acting that is common to all natural agents is based upon some intrinsic and natural necessity; but this mode of acting is through immediate contact and proximity; therefore, this is an indication that this sort of proximity is a necessary condition for any natural agent's being able to act.

11. *Various arguments for the necessity of the agent's presence to the patient.*

9. See *DM* 30. 7.
10. See §§ 24–28 below.

Now an [a priori] argument for this necessity has been proposed by certain authors. Just as a thing cannot pass from one place to another except by passing through a medium, so too an agent's action cannot be immediately transmitted to a distant thing unless it first attains to the medium and then through the medium—continuously, as it were—arrives at the distant thing.

However, to my mind, this argument is unconvincing. For it is not the case that numerically the same action passes through the medium to a distant thing, in the way that numerically the same body passes through the medium to a far-off place. Hence, it is correct to say, not that the action passes to the far-off place but rather that the action is educed by the agent's power from the potency of a distant subject. The above argument or analogy does not disclose any contradiction in this.

12. Others derive an argument from a finite agent's limitedness: namely, that it is because of the weakness of a finite agent's power that it requires the presence of the patient in order to act.

This argument can be confirmed as follows. If an agent were able to act [immediately] on a distant thing, then for the same reason it would be able to act /654b/ over any distance whatsoever. For if it requires no action on the medium, then what difference does it make whether the patient is more distant or less distant?

First of all, however, the authors of this position—and especially St. Thomas—do not limit it to finite agents but also require the relevant condition in the case of God. Therefore, this condition does not stem from the limitedness of [the agent's] power.

Second, what seems to arise from the limitedness of [the agent's] power is at most a limited sphere [of activity]. But why should one infer, from just any limitedness of power whatsoever, such a strong limitation to a *proximate and immediate* patient, given that the notion of an efficient cause does not as such require this restriction—especially in light of the fact that, as we were arguing above, not all powers are equally limited?

For this same reason, the inference made in the confirmation does not appear convincing. For those who deny that the highest degree of proximity is absolutely necessary for an action do not deny that this sort of proximity is expedient for an agent's acting in the most excellent way. In fact, they even assert that such proximity is necessary in order for an agent to act with all its power and to the full extent of its power. And this, they think, is the reason why, all else being equal, natural agents act uniformly nonuniformly through space.[11]

11. See §9 above, where the proponents of the first position claimed that their view could better handle the fact that a natural agent has a limited sphere of activity and that its

And so nothing of what was inferred in the above confirmation follows. For it is clear without doubt from the terms themselves that it takes more power to overcome a distant thing than to overcome a proximate one. And, by the same token, it will take more power to overcome a more distant thing than to overcome a less distant one—just as it takes more power to throw a rock to a more distant place.

That is why in the place cited above, ad 8, Capreolus claims that the explanation for [the necessary condition in question] should be sought not in any imperfection in the power of the agent and the recipient or in the degree of that power but rather in the fact that the agent is in some sense the act of the patient itself and that the patient is in some sense in potency with respect to the agent. But act and potency demand by their very nature to be nondistant [from one another]—in order, that is, to be able to exercise the roles of act and of potency between themselves.

Even though this argument will not suffice to convince a presumptuous mind, nonetheless, given sufficient experience of the matter, it seems to me to get closer to, and to suggest more completely, the proper explanation for the requirement in question.

But in order for us to clarify this point more fully and to defend Aristotle's position, we must explain the various modes of proximity and distance, as well as the various modes of acting on a distant thing through a nearby thing.

THE RESOLUTION OF THE QUESTION

13. *Various modes of distance and proximity of an agent with respect to a patient.* Thus, one should note that a patient can be distant from an agent by virtue of the fact that a completely vacuous space lies between them. Even though this /655a/ does not occur naturally, an agent and a patient could nonetheless be conceived of in this way; and one has to explain, with respect to them [as so conceived], how they would in that case be related as regards action. For this would contribute in no small way to explicating the matter at hand.

Second, a patient can be distant from an agent in such a way that the space

---

effects decrease in intensity as one moves away from the agent along a continuous spatial path. The phrase 'uniformly nonuniformly' (*uniformiter difformiter*) is used to characterize an agent's activity in cases where the effect decreases in intensity continuously as one moves farther away from the agent. The successive effects are 'nonuniform' because they differ from one another in intensity; they are 'uniformly nonuniform' because they are ordered in a continuous series from the most intense to the least intense as one moves away from the agent.

interposed between them is not vacuous but is instead filled with a sort of body that nothing can act on.

Third, it is conceivable that an agent should effect something in the medium but not through the same power—as, for instance, if it effected something in the air by means of light but effected something on the earth by means of its substantial form.

Fourth, and finally, it is conceivable that a distant patient should be joined to an agent by a medium which is such that the agent acts on it, too, and through the same power. This can be conceived of as occurring in various ways.[12]

First, it might happen that the remote agent introduces the action immediately only into the patient that is next to it, and that through the quality impressed on that patient the action is effected in a remote patient—with the result that the action, insofar as it exists in the remote patient, is related *per se* and immediately only to the power or quality that was impressed on the part next [to the agent], whereas it is related to the agent itself only remotely and only insofar as the agent gives or conserves the power in question.

Second, it is conceivable that, through the mediation of the power conferred on the part next to it, the agent should act on the remote thing by having a simultaneous and actual influence, along with that power, on the remote part, in such a way that (i) [the agent] is able to attain to the remote thing through that power and not without it and that (ii) in the absence of the actual influence of the agent itself, the power in question, even if it is conserved there, is likewise not by itself sufficient for the action that is effected in the remote part.

Third, it is conceivable that the agent's action should necessarily be diffused to the remote thing through the proximate thing, not because it is necessary for the proximate part of the patient to effect something in the remote part but solely because of a necessity of order (as I will call it)—a necessity that can arise either (i) on the part of the agent, which by its nature determines for itself this mode of acting through an uninterrupted line, as it were, or else (ii) on the part of the patient, which, when applied to a natural agent, must necessarily be acted upon in a nearby part before being acted upon in a remote part.[13]

12. In order to understand Suarez's position in all its subtlety as presented below, it is important to keep firmly in mind the three distinct modes of acting delineated here.

13. Note that on this alternative no part of the medium acts on anything. So, given the assumption that the distant patient is joined to the agent by a medium which is acted on by the agent, the three possible modes of action are these: (1) the agent acts just on the part of the medium next to it, and the other parts of the medium by themselves carry the action

First Assertion

14. *There is no action on a distant thing when a vacuum is interposed; the reason why all bodies abhor a vacuum.* First of all, then, one should assert that an efficient cause can effect nothing in a distant patient if a vacuous space is interposed [between them]. This assertion is generally accepted, so that even the authors of the first position do not seem to deny it. For although Scotus countenances certain actions that generate something from a distant matter, he nonetheless claims that [in such cases] some other action has to be diffused through the medium—even though /655b/ he concedes this only with respect to natural agents.

Now the assertion cannot be proved by appeal to positive experience (as I will call it), since a vacuum of this sort never actually exists between bodies. However, it can be proved by appeal to negative experience (as I will call it) and to the providence of nature as a whole or, rather, to the providence of the author of nature, who established things in such a way and instilled in them an inclination or motion of such a kind that they completely shun a vacuum even if they have to desert their proper places. The principal reason for this seems to have been in order that certain bodies might be able to exercise their actions through other bodies and in order that distant bodies might, through intervening bodies, partake of the influence of other bodies and especially of the celestial bodies. This is clearly suggested by Aristotle in *Meteorology* 1, text 1 [339a20–22], where he says: "It is necessary for it (read: the inferior world) to be proximate in some way (read: through the intervening elements) to the highest revolutions of the heavens, so that all of its power might be established and governed from there."

Nor will it be satisfactory to reply that it was not because of an absolute necessity but only for the sake of greater fittingness and utility that nature abhorred a vacuum and procured the contiguity of bodies in so solicitous a manner. This is so because such a great solicitude on the part of nature suggests a greater necessity and also because, if it were true that natural agents are able to attain to a distant thing in the absence of a medium, then it would oftentimes be more useful, as far as action is concerned, not to have a real medium interposed. For in keeping with what will be said in a moment, the sphere [of activity] would be more unobstructed, and the agent's power would be less occupied with it.

15. The assertion is proved, second, by another sort of experience, which, even though it is taken from something completely contrary [to a vacuum], seems nonetheless to have the very same foundation. If the space interposed

_____

to the distant patient; (2) the agent acts along with the parts of the medium on the distant agent; (3) the agent alone acts on the distant patient after having acted on the parts of the medium.

between an agent and a patient is filled with a body that interrupts the agent's action, then the agent's action on the distant patient is completely thwarted, even if the patient is otherwise situated within the agent's sphere of activity. Therefore, for the same reason, if the medium were completely vacuous, the agent's action would not be able to pass through it to the distant patient, since the action would be no less interrupted by a vacuum than by a plenum of the sort in question.

One might reply that the reason why this sort of interposed body impedes action on further bodies is not that it interrupts the agent's action but rather that the agent's entire power is occupied (as I will put it) with that body—from which it follows that the agent's sphere [of activity] is terminated there. For [those who make this reply] claim that the sphere of activity is not always the same—that is, is not always of the same magnitude or distance—but instead [varies] according to the susceptibility or resistance of the medium. For it can happen that a body which is a foot in diameter /656a/ offers more resistance because of its density than does a large but rarified body, and thus in itself limits and terminates the agent's sphere [of activity].

However, even though this reply may have an appearance of truth when the interposed body genuinely plays the role of a patient that the agent's power is occupied with overcoming and (as I will put it) penetrating, nonetheless, when the interposed body is altogether insusceptible to such an action, so that the agent's power is in no way applied to it in accord with that action, how is that body able to inhibit the action or to keep the agent from acting on further bodies? An example is the illuminating sun, whose action is impeded when an opaque body is interposed in a window—a body which is not susceptible to light and which resists its own illumination not positively but negatively through an insusceptibility, in just the way that a vacuum, too, is said to resist [an agent], though on different principles. Thus, the sun's illuminative power is not occupied, as it were, with striving and acting with respect to the body in question; instead, it simply does not act on that body, just as it does not act on a vacuum, either. Therefore, the body does not impede the action's transit (as I will put it) in any way other than by interrupting its continuation and its line or radius, as it were. Therefore, an equivalent impediment arises from an interposed vacuum.

This sort of experience seems to me to be very effective for proving the posited thesis. However, later on we will discuss an [a priori] argument for that thesis.

Second Assertion

16. *That which cannot effect anything in a filled medium will not effect anything on a distant patient.* On this basis it is asserted, second, that when a patient is separated from an agent by a real interposed medium, then the agent can-

not effect anything in the distant patient unless it can also act on the whole medium.

This is manifestly obvious from what has been said. For, first of all, if the interposed medium were not necessary for sustaining and, as it were, transmitting the agent's action, then that medium would be related altogether *per accidens* to the action. Thus, it would make no difference whether the medium were a real medium or a vacuum.

Second, the assertion is proved from the experience of a dense interposed body, which impedes the further transit of the action only because it is not susceptible to the agent's action.

Third, the principle we inferred from the case of a vacuum was simply that an agent's action is interrupted in a vacuum and that this is sufficient to impede the action. But this same sort of interruption occurs when the medium that is proximate to the agent is not susceptible to its action or influence. Therefore, etc.

And so we see that the sun illuminates the earth only /656b/ by illuminating all the intervening bodies. And if at a given time the moon, which the sun cannot penetrate with its light, is interposed [between the sun and the earth], then the action of illuminating does not reach the earth.

Third Assertion

17. *The power by which the agent acts on the distant thing must also be the power by which it acts on the medium.* I assert, third, that in order for an agent to effect something in a distant patient, it is not sufficient that it act on the medium through a different power—that is, through a wholly distinct action; instead, it is necessary that (i) it begin to act on the medium next to it through a power that is the same as, or subordinated to, the power by which it acts on the distant thing and that (ii) it diffuse the action—that is, the influence— through the whole medium all the way to the distant thing.

This assertion is directly contrary to Scotus and the others. Nonetheless, it is proved from what was said above. For in order for an agent to act on a distant thing, it must antecedently (either in time or in nature[14]) act on the nearby medium and continuously on the whole medium; therefore, it is

14. Suarez probably has in mind here the view, held by many ancient and medieval thinkers, that light is propagated instantaneously by the sun. In such a case the action on a nearby patient would not be temporally antecedent to the action on the distant patient. Nonetheless, Suarez argues, the former action would at least be prior in nature to the latter; i.e., the distant thing is acted on only because the nearby thing is being acted on, but not conversely. Perhaps this is shown by the fact that the action would be interrupted by the imposition of an impervious body between the nearby and distant patients.

necessary for this uninterrupted action to flow forth in some way from one and the same power on the part of the agent.

The consequence is evident from the fact that if there are two powers and two actions emanating from them, then formally there are two agents there, even if they are materially one by reason of a single suppositum or subject. Therefore, in order to be able to act on a distant thing through a given power, it is not sufficient to act on a nearby thing through another power.

This latter consequence is proved by the fact that these [two] actions are related to one another only concomitantly, and it cannot be claimed that the one is continued by the other or that it is effected without interruption. For example, even though a fire can act both through its heat and through its dryness, nonetheless, in order for it to act through its heat on a distant patient, it is not sufficient for it to act through its dryness on the nearby medium. For this is *per accidens* as far as the heat's action as such is concerned. Therefore, it must act through its heat on the nearby medium, since this is *per se* necessary for the continuation of the action.

In fact, even though it could happen that the one power's action is necessary, on the part of the patient, in order for the other power's action to be able to attain to that patient—as, for example, if the action of, and the disposition for, the dryness were necessary for the heat's action—nonetheless, the fact that the one power acted antecedently to dispose the distant thing would not be sufficient for the other power to act immediately on that distant thing without effecting anything in a nearby thing. For the disposition in question is merely a material disposition; and it makes no difference that it proceeds from another power existing concomitantly within the same subject, since the first power's action is not thereby being effected continuously through the whole medium. But it was proved in the two previous assertions that this is what is necessary for the action. /657a/

18. *Things to be noted.* There are, however, two things that must be noted here. One is that when we say that the action has to emanate from a single power, this does not mean that the power in question must be a single form or a single entity. Rather, it means that the power must be the adequate principle of a single action, even if it comprises more than one form—regardless of whether these forms are acting as equals or are subordinated [the one to the other].[15]

The other thing to be noted is that when we say that the action on the

---

15. Suppose two distinct fires produce an effect that neither could produce by itself; in that case they would be 'acting as equals' (*aequaliter agentes*). By contrast, in §31 below Suarez claims that the sun produces heat by the mediation of light; hence, in this case the two forms—viz., heat and light—are such that the former is subordinated to the latter.

nearby and remote things has to be a single action by continuation, as it were, this should not be taken to mean a strict and physical continuation of the sort that occurs in an act of illumination when the medium is continuous; rather, it is sufficient that there be a continuation according to some sort of subordination and causality. For when an agent is operating out to a given distance, it is not necessary that it should produce the same type of quality over that whole distance, since it is possible for it to effect one quality in a nearby body and a different quality in a remote body. For example, the sun produces only light in the celestial bodies that are below it, but it produces heat as well as light in the air all the way to the earth; and within the earth, because of the latter's depth, it produces only heat and not light, and then it effects other forms by means of this heat. One can see the same thing in the case of other astronomical bodies; they have their own proper modes of influence, which they diffuse all the way to the bowels of the earth, and yet they do not effect the same thing in all the intervening bodies. Instead, they effect in each body, according to its susceptibility, that which is proportionate to that body's disposition. So, then, since the qualities or termini produced in the diverse bodies are themselves distinct, the efficient causality cannot be diffused in the manner of a single continuous action. Still, it is necessary that (i) it be through the quality produced in the nearby body that [the agent] produces the other quality in the remote body and, similarly, that (ii) it be through this latter quality that [the agent] produces the quality in the more remote body. And this is the sense in which the action is said to be continued according to subordination and causality. For since, as was shown in the previous assertions, the action has to be effected continuously in the manner of a single action, and since a continuation in the same species of action or quality is not required, it is necessary for this to happen through the emanation of one action from another. Otherwise, the action effected in the distant thing will have no connection with the action effected in the nearby thing, but instead these actions will be related to one another wholly *per accidens*; the argument adduced in the third assertion proves that this cannot be the case.

Fourth Assertion

19. *Some agents can act immediately on an extended space and on all its parts.* Fourth, I assert, that even though (i) it is necessary for /657b/ an efficient cause to be close to and nondistant from the patient on which it first acts, nonetheless, (ii) it is not certain that it always acts on a distant thing through the nearby thing as through an instrument or power of acting, but instead it is probable that it sometimes acts immediately through its own proper power on the whole of some patient; and similarly, (iii) when it does act

on a distant thing through a nearby thing as through an instrument, it is necessary not that it act through that nearby thing as through an instrument that is separated in its causing but instead that it act through it as through a conjoined instrument, in such a way that by one and the same action the agent itself has an immediate influence along with the power that is diffused through the medium.[16]

The first part [of this assertion] is Aristotle's thesis itself, as well as the common position that we have been defending. And apart from Aristotle's inductive argument, this thesis is manifestly proved by the preceding assertions and by their proofs, which showed that an agent cannot diffuse its action all the way to a distant thing except in the manner of a single uninterrupted action. Therefore, it is necessary for the action to begin from an altogether close and nondistant patient; otherwise, it would start out as interrupted from the beginning.

And this claim is highly confirmed by certain experiences through which we see that the agent intends *per se* only an action on a remote thing and yet does not exercise that action except through a medium, even though the action, insofar as it is effected in the medium, would be completely useless were it not for the fact that it serves as that through which the action is transmitted to the distant patient. For example, a visible object does not diffuse its [sensible] species to the eye except through a medium. There are several evident indications of this. One involves a mirror, in which a reflection of those species is effected; a reflection is also effected in water. Such a reflection could not be effected if the species were not multiplied all the way to the bodies in question. Another indication is that the species are either distorted or transmitted properly according to the disposition of the medium. Likewise, there is the point mentioned above: namely, that if for any reason some part of the medium is insusceptible to the species, then the action is prevented from reaching the eye. Still, this action of the [sensible] species is, *per se* and by the intention of nature, wholly ordered to the eye, since it is in the eye alone that the species can have the effect for which they were instituted. Therefore, the action of the species in the medium would be useless were it not necessary in order for the action to be able to reach the distant eye through it. This, then, is an indication that it is because of this necessity that such an action is effected [in the medium]. And the same judgment must be brought to bear on every similar action, even in cases where it is not supported by such evident experiences.

20. *An inference from all that has been said.* From all this I infer that an efficient

16. Part (i) of this assertion is defended in the rest of §19 and in §20, part (ii) in §§21–22, and part (iii) in §23.

cause's natural mode of acting is, as it were, through a continuous line /658a/ of action from what is nearby to what is distant. And given the experiences just adduced, the fact that by its very nature the [efficient] cause determines for itself this mode of acting should serve as a sufficient reason for the above assertion, even in the absence of other reasons.

For we often make judgments in this way about the natures of things on the basis of what we experience, even if we are not able to supply any deeper explanation for the natural condition in question. For example, an object of sight multiplies species only along straight lines, whereas an object of hearing does this along bent lines too and through any sort of opening whatsoever, as is obvious from experience—from which we correctly infer that this is the natural mode of acting for such objects. A sufficient explanation for this is that such a property follows upon the nature of the two sensory organs. Still, we are trying to provide an explanation for this nature when we say that sound is a certain quality that follows upon motion and imitates the latter's nature, and that this is why it is able to proceed along any path whatsoever; color·, on the other hand, acts in a more tranquil and subtle manner, and this is why it diffuses species only along a straight path.

So, too, in the present context, if we wish to provide an explanation for, or conjecture about, the relevant natural condition of agents, then we should certainly not disdain the explanation of Capreolus's that was mentioned above.[17] For every act needs to be joined with a potency in order to exercise its causality on it; therefore, just as an intimate union [with matter] is required for a form's act, so too an efficient cause's act requires at least a lack of distance—not because of any imperfection but rather because of the perfection included in the notion of an act or actualization. Alternatively, if [the condition in question] must be traced back to some imperfection, then that imperfection must lie on the side of the effect, which, because it is dependent on its cause, must be joined to that cause and nondistant from it in order to be able to emanate from it—just as a stream must be joined with its source in order to emanate from it.

On this point, too, one can discern a certain latitude according to the varying perfections of the causes. For corporeal causes and effects cannot be immediately present to, or nondistant from, one another according to themselves as wholes, and so, failing this, they are proximate to one another according to their outermost [parts]. On the other hand, created spiritual entities are conjoined with, or present to, their effects or patients according to themselves as wholes—though it is not always necessary for them to be intimately present to the whole patient and to all its parts, since it is possible

17. See §12 above.

for them to be present to one part and to act on the whole through that part, in the way in which an intelligence that moves a celestial body is thought to exist in the eastern part. By contrast, wherever God acts, he is present as a whole and in the whole patient, not only because of his immensity but also because of the perfection of his acting, as we will see below /658b/ in its own place.[18]

Now I said that the mode of acting in question—namely, by initiating the action from a nondistant patient, is connatural to an efficient cause, since we are not at present discussing whether God can supernaturally change this mode of acting. We do believe, however, that [such a change] is not repugnant to divine instruments, even if it cannot be connatural to any created agent. I have discussed this in *Summa Theologiae* 3, vol. 1, disp. 31, sec. 7.

21. And from this one can see further that from the necessary proximity between the agent and the patient it does not immediately follow that it is also necessary for the agent to act on the remote part of the medium through the nearby part as through an instrument. For it will be sufficient if it acts through it as through a medium that is necessary for the continuation of the action—that is, for the action's being effected without interruption. For no more than this is proved by either the experiences or the arguments adduced so far.

Thus, when an action through a medium varies in its proximate and remote patients according to various qualities and termini on the part of the action, then, as we were saying before,[19] it indeed seems necessary for the power diffused in the nearby medium to be an instrument for acting on the remote patient, since otherwise there would no *per se* continuation or subordination of the actions with respect to one another. On the other hand, when an action as a whole is of the same species in both the proximate and remote parts of the medium, then it does not seem necessary *per se*, at least by reason of the necessary proximity between agent and patient, that the nearby part should be an instrument for acting on the remote part. For, as we have shown, an action of this sort has of itself the continuity and integrity required by [an efficient] cause's natural mode of operating.

I said "at least by reason of the necessary proximity" because if a quality diffused through the medium effects what is similar to itself, then in reality it follows that insofar as the quality exists in the nearby part, it can be of assistance in acting on the remote part—either in the manner of an instrument or in the manner of a partial agent. However, [such assistance] can be, as it were, *per accidens* and merely concomitant with the primary agent's action.

18. See *DM* 30. 7.
19. See §18 above.

22. For this reason, if it happened that a quality diffused through a medium did not effect what is similar to itself, then it would be necessary only that the nearby part be a medium with respect to the action and not that it be an instrument. Now I am not certain whether this ever happens; however, I do not see any contradiction that arises by reason of the necessary condition for acting that we are now discussing: namely, proximity. And there may be an example in the case of the object of vision. For it seems that the species are multiplied through the medium all the way to the sensory organ, in such a way that a species received in a diaphanous medium does not effect /659a/ anything similar to itself. This seems to be proved by the fact that the object cannot effect its species beyond a certain distance—which would not happen if a species received in the medium effected what is similar to itself. This argument was touched upon in the foundations for the first position; and in the replies [to the arguments] we will investigate how compelling it is.[20]

Another possible example has to do with the impetus impressed on a projected rock. For the one who throws the rock has contact with only one part of it, and yet the impetus is received not just in that part but in the whole projected body. Nor does the part of the impetus impressed on that part effect another similar impetus in a nearby part—both because (i) an impulse does not effect another impulse but instead effects only local motion, just as heaviness does not effect heaviness but instead effects local motion, and also because (ii) an impulse is impressed only through forceful contact, whereas one part [of a rock] cannot have contact of this sort with another part that is continuous with it. Therefore, it seems probable that, by means of contact with just one part of the movable thing, the thrower impresses the impetus immediately on the whole of that thing and on each of its parts.

But whatever the truth may be with regard to the specific examples, still, generally speaking, it is not the case that in order to preserve the axiom about the necessary proximity of the agent and the first patient, we are forced to say that it is necessary for there to be efficient causality by one part of the patient on another. However, when we discuss the arguments for the first position, we will investigate the question of whether there are any experiences or arguments which adequately prove that this sort of efficient causality does not always intervene or that it is not *per se* necessary.[21]

23. *The parts of the medium that are closer to the agent do not act on the remote parts without the help of the agent.* Finally, the last part of the [fourth] assertion also depends partially on this point. For even if the nearby parts of the medium do act on the remote parts, experience seems to prove that

20. See §9 above and the reply in §§47–48 below.
21. See §31 below.

they do not act merely by the power received in them and that they do not altogether lack the primary agent's actual influence. Otherwise, the same nearby medium would not have so strong an action on some parts and [yet] so weak an action on other parts that are equally close to it but unequally applied with respect to the primary agent.

This will have to be examined more closely in the replies to the arguments. For the present we are claiming merely that it does not follow from the proximity under discussion, or from the necessary condition for acting that we are now dealing with, that the agent acts on a distant part [of the medium] only through the power received in a nearby part as through an instrument that is separated, as it were, in its causing—that is, as an instrument that acts through itself alone without the principal agent's actual influence. This is so because (i) it is not necessary for the patient to be absolutely proximate to an agent from which /659b/ an action emanates continuously and without interruption and also because (ii) in a case like this the [principal] agent and the power received in the medium constitute, as it were, a single integral agent that touches the other [remote] part and so can act on that part through all its power.

I will clarify this by an analogy. When a fire heats the air that is close to it, it does not act on the air merely through the heat that it has on the last surface at which it touches the air or through any single nearby part of itself, no matter how much quantity that part is imagined to have—which can only be determined purely arbitrarily. Therefore, the fire acts immediately through the entire heat that it has within itself and within all its parts (I am assuming that all these parts lie within its sphere of activity); and yet not all the parts of the fire that acts are immediately proximate to the air that is acted upon. However, since all of them together constitute a single agent that is contiguous at its outermost boundary with the air being acted on, this is sufficient for its being the case that all those parts influence the patient immediately in the manner of a single integral agent. And the same would hold true if two fires, discontinuous from one another, were applied to the same part of a patient, so that a single action emanated from the two of them together as from a single integral agent.

Therefore, one can likewise see that the agent and the patient's first part, insofar as the latter is already the subject of its own quality, act together in the manner of a single agent and have an influence further into the patient— regardless of whether they are concurring as two partial agents or as a principal agent and an instrumental agent. But all these things will be further elucidated in the replies to the first position.[22]

22. See §§47–48 below.

REPLIES TO THE ARGUMENTS FOR
THE FIRST POSITION

On Substantival Generation

24. *Which agent is present in substantival generation.* As for the first sort of experience,[23] which has to do with substantival generation, the common reply is that the accidents that are present nearby effect the substantival generation in the power of the substantial form, even though the latter is off at a distance.

This reply faces the problem discussed in section 2ˑ. For even if the accidents can be instruments for effecting a substance, they nonetheless cannot be sufficient principles if they are separated with respect to their causality. And so if a far distant substantial form cannot in any way have an actual influence along with the accidental power in generating a substance, then it cannot through the accidents alone be a sufficient principle for such a generation.

For this reason one can plausibly claim that (i) the instrumental power diffused by a celestial body all the way to the earth's place, where substantival generation occurs, acts not as a separated power but as a power that is conjoined in causality /660a/ and that (ii) the celestial body's form has an actual influence along with that power as long as the effect does not otherwise surpass the celestial body's form in perfection. Nor does it follow from this that the celestial body acts immediately on a distant thing. For it does not act except insofar as it is conjoined to its power as diffused through the medium all the way to the distant patient.

You will object as follows: The [substantial] form of a celestial body and that same body's accidental power are diverse powers of acting, whereas the whole alteration that preceded [the generation] was effected by the celestial body by means of the accidental power alone. Therefore, this power is not sufficient for the celestial˙ body's˙ being able afterwards to have an influence on the substantival generation of another by means of its own substantial form.

I reply that it is not the case that the celestial body's [substantial] form and its accidental power are two powers that are conjoined only concomitantly and, as it were, *per accidens*. Rather, they are ordered to one another as a principal principle and an instrumental principal. And so even though the substantial form attains to the generation that is effected in the distant place, it does not act on the distant thing formally and properly, since it is conjoined to it by the mediation of its [accidental] power.

23. See §3 above.

This will be clearer and more straightforward if one holds that a celestial body's substantial form concurs *per se* as a principal principle not only in the eduction of the substantial form but also in the previous alteration; we claimed above that this is probable.[24] However, if someone should find this claim disagreeable, then it will have to be asserted that in generations of this sort the celestial body concurs only instrumentally through an accidental power which is diffused through the medium, and that it is assisted by some higher agent in bringing these generations to completion.

On the Alteration of the Body by the Imagination

25. As for the second argument, which concerns alteration,[25] I deny what is assumed: namely, that certain causes alter a distant thing without altering a nearby thing.

To the first example, which has to do with the imagination, one may reply that we are talking about either (i) the body of the very animal to which the faculty of imagination belongs or (ii) the body of another [animal].

If we are talking about another's body, then I deny that one [animal's] faculty of imagination has the power to alter another animal's body. No credible experience has been adduced thus far that proves this claim. Nor is the claim probable on the basis of any argument. For an act of the imagination is an immanent act, and there is no way for it to have the power to alter another animal's body naturally.

If, on the other hand, we are talking about the body belonging to the very animal that is operating by means of the faculty of imagination, then one should reply that the imagination moves the body only by the mediation of the sentient appetite, upon whose motion the humors and vital spirits by which the body is altered are stimulated. However, the motion /660b/ of the [sentient] appetite via the imagination is not an alteration but a certain vital affection. (I will explain this below.[26]) Now since the [sentient] appetite resides in the heart, which is a principle of motion both for the animal itself and for the vital spirits, it can readily stimulate a motion or alteration of the sort in question—not by effecting anything immediately in a distant thing but rather by the mediation of the nearby parts. However, in this sort of motion a special factor intervenes as well, since [the motion] is effected by a natural sympathy among the faculties that are rooted in the same soul, as will be explained below.[27] (I discuss this at greater length in *On the Soul* and

24. See *DM* 18. 2. 36–37.

25. See §4 above. The examples brought up in §4 will be discussed from now to §33.

26. See §§39–40 below.

27. See §40 below.

Summa Theologiae 1–2, q. 22, and it is touched on by St. Thomas in *De Veritate*, q. 26, a. 6, ad 11.[28])

On Enchantment

26. As for the second example, there are those who reject this power of enchantment. However, there is no reason why we should deny an experience that is attested to by both philosophers and physicians and that is generally accepted by common sense. Therefore, we grant that enchantment can occur naturally.

The way in which this enchantment works is clarified by St. Thomas in *Summa Theologiae* 1, q. 117, a. 3, ad 2, and in *Contra Gentes* 3, chap. 103. First of all, one should claim that the enchantment is not effected by the very act of seeing as by a principle through which an alteration is effected in another. For, as we were saying before in the case of an act of the imagination, an immanent act does not act *per se* on anything.

Second, one should claim that the alteration in question is effected by some toxic quality which is such that either (i) it exists in the eye or else (ii) it exists in the body's internal disposition, constitution, or humors and is communicated by the vital spirits, which are moved by the combination of the imagination and the mind's attentiveness and which reach the eyes. At that point what happens, in turn, is that the nearby air is infected by these spirits and that the alteration reaches out to a fixed distance and in this way does harm to another, even though the latter is some distance away. And perhaps it sometimes happens that the infected spirits themselves are emitted all the way to the person on whom [the agent's] gaze is directly fixed and so harm him more readily and more vehemently. Also, in the places cited above, Aristotle suggests that an enchantment is sometimes effected by an exhalation that has been contaminated and then transmitted all the way to the other person.

These, then, are the ways in which an enchantment can be effected naturally without any immediate action on a distant thing. I leave to one side something noted by St. Thomas in the places cited above: namely, that this kind of harm sometimes occurs because of the malice of demons, who cooperate in inflicting damage of this sort in accord with some secret pact. St. Thomas also notes that this type of alteration occurs more easily in infants and children, since they are more readily susceptible to various sorts of external impressions because of their delicate bodies. /661a/ Several examples of this kind of action can be found in Pliny, *Naturalis Historia* 7, chap. 2, and 33, chap. 10; in Abulensis, *Paradoxes* 4, chap. 16; and in Richard, *Quodlibeta* 3,

28. This reference to the *De Veritate* seems to be inaccurate.

q. 12. The same should be said, *mutatis mutandis*, about any sort of harm that poisonous animals inflict by means of either their glance or their scent.

Likewise, the same thing holds for the third example, the one having to do with the torpedo fish, about which Pliny says explicitly that "it affects the members of one's body by a certain odor and exhalation." It does not, then, act immediately on a distant thing; instead, it acts either by altering the medium or else by exhaling some noxious vapor. And the fact that it is said to hide itself in the sand or in the mud is irrelevant, since we do not have to interpret this to mean that it hides itself so completely in the earth that it does not leave its head or mouth uncovered in order to do harm.

Whether an Agent Can Act on a Distant Thing More Intensely than on a Nearby Thing

27. *Why the bottom of a kettle is cooler than the boiling water above it.* As for the fourth and fifth examples, one has to explain (i) whether and how it is possible for an agent to act more forcefully on a distant thing than on the nearby medium and (ii) whether in such a case this more forceful alteration is effected immediately in the distant thing without the cooperation of the medium.

In *Problems* 24.5 [936a31–35] and 24.8 [936b13–21], Aristotle notes that when water is heated in a vessel, at the beginning of the process of heating, while the water is still cold, the bottom of the vessel feels hotter, whereas afterwards, when the water has now become so hot that it scorches the hand, the bottom of the vessel is more temperate, so that it can be held by the hand. He explains this as follows. At the beginning of the action, when the water is cold, all the heat is confined to the bottom of the vessel and is not allowed to rise. But when the water then becomes hotter, the heat is allowed to exhale, as it were, and to rise, and this is why the bottom of the kettle becomes temperate. (It is for this reason, he says in the same place, that baths are hotter in the winter than in the summer.) And so what happens as a result is that as the action proceeds and as the water becomes very hot and is rarified by the process of heating, the hotter parts rise upward, while the denser and colder parts sink downward and cling to the bottom of the vessel and moderate it. And this is why it is judged to be less hot.

However, what is meant by the word 'heat' here is not just the quality or accident of heat, since this quality cannot rise or sink or be prevented from rising except by reason of its subject. Instead, what must be meant are the hot vapors or exhalations that are induced by the fire's action. Nor can this rising or sinking be explained merely metaphorically. That is, [one cannot claim] that the heat is said to be prevented /661b/ from rising only in the sense that the patient inhibits the process of heating from progressing further toward a higher part of the water. For on this interpretation, the explanation would carry no weight: namely, that the bottom of the kettle is hotter at the beginning because at that time the heat is being prevented from rising any further. For the fact that the action proceeds further does not at all by itself prevent the lower part from remaining equally hot—as is *per se* evident. Therefore, the explanation must be understood to be referring properly to certain hot vapors, which, as long as they are being detained because of a very cold, dense nearby body, bring it about that the heat of the lowest part is greater and is sensed more vehemently. But when, after the nearby body has been heated and consequently rarified, they are permitted to rise, less heat is sensed in that lowest part—especially given the fact that in the pores where those vapors were located before, their place is taken by the colder parts of the water, which, since they are heavier, naturally sink more. And it is because of this that the heat is more moderate as well.

28. Now on the basis of the Philosopher's explanation, thus expounded, it is easy to see that what one learns from the experience in question is that an agent acts more intensely on a distant˙ thing than on a nearby˙ thing only by transmitting some proportionate agent that proximately effects that intensity. For in the cited example, when the bottom of the vessel becomes extremely hot at the beginning of the action, this is due to the nearby fire and to the fiery or hot vapors contained in the very pores of the bottom of the vessel, whereas when, as the action proceeds, the higher parts of the water seem hotter, this is due not only to the remote fire (even though its action is of great assistance) but also to the hotter vapors that are rising and penetrating the water itself and thus heating it more forcefully. In addition, when the water itself begins to get hotter near the bottom of the vessel, it immediately rises as it is made lighter, whereas the heavier and colder water that was higher up sinks. And this is how it comes to be that the more distant part of the water is hotter—not because it is heated more when it is thus distant but rather because it was previously close [to the fire] and was made hotter there. But it is never the case that the part of the water that is close to the bottom of the vessel produces heat more forcefully than does the vessel itself (or its bottom) through which the action is transmitted—except perhaps at the end of the action, when the water is now completely overcome [by the fire], with the result that all of it is evaporated and corrupted. This stems from the fact that by reason of its moistness, it is more readily converted into air or into some impure mixture. Likewise, since the water is less dense than the vessel, the rising hot vapors or exhalations penetrate it more easily. /662a/ It also helps if there is some air circulating around. And so the whole entire action, as well as its intensity, is always effected through some medium.

29. *Why the papyrus is less hot than the oil on it; why the flaxen fiber is ignited even though the air that lies between it and the fire is not ignited.* One should deal in the same way with the similar experiences adduced above, including the one that has to do with the oil which seems to be hotter than the papyrus by the mediation of which it is heated. For as soon as the oil begins to be heated, it, too, is readily rarified and penetrated by the rising vapors, and it, too, rises immediately as it is made lighter and more subtle, whereas the larger and moister parts descend. And so the same thing happens in this example that happened in the above example.

Now as far as the flaxen fiber is concerned, the claim that it is ignited by the mediation of the interposed air even though the air itself is not ignited is not quite so obvious from experience. For perhaps the air is indeed antecedently ignited, even though this is not perceived by the senses as it is in the case of the fiber because of the latter's density. And the same can be said about the example concerning the root of the herb aproxis and the one concerning the pitch naphtha.

30. However, one could reply in a different way by admitting what is assumed in the argument: namely, that the remote matter is ignited without the nearby matter's being ignited, and by claiming that this stems from the disposition of the matter without its being the case that the fire acts more intensely on the remote thing than on the nearby thing.

This will be easy to explain if we presuppose that it is not necessary for the highest degree of heat to exist antecedently in a given matter in order for it to be ignited but that instead it is sufficient that there be an antecedent heat intensified to a degree such that (i) the form of a flaxen fiber, for instance, cannot be conserved along with it and that (ii) if enough dryness is adjoined to it, then it adequately disposes [the fiber] for the introduction of the form of fire. In this way, then, it can happen that the air in between is hot to degree seven and yet, because of a lack of dryness, is not ignited, whereas as soon as the fiber reaches that same degree, it is ignited. And so the action of the fire that produced the heat was never more intense in the remote matter than in the nearby matter but had a different effect [in the remote matter] because of a different disposition on the part of the patient.

You will object that at the very instant at which the [remote] matter is ignited, it is already hot to degree eight.[29]

I reply that even if this is so (for it is not certain as far as the first instant is concerned), it stems not only from the distant fire's action but also, via a natural resulting, from the form [of fire] that has now been engendered.

---

29. I.e., by the very fact that the subject bursts into flame at a given instant, it is hotter than it was immediately before that instant.

This resulting is effected instantaneously if there is no further resistance on the part of the matter. (This is what should be claimed to occur if we assume that all the accidents perish in a case of corruption.[30] If, however, /662b/ some degree of a contrary quality can remain, then a temporal interval will intervene—albeit a very brief and imperceptible one, given that the resistance is minimal and the activity great.)

But what about the action of the substantial form itself, an action that is effected in the distant matter and not in the medium?[31] The common reply is that this action is effected via a natural resulting, assuming that there is a sufficient disposition [on the part of the matter], or else that it is effected in the power of the substance by the accidental dispositions that exist there.[32] We, however, must reply, in keeping with the first assertion, that (i) the fire's form is able to attain to that place along with its power and to have a simultaneous influence on the eduction of the form or else that (ii) if the substantial form does not have this power, then the concurrence must be supplied by some higher cause—so that when it happens that a given thing is heated through a motion to such a degree that it is ignited, the introduction of that form is attributed to some universal cause.

31. *Another way of explaining the adduced experiences.* There is another possible way of replying to the experiences in question: namely, by admitting that it is possible for an agent to effect a quality more intensely in a distant patient than in a nearby patient, yet not by acting immediately on the distant thing but instead by acting through the medium. This mode of action can be conceived of in two ways.

First, it can be conceived of in such a way that the medium does not serve as an instrumental or partial co-efficient cause for acting on the remote thing, at least as regards the degree of the greater intensity that is effected in the remote part. However, this way of talking is not sufficiently consonant with the opinion we are defending. For it clearly follows that the action [on the distant thing], insofar as its intensity is of a given degree, is effected by the remote agent immediately in the distant patient without any action on the medium or through the medium. For the weak action that is effected in the nearby medium does not contribute *per se* to, and is not continuous with, the action on the distant thing—except, at most, up to the same degree of intensity. For example, if the whole medium and the distant patient were antecedently hot to degree four without any action on the part of the fire,

30. For background here, see *DM* 18. 2, n. 25.

31. The action in question is the generation of a new fire, which takes place in the distant patient but not, *ex hypothesi*, in the medium.

32. For more on what it is for an accident to produce an effect 'in the power of the substance', see *DM* 17. 2. 19.

and if afterwards the fire, when applied, immediately intensified the heat in the distant patient but not in the medium, then without a doubt that action would be immediately on the distant thing. Therefore, the same will hold even if the heat of degree four is effected by that same fire.

Alternatively, one can claim that the agent, through the power impressed on the medium, effects a more intense quality in the remote patient than in the medium itself because of a greater susceptibility or disposition and /663a/ a lesser resistance [on the part of the patient].

Now the power in question can sometimes be a quality of a different type from the other quality that is being intensified, and in such a case the matter presents no difficulty. For instance, in the example posited above concerning the mirror and the air that are heated by the sun, because the action of heating is effected by the mediation of light, it can happen that by the mediation of the air's light (as by the mediation of a power of acting) the sun heats the distant mirror or some other similar thing more forcefully than it heats the nearby air, and this because of a greater susceptibility and disposition on the part of the patient. And I see no contradiction in this. For just as a cause that acts through a diffused power can have an effect on a remote thing that it does not have on a nearby thing—as everyone concedes, and St. Thomas explicitly so in *Sentences* 2, dist. 15, q. 1, a. 2, ad 6, as well as the Commentator in *Physics* 9 and *On the Heavens* 2, comment 34—so, too, a fortiori, it can alter a remote part more intensely than a nearby one.

Alternatively, and lastly, one can conceive of this as happening by means of a quality of the same type—as, for example, when the sun, by means of the weakly illuminated air, illuminates a mirror more intensely, so that the light of the air in between, though weak in itself, concurs, insofar as it is conjoined to the first agent (whether as an instrumental or a partial cause), in effecting the light in the mirror, even to a degree of intensity greater [than its own]. Such a mode of acting is more difficult to countenance, since it assumes that a weak quality, at least insofar as it is conjoined to a prior agent, is able to concur in producing a quality of the same type to a degree of intensity which is unequal to its own and exceeds its own. The question of whether this can possibly happen will be examined in the next section, where we will have more to say about the example of the mirror and about the mirror's reflective action.[33]

Why an Agent Acts More Efficaciously along a Straight Line
32. As for the other experiences adduced in the confirmation of that second argument,[34] I reply that the second part of the last assertion is persuasive to a

---

33. See *DM* 18. 9. 33–38.
34. As noted above, these examples are found in §4.

sufficient degree of plausibility.[35] Nor has any other feasible reply or way out occurred to me. For I do not see why the presence of the sun along a straight line with respect to a given remote part of the air should be conducive to a greater illumination of that part except because the sun itself simultaneously has an influence, together with the air that is closer to it, on that [part], whereas it is not able to have such an influence on another part of the air that is positioned off to the side of, say, a window and not along a straight line, even though this latter part might be equally close to the medium in question.

Perhaps someone will claim that the light received in the medium acts in the power of the sun on the part of the air that is directly opposite the sun along a straight line, /663b/ whereas it acts only by its own power on the other part that lies off to the side, and that this is why it illuminates the former part more than the latter.

But this claim is wholly gratuitous and arbitrary, and it is impossible to discern what realities underlie these words or what the distinction in question consists in, given the assumption that the sun itself does not have an actual *per se* influence on either of the two parts. For, given this assumption, what is it to act "in the power of another" if not to act as a power that is diffused by that other and that takes its place? But the power that is diffused in the medium is one and the same power. Therefore, it acts in place of the sun, and as a power diffused by the sun, on *every* part of the medium. Therefore, it acts in the power of the sun [on every part] equally. Nor is it possible to explain what difference the sun's situational position or presence (as I will call it) makes, so that because of it [the diffused power] might be said to act in the power of the sun on the one part and not on the other—unless the sun itself has a greater *per se* influence by reason of being applied in the way in question.

33. I confirm and clarify this, lastly, as follows. When an accident acts in the power of another without the actual influence of that other, if such an accident were conserved in the absence of the other thing in whose power it is said to act, it would still be able to have the very same action. This is obvious in the case of a heaviness or an impetus that effects motion in the power of the thing that generates [the heaviness] or impresses [the impetus]. And the same holds for the heat that exists in water, if that heat is said to

---

35. The relevant part of the fourth assertion reads as follows: "When it does act on a distant thing through a nearby thing as through an instrument, it is necessary . . . that it act through it as through a conjoined instrument, in such a way that by one and the same action the agent itself has an immediate influence." See Suarez's defense of this claim in §23 above.

produce heat in the power of a fire. Indeed, those who claim that a maximal heat effects the form of [a new] fire in the power of [a preexisting] fire—in the above sense, that is, without any other actual influence on the part of the [preexisting fire]—claim as a result that the heat as separated from the fire and the heat as conjoined to the fire are equally able to effect the form of another fire in the power of [that preexisting] fire.

And so, as regards the case under discussion, if the light received in the part of the air closer to the sun produces light in another part [of the air] in the power of the sun according to the sense in question, then if this light were conserved in the one part after the sun had been removed from the medium, it would illuminate in the very same way the same part [of the air] that it now illuminates. But the consequent is plainly false, both because (i) if it were not false, then the light would even now [when the sun is present] illuminate equally the part of the air that is close to itself but does not lie directly opposite the sun, since the sun is now in fact no more absent from this part, or absent from it in any other way, than it would be absent from that other part mentioned above if it were completely removed, and also because (ii) in the case of fire and heat the opposite is obvious from experience, as was noted in that same confirming argument we are now discussing.[36]

Therefore, one must claim, it seems that (i) the sun has an actual influence along with the nearby part of the medium in the illumination of the part that is directly opposite it, whereas it is not able to have an equal influence on the other part that lies off to the side, even if the latter is equally close to the air that serves as the medium, and that (ii) this is why those parts are not equally illuminated or equally heated. /664a/

On the Action of the Magnet and Similar Actions

34. As for the third argument,[37] which concerns local motion, the primary and principal experimental evidence has to do with the magnet. In *Physics* 7.2, q. 1, the Conimbricenses bring together in an erudite manner many considerations regarding the magnet, as well as regarding several of the other experiences we are discussing here.

Briefly, however, as far as the present issue is concerned, we will grant that an attraction is effected by the magnet as by an efficient cause. For in *Quaestiones Naturales* 2, chap. 3, Alexander [of Aphrodisias] concluded that iron is attracted by a magnet only as by an end and that it moves itself toward the magnet by an intrinsic and innate power as if by a natural heaviness. However, this claim is rejected by Albert, *Metaphysics* 2, tract 3, chap. 6; by St.

36. See the last paragraph of §4 above.
37. See §5 above.

Thomas, *Physics* 8, lect. 3, text 10; and by Galen, *De Facultatibus Naturalibus* 3, last chapter.

It is rejected, first of all, because a natural motion is effected by an intrinsic power from any distance whatsoever, as is obvious in the case of earth and fire, whereas iron tends toward a magnet not from any distance whatsoever but [only] from a set and definite distance. Therefore, it does not tend toward it but instead is drawn toward it.

Second, iron is moved toward a magnet only when [the iron and the magnet] stand in an appropriate ratio of quantity to one another. For a large mass of iron is not attracted by a small magnet. Therefore, [the iron's movement] is due to an action which does not follow when there is a relation of less inequality [between the agent's quantity and the patient's quantity].

Third, it is said to be obvious from experience that if a magnet is smeared with goat's blood or with garlic juice or onion juice, then it cannot attract iron. Therefore, this is because its attractive power is thereby weakened.

35. One should add further that the magnet impresses on the iron a certain quality, productive of motion, by which it draws it to itself. This is what all the authors teach. For just as the projection [of a body] is effected by means of an impressed quality, so too with attraction. The difference, however, is that the impulse is impressed [on the projectile] by means of immediate quantitative contact, whereas the attractive quality in question is not. The reason for this is that [these two qualities] were instituted by nature for the sake of contrary effects. For by means of an impulse the movable thing is separated from the mover, which touches it, whereas by means of an attraction the movable thing is drawn toward the mover until such time as it comes into contact with it.

Further, this attraction on the part of the magnet is such that it not only draws the iron to itself *per se* but also communicates a participation in its power to the iron itself. For an attracted piece of iron draws another piece of iron to itself, and that one attracts still another, so that they form a chain, as it were, in the way Augustine reports in *De Civitate Dei* 22, chap. 4, and as we ourselves have also experienced at times. This, then, is a clear indication that the magnet impresses on the iron /664b/ a quality that has the power both to move the iron itself and also to effect another similar quality by which this iron likewise attracts iron to itself.

36. Lastly, by way of reply to the argument under discussion, we should add that the magnet impresses this quality on the iron only through a medium—more specifically, by altering the medium all the way up to the iron. For even though this alteration of the medium is not perceived through sensory experience, nonetheless, since it can be readily effected, we infer on

the basis of other experiences and arguments that an efficient cause's natural mode of acting is preserved in this sort of alteration too.

Nor does the fact that the medium itself is not drawn toward the magnet constitute an objection, since it is not necessary for a quality that is diffused through a medium to have the same effect in the medium that it has in the distant patient. For, as was explained above,[38] because of different dispositions on the part of the patients it can happen that a power diffused through a medium effects in a distant body a new quality (or an intensity of a quality) that it does not effect in the medium itself. So, too, in the case under discussion it can happen either that (i) the quality diffused through the medium is not of the same type as the quality impressed on the iron itself or else that (ii) even if it is in itself of the same type, it does not have the same attractive effect in the medium that it has in the iron, and this because of the iron's aptness or disposition.

37. The only possible problem is another sort of experiential evidence on the basis of which it is clear that the magnet alters the iron even when a dense medium is interposed between them—as is also perceived through sensory experience and as Augustine reports in the place cited above, where he says that if the iron is placed on top of silver and the magnet is placed underneath them, then the iron moves with the motion of the magnet "by a rapid back-and-forth motion as one jiggles the magnet, even though the silver in the middle is not being acted upon at all." For it seems unlikely that the magnet can alter and penetrate the whole of so dense a medium.

Still, when Augustine says "even though the silver is not being acted upon at all," he clearly means the sort of reception of an action that can be sensed in the way that the iron's motion and shaking are. However, Augustine says nothing here about invisible alterations. Nor is it very hard to believe that a magnet might penetrate an interposed body with its action of alteration, given either that the body is porous, as a piece of wood is, or that it has little thickness, as was perhaps the case with the silver mentioned by Augustine— just as celestial influences, too, penetrate even the most dense bodies and over a great distance because of their great power of acting. For the magnet's power is thought to be a sort of participation in a celestial property, as St. Thomas says in *De Veritate*, q. 5, a. 10, ad 5, /665a/ and in the disputed question *De Anima*, a. 1. Perhaps it can also happen that the [magnet's action], even if it does not penetrate the whole of the dense body, reaches the iron along a continuous path by means of the surrounding air.

One should also make the same judgment about the amber that raises

38. See §§30–31 above.

chaff upwards. And the same holds for quicksilver, which attracts particles of gold, and for any other similar thing, or for a medicinal root or herb that has the power to attract or even to expel something.

38. *The delayer fish that detains a boat.* Now as far as the ship-holder's action of detaining is concerned, even though this is in other respects a remarkable effect of nature—for it is extremely difficult to explain by what power so small an animal can retard so forceful a mass—nonetheless, in the present context it presents no difficulty at all, since Pliny explicitly says that "[the ship-holder], with no exertion of its own, does not do this by pulling or in any way other than by adhering." Therefore, it does not produce any effect in a distant thing.

Now the question of what [the ship-holder] impresses on the boat in order to detain it is discussed at length by Scaliger in *Contra Cardanum*, exer. 218, and, in reply to him, by the Conimbricenses in *Physics* 7, chap. 2, q. 1, a. 5. My own view is that the matter is an extremely mysterious one that has to be traced back to some power of a higher type which has a force of such a nature and magnitude for resisting the boat's impulse that it cannot be weakened by that impulse. However, I am not certain whether the animal does this by impressing on the ship some quality that weakens the force of the ship's impetus or whether it does it merely by adhering through a power that is innate to itself, in the way that a man keeps a suitably-sized rock from falling or, finally, whether this fish has so great a power to hold itself in position and, as it were, adhere to its place that it cannot be dragged away or dislodged even by what is impelling the boat. But in whichever of these ways the effect is brought about, there is no doubt that it stems from a remarkable and mysterious power, perhaps with the aid of some special and connatural celestial influence. Indeed, at the end of *Hexameron* 4, chap. 10, Ambrose, following Basil in *Hexameron*, homily 7, remarks that it is "by the Creator's good pleasure and power that so small an animal has received such great strength."

On the Action of the Imagination and Similar Actions

39. The ones who work at refuting the fourth argument[39] are those who believe that a cognition existing in the imagination concurs as an efficient cause, by means of its own proper physical influence, with respect to an act of the appetitive faculty.

Hence, there are some who locate both of these faculties together, either in the brain or in the heart, so that they might be close to one another and be able to act on one another—even though the more correct teaching has it

---

39. See §6 above.

that the imagination exists in the brain and that the appetitive faculty exists in the heart, /665b/ as will have to be proved at more length in another place.

Others claim that certain (I know not what) qualities are diffused from the brain by an act of the imagination all the way to the heart, in order that they might affect the appetitive faculty. But this looks fictitious. For the qualities in question are not the species of the object or of the imagination's act itself; such species would be useless, since the appetitive faculty cannot make use of species. Nor can they be qualities of a sort which, as it were, transfer the imagination's cognition of an object to the appetitive faculty. For the appetitive faculty itself never perceives such a cognition. Nor can one faculty's cognition be made manifest, either formally or objectively, to another faculty except by means of another species or by means of a self-cognition.

Finally, there are others who, convinced by this last argument, claim that a cognitive act existing in the brain has an influence on the appetitive faculty by an immediate action through proper efficient causality. And they do not deem this problematic, given that these two faculties are conjoined in the same soul, which is the principal principle of the action in question. For just as a principal power is able to cooperate with its instrumental power even if the latter is diffused to a distant place, so too, conversely, an instrumental power is able to cooperate with a principal power even in a distant place if the principal power itself has been diffused to that place—as long as there is, in that very same part where the action occurs, another instrument that is more proper to and proportioned to the action in question.

Given the first fundamental assumption posited above,[40] this reply is less implausible than the others, and in the case of God's instruments it is usually added that they are able to attain immediately to a distant thing because the principal power is present there. However, absolutely speaking (whatever the case might be with regard to miraculous actions), the reply is not satisfactory, since it already allows for an efficient causality—on the part of some form or quality, that is, act—which leaps to a distant thing by a jump, as it were, without a continuous action through the medium.

40. And so we ourselves will avoid these difficulties straightforwardly by denying that a cognition concurs as an active cause with respect to an act of the appetitive faculty. Instead, it concurs only as a condition that represents an object and is such that, once it is posited, the appetitive faculty effects its own act by virtue of the natural sympathy between the faculties in question.

The fact that these faculties are rooted in the same soul fits in very nicely with this. For it is the soul (or the suppositum through the mediation of the

40. The fundamental assumption alluded to here is that the imagination acts as an efficient cause on the appetitive faculty. In §40 Suarez argues against this assumption.

soul) which operates as the principal cause and makes use of those faculties. And so when [the soul] perceives an object appropriate to itself through
the one faculty, it desires that object through the other faculty—not, to be
sure, because it acts through the one faculty on the other but rather because through the one faculty it is stimulated by an object to operate through
the other faculty, where the stimulation takes place not through a genuine
change stemming from an efficient cause /666a/ but instead through a metaphorical change which stems from a final cause and which thus requires a
proximity of life, as I will put it, and not a proximity of place.

And the same thing should be said, *mutatis mutandis*, about the appetitive faculty and the moving faculty. For even though one could claim that
every motion begins from the heart and proceeds by means of the [animal]
spirits and nerves to the part in which the motion appears or is exercised,
nonetheless, as far as the present point is concerned, the application of the
moving faculty by the appetitive faculty takes place not through a proper
and physical action of the one faculty on the other but rather through the
subordination of the faculties within the same soul. It is in this way, too, that
the intellect and the senses are applied to their operations by the will and
the appetitive faculty—a point discussed at length by philosophers in *On the
Soul* and by theologians in *Summa Theologiae* 1–2.

However, in the case of the efficient causality of the sensible species within
the internal senses by the mediation of the external senses, there is another
and far different explanation. For in this case there is a real and proper efficient causality that has to be effected through a medium—in the way in
which visual species are said to extend from the eyes to the common sense
via the optic nerve. For this action on the part of such species is not properly
a vital or immanent action but is instead an action that proceeds from without by means of those instruments. And so it is properly diffused through a
medium in the way that other natural actions are.

On the Action of a Spiritual Entity on a Body

41. Thus far we have been talking about corporeal agents and patients in
relation to one another. The fifth argument,[41] however, is about the action of
spiritual entities on bodies and among themselves.

As regards the first part, the one concerning the action of spirits on bodies,
one should claim, speaking consistently with what has gone before, that an
intelligence's immediate proximity to a body is necessary in order for him to
be able to move the body locally. (I am assuming that a created spirit cannot

41. See §7 above.

exercise any other sort of action on a body, a point that I will prove below when I discuss intelligences.[42])

Thus, if, in order to move a given body, an angel is able to impress an impetus by means of another body which he does not move locally, then, to be sure, in this sense it is sufficient, in order to move a body locally, that the angel be present to that body by an immediacy of power. However, he must still be present by an immediacy of suppositum to the body on which he first began to impress the power. On the other hand, if (as I deem more probable) an angel is not able to impress this sort of power through the mediation of intermediate bodies that are not themselves moved, then an angel who effects a motion must be proximately present, by an immediacy of suppositum, to the relevant body, which he moves immediately.

It is in this sense that philosophers claim that every intelligence /666b/ that moves a celestial body is present to the sphere that he moves. So, too, theologians claim that the angels are present by suppositum to the bodies which they assume and in which they appear. And as often as Scripture says that an angel moves or carries off a given human being, it indicates that the angel is substantivally present there or that he is moved along with the thing that he moves. This would not be necessary if the angel did not have to be present to the place where he effects motion. And St. Thomas clearly presupposes this point in *Summa Theologiae* 1, q. 52, and q. 53, and q. 55, a. 2, ad 3, and q. 113, a. 6, ad 3, and even more clearly in the places to be cited below.

42. Nor does the fact that a spiritual entity has no position constitute an objection. For [such an entity] has a substantival and real delimited presence in accord with which he must be conjoined to a patient when he acts on that patient. I am not at present discussing the question of whether the operation itself constitutes the nature of this presence (a claim that some theologians seem to make) or whether, conversely, this presence is of itself prior to or even independent of the operation (a claim that many affirm and that seems to me more plausible). Instead, I am asserting that for such an operation it is necessary that there be a substantival presence, which is perhaps what St. Thomas meant by "spiritual contact with a body" in *De Potentia*, q. 6, a. 7, ad 12, and more explicitly in *De Malo*, q. 16, a. 1, ad 15, where he says that an angel does not act immediately on a body that is distant from himself and where he alludes to Damascene's claim that "where an angel is, there he operates." (See Damascene, *De Fide Orthodoxa* 1, chaps. 16 and 17, and *De Fide Orthodoxa* 3, chap. 2.)

42. See *DM* 35. 6.

43. Again, the fact that an angel effects motion through his intellect and will does not constitute an objection, since, as I will explain below in its own place,[43] he does not effect motion through these powers in the sense that he proximately elicits the motion; rather, he effects motion by directing and applying his executive power, which must itself be conjoined to the patient.

This reply is suggested by St. Thomas in the place just cited from the *De Potentia*. For after having posed the objection in argument 12 that that which effects motion must exist together with that which is moved, whereas an angel does not exist together with a body by virtue of his willing that the body be moved, he replies: "The angel's command requires the execution of a power; hence, it is necessary that there be a certain spiritual contact with the body that he moves." And in *Quodlibeta* 6, a. 2, in the reply to the second argument, which was similar [to the above argument], St. Thomas says that an angel's action is rooted in his essence, from which the power and the operation proceed, and that therefore it is necessary that the angel's substance be conjoined in some way to the things that he moves, since that which moves and that which is moved have to exist together.

This is further explained by the fact that if efficacy in effecting motion had to be conceived of by analogy with /667a/ the will's attainment of its own object, then just as an angel's will is able to will a thing indifferently, no matter how close or how distant it is, so too by the efficacy in question he would be able to move bodies, nearby and far-off, from any distance whatsoever. But the consequent is plainly absurd. For given that an angel has a finite power, it is improbable that he can operate equally on a thing no matter how far away it is; rather, he has a limit to his sphere of activity. Therefore, just as the moving faculty is related to its subject differently from the way in which the will is related to its object, so too with the absolute condition of closeness and distance. For a moving faculty has a real and *transeunt* action on the subject that it moves, and so it must be really nondistant from it. But it is different with the will insofar as it is related to an object, since it does not really act on the object and does not really affect it.

On the Action of Spirits on One Another

44. The second part of the argument in question had to do with the action of an angel on another angel or on a separated soul. Such action can include speech as well as local motion.

As far as the local motion is concerned, the explanation is the same as that for the motion of a body; nor do I see any assignable reason for differentiating between them. Thus, in the place just cited, St. Thomas is claiming in general

43. See ibid.

that an angel's substance has to be conjoined to the things he moves. For he did not say "to the *bodies* he moves," but instead "to the *things* he moves," in order to indicate that the teaching was a general one. (I am assuming that he is talking about a case in which one angel moves another by truly and physically effecting motion in that other. For if he is moving the other angel only morally by means of a command, then he requires only the sort of presence that suffices for a command, the explanation of which is the same as that for speech, since a command is effected by means of speech.)

45. *How angels speak with one another.* Now as far as the speech of one angel to another is concerned, we cannot talk about it expressly here, since it is a theological matter and is difficult to explain.

However, speaking in general, one can proceed in either of two ways in this matter. One way is by claiming that the speaking angel does not effect anything in the angel to whom he is speaking. And on this view the reply [to the argument] is straightforward within the present context, since the angel to whom the other is speaking is related to him not in the way that a subject or patient is related to an agent but instead in the way that an object is related to an immanent act. And so it is not surprising that speech should be able to occur immediately with respect to an angel no matter how far away he is.

Now in reply to the relevant argument one must, according to this mode of explanation, claim that the one angel's speaking and the other angel's being stimulated are effected not through a *transeunt* action by the one on the other but rather through /667b/ a certain natural sympathy, as it were. For when the one angel wills that the other perceive his act or his thought, the other immediately makes use of the species that he himself previously had of that act or thought in order to attend to the speaker. Nor do I see any other way in which this position can be explicated.

From this, however, it immediately becomes apparent how serious a problem there is with this position: namely, that faculties rooted in different essences or substances should have a natural sympathy and connection among themselves, along with a concomitance in acting that is not causal and yet is infallible and *per se*—and this in the absence of any action by the one on the other. And this problem is attended by another: If an angel has innate species of another angel's acts, then why is he not able, if he so wills, to intuit those acts as soon as they exist, even if the other angel does not stimulate and, as it were, apply him by his own decree or volition? Again, there is a problem regarding the illumination by which one angel not only speaks to but also teaches another. For even if the natural sympathy in question is granted, it does not seem sufficient for this sort of illumination. Finally, whatever might be true of speech taken in the strict sense, the problem can be extended to every action on the part of an intelligible species. For it is probable that the one angel, insofar as he is an actually intelligible object, is of himself able to impress a species of himself or of his own acts on the other angel if the latter lacks such a species. And whatever is true of angels among themselves redounds even more to the case of a soul that is separated from its body. Therefore, given that such an action is posited, the entire problem remains if that action is not impeded by distance.

46. The second possible mode of explanation is to countenance an intellectual action by one spirit on another through the real effecting˚ of an intelligible species or else through the real effecting˚ of an intensification or modification of such a species. Given this presupposition, there are still two possible replies to the problem at hand.

First, one might exempt this sort of action from the general rule handed down above. St. Thomas intimates this way of replying in the place cited above from the disputed question *De Anima,* as well as in *Quodlibeta,* q. 6, a. 10. The explanation he suggests in both places is that the ordering relations among angels play the same role that position plays among bodies, and so a purely intellectual action depends not on position or on a medium but rather on a natural ordering. And in *Summa Theologiae* 1, q. 107, a. 4, he adds that the intellect's operation abstracts from place and time and that for this reason speech effected through an intellect is not impeded by distance. And this can be confirmed by the fact that it seems incredible that one angel should not be able to speak to another unless they are nondistant from one another in substance and suppositum. For the sort of action in question cannot be transferred through a medium.

However, this position /668a/ seems in fact to be insufficiently consonant with all that has been said, since it severely weakens the principle that has been posited and the whole rationale for that principle. Likewise, even though angels do not have position,[44] they do nonetheless have substantival presence. Thus, no differentiating reason has been given for excluding the necessity of this sort of presence for the action under discussion; [but in the absence of such a reason] a lack of distance between angels would likewise not be necessary in order for one to move or detain another with respect to place. Again, on the explanation in question God would not, by reason of the action by which he creates and illuminates an angel, be intimately present by his essence in that angel; instead, he would be present only by reason of his immensity—which is contrary both to St. Thomas and to the more correct account, as we will see below.[45] The inference is obvious from

44. The reason is that having position presupposes having parts.
45. See *DM* 30. 7.

the fact that God, too, acts on an angel as a spirit acting on a spirit. Therefore, the same explanation holds for him. For these reasons, then, the last way of replying is probable: namely, that nondistance is necessary for this action [of God's] too, as well as for angelic speech, if the latter requires the sort of [genuine] action in question.

I will leave it to others to judge which of these positions is the most probable, absolutely speaking. I assert only that this third position is more consonant with the matter we are now discussing—unless one chooses the first position, whose problems are extremely difficult to resolve.

On the Sphere of Activity

47. The last problem, which is posed in the sixth argument,[46] is quite easily solved by appeal to the second and third parts of the last assertion,[47] which the argument itself plausibly supports without proving anything contrary to the earlier assertions. For even though we grant that each agent has a natural sphere of activity with a determinate magnitude, within which it is able to act *per se* and by its own power and action, it does not follow that it can act immediately on a remote part of that sphere without acting on a nearby part. For it can act only by an uninterrupted action which it initiates in a patient that is close to and nondistant from it and which it diffuses continuously throughout the whole sphere of activity. For every efficient cause whatsoever determines this mode of acting for itself. Nor is it problematic that all causes, even though they are unequal in power, should equally determine for themselves this sort of proximity on the part of the patient. For this condition does not stem just from the limitation or imperfection of the power but instead stems from the nature of [efficient] causality. By contrast, the limitation of the sphere of activity stems from the limitation of the power, and so, other things being equal, corresponding to inequalities in power there will also be unequal spheres of activity.[48]

46. See §§8–9 above.

47. See §19 above. The second and third parts of the fourth assertion read as follows: "It is not certain that [the agent] always acts on a distant thing through the nearby thing as through an instrument or power of acting, but instead it is probable that it sometimes acts immediately through its own proper power on the whole of some patient"; (iii) "When it does act on a distant thing through a nearby thing as through an instrument, it is necessary not that it act through that nearby thing as through an instrument that is separated in its causing but instead that it act through it as through a conjoined instrument, in such a way that by one and the same action the agent itself has an immediate influence along with the power that is diffused through the medium."

48. The qualification "other things being equal" is important here, since Suarez indicates in §48 below that an agent's sphere of activity cannot be defined merely in terms of the

However, the argument in question does seem to prove correctly that natural agents are not limited to acting *per se* and by their own proper power on just the last surface /668b/ of a body that is contiguous with them. Rather, they can act in this way within a set space which they are able to attain to by their own power, even if—whether *per possibile* or *per impossibile*—one part of the medium does not act on another part. This is what we claimed in the final assertion.

48. Still, the argument does not prove—though it apparently intends to prove this as well[49]—the impossibility of the mode of acting whereby the agent acts on a remote part [of the medium] through a nearby part over the whole space, in such a way that no matter how we divide, via parts of the same ratio, the remote part from the nearby part (indeed, even if we divide the proximate surface from all the rest of the magnitude[50]), the effect will always be able to proceed actively to what is remote through what is nearby. For there is no contradiction involved in this mode of acting, since (i) the quality received in the medium or in any part of the medium or in the surface is able to be active; (ii) the patient is likewise apt to receive such a quality; and (iii) the remote part stands to the nearby part in a relation that is appropriate for it to be able to be acted upon by that nearby part. For the action proceeds uniformly nonuniformly from the beginning of the sphere to the end. Therefore, there can be a concurrence of all the elements required in order for it to be the case that the action is always being effected on what is remote through what is nearby. Nor can the infinity of the proportional parts constitute an objection, since there is a similar infinity in the action's progression.

We do not assert, then, that this mode of acting is impossible. Rather, we assert, first of all, that (i) it is not necessary that *every* agent should require the proximity and nondistance of the patient on which it acts primarily[51] and that (ii) it is not sufficient to define the sphere of an agent's *per se* activity

---

quantity and limitation of its power. One must also take account of its characteristic manner of acting on the medium, where the different alternatives are (apparently) those laid out in the last three paragraphs of §13 above.

49. Suarez infers this intention from the first confirmation in §8 above.

50. I.e., Suarez is even willing to grant the objector that the agent acts *by itself alone* only on the proximate surface of the patient.

51. So Suarez is in effect claiming that the agent can be said to act *per se* and primarily on more than just the part of the medium that it *first* acts on, as long as it itself has an influence, along with the qualities impressed on the closer parts of the medium, on the remote parts. Still, its action must always proceed continuously from the nearby parts to the remote parts.

in terms of the quantity and limitation of its own power.[52] Second, we assert that even when an action does proceed in the above manner through a nearby part [of the medium] to a remote part, it is not the case that it is effected by the one part on the other in such a way that the agent does not actually and simultaneously act together with all the parts within its sphere of activity—and so its action on the remote part by means of the nearby part is more efficacious than it would be if the nearby part were acting by itself on the remote part through the power received in it. Both these points were made in the last assertion and seem to be proved sufficiently from everything that was said and contained in that last problem.[53]

52. This qualification is a bit puzzling. As mentioned above in n. 48, he apparently has the differences among modes of action in mind here. Perhaps his thought is that an agent's sphere of activity may depend not only on its own power but also (depending on its mode of activity) on the power that it imparts to the medium.

53. This seems to be a reference to §23 above.

Section 9

Whether, in Order to Act, an Efficient Cause Requires a Patient That Is Dissimilar to It, and in What Proportion

1. *Difficult arguments against the affirmative answer; first argument.*[1] An argument that poses a problem can be taken, first, from what was said in section 7*, where it was shown that sometimes an agent acts on itself, even with respect to the same part.[2] But it is impossible for one and the same thing /669a/ to be dissimilar to itself with respect to the same part. Therefore, it is not necessary that the patient always be dissimilar to the agent.

Perhaps someone will reply that when a thing acts on itself, it always operates through a power that is of a different type from the form that it effects in itself, and so it is dissimilar to itself at the beginning of the action because it does not [yet] have that form formally but instead has it only virtually.[3]

2. *Second argument.* But against this I argue, second, as follows. Sometimes a thing even acts on itself through formally the same quality. For when the heat or coldness of a given body is surrounded by a contrary agent, it is wont to intensify itself and, as it were, brace itself for resisting or subduing that other agent. This is clear in the case of the belly's heat, which for the reason noted is stronger during the winter—as is evident from experience and is attested to by Hippocrates in aphorism 15. The same thing is evident in the case of the air in caves or deep places, which is hotter during the winter.

Nor can this be attributed to the extrinsic agent, since that agent is a contrary and cannot intensify a quality that is opposed to it. Nor, again, can it be attributed to a natural emanation from an intrinsic form. For that sort of emanation is of itself always as great as it is able to be, since it is purely natural; besides, there is no reason why it should increase because of a surrounding contrary—indeed, it should thereby be impeded instead. In addition, the type of action in question occurs not only in natural subjects but also in preternatural subjects, since it is also the case that the water in wells becomes hotter in the winter.[4]

---

1. The reader might want to go first to §5, where the nature of the problem is clarified, and then return to §1.

2. See *DM* 18. 7. 45.

3. See *DM* 18. 7, n. 7, for an explanation of the distinction between the formal and the virtual possession of a quality.

4. Heat is preternatural to water because water by its nature tends to be cold.

3. *Third argument.* Third, there is a similar argument: Sometimes one thing acts on another that is similar to it in quality and intensity, even though the action is effected by means of the same quality. The assumption is evident from the standard example concerning iron, which, even if it does not in itself have the highest degree of heat but instead has, say, only a heat of degree six, intensifies a similar heat in chaff or flax in such a way that it ignites it. And, likewise, the heat and light in a medium are wont to be intensified by the heat or light of a far-off body through reflection, even if that body is not in itself intensively hotter or brighter. For example, when the sun directly heats the atmosphere and the earth, the atmosphere's heat is intensified through reflection from the earth and, similarly, the atmosphere's light is intensified through reflection from a mirror, and so forth—even though neither the heat in the earth nor the light in the mirror could possibly be more intense than the heat and light that exist in the atmosphere because of the sun's action. For they are more distant from the sun than the atmosphere is.

4. *Fourth argument.* Fourth, if the dissimilarity in question were necessary for any reason at all, it would be especially so in order that the agent might surpass the patient in the power to act. But the dissimilarity is not necessary for this reason, /669b/ both because (i) it can happen that this superiority of power stems from some other source—namely, from a greater density or other condition on the part of the subject—and especially because (ii) such an excess [of power] on the part of the agent does not always seem necessary—otherwise, a patient would never be able to react upon its agent. For either the patient is surpassed by the agent in power or it is not. If it is not surpassed and is nonetheless acted upon by the agent, then it is straightaway the case that an excess of power is not required in the agent. On the other hand, if the patient is surpassed and yet reacts on the agent, then an excess of power is not required in order for it to react. But a reaction is a genuine and proper action and an instance of efficient causality. Therefore, an excess of power is not always necessary for efficient causality; therefore, a dissimilarity in form—that is, in the principle of acting—is not always necessary either.

Lastly, it can happen that the action is coeval with the agent, as in the sun's action of illuminating. But in such a case there is never a dissimilarity between the agent and the patient, since they have always been similar to one another.[5]

---

5. As mentioned in *DM* 18. 8, n. 14, since according to one standard medieval view, the sun's light is propagated instantaneously, a body within the sun's sphere of activity will always have been illuminated. See §6 below for Suarez's solution to this difficulty.

T H I N G S   T O   B E   N O T E D   F O R   T H E   R E S O L U T I O N
O F   T H E   Q U E S T I O N

5. *One must attend to the dissimilarity between the agent and the patient at the beginning of the action.* It should be noted that when we ask whether an efficient cause requires a patient that is dissimilar to it, we are talking not about the conclusion of the action but rather about its beginning: that is, about the disposition and relation that must be present antecedently between the agent and the patient in order for an action to occur. For we are investigating here the conditions required for acting, not the conditions that follow upon an action. Besides, at the end of an action the comparison will be not so much between the agent and the patient as between the effect and the cause. It follows that a dissimilarity at the end of an action cannot be part of the notion of an efficient cause. To the contrary, the agent's intention is to make the patient similar to itself; and if at times this is not perfectly accomplished, it is because of the imperfection of the effect. This imperfection sometimes arises from a weakness in the power of an agent that is unable to overcome the patient's resistance, and it sometimes arises from a lack of receptivity on the part of the patient along with a more noble power on the part of an agent that is a universal or equivocal cause acting through a higher type of form which the effect is unable to receive according to the same notion—with the result that the effect is made similar according to some analogous or general notion but not according to the complete notion.[6]

6. *An action can be coeval with the thing that acts.* Again, one should observe that when we look for a dissimilarity that has to be present antecedently between the patient and the agent, we are talking about a priority not in time or duration but rather in the order of nature and causality. For even though the former sort of priority* is often present, it is not necessary *per se,* /670a/ as the last argument made at the beginning aptly demonstrates.[7] For it is not to be doubted that an action can be coeval with its agent when it does not require successiveness and is effected without resistance. Hence, if the action in question is a natural action and of such a kind that it can make the patient perfectly similar to the agent, then it will perfect that similarity from the beginning. For as soon as a natural agent exists, it acts to the full extent possible, and so if it acts without resistance, it produces a perfect effect from

---

6. E.g., craftsmen communicate to their artifacts various accidents that they themselves do not have in a univocal sense. Still, the artifacts have characteristics that are patterned after the conceptual models which the craftsmen have in mind when they fashion them.

7. See the last paragraph of §4 above.

the beginning. Therefore, as far as real duration is concerned, the patient in that sort of action is never dissimilar to the agent. However, it can still be thought of as being dissimilar in the order of nature, since such a patient would not of itself, prescinding from the agent's action, have a similarity to the agent. And so it is not the case that the action in question is effected with respect to the patient insofar as the latter is already similar; to the contrary, it is the action that makes the patient similar, and so the action is, formally speaking, effected by that which is dissimilar.

THE RESOLUTION OF THE QUESTION

7. *Each thing acts on what is dissimilar to it in form and similar to it in matter.* Given that the sense of the question has been thus explicated, its resolution is straightforward: One should claim that an agent cause is unable to act on a patient except to the extent that the patient is dissimilar to it in form—that is, in the terminus of the action.

This is in effect a first principle in philosophy. Aristotle propounds it in *On Generation and Corruption* 1.7, text 46 [323b2–7], where he says that the vast majority of earlier thinkers had affirmed by unanimous consensus that no similar thing is acted on at all by a similar thing "because the one is no more an agent or a patient than the other." And in text 48 [323b21] he confirms this by arguing that otherwise, for the same reason, the same thing would be affected by itself. He subsequently clarifies this by explaining that the required dissimilarity is a dissimilarity with respect to form or species. For what is required in the matter or genus that serves as the subject is, by contrast, a similarity between the agent and the patient—a point that we will explain a little further on.[8]

Aristotle presupposes this same principle in *On Generation and Corruption* 1.9 [326b31–33], when he says that an agent acts insofar as it is in act whereas a patient is acted upon insofar as it is in potency. He also teaches this in the whole of *Physics* 1, as well as in *Physics* 3, at the beginning [1.200b12–201b15]; in *Physics* 7, from text 35 onwards [249b27–250b8]; and in *Physics* 8, from the beginning. And in these places the commentators generally agree—even though, as we will see when we reply to the problems, some of them do not correctly explain the principle in the case of certain particular actions.

8. *An argument for the thesis; absurdities follow from the opposite of the thesis.* The argument for this assertion has already been touched upon. An agent

8. See §11 below.

acts insofar as it is in act, and it requires for its acting a patient that is in potency. But that which is in potency as such /670b/ is dissimilar to that which is in act as such. Therefore, etc.

The major premise is obvious as far as its first part is concerned. For to act is to give or communicate *esse*, and so it is necessary that such *esse* be presupposed to actually exist in the cause—either formally or eminently, depending on the mode and dignity of the agent.[9] For no one can give what he does not in any way have within himself.

And it is by almost the same argument that the other part of this same premise is proved. For when an agent communicates its *esse* to a patient, it reduces that patient from potency to act. Therefore, the patient, insofar as it is subjected to such an action, is assumed to be in potency. This is why in *Physics* 1 privation is posited among the principles of generation that are necessary on the part of the matter. These principles are, *mutatis mutandis*, necessary for *any* change or action that is effected in a subject.

In addition, Aristotle elegantly confirmed this thesis from absurdities. For if the thesis were not true, then there would be no reason why, given two similar things, the one should act upon the other, rather than vice versa. Likewise, the same thing would be able to intensify itself. Again, actions would have no conclusion; instead, following a complete battle between the contraries, after victory had been achieved and the patient had been made similar [to the agent], the action would then begin once more. Briefly, as Aristotle puts it, in this way nothing would be able to be overtaken either by destruction or by motion.

COROLLARIES OF THE PRECEDING RESOLUTION

9. From these arguments it follows, first, that the dissimilarity that is *per se* necessary between an agent cause and a patient is just the dissimilarity that obtains between a disposition and [the corresponding] privation—that is, between a thing as constituted in actuality and as existing in potency. For if one presupposes in the patient a capacity for receiving a given form, and if the agent has the power to produce that form, then the agent requires no dissimilarity on the part of the patient other than its lacking the form. For no other sort of dissimilarity can be universally required either by the nature of

---

9. A univocal cause communicates a form that it itself has formally—i.e., as an actual perfection of itself—whereas an equivocal cause communicates a form that it itself does not formally possess, even though it possesses it eminently or in a higher way. For an explanation of the distinction between univocal and equivocal causes, see *DM* 17. 2. 21.

motion or action or by any other general principle. Hence, it is not because of the nature of an efficient cause as such that among generable and corruptible things one finds not only this sort of dissimilarity but also a positive opposition and contrariety; rather, it is because generable and corruptible things are instituted in such a way that (i) they are able to have reciprocal conflict and action among themselves and that (ii) they are able, in keeping with their species, to be generated and corrupted by one another.

However, one should keep in mind that among efficient causes some are univocal whereas others are equivocal; we have already explained these terms above.[10] (We are talking at present about principal causes, since the doctrine concerning principal causes is easily adapted to the case of instrumental causes.) /671a/ Thus, it is among univocal causes that the condition in question applies formally and most properly. For when an agent introduces into a patient a form of the same type as that through which it acts, it presupposes within the patient a lack of that form, and, consequently, it presupposes a formal dissimilarity to the patient.

10. An equivocal cause, by contrast, does not induce in the patient a form that is of the same type as, and thus formally similar to, the form of its own through which it acts. And so it does not properly presuppose within the patient a formal dissimilarity—that is, a lack of the same species of form that the cause has within itself. Instead, it presupposes a dissimilarity between (i) the patient *qua* subject to the action and (ii) the patient *qua* perfected by the action—and, consequently, it also presupposes within the patient an absence of the sort of similarity that can obtain between a given form taken formally and another form that contains that form eminently.[11]

The reason for this is clear. First, an equivocal cause does not effect a formal similarity but instead effects only an "eminential similarity" (as I will put it). Therefore, it is only the corresponding dissimilarity that it antecedently requires, since only the privation of the form that terminates the agent's action is necessarily presupposed for the action. For the patient's lacking a given form that exists formally in the agent is not required for an action unless the patient is going to receive that form formally—that is, unless it is going to receive a form of the same type. Rather, what is necessary is only that it lack the form that is going to be introduced in it and that is going to be the terminus of the action—even if that form exists only virtually or eminently in the agent. For the privation required for an action is not for-

10. See ibid.

11. I.e., in the case of equivocal causality it is required that the subject lack the form which the agent is able to communicate, so that the agent possesses not that very form but rather another form (i.e., a power) which contains that form eminently.

mally opposed to the form that is the principle of the action; rather, it is opposed to the form that is going to be the terminus *ad quem* of the action, since a privation of this sort has the nature of a terminus *a quo*. Therefore, the dissimilarity that is required between a patient and an equivocal agent does not have to be a formal dissimilarity; rather, as has been explained, an eminential dissimilarity is sufficient.

It is for this reason that a heavy body is able to move another heavy body downward, even if they are similar in heaviness or even if they are both moving downward together and are similar in this respect as well. For the formal terminus of this action is not heaviness but rather a lower "where," which is in some sense virtually contained in the heaviness. And so it is the privation of that "where," not the privation of heaviness, that is necessary for this motion.

The same holds for all similar cases, especially for immanent acts, in which the faculty's action is always equivocal.[12] It is commonly said of such an action that it tends not so much to produce something similar as to produce something proportionate—that is, a second act that is consonant with the first act and that constitutes the perfection of that in /671b/ which it is contained virtually and eminently but not formally.[13] And so in this sort of action, too, only the aforementioned eminential dissimilarity is presupposed between the active and passive principles as such. That is, what is presupposed is that [the active principle] contains eminently an act that [the passive principle] does not have formally until it receives it from the active principle. This sort of dissimilarity is always present, regardless of whether the principles in question are distinct in reality from one another or are only conceptually distinct—as will become clearer in the reply to the first argument.[14]

11. *The sources for an action's not occurring between two things.* Second, it follows from what has been said that efficient causality requires *per se* that the agent cause should have power over the patient and with respect to the patient's receptivity, since otherwise it would be impossible for an action to follow. This point follows from what has been said, since the reason why the aforementioned dissimilarity between the agent and the patient is necessary

12. In an immanent act the power whereby the act is elicited is distinct from the act which is elicited. The power (or first act) is a quality of one type, whereas the elicited act (second act) is a quality of a different type and not a power.

13. For an explanation of the distinction between first and second act, see *DM* 18. 3, n. 4. Also, for some background on the distinction between virtual and formal containment, see *DM* 18. 7, n. 7.

14. See §14 below.

is so that the agent, to the extent that it is in act, might have the power to subject to itself the patient, which is only in potency. And it is confirmed by the fact that just as it is impossible for a form to inform matter unless it has an informative power proportionate to the matter, so too an agent cannot within its genus actuate a subject unless it has power over it. For a second act always requires a proportionate first act.[15]

Now in order that this might be more fully explained, one should note that there are four possible sources for an action's not following between two given things—I am talking about natural agents.[16]

First, if there is no active power in them.

Second, if there is power in the one but no capacity in the other for the form which the first is able to effect. This is why fire cannot produce heat in a celestial body.[17] And the reason why Aristotle posited *privation* rather than *negation* as a principle of generation or change is that it must exist in a subject that has a capacity [for the corresponding disposition]. This is also why he claimed, in *On Generation and Corruption* 1 [6.322b5–22], that what is required between the agent and the patient is a dissimilarity in form along with a similarity in matter by reason of which the patient has a capacity for the agent's form.

However, this is not true of all agents in the same way. For a celestial body acts on lower things here below even though it does not agree with them in matter; and an intelligence moves a body with which it does not agree in matter. Thus, in the case of agents that act by a univocal and corruptive action the proposition in question is true without qualification, and it is properly these agents that Aristotle was talking about. For in the same place he said that an agent which agrees with the patient in matter is also acted upon by the patient, but that this is not so in the case of a higher agent that does not share in matter. Thus, in the case of things that act by an equivocal action /672a/ all that is required is an agreement with respect to some common notion. For we are talking about created agents, none of which can alter or generate another unless there is some sense in which they agree in matter— at least in general, since it is necessary that both be material. This is also seen in the case of local motion, since that which produces the motion and

15. See *DM* 18. 3, n. 4.

16. The term 'natural agent' is here being used in contrast to 'free agent'.

17. Suarez is assuming here that celestial matter—i.e., the matter of the celestial bodies— is of a different type from the matter of which terrestrial substances are composed. In particular, whatever is made of celestial matter is subject just to local motion and not to any other sort of change—i.e., alteration, augmentation, generation, or corruption. See *DM* 13. 11.

that which is moved always agree in some sense in the capacity to receive a motion that is proportionate to oneself. For no created thing can effect local motion unless it itself is also movable, as is clear in the case of bodies and as we will explain below in the case of the intelligences as well.[18] But this is in some sense extrinsic to the notion of an agent. What is intrinsic, by contrast, is that the patient should have a capacity for that form with respect to which an active power exists in the agent.

12. Third, an action will be impeded once the capacity in question has been reduced to actuality. For in that case, too, the agent's power over the patient ceases, and this by reason of the fact that the agent has already effected everything that it was able to effect. This dovetails with what we said before: namely, that nothing can act on what is similar to itself insofar as it is similar—which is true for both univocal and equivocal agents, as long as we are talking about the appropriate sorts of similarity that can exist between those causes and their effects, as is clear from what was said above.[19] For the analogous argument stems from the same root: namely, that the whole power of a given cause has already been exhausted in a given patient, and so there is nothing left for the cause to do.

You will object that even if the patient is in act with respect to a given form or quality, it is still possible for the agent to retain the power to introduce another similar form; otherwise, the whole question under discussion will be reduced to the question of whether two accidents that differ solely in number can exist in the same subject.[20]

I reply that this is not possible, since after the capacity of the subject has been fulfilled by one act, it no longer remains in potency with respect to another similar act; and in this regard it is true that the question under discussion is closely connected with the question about several accidents, differing solely in number, in the same subject. For if two substantial forms, differing either in species or only in number, could exist in the same matter, then a natural agent would be able to induce the second form in a matter that had only the first. Therefore, similarly, if a subject could have two completely similar accidents, then even if it had one of them, it could still receive the other one from a similar agent or even from itself. And this is why we claimed above—in Disputation 5, section 9—that it is impossible that accidents which are altogether similar to one another and diverse solely in number should be received together in the same subject. /672b/˙

13. Fourth, and lastly, assuming that there is a power on the agent's part

18. See *DM* 35. 4. 15.
19. See §§9–10 above.
20. On this question, see *DM* 5. 7–9.

and a capacity on the patient's part along with a dissimilarity and privation, the action can still be impeded because of the patient's resistance. On
this point one should note that resistance on the patient's part is not *per se*
required for an action as such—just as we have likewise claimed that contrariety or positive opposition is not necessary. For a privation as such puts up
no resistance but instead prepares the way for an action. Therefore, whatever it is that puts up resistance is traced back to a positive opposition or
repugnance and so is not *per se* required for an action—to the contrary, of
itself it impedes or retards the action. Hence, the fact that an action is successive and not instantaneous stems from the patient's resistance unless the
action involves local motion, which this sort of successiveness is endemic
to—as is clear from philosophy and as we will explain below in the treatment
of action and passion.[21] So from this it follows that when, over and beyond
the dissimilarity of the patient, there is also resistance, then if that resistance
is great enough to surpass or equal the agent's power, the action is impeded.
And this is why it is a common philosophical axiom—and, as it were, a first
principle—that in order for anything to be effected, there must be a 'relation
of greater inequality'—that is, a relation in which there is more power in
the agent than there is resistance in the patient. This is taken from Aristotle
in the places cited above, since an agent *qua* agent overcomes the patient,
at least with respect to that which it is effecting. For this reason, then, it is
necessary that the agent should surpass the patient in power. Otherwise,
how would the agent be able to overcome the patient? This will be explained
more fully in the reply to the fourth argument.[22]

REPLY TO THE ARGUMENTS

Reply to the First Argument

14. Thus, it remains for us to give a satisfactory reply to the arguments.

The correct reply to the first argument was given [in the place where the
argument was set forth],[23] and that reply has been clarified by everything we
have said. In addition, it can be explained more fully as follows. One and
the same thing is able, at the same time and according to the same part [of
itself], to be both in first act and also in potency with respect to second act—
or, as others put it, to be both in virtual act and also in formal potency.[24] And

21. See *DM* 48 and 49.

22. See §39 below.

23. See §1 above.

24. See *DM* 18. 7, n. 7, for a description of the distinction between virtual act and formal
potency.

to the extent that [the agent and the patient] are distinguished according to these two notions, whether in reality or only conceptually and relationally, the thing in question bears a certain dissimilarity to itself—not a proper and formal dissimilarity but an eminential and virtual dissimilarity, which, as we have explained,[25] is enough for an action.

Reply to the Second Argument: On Antiperistasis

15. *The opinion of some.* The second argument[26] takes up the common problem concerning antiperistasis. This is a purely physical problem, /673a/ that is normally treated expressly in *On Generation and Corruption* 1.7, and so I will [just] touch upon a few points necessary for the present context.

In reply to this argument, there are some who claim that even though one and the same quality cannot intensify itself by a direct action, it can nonetheless do so by a reflexive action. This reflexive action, they claim, occurs as follows in such a case. A hot thing, say, when beset by its contrary, emits toward that contrary certain species that serve as instruments for acting on it; however, since the contrary itself resists those species, they are reflected back toward their own agent and thus intensify it. So claim Marsilius, *On Generation and Corruption* 1, q. 17 and 18; Albert of Saxony, *On Generation and Corruption* 1, q. 15; Paul of Venice, *Summa de Generatione*, chap. 23, and *Summa Meteorologiae*, chap. 3; and others.

However, this position makes incredible claims and does not solve the problem. For, first of all, it conjures up intentional species without any basis. Then it makes them the instrument of a material alteration, which is unheard of. Again, it has them going and returning even though they are accidents—unless, perhaps, one claims that they are little bodies of some sort, which is even more incredible, or unless one claims that this 'return' is a metaphorical one that occurs by virtue of a reaction, which cannot be true, as will now become obvious as we argue for the second part [of our criticism]—namely, that the problem is not solved [by this reply].

This is clear, first of all, from the fact that these species, whatever they might be, are instruments of the agent from which they emanate. Therefore, they act in the power of that agent. Therefore, in acting they cannot surpass its power. So how can they intensify that agent, even if they do return to it?

Second, this sort of action often occurs without any diffusion or action through a medium—namely, when the contrary agents are very close to one another and the power of the first is strengthened within it. In such a case there are no species that could return to it, since there are no species re-

25. See §§9–10 above.
26. See §2 above.

ceived in the contrary agent, as the reply supposes. (For it is because of the contrary's resistance that the species are claimed to return to their source.) Nor are there any species in the medium, since there is no medium.

Finally, this sort of action sometimes occurs with respect to a subject that has an aversion to the quality in question, as in the case of the water in a well. Therefore, it cannot occur through that subject's reflexive action.

16. *The opinion of others, along with a refutation.* Thus others claim that, through a natural desire for its own conservation, the one contrary, when surrounded by the stronger contrary, collects and unites itself and turns its action upon itself in order to protect itself. And Niphus, in *On Generation and Corruption* 1, his own text 195, examination of problem 2, adds that the one contrary has of itself the power to act throughout /673b/ a given sphere and that, because it is prevented by the surrounding contrary from diffusing that power beyond itself, it turns it toward itself and so intensifies itself.

However, this opinion, too, is not only false but does not solve the problem. This is proved by the fact that it straightaway concedes not only that what is similar acts on what is similar but also that one and the same thing acts on itself with respect to the same formal quality. And it makes no difference if one replies that this happens because of the surrounding contrary and, as it were, because of fear of that contrary. For there either is or is not, within that quality itself, an intrinsic natural power for the action in question. If there is, then the quality will effect the action and intensification within itself from the beginning and at all times, apart from the occurrence of the contrary. For a natural power, as long as it is not impeded, naturally exercises all its force apart from any other occurrence. On the other hand, if there is not within the thing a power sufficient for the action, then it will not effect the action even if its contrary is pressing upon it.

A similar argument is adduced by asking whether or not this greater intensity is natural to the thing and to the quality. For if the intensity is natural, then the thing will always have it emanating from its intrinsic nature and will not wait for the exigency of protecting itself from a contrary in order to effect it. On the other hand, if the intensity is preternatural, then it cannot stem intrinsically from the very quality itself.

17. Again, I ask whether or not this greater intensity, acquired from within upon the occurrence of the menacing contrary, is such that if the contrary is removed before it diminishes, then it persists in the thing. For if it does persist, then this is an indication that it is natural and that it would have existed *per se* from the beginning and at all times, apart from the contrary agent, if there had been no impediment. On the other hand, if it does not persist, then it could never have been effected from within, since a perfection that emanates from within is not removed in the absence of an extrinsic agent.

Finally, it is hard to know what is meant by the words "the agent collects and unites itself to a greater degree" or "it turns its action upon itself." For they might mean that the agent condenses itself and retracts all its parts into a smaller place. But this is easily disproved by the arguments already given when they are applied *mutatis mutandis*. For this motion or contraction is either natural or nonnatural. If it is natural, then it will always exist in the thing, speaking *per se*; if it is nonnatural, then it will not be effected from within because of a menacing contrary. This is confirmed by experience as well. For we do not find motions of this sort in all things that are acted upon by their contraries; but it would have to occur in *all* of them if it stemmed naturally from the force of a desire to protect oneself from a contrary.

Moreover, what was added [by Niphus]—namely, that the agent turns /674a/ its action upon itself because it is prevented from diffusing it—has no plausibility at all. For from the fact that an agent ceases to act upon another, it does not follow that it is capable either of acting upon itself or of effecting a greater intensity. Otherwise, a thing existing in a vacuum would intensify itself by the very fact that it is unable to act upon another. Likewise, effecting a greater intensity exceeds the agent's proper power. Therefore, even if an agent is prevented from issuing forth in an action proportionate to itself, it does not thereby follow that it can effect within itself an action that exceeds its proper power.

18. Thus, there are others who, finding no way to explain the action in question, deny that such an action exists in reality. And as regards the experiences, they reply that they are apparent and not real, and they contrive causes for the various appearances of this sort—causes that are fictitious and incompatible with sense experience. Still, Galen, *De Simplicium Medicamentorum* 3, faculty 3, was inclined toward this position.

19. *Two ways of explaining action through antiperistasis; why baths and an animal's belly are hotter in the winter; why the same holds for the water in a well.* Therefore, one should claim that there are only two ways for a given quality to be intensified upon the occurrence of a surrounding contrary: namely, either (i) by an extrinsic agent which is detained or trapped there upon that occurrence or, conversely, (ii) because in virtue of that occurrence a corrupting extrinsic agent withdraws and the thing immediately reduces itself from within to its natural state, which calls for the greater intensity in question. And so it follows that a quality never intensifies its very self.

We touched upon the first of these ways in the preceding section,[27] where, drawing from Aristotle, we said that baths are hotter in the winter because the heat in them is trapped by a colder medium and is prevented from

27. See *DM* 18. 8. 27.

rushing outward—something we explained in terms of hot exhalations. So, too, an animal's belly is hotter in the winter because the animal spirits are held within by reason of the fact that the air's coldness compresses the skin and the pores, as Galen noted when he was explaining the aphorism cited above from Hippocrates and as Aristotle elegantly explained in *Problems* 2.29 [869a19–22], where he gives other examples. This same cause is, I think, the source of the fact that the water in a well is hotter in the winter: namely, because some of the hot exhalations generated in the depths of the earth are prevented from rising when, because of the greater coldness, the medium is denser and thicker.

20. However, there are two problematic aspects of this last experience. One is this: Where do these exhalations come from? The other is this: How, given that they are very rarified, are they able to act on water that is extremely cold?

To the first of these problems one should reply that it is by the power /674b/ of the sun and other celestial influences that these exhalations are generated from the earth, which, because of its density and because of its dryness (which is greater, speaking *per se*, in its lower parts), is an appropriate matter for having such exhalations produced from it. And perhaps most of these exhalations, having been generated there during the summer, are afterwards retained there longer for the reason mentioned above. Moreover, since they are more subtle than water, they will easily mix with it when they try to rise, and so they will easily be able to temper its coldness, at least by continually reacting upon it. Perhaps, too, the air trapped in the depths or pores of the earth, given that it is hot by its nature, is made even hotter for this same reason and assists in the action.

The second way in which such an action occurs is illustrated by other examples.[28] The first has to do with the water in a well being colder in the summer by reason of the fact that the hot exhalations by which it could be heated do not stop there but instead rise quickly—both because (i) the medium, by virtue of the fact that it is hotter and more rarified, does not impede them and also because (ii) during that season the exhalations are more subtle due to the stronger influence of the sun. And so when the contrary agent is removed, the water becomes colder from within—not colder than its nature calls for but colder than it was beforehand when it was being acted upon to a greater degree by its contraries. This is also how it happens that cold water becomes colder when it is exposed just a little to the sun during the summer. For the extrinsic heat effects some rarification in the medium or on the water's external surface or in the vase that contains the water,

---

28. Having solved the two problems posed in the first paragraph of §20, Suarez now returns to the second of the alternatives mentioned in the first paragraph of §19.

and if at that time some hot vapor was surrounding the water or had been mixed with it, it evaporates more readily, and as a result the water reduces itself more toward its natural state. And perhaps, in addition, the water is more condensed not only for the reason just stated but also by virtue of its having an occasion to avoid a vacuum; and the coldness increases because of this too. (See Aristotle, *Problems* 24.13 [937a25–33] and *Meteorology* 1.12 [347b34–349a11].)

Therefore, all similar experiences can be explained in one of these two ways, with the result that it is never necessary to admit that one and the same thing intensifies itself with respect to the same quality. For when this intensification comes from within via a natural emanation, it is attributed to the generating thing.[29]

Reply to the Third Argument: Whether a Multiplicity of Agents or an Agent's Density of Matter Contributes to the Intensity of an Action

21. *The affirmative answer of certain authors.* In the third argument two problems are raised.[30] One is this: Is a quality that exists in a denser subject able to intensify beyond its own degree of intensity a quality similar to itself that exists in another, more rarified, subject? /675a/ Alternatively, and this amounts to the same thing: Can several partial agents or several parts of the same agent, by virtue of a greater application to one and the same patient that is similar to them in a given quality and equal in the degree of [that quality], intensify that patient's quality?

There are many who answer affirmatively: for example, Marsilius, *On Generation and Corruption* 1, q. 19; Soto, *Physics* 2, q. 2; and Niphus, *On Generation and Corruption* 1, his own text 195, prob. 2, q. 2. Their argument is that an agent's power increases not only according to the intensity of its form but also according to its multiplicity, since Aristotle says in *Physics* 8, text 80 [266b1–5], that within a greater magnitude there exists a greater power; therefore, if the whole of that power is applied to the same patient to a greater degree, as happens when the agent is more dense, then it will produce a greater effect as well.

This is confirmed by the common example, adduced above,[31] of a red-hot piece of iron, as well as by the example of two things that are equally luminous and equally applied to one and the same part of the air. Likewise, it is confirmed by the example of a multiplicity of equally intense acts, which

29. For more on natural emanation and the attribution of its effects to the generating thing, see *DM* 18. 3. 3–14.

30. See §3 above. Suarez deals with the first of the two problems in §§21–32 and the second in §§33–38.

31. See §3 above.

intensify a habit, as well as by the example of equal drops of water, falling in exactly the same way, which eventually hollow out a rock.

Second, it is confirmed by the fact that in the winter the air freezes water because, no doubt, it intensifies the water's coldness beyond that degree of coldness that the air has within itself. For if the air were just as cold itself, it would likewise be condensed and turn into water.

22. The authors in question do not think that this position of theirs is contrary to the doctrine that has been handed down concerning the required dissimilarity between an efficient cause and its patient. Instead, they claim that just as what is similar acts on what is similar to it in form as long as the latter is dissimilar to it in degree of intensity, so too it is possible for what is similar both in form and in degree of intensity to act on another similar thing as long as the latter is dissimilar to it in power and potency. But this is what happens in the present context. For even though a very dense thing that is hot to degree four does not exceed an equally hot air or an equally hot hand in degree of intensity, it nonetheless does exceed them in strength and power. For, as was said above,[32] strength or power is not measured by intensity alone. This is clarified further by the fact that the dense hot thing in question has the power to produce in another thing the whole form that it has within itself. Therefore, because it is unable to multiply that form in a more rarified patient because of the latter's incapacity, it increases it intensively.

23. *The position just laid out is refuted; the resolution of the question.* I judge this position to be false and contrary to the posited principle, which must be understood to have the following meaning: Nothing can act in any way upon another similar thing with respect to that very form in which they are similar; nor can it add any perfection or intensity to that thing as long as they are assumed to be *perfectly* similar—that is, similar not only in species /675b/ but also in degree of intensity, what Aristotle, in the place cited from *On Generation and Corruption*, expresses by saying, "If they are *altogether* similar . . . ."

As for the argument they adduce, one should reply that a multiple form with an equal intensity, whether it exists in one very dense agent or in many agents no matter how they are applied, is not sufficient to intensify a similar form in another thing beyond the degree of intensity which that form has within the agent. This is the more common position and is held by Paul of Venice, *Summa de Generatione*, chap. 23; by Albert of Saxony, *On Generation and Corruption* 1, q. 15; by Astudillo, *On Generation and Corruption* 1, q. 21; and, most thoroughly, by Vittoria, *Relectio de Augmento Caritatis*.

32. See §21 above.

24. An a priori argument [for this reply] has just now been touched upon. By its action the agent intends to assimilate the patient to itself, and when this goal has been attained, its action ceases. But if the patient has been made similar both in form and in degree of intensity, then it is already perfectly similar. Therefore, the action does not proceed any further.

Nor can one reply that because the patient has not attained as great a *multiplicity* of forms as exists within the agent, there is not yet a perfect similarity. For a form's multiplicity or paucity is irrelevant to the nature of the form or quality itself but instead derives from the subject—that is, the quantity—and so this is not a dissimilarity in form but rather an inequality in quantity. For one white thing will not be said to be *dissimilar* to two white things by reason of the fact that it is not as many as they are; instead, it will be said to be *unequal* to them. But it is not this sort of equality that is intended by the action; rather, it is a similarity in form. What's more, the first sort of similarity (or, rather, equality) is impossible once the subject's capacity for rarity or density is presupposed or, what amounts to the same thing, once it is assumed that the patient is one and the agents are many. Nor is it true that this inequality can be counterbalanced by a greater intensity, both because (i) they are quantities or perfections of different types and because (ii) what will happen instead is that because of that greater intensity there will be a new dissimilarity in degree of intensity, even while the same inequality in the multiplicity of the form remains.

25. The second argument is that in a languid form, in whatever way it might be multiplied in many and diverse subjects or in many parts of the same subject, there is not enough power to effect a greater intensity in a similar form. Therefore, etc.

The antecedent is obvious, first of all from the fact that such a power does not exist there *formally*, since the relevant intensity does not exist formally in that form. For I am assuming that the intensification [of a form] is not a summation of several similar degrees of intensity in the same part of the subject but is instead a proper and *per se* augmentation of the same quality within the same /676a/ part of the subject. For example, there would be no such augmentation to degree eight even if two heats of degree four were posited in the same part of the subject; I will explain this in its proper place below.[33] Therefore, the perfection in question is all the less able to exist formally in a multiplicity of languid forms that are in many subjects or in many parts of [the same] subject.

It is likewise not the case that the power exists there *eminently*. For according to its species the form in question is of the same type, whereas according

33. See *DM* 46. 1.

to its degree of intensity it is of a lower type in each part of the subject and, as a result, it is of a lower type in all of them even when they are taken together. For it is not the case that there is a more eminent power in many things of the same type than in each one separately, since an eminence of power requires a form or nature of a higher type.

Nor, again, can one claim that the intensity in question exists *virtually* in that form by reason of its multiplicity. For virtual (as opposed to eminential) containment is attributed only to an instrumental power. But the intensity in question cannot be attributed in this way to a multiple form that is both of a lower intensity and of the same type, because (i), as was explained above,[34] when such a form effects something similar to itself, it behaves not so much as an instrument as a proper principle of acting, and also because (ii) it is impossible to identify a principal agent in whose power it is said to produce the effect in question. Indeed, this multiple form is not in its own right instituted to be an instrument of any action but is instead a sort of aggregation of instruments of the same type.

26. *Absurdities follow from the opposite position.* I argue, third, from absurdities. For from the opposite position it follows, first, that three things that are hot to degree four can heat one another to the highest degree if two of them, having been joined together, intensify the heat of the third to five degrees, and if that one in turn makes the other two similar to itself, and if they proceed in this way to the highest degree.

Second, it likewise follows that water that is hot to degree four in each of its parts can render itself hotter to any degree whatsoever. For the two outermost parts, say, will act on the middle part and intensify its heat, and it in turn will act on the outermost parts, and the action will proceed in this way to the highest degree. However, these and similar consequences are plainly false and contrary to experience.

It follows, third, that a habit is intensified by languid acts in such a way that it is inclined toward a more intense act—which, I assume, is also false.

27. In order to reply to the foundation for the contrary position, we should note, first, that it is one thing for the power of acting to increase because of the multiplicity of a form /676b/ and another thing for it to increase with respect to its ability to produce an intensively more perfect effect. For the former is the more general, and the authors of the position in question incorrectly infer the latter from it. Thus, in the first of these modes of increase the power to act is increased extensively rather than intensively, and so it is increased not in such a way that it can produce an effect more intense than the very form that is the principle of acting but rather in such a way

34. See *DM* 18. 6, esp. §4.

that, other things being equal, it can produce its own exactly corresponding effect more easily, more quickly, more forcefully, and at a greater distance. Hence, one can say that it is increased with respect to the *mode* of production but not with respect to the *thing* that it is able to produce. Similarly, when the density of the parts of the subject is joined to a multiple form, it greatly facilitates this mode of action, since the entire multiple form is better applied to the patient and so is conducive to a prompter action. However, [the density] cannot by itself be conducive to a better effect than that contained in the power of the form, since the application in question is a condition that is *per se* conducive to acting only if the power is presupposed.

28. Second, one should note that we are talking about a multiple form that is altogether equal to the patient's form in essence and degree of intensity. For if the agent's quality happened to be of a different type, with respect to essence and species, from the form effected in the patient, and if it contained the latter eminently, then, as was mentioned above,[35] even if it were languid within its own order, it could still be a principle for effecting a quality of a lower type that was intense within its own order. For that higher quality, whatever its degree of intensity, would by reason of its essence be able to contain eminently the entire range of the lower quality. Nor, in that case, would a similar thing be acting on a similar thing, even if, say, a quality of degree one intensified a quality of degree one. For the qualities would be of different types, and there would be a sort of ratio [between them] rather than a proper similarity.

Next, it is also possible for a multiple form to be conducive to a more intense effect when the effect does not correspond exactly to the intensity of the agent's form. For instance, when a single lamp illuminates the air, it does not produce in the air as intense a light as it has within itself, and so it may well happen that two lamps of equal intensity to one another, taken together, should produce a more intense light in the air than either of them could produce by itself. For in that case the arguments adduced above do not apply, since the patient is never made perfectly similar to the agent. Therefore, when an agent has not only a greater multiplicity of form but also a more intense form, it can have the power to intensify the effect. Thus, in each thing that acts *per se* there will be a form /677a/ that is productive of the whole intensity in question, whereas the fact that one of them, acting by itself alone, would not produce the whole effect could stem either from an indisposition on the patient's part or from the distance or from some other similar cause. And in such a case an intense multiple form could very well

35. See §§9 and 25 above.

be conducive to the production of a more intense effect, though an effect that does not exceed the intensity of the cause.

29. *Whether two similar but unequal agents can assist one another with respect to an action.* A more difficult problem is this. If two unequally intense agents concurred simultaneously, could they assist one another in producing a more intense effect which, though it did not exceed absolutely the total intensity of the cause, would nonetheless exceed the intensity of the partial agent that has the less intense form—with the result that even though a languid quality, no matter how many times it is multiplied, cannot *per se* intensify a quality similar to itself in degree of intensity, it can nonetheless, with the concurrence of a more intense quality, assist and cooperate in such an intensification?

In such a case, once again, the arguments made above do not seem to apply. For in a total agent of this sort there is an absolutely more intense form and a power sufficient for the effect, and the lower degrees of the quality, when conjoined to the higher degrees, can concur with respect to any degree whatsoever of another similar quality. For example, when a hot thing of degree eight intensifies a heat of degree four, it concurs with respect to, say, degree five not only by means of degree five (or higher degrees) of its own heat but by means of *all* its heat—just as, conversely, when it produces degree one, it effects it not by means of degree one of its own heat but by means of *all* its heat. An indication of this is that, other things being equal, a thing that is hot to degree eight has more power to effect degree one (or degree five) than does a thing that is hot to degree one (or degree five), since it will overcome greater resistance and act more forcefully. Therefore, this is an indication that (i) it is not acting only by means of a similar degree and that (ii) the other degrees are truly concurring with respect to that action and are not related to the action [merely] concomitantly and, as it were, *per accidens.* The reason for this is that in order for all the degrees of heat to assist and concur, it is enough that the essence of heat should exist in each and every one of them, even though the unique similarity that exists between degrees of altogether the same type does not exist in each of those degrees. For it is enough that the latter sort of similarity should exist in the *whole* form that is the principle of acting. So too, then, several languid forms, when conjoined to a more intense form, will be able to concur with the latter in producing a more intense effect.

This position, then, is plausible, and the arguments made above do not militate against it, as will easily be seen from what has been said. What's more, it can help save certain /677b/ experiential data, as was mentioned above and as we are also about to see.

30. Still, the position is not entirely free of difficulties. For if a languid form, when conjoined to a more intense form, acts to intensify what is similar to itself, then why will it not rather act to intensify itself? Again, if this position were true, then a thing that is hot to degree eight and equally close to two things that are hot to degree four would act with and through the one to intensify the other, and vice versa.

However, one could reply that it is because of the particular disposition of the patient or of the partial agent that a languid partial agent cooperates with a more intense agent to intensify a similar form within a given distinct subject rather than within itself or to intensify one subject rather than another similar subject. This will become more readily evident from what will be said below. Therefore, this position is plausible. More on this below.[36]

31. *How red-hot iron generates fire.* The foundation for the contrary position has been sufficiently taken care of by these considerations.

As for the first experience that we adduced, the one about the red-hot iron,[37] the common consensus of all philosophers, as well as the reply, is that fire is contained within the pores of the iron, even though it is hidden from us. The greater intensity that we readily experience with our senses derives from this fire that is contained in the pores of the red-hot iron, though the vehemence and quickness of the action stem from the combination of the iron and its density. Now one indication that there is fire contained and enclosed in the pores of the iron (as we have just now claimed) comes from lightning, which always derives from fire, as Plato said in the *Timaeus*. Likewise, this same point can be proved by an argument that is not at all to be scorned: namely, that since iron has pores in which air would normally exist, it follows that when a vehement heating action occurs, the air will be turned into fire by the force and efficacy of such an intense and vehement heating action. And, finally, so vehement a heating action never occurs in any matter or subject that is susceptible to such a heating action unless some exhalations are secreted by it and then ignited—that is, turned into fire.

There are others who reply with a far different argument: namely, that the highest degree of heat exists in the iron, and this in the absence of the form of fire because of other dispositions that are repugnant to fire and that conserve the form of iron there. But it is hard to believe that these dispositions, which exist connaturally in the iron as in a subject that is proportionate and connatural to them, would not also impede such a great intensification of the heat, since by nature they are repugnant to it as well.

36. See *DM* 46.

37. See §21 above. The puzzle is that the red-hot iron is able to ignite various substances even though, apparently, it does not itself have heat of the intensity required for fire.

Above I intimated yet another reply: namely, that in matter that is dry and properly disposed fire can be generated without a prior maximal heating action.[38] This reply can be /678a/ easily defended, and, if it is accepted, then it does not follow that the highest degree of heat is present in the iron. However, the first reply is sufficient.

32. *Whether languid acts strengthen a habit.* As for the experience having to do with languid acts,[39] one may reply that in fact experience proves just the opposite, since according to the common position such acts do not intensify or augment a habit—though this requires a longer explanation, which we will provide more explicitly in its own proper place.[40]

As for the other experience, the one that has to do with the falling drops of water, one may reply that all the individual drops do something, since little by little they dispose the subject, which they render a bit more soft. Otherwise, if the subject remained equally indisposed, then the second drop could not do anything more than the first, nor the hundredth anything more than the third. Still, each drop acts on a dissimilar patient, since, for example, the patient was of itself dry and at the beginning began to be moistened in proportion to the capacity and power of [one] falling drop; and because the subsequent drops find the patient more disposed, they effect more, despite the fact that none of them acts beyond its own proper intensity and power.

As for the third experience, the one having to do with the ice, one should, first of all, deny that the air makes the water colder than it itself is cold; rather, the most it can do is prevent the water from being heated in any way by an extrinsic agent, and then the water itself reduces itself to the greatest degree of coldness that it can have by its nature. Now if that degree of coldness is sufficient for its freezing, then straightaway the freezing does not result from the air; on the other hand, if it is not sufficient (as indeed it seems not to be, since otherwise water in its natural state would always be frozen), then some other cause of the freezing besides the air will have to be sought, while the air will be said only to cool the water. Now my own view is that the freezing stems from a diminution of the water's moistness and to that extent stems from some desiccating celestial influence. For it is this dryness, modified and tempered in the relevant way, which, along with a given density and coldness on the part of the matter, brings the freezing to completion. Therefore, in this case there is no quality that is intensified by a more languid quality of the same type.

38. See *DM* 18. 8. 30.
39. See §21 above.
40. See *DM* 44. 10.

Reply to the Third Argument: On Reflexive Action

33. The second problem raised in that same [third] argument has to do with reflexive action.[41] Some claim that in a reflexive action a languid form is able to intensify its very own self, not to mention that which is similar to itself—a position which, understood in so absolute and universal a way, we rejected above, and against which we will once again direct some remarks in a moment.

There are others who claim that it is through reflection that, for example, solar rays are multiplied with respect to the same part of the medium. For, they claim, it is because these rays are of themselves able to travel further, thus acquiring a greater sphere, /678b/ that when they meet a body that prevents their being further diffused, they return to the same patient from which they reverberate, and thus reflection occurs.

However, unless these claims are being made metaphorically, they are plainly false and manifestly contrary to reason. For the rays are imagined to be certain little bodies that have their origin from the sun—a view which, when applied to every agent, found favor with Democritus but was rejected by Aristotle and all the philosophers, as St. Thomas noted in general in *Summa Theologiae* 1, q. 115, a. 1, and specifically with regard to light in *Summa Theologiae* 1, q. 67, a. 2.

34. *The first way of answering the question is disproved.* There are two possible ways to understand the claim that action on a medium is more intense because of reflection.

The first way is this: When a principal agent is acting within a smaller sphere, it acts more intensely in the parts of that sphere than it would if its action were diffused throughout a larger sphere. This principle by itself indeed seems plausible. For when a finite power is applied to several things, it is weaker in each of them. Therefore, conversely, when it is concentrated on fewer things, it will act more forcefully in each of them. Therefore, it will also act more intensely, though still within the range of its own power and intensity. Thus, even though the fire that is heating this room could at this time be heating a much larger sphere, nonetheless, because its action is confined within the limits of the room, it produces a more intense heat in this air than it would otherwise produce. And the same thing holds, *mutatis mutandis*, for the sun's illumination.

Now even though in a case like this the intensity is said to be greater because of reflection, nonetheless, reflection as thus expounded is in fact, on the part of the body in which it occurs, merely an impediment to the action's

41. See the second half of §3 above.

proceeding further, whereas on the part of the principal agent it is a more efficacious action and a greater application of its own power.

35. However, this way of explaining reflection and action through reflection, even though it is plausible in what it affirms, nonetheless does not seem sufficient by itself to preserve everything that experience reveals in the sort of reflection under discussion. For, first of all, if the body in which the reflection occurs were serving merely as an impediment to diffusion by reason of which the primary agent's power—concentrated, as it were, on a smaller sphere—acted more strongly on that sphere, then each body that was placed at the same point and that equally impeded the sphere's being extended would produce an equal reflection. For each of them would present to the primary agent an altogether equivalent occasion for intensifying its action more strongly and, as I will put it, for redoubling its efforts. But the consequent is manifestly contrary to experience, since, for example, a black thing does not, all else being equal, effect as great a reflection of light as a white thing does; /679a/ nor does a white thing effect as great a reflection of light as a mirror does.

Second, if reflection occurred only in the way in question, then it would have to occur in equal proportion throughout the whole sphere, since this stronger action or application of power would occur in equal proportion throughout the whole sphere. But the consequent is contrary to our manifest experience, since a stronger reflection occurs in the parts of the sphere that are closer to the body by which the reflection is effected, as is sufficiently obvious *per se*.

36. *The body that reflects the action truly acts on that against which it reflects the action.* Thus, it seems necessary to say that in the sort of reflection just spoken of there is a proper efficient causality on the part of the body in which the reflection occurs˙. For that body receives an active form or quality from the primary agent, and, affected by that quality, it in turn acts on the patient that is proximate to it—that is, on the very medium through which the agent's original action has reached it. And this is why the agent's original action is called a direct action, whereas this second action is called a reflexive action.

Now this way of explaining reflection is proved in no way other than by means of a sufficient enumeration and from the fact that it is *per se* plausible and does not involve any contradiction. For it often happens that a given thing acts in return by means of a form that has been received from without. For example, hot water acts through heat.

However, this explanation is not without its own problems. For, first of all, given that the medium receives the very same quality from the primary agent, one might ask why the medium does not act upon that other thing whereby the reflection is said to be effected rather than being acted upon by it. The reply is that this stems from the particular disposition or condition of the given body and the given quality. For example, as experience teaches, light seems not to be active *per se*—or at least not equally active—unless it is received in a dense, polished body. For the reason why the moon, when illuminated by the sun, produces more light than the other parts of the heavens do is that it is bright to the degree that it is also dense. Therefore, it is because the reflection of light always occurs in a dense body with respect to a rarified medium that the action in question is effected by this sort of body rather than by another. Something similar holds in the case of the reflection of heat. For such a reflection is commonly effected by a denser body, which, as was explained above, acts more forcefully because of a multiplicity of matter.[42]

37. *A problem is resolved.* But then a second problem arises. For it follows from this either that (i) the primary agent heats or illuminates the distant thing more intensely than the nearby thing because of the latter's disposition or else that (ii) the distant thing in which the reflection occurs intensifies a similar quality in the medium solely because of a multiplicity of matter, even though that quality is less intense, or at most equally intense, in it. /679b/ But both these alternatives are inconsistent with what has been said above.

This is the argument that especially moves those who claim that in a reflexive action what is similar in degree of intensity is intensified by what is similar to it or that the same thing is intensified by itself. But this claim was in part impugned above, and, what's more, it can easily be refuted. For a reflexive action is a true action, and it cannot be effected in the absence of a sufficient power, and there is nothing special about it except its name. For it is an action that is turned back toward the agent from which the form that effects the reflexive action is directly received.

And so one could reply that this sort of reflection is never effected except either by means of a quality of a diverse type or with the assistance of some similar quality. For example, when a mirror produces heat by means of light through a reflexive action, then the reflection is said to be effected by means of a quality of a diverse type, and the problem just mentioned easily disappears, as was explained above.[43] For even though the light in the mirror is not more intense than the light in the air, it can produce heat more intensely because it is a quality of a higher type and, in addition, is assisted by the subject's density and by the multiplicity of a more strongly applied form.

By contrast, when the reflection occurs among instances of light them-

42. See §§23–25 above.
43. See §§9, 25, and 28 above.

selves, the reply just given is irrelevant, and for this reason there will be some who claim that there is really no such thing as a reflexive action whereby the light of the medium is made greater, but that it appears that there is such an action because the shiny (or white) body in question affects vision more strongly. But this claim seems incredible. For we experience that the air itself shines more brightly when a reflection occurs and that the objects positioned within it are seen better.

Again, one could claim that it is not the case that the light in the medium is intensified but that a new light is effected by the body through reflection, and that it is not problematic that two instances of light should exist simultaneously in the same part of the air. For example, when a reflection is effected in a mirror, it is probable that a new visible species of the same object is caused in the medium through the reflection. However, this multiplication of instances of light, even though it finds favor among those who study optics, is not accepted by philosophers; nor is it consonant with the things that were said above concerning the individuation of accidents.[44]

Thus, alternatively, one could claim that the light received in a dense body is of a different type from that which is received in the air—which is difficult to believe. Or, again, one could claim that the light is assisted by some quality of the subject's. But all these claims, as well as others that could easily be thought up, would be affirmed without any basis in order to evade the problem rather than to clear it up.

38. Therefore, it seems that some of the aforementioned consequences will have to be conceded, as long as one keeps in mind that a languid quality intensifies what is similar to itself not by itself alone but in the power of, and with the help of, the principal agent. For it was shown above that this is plausible.[45]/680a/

So if, for example, we claim that because of the subject's greater susceptibility the sun illuminates a distant mirror more intensely than it illuminates the air in the medium, with the medium itself assisting as an instrument or partial agent, then it is easy to see that the mirror, illuminated in this way, in turn acts on the air close to it and intensifies the light in it. For it is unproblematic that a certain degree of intensity should be effected in a given quality by one agent and that other degrees of intensity should be effected in that same quality by another agent, as long as the agents are acting (i) by diverse actions and (ii) not equally primarily but in a certain order—as happens in this case.

On the other hand, if we claim instead that in the direct action the distant

44. See DM 5. 7.
45. See §§27–30 above.

mirror is not illuminated more intensely than the air in the medium, then we will have to say that because the mirror is more apt than the air to act through the light it receives, it is joined virtually to the primary agent as soon as it is illuminated and that it assists and is assisted by the primary agent in intensifying the air's light.

So these two modes of explanation can be plausibly defended—though, all things considered, the first seems more straightforward and also better at clarifying reflexive action and avoiding the problems.

Reply to the Fourth Argument: On Reaction

39. In the fourth argument[46] a problem is raised concerning reaction and the way in which the ratio [of greater inequality] required for efficient causality is preserved in it. However, this problem is treated at greatest length in *On Generation and Corruption* 1, and it depends especially on an understanding of the distinction between the potentiality to act and the potentiality to resist, a distinction that we will propound below when we discuss potentiality.[47]

For now I will briefly point out that to resist something is not formally to act upon it, since sometimes a thing can resist even though it does not effect anything in another. From this it follows that for acting it is not necessary that the one thing's power to act should be greater than the other thing's power to act; instead, all that is required *per se* is that the action of the one should surpass the *resistance* of the other. Therefore, it can ̇ happen that a patient reacts on its agent even though it is acted upon more forcefully by that agent. For even though it is surpassed in activity, it can nonetheless by its own activity surpass to a small degree the resistance of the other, and so it acts on the latter not insofar as it is greater than or equal to it but rather insofar as it is in some way inferior to it. However, these points will be better understood after the notions of active and resistive potentiality, along with their relations to one another, have been explained. We will present this explanation below.[48]

The last argument was answered above.[49]/68ob/

46. See §4 above.

47. See *DM* 43. 1.

48. See ibid.

49. The argument in question is found in the last paragraph of §4 above and was answered in §6 above.

Section 10

Whether Action Is the Proper Notion of Causing for an Efficient Cause—That Is, Its Causality

1. We have explained the principles and conditions that are necessary for an efficient cause's being proximately ready to cause. It remains for us to explain what it is by virtue of which an efficient cause is formally constituted as actually causing. This is what we call the proximate notion of causing: that is, the causality of each cause.

Now, as I have said repeatedly,[1] what is being discussed is not the relation *cause of* that is said to result once the effect has already been produced. For it is obvious that this relation is not the causality, since it instead presupposes the causality as the notion upon which it is founded. Thus, the discussion is about the causality insofar as it bespeaks, in our way of understanding, the proximate notion of the foundation for the relation. For it is this notion that constitutes and denominates an acting cause insofar as it is said to be prior in nature to its effect.

THE OPINIONS OF SOME

2. *First opinion.* The problem is whether this causality is the very action itself whereby the agent acts, or whether instead it is something else over and above the action.

Now some Thomists deny that an agent's causality is the action itself: for example, Soncinas, *Metaphysics* 5, q. 4, and Javellus, also in *Metaphysics* 5, q. 4, where he refers to Hervaeus, *Quodlibeta* 2, q. 1, and *Quodlibeta* 4, q. 8.

One possible foundation for this position is as follows. The agent's causality must be different from the agent's effect, since the causality is not caused, whereas it is through the causality that the effect is caused. But the action is an effect of the agent's. Therefore, the action is not the agent's causality.

The minor premise is proved by the fact that the action is nothing in reality other than the effect insofar as it emanates from the agent.[2] Also, the action

---

1. See, e.g., *DM* 12. 2. 13.

2. Scholastic philosophers generally agreed on the dictum that the action exists in the patient (*actio est in passo*) and not in the agent. The reason is that the action modifies the

itself, even when taken formally, arises from the agent and from its power; therefore, it, too, is an effect of the agent's and stands in need of a causality whereby it is caused.

Second, an efficient cause still remains a true efficient cause after the action has been completed. For after the sun has produced gold, it is a true efficient cause of the gold, and it is true to say that the gold depends upon the sun as upon an efficient cause. And yet it is not the case that the action continues.

3. But if you ask these authors what the notion of causing is for this sort of cause, they reply only* that an efficient cause's causality is to give *esse* to the effect. However, since this formula is common to all the other genera of causes as well,[3] especially formal causes, they add the following gloss: "that is, to give *esse* by effecting" or "that is, to effect or to produce."

In this they seem to go wrong in two ways. /681a/ First, they are explaining the same thing by means of itself. Second, having been challenged, they fall back into the opinion they disapprove of. For what is it to effect except to act? And by virtue of what other than an action is a thing denominated as acting? Thus, to say that an efficient cause's causality consists in the acting itself is the same as saying that it consists in the action, except that by this latter phrase one explains more formally—that is, not just by means of the concrete term, the denomination 'agent', which is the same as the denomination 'cause that is actually effecting', but by means of the abstract term ['action'] and the denominating form.[4]

4. *Second opinion.* Thus, others, in order to distance themselves completely from the position just mentioned, claim that an agent's causality cannot be anything outside of the agent but must instead be a mode that is intrinsic to the agent itself. For in all the other types of causes a thing's causality is a mode of it that affects it intrinsically. By contrast, an action as such is not,

---

patient and is inconceivable in the absence of the effect produced in the patient. The present argument accepts this principle and attempts to show that the agent's causality is distinct from the agent's action.

3. In §10 below we get a partial account of how the causality of the efficient cause differs from that of the formal cause and the material cause. Suarez has already discussed these latter types of causes in *DM* 13–16.

4. In any given pair of corresponding concrete and abstract terms, the abstract term signifies a certain determination, whereas the concrete term is predicable of the individuals that have that determination. E.g., the abstract term 'whiteness' signifies a certain color, and the concrete term 'white' is predicable of the individuals that have that determination. So, too, in the case at hand. The abstract term 'action' is just the 'denominating form' associated with the concrete term 'agent'.

properly speaking, a mode of the agent but is instead something outside the agent itself.[5]

This is confirmed by the fact that the sort of action in question, which exists in the effect, is not found in every instance of efficient causality. This is obvious in the case of creation, and yet there is a true efficient cause there.[6] Therefore, an efficient cause's causality does not as such consist in the action but consists instead in something intrinsic to the agent itself, whatever that might be.

It is confirmed, second, by the fact that a single efficient cause has a single causality with respect to a single adequate effect, and yet such a cause often has several actions rather than a single action. For example, it is by a single causality that a fire generates a fire similar to itself, and yet in this case there is one action whereby it transforms the matter, another action by which it produces the form, another action by which it unites the form [to the matter], and another action by which it produces the whole composite. For all these actions can be distinguished in the generation of a human being, and the same line of reasoning seems to hold for the remaining cases. For the very distinction among the connections and relations points to a distinction among the actions.[7]

THE RESOLUTION OF THE QUESTION

5. *The causality of an efficient cause is the action itself.* Nonetheless, one should claim that an efficient cause's causality can consist in nothing other than the action. This is the position held nowadays by the most learned modern writers, and it is suggested by St. Thomas, *Metaphysics* 5, chap. 2, in these

5. Once again, the proponents of this position agree with Suarez that the *action* is not an intrinsic determination of the agent but instead exists within the patient or effect. But they insist that the *causality* is indeed a determination of the agent. So the agent's causality must be distinct from its action.

6. The assumption behind this argument is that there is no action unless there is a patient acted upon. But in creation *ex nihilo* there is no antecedently existing patient. For Suarez's reply, see §§9 and 11 below.

7. The Latin word translated here as 'connection' is *habitudo*, which is the most general term for a relation and includes within its range not only 'categorial' relations (*relationes*) among substances and accidents but also 'transcendental' relations—e.g., the union of matter and form and the inherence of an accident in a substance—which do not fall within the Aristotelian categories. For more on the distinction between transcendental and categorial relations, see *DM* 47. 3. 10–13 and 47. 4.

words: "An efficient cause is a cause of the end with respect to *esse*, since by producing motion it leads to that which is the end." And later on: "An efficient cause is a cause insofar as it acts." Albert is of the same opinion in *Physics* 2, tract 2, chap. 6.

This position is proved by the fact that an agent cause's causality is what constitutes it (or better: denominates it) as actually acting. But this /681b/ is the action and cannot be anything else. Therefore, etc.

The major premise is obvious from the very exposition of the question laid out above, as well as from the terms themselves. For a cause is constituted in the notion of a cause by its causality. But to be an actual efficient cause is the same as being something that acts.

The minor premise also seems clear from the terms themselves, since a cause is constituted as actually acting by that which is thought of as being immediately added over and beyond the power to act. For as long as a cause is being thought of as having just the power to act, it is not being thought of as actually acting. Therefore, within the scope of this sort of cause there must be something that is *per se* and necessarily required over and beyond that power. But this is none other than the action itself, since the action is such that (i) if it is removed, then the power cannot be thought of as actually acting, and (ii) if it is posited, then necessarily the power is actually acting. It is for this reason that in *Metaphysics* 5.15 [1021a15–27], Aristotle claimed that the relation *agent* is proximately grounded in the action. Therefore, it is the action that is the agent's proper causality.

6. Second, a given cause's causality is (i) that by virtue of which it attains to its effect proximately, *per se*, and intrinsically, and conversely, (ii) that by virtue of which the effect depends upon such a cause. For the causality is, as it were, a path to, or a stretching out toward, the effect.[8] Hence, it is situated between the cause and the effect as between two termini, since it is through the causality that the cause influences the effect and that the effect proceeds from the cause. But the action is that by virtue of which an efficient cause actually attains to its effect and that by virtue of which the effect depends upon its cause. For the causality is the very dependence of the effect produced upon the cause that is producing it—as we will explain in a moment and will discuss at greater length below when we deal with action.[9] Therefore, etc.

7. Third, this position is proved by a sufficient enumeration. An action is necessary for the sort of causality in question. And nothing else besides an action is necessary or, indeed, even plausibly imaginable. Therefore, etc.

8. The word translated here as 'a stretching out' is *tendentia*.
9. See *DM* 48.

I take the major premise to be certain, especially in the present context, where we are dealing with created causes. For it is only in the case of creation that the premise can be doubted. But right now we are not dealing with creation—though, as we will show below, the premise holds true for creation as well.[10]

The minor premise will become clear from the replies to the arguments for the opposed position. For now it can be briefly explained as follows. If the agent's causality is some other thing that mediates between the power to act and the action, then that thing is either (i) antecedent to the action and in some sense its root or (ii) subsequent to the action and something that results from it or (iii) concomitant with the action. But none of these alternatives can be plausibly asserted.

The first part is proved by the fact that whatever is antecedent to the action does not pertain to the efficient cause's actual causality but instead either (i) pertains to the notion /682a/ of causing in the manner of a principle *quo* or of causing in the manner of a principle *quod* or else (ii) pertains to a condition required for acting.[11] An indication of this is that if one stops with the whole of this antecedent thing and no action follows upon it, then the cause is not yet being thought of as actually causing—regardless of whether (i) this stopping is accomplished by the intellect's prescinding [from the action] or whether (ii) the action is suspended in reality, either supernaturally or because of the cause's freedom, after all the other prerequisites have been posited. On the other hand, as soon as the action is thought of as being posited in reality, it is impossible for the cause not to be actually causing.

The second part is easily proved in the opposite way. For whatever follows upon the action is either its terminus or something posterior to its terminus. Therefore, such a thing is much less able than the action itself to pertain to the primary agent's causality, since it is properly an effect of the cause in question, be it a primary effect or a secondary effect.

The third part is likewise easily proved. For if the thing in question is only concomitant with the action, then it is *per accidens* with respect to the action. Therefore, the action can remain even if this thing is excluded. Therefore, the agent's causality will remain even if this thing is excluded. Therefore, the causality cannot consist in this thing—especially in light of the fact that it is impossible to understand or explain what this thing might be which is

10. See §§9 and 11 below, as well as *DM* 20. 4.

11. I.e., anything antecedent to an action has to do either with the principles of action (dealt with above in *DM* 18. 2–6) or with the necessary conditions for action (dealt with above in *DM* 18. 7–9). The topic of the present section, by contrast, is that which formally constitutes the thing as an actual agent.

distinct from the action, from the action's principles, and from all the conditions antecedent to the action, but which is nonetheless necessary for the action. Nor can any plausible reason for this necessity be given.

Therefore, what remains is that it is the action alone that can be the agent's causality.

THE ARGUMENTS TO THE CONTRARY
ARE ANSWERED

8. *Whether the action can be called an effect of the agent's; an action does not come to exist through another action; an agent is constituted as actually acting through an actual action.* To the foundation for the first position [12] one may reply that the action is not properly and formally the very effect that is produced by the agent; rather, it is a mode of such an effect, distinct in reality from that effect.

A sufficient argument for this claim is that the effect can remain in the absence of such a mode; or, what amounts to the same thing, the effect can remain even if its dependence changes. For the mode in question is the effect's emanation from—that is, dependence upon—the acting cause. But it is possible for the effect to depend now on this cause and afterwards on another cause; and so with respect to one and the same effect the dependence within it can vary, and in such a case nothing varies except the causality of the agents. We said a few things above about this distinction between the action and the terminus, and we will say more in what follows, in part when we discuss creation and in part when we later discuss action and passion. [13]

However, if under the term 'effect' we include not only the thing produced /682b/ but anything whatever that emanates from the agent's power, then we grant that the action is in some sense the agent's effect, since it is dependent upon the agent—or, better, it just *is* the very dependence [of the effect] upon the agent. But to be an effect in this broad sense is not repugnant to the causality; to the contrary, in all the kinds of causes we have discussed thus far the causality is an effect of the cause. For the union [of form and matter] is an effect of the form and also of the matter within its own genus; and this union is the causality of each of them according to diverse transcendental relations. The general reason for this is that a cause is always such that a causality proceeds from it; and so even though the causality is not caused for its own sake, it is nonetheless caused concomitantly and so,

12. See §2, par. 3, above.
13. Creation is discussed in *DM* 20, action in *DM* 48, and passion in *DM* 49.

broadly speaking, is included under the effect. However, it is not thereby necessary that the causality be caused by another causality or that the action be caused by another action. For it is part of the notion of a causality that it should have an immediate transcendental relation to the cause and that it should be, as it were, a medium or link between the cause and the effect. And it is in this way that an action is related to its terminus and to the efficient principle or cause from which it emanates. But the action itself does not emanate by means of another action; otherwise, there would be an infinite regress. Rather, the action just is the very emanation itself. In the same way, the terminus of a motion comes to exist by means of the motion, but the motion itself does not come to exist by means of another motion, since it is the very path to the terminus.

From this it follows (by way of reply to the second argument[14]) that it is impossible for a cause to remain an actual cause once the action has ceased or been completed. To be sure, it is possible for a thing that was an actual cause to endure; however, it will not endure under the notion *actually causing* when it is not actually having an influence on the effect. Hence, neither can the effect in such a case any longer be truly said to depend upon such a cause. Rather, the effect is said to *have depended* on it at one time for its coming to exist—a dependence that it had only by reason of an action that also existed at the time when the effect emanated from its cause.

9. *The agent's causality is not a mode intrinsic to the agent.* As for the arguments posited afterward [for the second position],[15] we deny that an agent's causality must or can be an intrinsic mode of the agent itself, distinct from the action that emanates from the agent and exists in the terminus itself or in the patient.

This denial seems obvious in the case of natural agents that act only by means of *transeunt* action. For it is not the case that such agents change or that they acquire anything by virtue of the fact that they act. Nor is there any need to conjure up a mode of the sort in question, since the action is sufficient for the effect to emanate from its agent.

Now as far as things that act by *immanent* action are concerned, if they effect nothing other than the immanent act itself, then it is likewise obvious that within the acting faculty there is no other intrinsic mode distinct from the act itself or from the immanent action /683a/ that is the causality of such an act. For the immanent action itself emanates immediately from its principle; and whatever else might be added as a medium between the faculty, as sufficiently constituted in first act, and the action will be fabricated

14. See the last paragraph of §2 above.
15. See §4 above.

gratuitously, without any necessity, and beyond the whole of the common teaching, which recognizes within these faculties nothing except the acts themselves—that is, the actions, along with their principles, which are either species or habits.

What's more, within the will there is nothing actual in which the freedom of the will is primarily exercised except the action elicited by the will itself. Therefore, it is the action that is the effective causality of such a faculty. To be sure, because the thing that comes to exist through such an action remains within the faculty itself, it follows that this sort of action is a mode that affects the acting cause—but not because this is part of the notion of an agent's causality as such.

Finally, as regards those things that effect something outside themselves by means of an immanent act,[16] it might seem that the causality whereby such a cause effects something outside itself is an act or mode that remains within it. But this is not true. For the act that remains within such a cause is not the formal causality that constitutes the thing as actually causing something outside itself. Instead, this act is either (i) the proximate principle of acting from which the causality arises or else (ii) the application of that proximate principle.[17] This can be seen in the case of God himself, of whom it is especially true that he effects something outside himself by means of an act that remains within himself. For even though this act is eternal and immutable within God, its actual causality is nonetheless posited in time, since God is not actually causing until the effect comes to exist. And so such a causality cannot be anything within God himself, who cannot be changed; rather, the causality exists within the creature that comes to exist or is changed.[18]

Therefore, an agent's causality is never a mode that intrinsically affects the agent itself as such.

10. Nor, indeed*, is it necessary that there should be a similarity on this point among all the genera of causes. For they do not all have the same nature. Material and formal causes are intrinsic causes, whereas an efficient cause is by its nature an extrinsic cause. What's more, if we compare the mat-

---

16. What Suarez has in mind here are immanent acts of intellect and will (e.g., intention, deliberation, choice) that lead to bodily motions.

17. So Suarez's reply is that some immanent acts of intellect and will are themselves causes of bodily movement, or at least acts that apply the causes of bodily movements to their appropriate patients. But the causality involved here exists in the bodily patients and is distinct from the causality that produced the immanent acts themselves.

18. So God's immanent act of will remains within himself, but it is also a cause of things outside himself. Insofar as these latter things are caused, God's action—i.e., causality— exists within them rather than within God.

ter and the form to one another, the latter is in some sense more intrinsic, since it is more proper and since it determines the matter by affecting it.

For this reason there is an analogous dissimilarity among the causalities belonging to these causes. For the form's causality is an intrinsic mode and is really the same as the form,[19] whereas the matter's causality can be called intrinsic to the extent that it exists within the matter itself, though it is not a mode that is identified with it as in the case of the form. By contrast, the causality of an agent is *per se* extrinsic and just as distinct from the agent as the effect is. /683b/ And if such a causality sometimes remains within the agent or is only modally, and not really, distinct from the agent, this is accidental to the notion of an agent as such and stems either from the fact that the agent is simultaneously the patient or from the fact that the thing that comes to exist is not altogether distinct from the agent but is instead a mode of the agent.[20]

11. As for the first confirmation,[21] I deny what is assumed. For even in the case of creation the causality consists in the action, as is proved by the argument adduced a short while ago.[22] For since this causality is temporal, it cannot consist in a mode intrinsic to the agent; therefore, it must consist in the extrinsic action. Now later on we will explain what this action is and what subject it exists in.[23]

12. To the second confirmation[24] one may reply that the argument can be turned the other way around. For whenever there is formally a single cause—that is, a single causality—there is a single action; and, conversely, when the actions are multiplied, the causalities are multiplied too. This is an indication, then, that the sort of causality in question consists in the action.

Therefore, if the generation of a fire is taken to include the antecedent alteration as well as the substantival generation, then we by all means grant that these are two actions; but in the same way there are two causalities. On the other hand, if we are talking only about the causing of the substance, then we deny that there is more than one action here. Rather, there is one and the same action whereby (i) the whole composite comes to exist, whereby (ii) the form is educed from the potency of the matter, and whereby (iii) the form is united to the matter. For what are conveyed in all these [descriptions]

19. For more on the modes of identity and distinction, see *DM* 18. 2, n. 31.

20. E.g., when an animal moves itself, it acquires a new "where," which, according to Suarez, is a mode of such a substance rather than a separable accident.

21. See §4, par. 2, above.

22. See §9 above.

23. See *DM* 20. 4.

24. See §4, par. 3, above.

are merely the several connections that one and the same action bears to its subject, to its formal terminus, and to its total terminus.

However, in the case of the generation of a human being there is a special reason (whatever some might claim) for distinguishing the action whereby the form is produced from the action whereby it is united [to the matter].[25] For this particular form does not depend on the matter as on a proper cause of its production but does depend on it within the union. Still, the action whereby the form is united to the matter is not distinct from the action whereby the composite is effected, since the composite cannot be effected in any way other than by uniting the form to the matter. (See Scotus, *Metaphysics* 7, q. 10; Antoine André, q. 13; Zimara, theorem 100; and Durandus, *Sentences* 2, dist. 1, q. 4, reply to the last objection.) /684a/

25. This is so because the rational soul—unlike material souls such as the vegetative and sentient souls—cannot be educed from the potentiality of the matter but must instead be created *ex nihilo* by God.

Section 11

Whether an Efficient Cause Corrupts or Destroys a Thing by Effecting Something, and How

1. If the very term 'efficient cause' is considered attentively, it seems to signify not a cause that takes away *esse* but a cause that gives *esse*. This is why in everything that we have said thus far about this cause we have been explicating the causality of this cause only insofar as it gives or pours forth *esse*. However, since philosophers ordinarily speak of the efficient cause in such a way that they judge it to effect not only the generation of things but also their corruption—where this involves not a giving of *esse* but rather a taking away of *esse*—it follows that in order to complete the present disputation we must say a few words about corruption as well and explain (i) whether it, too, is an instance of true efficient causality and (ii) what causality or power it is effected by.

2. *Different ways of destroying things.* Now one should note that there are two ways in which a given thing can be corrupted or cease to exist: first, because the non-*esse* of the one thing is consequent upon the *esse* of some other thing; second, because the thing is absolutely deprived of its *esse* immediately, as it were, and without this being consequent upon some other *esse*.

A piece of wood is corrupted in the first way when a fire is generated from it, since the wood's *esse* cannot exist together with the fire's *esse* in the same thing. By contrast, it is in the second way that the light in the air is corrupted by the absence of the sun. For no *esse* that is repugnant to the *esse* of a bright thing is being introduced into the air; instead, the form in question simply perishes when the cause that was conserving it withdraws. And even though one could claim that the sun's *esse* in the other hemisphere is itself naturally incompossible with the light's *esse* in the air of this hemisphere, nonetheless this is so in an exceedingly indirect and extrinsic and accidental manner—due to the absence of a necessary condition for acting and not to any incompossibility that exists intrinsically and *per se* between the light and a particular "where."[1]

---

1. The relevant necessary condition for acting is that the patient be susceptible to the sun's action. But when the Eastern Hemisphere is facing the sun, the Western Hemisphere is not susceptible to being illumined by the sun.

THE RESOLUTION OF THE QUESTION

3. *Nothing is ever destroyed directly by a positive action.* Given this, there are two principles that seem certain. The first is that a thing's being corrupted and ceasing to exist is never effected through an instance of *positive* and *proper* efficient causality except insofar as the absence of the one *esse* is consequent upon the effecting or positing of some other *esse*.

This is proved by the fact that an instance of positive efficient causality occurs only through a positive action. But a positive action does not tend immediately and *per se* toward non-*esse*. Therefore, the corruption or destruction of a given thing cannot be effected positively through such an action except insofar as /684b/ some other thing's *esse*, which is necessarily connected with the non-*esse* of the first thing, is effected through that action.

The major premise is proved by the preceding section [of this disputation],[2] and the same point is obvious from the terms themselves. For efficient causality and action are the same thing, as are that which effects and that which acts.

The minor premise is proved from the fact that, as will be shown below in its own place and as no one denies in the case of *transeunt* actions, an action that is real—that is, positive (for they are the same thing)—necessarily tends toward a real terminus.[3] But a real terminus receives some real *esse* through the action; this is why it is the action's terminus.

Hence, not even those who deny that there is a real terminus in the case of immanent actions can deny that the very action itself, insofar as it is effected positively, receives some sort of real *esse* from its own efficient cause.[4] But if something is corrupted immediately through such an action (that is, without the production of any other terminus or thing), then this is so only insofar as that action's *esse*, whatever it might be, is incompossible with the other *esse* that is destroyed. Therefore, it is true without exception that whatever is destroyed through an instance of positive efficient causality is not destroyed immediately but is instead destroyed only in consequence of some other *esse* that is effected through the action—and this consequence is always grounded in some repugnance among the things in question.

This is confirmed by the popular axiom that no agent operates insofar as it aims toward an evil. But non-*esse* as such has the nature of an evil.[5] There-

2. See *DM* 18. 10.

3. See *DM* 48. 2.

4. For a discussion of whether an immanent act has a real intrinsic terminus, see *DM* 48. 2. 5, as well as *DM* 18. 4. 5.

5. This follows from the fact that a thing's *esse* or type of existence is a good for it.

fore, it is never the case that an instance of positive efficient causality aims *per se* toward non-*esse*; rather, it aims toward some *esse* from which some other non-*esse* follows.

4. *An objection is answered*. You will object that even though this is true in the case of natural agents, it is nonetheless not true in the case of voluntary agents. For God is able to will that a given thing not exist, not in order that some other thing should exist, but simply in order that the thing in question should not exist. And it is often the case that one human being intends the death of another in this same way. Hence, among nonnatural agents it often happens that an action is aimed *per se* and primarily toward destruction.

One may reply that even though it is possible for a voluntary agent to *intend* the destruction of a thing *per se*, it is nonetheless not possible for it to *execute and effect* that destruction through an action which of itself aims primarily toward non-*esse*—and this for the reason mentioned above. Hence, even God himself, when he wills to destroy a given thing, will either achieve this through a mere suspension of his influence without any positive action or else, if he wants to use a positive action, will necessarily effect something from which the corruption in question follows. On the other hand, a human being, who is unable to destroy a thing through the mere suspension of his influence because the thing does not depend upon him for its *esse*, always makes use of actions that in general are nothing other than bodily changes of place that aim directly and *per se* toward their proper termini. /685a/ And thus the corruption or destruction follows *per accidens* and is such that even though it is intended *per se* as far as the agent's extrinsic intention is concerned, it is nonetheless effected *per accidens*—that is, as a consequence—through the sort of action in question.

5. *The directly intended destruction of a thing is effected through an absence of efficient causality; an Aristotelian axiom is explicated*. The second principle is this: When a given thing's ceasing to exist is not the consequence of the positive effecting of some other thing but is instead effected by itself *per se*, then this ceasing to exist is brought about not through an instance of proper efficient causality but through an absence of efficient causality.

This principle follows from the preceding one. For a positive action exists only as ordered toward some positive *esse*. Therefore, when no *esse* is communicated, there can be no positive action. But in the type of ceasing to exist and corruption under discussion no *esse* is communicated, but instead *esse* is simply removed. Therefore, it cannot be brought about through a true action. Therefore, it must necessarily be brought about through the absence of an action, since there cannot be any other mode of causality that pertains to an efficient cause.

You will object that this latter sort of cause, which is such that it removes a *per se* cause, appears to be merely a *per accidens* cause. But a cause of the kind of corruption under discussion is not just a *per accidens* cause but a *per se* cause. Therefore, this sort of corruption occurs through proper efficient causality as well as through the absence of a cause.

The minor premise is obvious both (i) from Aristotle's claim that just as the presence of the sailor is a cause of the ship's being conserved, so the absence of the sailor is a cause of the ship's sinking,[6] and (ii) from the fact that the effect in question cannot be traced back to a cause that is more proper and *per se*. And this seems to be the basis for the common axiom, "If an affirmation is a cause of the affirmation, then a negation will be a cause of the negation," which is evident especially in the case of causes that are proper, *per se*, and adequate.

The reply is that from this very axiom one can infer that what is to be sought as the *per se* cause of the corruption (if indeed it can have such a cause) is not something that is positively acting but rather something that is not acting, since a cause must be proportioned to its effect. Thus, even in Aristotle's example the sailor's absence is not an acting cause but rather a nonacting cause. Therefore, if this absence is compared to the ship's sinking insofar as the latter is a positive effect, then it is only a *per accidens* cause of the sinking as long as we consider the matter truly and physically—though it would be judged a *per se* cause morally and by imputation if the sailor were obligated to be present. On the other hand, if the sailor's absence is compared only to the absence of assistance or protection for the ship, then the former negation could be called a *per se* cause of the latter negation. For they are proportioned to one another, and there is an intrinsic and immediate connection between them. Therefore, in this sense, if a *per se* cause is at first pouring forth *esse* and afterwards withdraws its influence, it will be called /685b/ a *per se* cause of such an *esse*'s ceasing to exist—not because it effects the ceasing to exist by a positive action but because it is, in a proportionate way, a proper principle and source of such a ceasing to exist.

Hence, a privation is such that just as it is said to exist not through a positive *esse* but rather through the absence of an *esse*, so too it is said to be effected not through a positive action but through the absence of an action. And, analogously, a *per se* efficient cause of a privation is called a *per se* cause not because it effects the privation positively but rather because it withdraws the influence by virtue of which it had been a *per se* cause of the *esse* that

6. The assumption being made by the objector is that the ship's sinking is a positive effect consisting of the local motions and alterations of various bodies. Below Suarez carefully distinguishes the sinking of the ship thought of in this way from the "absence of assistance or protection for the ship."

is destroyed through such a corruption. Indeed, every cause that destroys another by effecting something positively is as such—that is, insofar as it is an efficient cause—a *per accidens*, rather than a *per se*, cause of the other's destruction.

COROLLARIES OF THE FOREGOING DOCTRINE

6. *A change, but not an action, occurs in any destruction of a thing whatsoever.* From these principles we can infer a few things that are worthy of note about the changes or corruptions of things.

It follows, first, that in every case of corruption—that is, loss of some real *esse*—there is a change but not necessarily always an action. This is evident from the second principle posited above, taken together with the definition of a change. For, as Aristotle attests, a thing changes when it is different from the way it was before. Thus, when the air goes from being illuminated to being dark, it changes. Therefore, some change occurs in it. And yet this change is not brought about through an action, as is obvious from the second principle posited above. Therefore, in this case there is a change without an action, and the same holds for all similar cases.

Now the reason is that the change in question is purely privative and not positive. It follows that this occurs only in the case of accidental changes, as long as we are talking about change properly and in keeping with the ordinary course of nature. For the subject of an accident can sometimes lose that accident even if it does not acquire another accident, whereas the subject of a substantial form cannot change substantivally by losing one form unless it acquires another. And this is why I said "as long as we are talking about change properly and in keeping with the ordinary course of nature." For God could suspend the influence of a substantial form even while conserving the matter; or, if the term 'change' is extended to include annihilation, he could change a thing completely from *esse* to non-*esse* without any action at all.

On this point one should also note the following difference between free causes and natural causes. Because of their intrinsic dominion and power, free causes are able to suspend their influence without any prior action or change either within themselves or within another thing. And so they can cause the sort of privative change in question /686a/ either within themselves if they are themselves changeable, as in the case of created causes, or within other things, as in the case of God. By contrast, natural causes cannot suspend their influence unless there is a prior change in some other thing that was required for their acting. And so even though they sometimes alter a subject in the aforementioned way without acting on it, nonetheless, it is always the case that some other action occurs, either with respect to that same subject or with respect to another subject. For example, the sun destroys the light in the air by withdrawing its influence only if there is some prior action whereby the sun itself moves or by which a shutter is closed, and so forth.

7. *An action that aims secondarily at destruction is always dependent on a subject; annihilation cannot take place in a subject.* Second, from what has been said it follows that whenever a thing's corruption or ceasing to exist is effected through a positive action that of itself has the role of causing such a corruption as a consequence, it is necessary for this action to be effected in a presupposed subject.

The reason for this is that a corruption or ceasing to exist is effected by virtue of a physical action (for this is what we are talking about) only because the *esse* that is effected through such an action has a natural repugnance to the *esse* that is destroyed. But there can be such a repugnance only relative to the same common subject, which remains as the subject of both termini. For among things that subsist *per se* and have no ordering to a [common] subject there cannot be a natural repugnance by virtue of which it is impossible for them to exist at the same time. Therefore, it is necessary for an action of the sort in question to exist in a presupposed subject.

From this it follows that annihilation, properly speaking, cannot be effected by God through a positive action, since annihilation leaves behind nothing of the thing in question which could serve as the subject of the action.[7] Likewise, either (i) the action would be effected in a subject, in which case it would not destroy that subject and, as a result, would not effect an annihilation, or else (ii) it would be effected without a subject, in which case nothing could be effected through it which would be repugnant to the entire *esse* of some other thing. Therefore, nothing can be annihilated through such an action.

Someone might object that the action whereby the rational soul is effected does not exist in a subject, and yet the corruption of something else— namely, the embryo—follows upon it.[8]

One may reply by denying the minor premise. The corruption of the embryo properly follows instead either (i) from the action whereby the matter is sufficiently disposed for the introduction of the rational soul or (ii) from the

---

7. On this score annihilation is distinct from corruption, in which there is a perduring material substratum or subject.

8. The assumption is that the human embryo has only a sentient soul and so ceases to exist when this soul is succeeded by a rational soul.

action whereby the soul itself is united to the body or (iii) from both these actions, each within its own genus, as will be explained below.[9] But these actions both exist in a presupposed subject. The creation of the soul, on the other hand, is presupposed in the order of nature only for the action that unites the soul to the body, whereas it is naturally consequent /686b/ upon the action that disposes the matter.

Someone could pose a more difficult objection having to do with the action whereby the bread is converted into the body of Christ. This is not an action in a presupposed subject, and yet by virtue of this action the substance of the bread ceases to exist.

Now this is a deeper problem than can be treated in this place, and it was in order to exclude it that I stipulated that the discussion would concern natural action and natural ceasing to exist—whereas this whole mystery [of the Eucharist] is supernatural. Still, in the case of this mystery I believe it to be true nonetheless either that (i) the bread's ceasing to exist does not follow here solely by virtue of a physical action and of a natural connection among the things or that (ii) if some such action does occur here, then it is in some way directed toward a subject, and the bread's quantity, which is conserved without a substance, assumes the role of such a subject—as I have argued at greater length in the proper place.[10]

8. Third, I infer that whenever a corruption or ceasing to exist is effected through a positive action, there is a single noncomplex action but two partial changes, one positive and the other privative.

For as Aristotle taught in *Physics* 5 [1.224b35–225a12], there are three ways in which something can change. The first way is from having some form to lacking it, and, as has been explained,[11] in such a case a change is effected but, speaking *per se*, no action occurs. Instead, there is an absence of a conserving action.

In the second way, the change is from a pure privation to the having of the form—for example, from being dark to being bright. And just as there is a single action in this sort of case, so too there is a single noncomplex change.

Third, something can change from having one form to having another form, as when a thing goes from being hot to being cold or from being wood to being fire. And in such a case (i) there is a single noncomplex action whereby the form being introduced *de novo* into the subject is educed from or united to that subject—for, as we have explained, no further action is necessary in order to expel the other form—but (ii) there are two changes

9. See §8 below.

10. Suarez deals with this question explicitly in *Summa Theologiae* 3, q. 75, disp. 49.

11. See §5 above.

effected, since the subject falls under two different descriptions: namely, 'lacking a form that it previously had' and 'having a form that it previously did not have.' These two changes are distinct from one another to such an extent that they are sometimes separated in reality, as was just explained with respect to the first two modes of change. Again, the one change is the generation of a substance or accident, whereas the other is the corruption of a substance or accident; or, alternatively, sometimes the one change is an intensification, whereas the other is a remission. And, finally, the one change is positive, whereas the other is privative. Hence, the changes differ from one another to the same extent that the introduction of the one form and the privation of the other form differ from one another. However, these changes can be called 'partial' changes because, physically speaking, they constitute a single complete transition from one positive terminus to another—a transition which, in philosophy, /687a/ is called the conversion of the one thing into the other.

You will object as follows: Just as both a positive change and a privative change occur in this case, so too there is both a positive action and the absence of the action by which the opposite form was being conserved by natural causes or at least by God (for this latter is always necessary). Therefore, the notion of an action and the notion of a change are the same.

One may reply that the only difference is that the notion of a change is preserved in the new privation insofar as it is in a state of coming to be, whereas the notion of an action is not at all preserved but instead requires a positive influence. This is clear from their definitions and essential notions.

9. Fourth, one may infer that a corruption effected through an instance of efficient causality is effected by the very same principles (be they principal principles or instrumental principles), accompanied by the very same conditions, that effect the generation or production upon which this sort of corruption follows.

This is proved from what has been said. For there is no efficient causality or action with respect to the corruption other than that which there is with respect to the production. Therefore, it is through the very same principles whereby the one *esse* is effected that the other *esse* is removed. And no principle can concur positively in removing one *esse* except insofar as it concurs in giving some other *esse*.

It was on this basis that we claimed above,[12] in opposition to some modern thinkers, that the form introduced into the patient by the agent does not concur as an efficient cause in expelling the opposite form—for example, that the heat introduced in the patient does not concur as an efficient cause in ex-

12. See *DM* 18. 2. 19.

pelling the coldness, and so on for the other cases. For the form introduced into the patient is not an efficient principle of its own generation. Therefore, neither is it an efficient principle of the corruption of the opposite form.

Again, if the efficient causality in question is positive, then something positive is effected through it. But the form introduced into the patient does not positively effect anything by means of which it expels the other form. Instead, the expulsion of the other form follows immediately [upon the introduction of the new form]. Therefore, etc.

10. *How one body impels another locally.* Hence, there is no analogy with the customarily adduced case of one body's expelling another from the same place, where the one seems to expel the other as an efficient cause. (See Soto, *Physics* 2, q. 4.) For even though in *Sentences* 4, dist. 12, q. 3, Scotus seems to deny that the one [body] expels the other as an efficient cause, nonetheless, the fact of the matter is that the two cases are not similar.

For the two bodies are in contact with one another, and the one impels the other; and the expelled body loses its place not through a mere ceasing to exist but through a real change and through a real inclination toward the other place to which it is moved by the expelling body as by an efficient cause. And so what is involved here is not merely the formal incompossibility of those bodies being in the same space /687b/ but also a special positive action whereby the body expelled from the one place is transported to the other—an action that is distinct from the action whereby the second body is introduced into the first body's place.

But it is different when a form introduced into a single subject expels another form. For the form that is expelled is not changed positively; instead, it just, privatively, ceases to exist. Thus, there cannot be a special efficient causality here. Therefore, there is only a formal expulsion here. And, in general, within its own genus every cause concurs with respect to the non-*esse* of the one terminus in just the way that it concurs with respect to the *esse* of the other terminus. Therefore, because the heat that is introduced into a subject heats that subject not as an active cause but only as a formal cause, it follows that it expels the coldness not as an active cause but only as a formal cause. But it is different with the heat that exists in the thing that generates heat, since that heat is a principle that effects another heat and expels the opposing coldness as a consequence.

Analogously, the heat produced in a piece of wood (and the same holds for every similar disposition), even though it excludes the directly opposed accidental form only as a formal cause, nonetheless corrupts the substance itself as a disposing cause. For it is in this way that it causes the introduction of the opposing [substantial] form and, as has been explained, a form concurs with respect to the non-*esse* of the one terminus within the very same genus of cause within which it concurs with respect to the *esse* of the opposing terminus. Hence, since an accident, by its own proper nature and power, has the role of preparing the way for a substantial form connatural to it, as well as the role of formally expelling the contrary disposition, it can be said to corrupt the substance by its own proper power within the genus of a disposing cause. So if the patient's accidents and dispositions also concur as efficient causes with respect to educing its [substantial] form, then they concur within this same genus of efficient causality with respect to the corruption of the other form; on the other hand, if they did not previously have any efficient causality with respect to the former, then they will not later have it with respect to the latter either.

And so it is true without exception that the only principles that effect the corruption are the ones that effect the generation—when, that is, the corruption is brought about through [positive] efficient causality. For if it is brought about solely through the absence of efficient causality, then it does not need a proper principle of acting; instead, all that is required is that whatever was the principle of producing or conserving the thing should stop acting.

Disputation 19

On Causes That Act Necessarily and Causes That Act Freely or Contingently; also, on Fate, Fortune, and Chance

In addition to all that was said about created efficient causes /688a/ in the preceding disputation, what remains to be discussed is the mode of acting that belongs to such causes. We have reserved this topic for the present disputation because it poses a special problem and because the frequently invoked distinction between necessary and contingent effects, as well as an understanding of a great many causes, depends upon it. Thus, we will discuss, first of all, causes that act necessarily, then free causes, and, finally, contingent causes. From all of this it will become clear what fate, fortune, and chance amount to among natural causes.

Section 1

Whether among Created Efficient Causes There Are Any That Act Necessarily, and What Sort of Necessity This Is

1. *There are causes that act necessarily once the things required for acting are present; what these required things are.* This question is easy, and so one should assert succinctly, first, that among created causes there are many that operate necessarily once all the things they require for operating are present.

This is obvious from experience and from a simple induction. For the sun illuminates necessarily, and fire produces warmth necessarily, and so on for the others. The reason for this must stem from the intrinsic condition and determination of [the agent's] nature, as we will explain in the next assertion.

Now the qualification "once all the required things are present" is added because what must be presupposed is a cause that is (i) sufficient, (ii) proximately ready [to act], and (iii) accompanied by all the conditions that are required for acting. For if one or another of these conditions is absent, then no action will follow—not, to be sure, because of an indifference or indeterminacy on the part of the cause but rather because of the absence of some co-cause or else because of the absence of a power or condition that is necessary for operating.

However, the action itself must not be counted among the things that are necessary for acting. This is evident *per se*, since otherwise one would not be asserting anything special about the causes under discussion; instead, one would be making a claim that is common to all things—not only to all agents but to all entities as well—namely, that if they have a form whereby they are constituted with such and such an *esse* or under such and such a notion, then the consequent that they are of that sort follows necessarily. For just as if someone has whiteness, then he is necessarily white, so too if someone exercises an action, then he necessarily effects something—where this is merely the necessity of the *consequence* (as they say): that is, a conditioned necessity, and not the necessity of the *consequent*—that is, an *absolute* necessity. The former kind of necessity is irrelevant in the present context, since causes cannot be distinguished with respect to it.[1] Therefore, in order

---

1. It is trivially and universally true that necessarily, if a given agent acts, then it acts. In the present context, by contrast, we are interested in the conditions under which it is true that a given agent acts necessarily, where the necessity attaches to the action itself absolutely.

for the discussion to be dealing with true and proper necessity, the action itself must not be included when a cause is said to act necessarily once all the required things are present.

From this it follows, a fortiori, that whatever is posterior to the action or consequent upon it must not be included either. This is obvious *per se*. /688b/ Indeed, properly speaking, nothing of the sort can be said to be necessary *for* the action; rather, it is said to be necessary *given* the action.

2. *The first and second things required for acting; the third; the fourth; the fifth.* Therefore, under the qualification in question one should include all and only those things that precede the action. Several of them are enumerated by the authors, as one can see in Scotus, *Metaphysics* 9, q. 14, ad 2; Antoine André, *Metaphysics* 9, q. 1, ad 2; and Zimara, theorem 112. They posit six conditions.

The first condition is that the cause have a full and sufficient power to act. This is evident *per se*, since an action must presuppose a sufficient power. And in order for a cause to act necessarily, it must be assumed to be unqualifiedly and absolutely capable [of acting]; but it cannot be absolutely capable [of acting] without a sufficient power.

The second condition is that the cause have a susceptible and sufficiently close patient. For created agents cannot effect anything except in a presupposed subject; and since they are finite agents, they require that this subject be within the proportionate sphere [of activity] beyond which they do not have the power to act.

The third condition, which follows from the second, is that if a medium is interposed between the agent and the patient, it be suitable for, and susceptible to, the agent's action. For we are assuming that agents cannot effect anything in a distant patient except through the medium.

The fourth condition is that there be nothing impeding the action that has an equal power to resist it. For nothing is able by acting to overcome [a patient] unless it surpasses it in active power, and accordingly it was shown above that a proportion of greater inequality is necessary for an action.[2]

The fifth condition is that the patient not yet be at the terminus [of the action]—that is, that the patient not yet have the whole form that the agent is able to effect. It is for this reason alone that heaviness does not produce motion in [elemental] earth that is located at the center [of the earth]. This condition is contained in the second one, since for an action the patient is required to be in a state in which it is susceptible to the action, whereas once it is at the terminus, it is no longer susceptible to the action. Indeed, this condition coincides with a condition that was discussed above: namely, that

2. On the phrase 'proportion of greater inequality', see *DM* 18. 9. 13.

the agent and the patient must at the beginning be in some way dissimilar to one another.[3]

3. *Sixth condition.* A sixth condition is added: namely, that any action which is naturally required beforehand be presupposed as already having been completed. For instance, even though a brute animal's appetitive faculty operates naturally, it is not always acting, since it necessarily requires an antecedent condition that is not always present. And, similarly, the faculty of sight does not act unless an object acts upon it beforehand.

This condition is implicitly contained in the preceding conditions. For when one action is required antecedently for another action, /689a/ it may well be because the power to act is brought to completion through it—as in the example concerning the faculty of sight, which must be acted upon antecedently by the object, since in the absence of a [sensible] species it does not have the complete power to act. There are many who say the same thing about the sort of cognition of an object which is required for an act of the appetitive faculty: namely, that it brings the [appetitive faculty's] power of acting to completion. However, it is more accurate to say that this cognition applies the object to the appetitive faculty in a sufficient and proportionate manner. For what we said in the second condition—namely, that it is necessary for the patient to be sufficiently close—must, in the case of immanent acts, be extended to the object, which serves as the matter toward which such acts are directed. And, in general, whenever an efficient cause requires other co-causes—even ones of different genera—in order to act, it will not be able to initiate its action unless all the required co-causes are disposed in such a way that they are able to concur, each within its own genus [of causality]. For the reason why a patient is required is that a created agent's action cannot be effected in the absence of a material cause. So, therefore, since the object (or a cognition of the object) is a co-cause required for a vital act of the appetitive faculty—regardless of whether it concurs as an efficient cause or as an end or as an extrinsic form or as the matter with respect to which (for concerning all these there can be different opinions, which are irrelevant at present)—it follows that the cognition of the object is an action that must precede the appetitive faculty's efficient causality.

4. *Seventh condition; eighth condition.* A seventh condition is added: namely, that the cause not be a free cause. However, we ourselves do not need this condition, since this is just what we claimed in the assertion: namely, that some causes are not free in operating but instead act of necessity once all the required things have been posited.

Again, an eighth condition can be added: namely, that the cause have the

3. See *DM* 18. 9.

necessary concurrence of the First Cause. Now this concurrence will be discussed explicitly below,[4] but as far as the present discussion is concerned, this condition either is not one of the prerequisites or else is contained in the above conditions as we have explicated them. For if we are talking about [God's] *actual* concurrence, then this concurrence is not distinct from the action itself, and so just as the action itself is not included among the antecedently required conditions for acting, so too neither is [God's] actual concurrence.[5] On the other hand, if we are talking about [God's] *aptitudinal* concurrence (as I will call it)—that is, about the First Cause being applied and conjoined in a way sufficient for his concurring—then on this interpretation the condition in question is indeed necessary, but it is contained in something we have already said: namely, that a necessary cause is one that has a complete power along with all of its co-causes.[6] For without the First Cause's power, a secondary cause's power either (i) is incomplete or else (ii), if it is said to be /689b/ complete and total within its own genus, is such that it needs to be conjoined with *all* the other required causes, no matter what their genus or type of causality might be. Therefore, what is included under this condition is every concurrence on the part of a higher cause to which the lower cause in question is essentially subordinated—regardless of whether this subordination among efficient causes exists only between created causes and the Uncreated Cause or whether it exists among created causes themselves as well. We will look into this below.[7]

5. *Whether any natural agents are indifferent with respect to more than one effect.* It is possible to add a ninth condition: namely, that the cause, if natural, not be equally indifferent with respect to more than one effect. For if it is, then by the very fact that it is a natural cause and not a free cause, it will not produce either effect by necessity, and, as a result, it will produce neither of them, since there is no more reason for it to produce the one rather than the other; and because it is not a free cause, it will not be able to be determined to the one effect more than to the other unless the indifference is removed from somewhere else.

Many examples are wont to be adduced, but we will present those which

4. The whole of *DM* 22 is devoted to God's general concurrence with secondary causes.

5. In concurring with creaturely causes, God cooperates with them in bringing about given effects. But since an action is, ontologically speaking, a mode belonging to the effect or the patient, God's action is identical with the relevant creature's action.

6. God's aptitudinal concurrence is his being ready and prepared to concur with the secondary cause in question. Strictly speaking, it is this aptitudinal concurrence that is naturally prior to the creature's action and a necessary prerequisite for it.

7. See *DM* 22. 5.

suffice to make clear the source of this indifference. The first example is that of a fire that exists at the center of the earth in the shape of a circle, each of whose parts is equally distant from an outermost place. Such a fire would not move in one direction rather than another, since there is no determining reason or cause. Nor would it move in every direction, since if it did, it would be divided into each of its parts.[8]

The second example is that of a perfectly flat piece of glass placed on top of a perfectly flat rock upon which another perfectly flat boulder falls. The boulder will not break the glass, since either it would divide it into all its parts, which is impossible,[9] or else there is no more reason why it should divide it into certain parts rather than into others.

The third common example is that of a brute animal presented with two equally desirable objects. It will not move toward either of them.

The fourth example has to do with higher causes that have the power to produce contrary effects. They cannot of themselves be determined to the one or the other effect if they are applied to acting while they have the sort of indifference in question.

A fifth and more difficult example concerns *every* natural cause. For even though a natural cause is determined to produce a form that belongs to a single species, it is nonetheless indifferent with respect to various individuals of that species.[10]

6. *Where the circular fire at the center of the earth tends toward.* Nonetheless, one should, it seems, reply that this [ninth] condition has rather to be traced back to one of the conditions posited above: that is, to the absence of one of those conditions. For the condition of indifference, taken just by itself, is in some sense incompatible with the proper determination of natural agents, since it is proper for them /690a/ to be determined to one effect. How, then, can they have this indifference of themselves?

Nor is it enough to reply that they are determined to one effect under some general notion, since in this sense even a free agent is determined to one effect: namely, to what is good in general. On the other hand, if one claims

8. According to the cosmological theory being presupposed here, the natural place of fire is the sphere of fire, which is the outermost sublunary sphere. In this example, each part of the fire has a distinct path, along a straight line, to that outermost sphere. Since each part of the fire is equally attracted along its own distinctive path, it resists any movement along an alternative path. So, the argument goes, the fire as a whole would not move in any direction at all, and, what's more, it could not move in every direction at once— presumably because it would then be divided into infinitely many actual parts, which is impossible.

9. This is impossible because the glass has infinitely many nonoverlapping parts.

10. This issue is raised in §11 below, as well as in *DM* 5. 3. 31 and 22. 1. 12.

that a natural agent is determined to a single species of effect but not to a single individual effect, then from this it follows, first of all, that the indifference found among such agents is at most the sort of indifference alluded to in the last example, and not the sort of indifference suggested in the other examples. And one can object even to the former sort of indifference, since the very idea that these agents have been established with a kind of indifference and that they are unable to determine themselves [to an individual effect] seems contrary to any fitting design on the part of nature. For on such a view they would of themselves be utterly incapable of acting.

What's more, in the first four examples, to the extent that they contain any truth, the failure to act seems to derive not from any indifference but instead from some impediment or from the absence of one or another of the necessary conditions posited above. For instance, in the first example it does indeed seem likely to me that the fire would not in that case be moved from within. But the reason for this derives from the equal degrees of activity and resistance that all the parts have. For' among the conditions required for [an agent's] acting by necessity was the condition that there be no equal power resisting the action. And yet in the case in question each part of the fire is equally inclined toward an outward motion along a line that is straight with respect to that part; and so among themselves the parts have equal degrees of activity and resistance, and this is why none of them moves. Nor would the parts be completely divided from each other by these, as it were, contrary propensities. For, first of all, the fire has a stronger inclination toward its own conservation than it does toward its [natural] place. Second, the division itself would have to be accomplished via local motion; hence, by the very fact that the parts cannot move, they cannot be divided either.

7. *Why the perfectly flat piece of glass, struck by the perfectly flat boulder, would have to shatter.* The second example cannot, first of all, occur naturally, since it is naturally impossible for one perfectly flat thing to fall on another [perfectly] flat thing in a way that is uniformly primary [with respect to each of its parts]—just as it is impossible for a flat thing to be separated from a flat thing in a way that is uniform [with respect to each of its parts], because either (i) there would have to be a vacuum or else (ii) the air would have to fill the whole of that [vacated] place instantaneously. So, too, it follows conversely that if a flat thing were to fall on a flat thing in a way that is uniform [with respect to each of its parts], then either (i) a certain parcel of air would be expelled as a whole instantaneously, with the result that it would reach a more remote spatial location just as quickly as it reached a nearby spatial location, or (ii) the air would remain in that place penetrating [the flat things] /690b/ or else (iii), assuming that the air remained in between them, the two flat things would not touch one another. Therefore, it must be the case that

the falling flat thing touches [the other flat thing] with one of its parts prior to touching it with another part.

However, the same problem could be raised about this very claim. If the thing is uniformly flat and uniformly heavy in each of its parts, then why does it fall and touch with one part prior to falling and touching with another part? For this reason one will surely have to look for some extrinsic cause of the asymmetry in question, given that bodies of this sort and a motion of this sort have been posited—for example, that the medium is not uniformly divisible in each of its parts, or something of this sort. Or else, of course, if no such cause is present, then one has to say that the flat [boulder], which falls uniformly [with respect to each of its parts], cannot expel all the air in between and for this reason can neither touch the glass nor break it. The reason for this may well be that when a minimal parcel of air is unable either to be penetrated or to pass through a volume of space as a whole all at once, it prevents any heavy falling thing from expelling it—just as, conversely, no force, however great, can separate two flat things all at once with respect to every part, since the air cannot rush in to fill the vacuum all at once. And so the reason why the effect does not follow in such a case is that the medium is sufficient to prevent it.

8. However, if, in pressing on with this problem, we assume either that the air vacates its place all at once or that the fall occurs in a vacuum, then we can make two plausible claims.

The first is that the [falling] boulder would naturally act to the full extent possible, and so it would not divide the glass but would instead compress it in such a way as to corrupt it and change it into another nature—just as we see happening with wheat that is ground by a millstone. However, the body that would thereby result might have˙ to be continuous. For if it were divided into particles in the way that meal is, then one could not give a natural explanation for why certain parts rather than others should be divided off except by tracing this heterogeneity or asymmetry in the effect back to some asymmetry in the contact and in the alteration resulting from that contact—an asymmetry arising either (i) from there being pores in the bodies themselves or else (ii) from certain other causes that were concurring there. Or, alternatively, if the contact in question were not enough to result in an alteration sufficient for corrupting the glass, then it would not be problematic—instead, it would be necessary—to claim that the glass would not be broken. The reason for this is that when one body falls on another, it does not fracture it except because of some local motion that is effected nonuniformly in the parts of the fractured body. For a fracture occurs when one part of that body—a part that can neither resist (because of a lack of power) nor give way or be deflected (because of its hardness)—is pressed down prior to another part. /691a/ But in the case described above the glass is unable to undergo local motion, since (i) it is being touched and impelled equally in each of its parts, and (ii) it is also being simultaneously and uniformly resisted in each of its parts by the body placed under it. Hence, if this latter body were not uniformly flat or uniformly solid, and if it yielded more easily in some part of itself, then the glass would be fractured at that part. And so in the example in question it would never be because of indifference that the action ceases; rather, it would be because of an impediment that puts up equal resistance.

9. *Which of two equal objects, presented in the same way, a brute animal will move toward.* In the third example one can likewise readily deny that the symmetry in question can occur naturally in all respects, since the objects cannot be equally proposed and considered simultaneously.

Alternatively, even if we grant that the equally desirable objects are represented simultaneously, we will claim that they are also loved simultaneously, but that the animal will nonetheless move to acquire the one before the other by reason of the fact that a motion in the one direction is apprehended as less difficult because of some circumstance.

And, finally, if we assume an apprehension that is uniform in *all* its circumstances—with respect to both the desiring [of the objects] and the execution [of the act]—then we will have to grant, it seems, that the animal's appetitive faculty does not have the ability to determine itself to the one object rather than the other, and this because of its lack of freedom. Hence, this lack of determination does not stem from any indifference; rather, it stems from (i) a natural necessity and determination in [the appetitive faculty's] mode of operating, along with (ii) the absence of a condition that is required in order for it to operate in that mode, an absence that derives from causes that are uniform within their own genus and that resist one another. For, as we claimed above,[11] the sentient appetitive faculty can operate only in conjunction with a sufficient proposal of and movement by the object. But this is lacking in the present case, since neither of the objects in question is apprehended *without qualification* as something to be loved and pursued, as is required in order for the appetitive faculty's effect to follow necessarily. Moreover, the reason why that sort of apprehension or judgment is not had in this case is that the objects mutually impede one another as long as they produce equal movement and resistance within their mode of causing. And so in this case, too, [certain of] the conditions enumerated above are absent.

10. *Why an equivocal natural agent produces this effect rather than that effect.* As for the fourth example, we can deny, first of all, that there is any natural

11. See §3 above.

cause that is of itself completely indifferent with respect to producing contrary effects. /691b/ To the contrary, as we shall see below,[12] Aristotle locates
the difference between free powers and natural powers in the fact that the
former are powers directed toward opposites or contraries, whereas the latter
are not at all like this but are instead directed toward just one or the other of
[a pair of] opposites.

This has to be interpreted as a *per se* claim, and one that depends on the
assumption that all other things are related in the same way [to the power in
question], since it can happen *per accidens* that contrary effects follow from
the effect of one and the same natural agent, as we explained above in the
case of antiperistasis.[13] Likewise, because of the diverse dispositions of the
matter, one and the same sun softens wax and hardens mud; and because of
differing concurrences on the part of [the other] causes, it also happens that
the sun concurs with respect to differing or mutually incompatible effects.
Nonetheless, given all the simultaneously concurring causes, the sun always
acts by a natural necessity and determination. Indeed, as far as it itself is
concerned, it always initiates the action in the same way: namely, by producing light and heat; and afterwards, depending on the disposition of the
patient or the concurrence of the other causes, the appropriate effect follows
by that same necessity.

It is in this sense that in *On Generation and Corruption* 2, text 18 [10.336a25–
31], Aristotle claims that one and the same natural agent, situated in the
same way (that is, both internally and with respect to other things), is apt
always to produce the same thing. Therefore, it does not follow from their
power to produce contrary effects that there is also an indifference within
natural causes. For they can never effect contraries by themselves alone but
only in conjunction with other things; once these latter things are posited,
the natural causes produce one or the other effect by necessity.

11. *How it is that any efficient cause produces, within the same species, this singular effect rather than that one.* In the fifth example there is a somewhat greater
ambiguity regarding the indifference or determination of each natural cause
with respect to individual or singular effects.[14]

On this issue there is the not implausible view that even though a natu-

---

12. See *DM* 19. 2. 22.

13. See *DM* 18. 9. 15–20.

14. The problem is this: Suppose a given agent in a given set of circumstances necessarily produces, say, the form of fire. Why is it that it produces *this* fire rather than some
other perfectly similar fire? This question is intimately related to questions concerning the
individuation of substances and accidents and is indeed raised by Suarez in his treatment
of individuation. See *DM* 5. 3. 31.

ral cause's power, considered absolutely, is indifferent with respect to many individuals in the manner of a cause that is higher and sufficient with respect to all those individuals, nonetheless, when such a power is applied to this particular patient in these particular circumstances, it is naturally determined to effect a given singular form. Moreover, when we say that a cause acts necessarily once all the required things are present, we are talking about all the particular things that are required for the action.

However, as I mentioned above,[15] it is more likely that this determination to a singular effect derives from the First Cause's concurrence and delimitation. Given such a concurrence and delimitation, one should claim that this condition too is included among the prerequisites for acting, on a par with those prerequisites that we have already explicated. For a secondary cause needs the First Cause's concurrence, /692a/ which is determined to a particular effect. Once this concurrence is furnished in first act and all the other required things are added,[16] a given [secondary] cause is necessarily determined to a given particular effect. And so on this view too there is no indifference that is incompatible with the action's being naturally necessary.

Nor is it the case, as the objection maintained, that this last type of indifference, according to which natural agents are unable to determine themselves to singular effects unless that determination originates with the First Cause, is contrary to the fitting design of nature. Rather, this is a natural imperfection and requirement on the part of such agents, and it is the type of subordination that they have to the First Cause, a subordination by virtue of which they are thought of as his instruments. And so just as they depend on the First Cause in their operating, so too they depend on him for the determination to produce this individual rather than another. Indeed, it is on the basis of this effect [of the First Cause] that we properly come to grasp that nature's work is the work of intelligence, and that an effect, no matter how necessary it is with respect to its particular cause, is nonetheless a free effect with respect to its Universal Cause.

Thus, it is clear from all these things that among natural causes there is, properly speaking, no indifference that conflicts with a necessity of acting in such a way as to preclude its being the case that, once all the other co-causes and conditions required for acting are posited, a natural cause acts of necessity without any sort of indifference at all.

15. See ibid.

16. The concurrence as furnished in 'first act' is equivalent to God's *aptitudinal* concurrence, while the concurrence as furnished in 'second act' is equivalent to God's *actual* concurrence. See §4 above.

WHICH CAUSES ACT NECESSARILY

12. Second, one should assert that all causes that operate without the use of reason operate as such with the aforementioned necessity.

This assertion is taken from Aristotle, *Metaphysics* 9.2 [1046b5–24], where the distinction he draws between rational and nonrational powers is that nonrational powers are determined to one effect whereas rational powers are indifferent with respect to opposite effects. Later on we will see what he means by rational powers and whether this latter mode of operating belongs to all of them. For the present we are asserting merely that every faculty which altogether lacks the use of reason exercises its operations by natural necessity.

This assertion can likewise be confirmed inductively, since it is clear from experience for all the various levels of things, all the way up to brute animals.

13. *Whether the sentient appetite of a human being acts freely or necessarily.* The only possible doubt has to do with the human sentient appetite, to which some writers attribute an alleged trace of freedom. Indeed, there are those who extend this trace of freedom to brute animals—a point that we will take up again below.[17]

However, on this issue, which is widely disputed in theology, /692b/ the truth is that if there is any participation in freedom within the human sentient appetite, this is so only to the extent that there is a participation in reason within the human [sentient] estimative faculty. On the other hand, if within the estimative faculty there is no true reasoning process (as in fact there is not), then within the sentient appetite, taken by itself, there is likewise no true freedom that excludes a necessity of operating once all the required things have been posited.

And so the induction made above is in fact confirmed and, as it were, completed by this example. Now, as we will see below,[18] the explanation for this is that the use of reason is the adequate root of freedom, and thus the absence of the use of reason is likewise the adequate cause of the absence of freedom and, consequently, the adequate cause of a necessity in operating. However, if we are looking for an intrinsic and, as it were, positive source of this latter mode of operating, then there is no source other than the very nature of the relevant entities or faculties, which by their nature have this sort of determination in their mode of operating because they are not perfect enough to be able to partake of a dominion over their own operations. In the

17. See *DM* 19. 2. 9.

18. For a discussion of the sense in which reason is the root (though not the subject) of freedom, see *DM* 19. 4. 4 and 5.

same way, an indifference in operating derives intrinsically and adequately from the dignity of the rational faculty, as we will explain below.[19] Moreover, just as the affirmation of the one is a cause of the affirmation of the other, so too a denial of the one is a cause of the denial of the other.[20]

14. Lastly, one can infer from this that the necessity in question is so strong that neither the intrinsic power of the faculty itself nor any other natural cause whatsoever is able to remove it or to prevent it from issuing in an act. To be sure, natural causes can, as we have explained, impede one another through resistance or through a contrary action, and in this way they are also capable of removing all the things that are required for acting. But once those things have been posited, natural causes cannot prevent the action of a necessary agent, since they do not have the power either to change the nature of things or to remove wholly intrinsic properties.

God alone seems to have this power. For it is through such power that he brought it about that the fire did not incinerate the three young men, and so on.[21] Still, if the matter is considered carefully, even God himself does not seem to be able to bring it about in the composed sense (as they call it) that a cause which by its nature acts necessarily should fail to act once all the things required for acting have been posited. Rather, he is able only to remove one of the required things; and in this way he is able to bring it about *simpliciter*—that is, in the divided sense—that such a cause does not operate. For instance, in the example cited, God prevented the fire's action by withholding his own concurrence from the fire—that is, by not applying his own power to operating along with the fire. But this is one of the prerequisites for the fire's being able to act. Therefore, it is not the case that God brought it about that the fire did not act even though all the required things had been posited; instead, he removed one of those things. For if God had decided on his own part /693a/ to grant his concurrence and had left all the other required conditions intact, then he would have been unable to prevent the action. For it involves a contradiction to remove that which is natural in the absence of any contrary efficient causality, or at least without withholding the assistance or efficient causality that is required on God's part. For how can a natural action be prevented if no impediment is posited? Or what impediment could there conceivably be if none of the impediments

19. See *DM* 19. 5.

20. The inference goes both ways—i.e., from having reason to being free and from not having reason to not being free—because having a rational faculty is an *adequate*—i.e., necessary and sufficient—condition for being free.

21. This is an allusion to the biblical story, in Dan. 3, of the three young men in the fiery furnace.

just mentioned were present? And so once the presupposition in question, explained as above, has been made, the action arises with such a strong necessity that it cannot be impeded except by removing some part of what has been presupposed.

Now the difference in this regard between God and other, created agents is that once all the things outside God that are required for the actions of natural agents have been posited, God is able by his own will alone to impede the action by withholding that which is required on his part. Other, created agents, by contrast, are not capable of this. Rather, it is only through some [positive] action or opposing resistance—or at least through some local motion—that they are able to pose an impediment or to remove the matter or some other necessary condition.

And so it is sufficiently clear what sort of necessity this is and how extensive it is.

Section 2

Whether among Efficient Causes There Are Some That Operate without Necessity and with Freedom

1. *Arguments for the negative reply.*[1] This question is very important and far-reaching, and to a great extent it depends on the theological problems that arise from the supernatural mysteries of grace and divine predestination. However, here it will be discussed only to the extent that it can be stated in terms of natural principles.

Thus, if we look to natural reason, there seem to be many arguments proving that there cannot be any efficient cause without an intrinsic necessity of acting.

The first argument is this:[2] The First Cause, from which all other causes emanate, operates by a necessity of nature, and nothing other than this is intelligible to natural reason; therefore, a fortiori, the same holds for all other causes that operate in subordination to the First Cause.

The antecedent is commonly supported by appeal to the views of Aristotle and other philosophers. Furthermore, it is evident to reason, since if God did not operate by a necessity of nature, then he would not be immutable, since he would be able to be different now from what he was before.

The primary consequence is proved as follows: A secondary cause does not act unless it is moved by the First Cause; therefore, if the First Cause necessarily moves a secondary cause to operate, then the secondary cause is necessarily moved /693b/ and thus operates necessarily, since an active motion cannot exist without a passive motion[3] and an actual act of moving [something] to operate cannot exist without an actual operation—both because there cannot be an act of moving without a terminus and also because a divine act of moving cannot be frustrated.

2. *Second argument.*[4] And from this there follows a second argument, which goes through even if we assume that the First Cause acts freely and not by necessity. For even though it properly follows from this assumption that the effects are not necessary with respect to the First Cause, nonetheless, one

1. The arguments that Suarez lays out here in §§1–7 form the subject matter of *DM* 19. 3–9 below.

2. This first argument is answered in *DM* 19. 3.

3. This is equivalent to saying that there cannot be an action unless something is effected by that action.

4. This second argument is discussed in *DM* 19. 4.

can, it seems, infer just as effectively that there is no other cause, subordinated to the First Cause, that does not operate by necessity. For no other cause operates without being moved by the First Cause, since every secondary cause needs to be moved by the First Cause. But every cause that is a moved mover operates by necessity. For its being moved is not within its own power but is instead within the power of the mover, whose act of moving is such that the moved mover can neither posit it nor impede it, whereas the moved mover's operating follows necessarily [from that act of moving], as we argued above.[5]

3. *Third argument.*[6] The third argument is this: It was shown in the preceding section that every cause that operates without reason acts by necessity.[7] Therefore, if there is any cause at all that acts without necessity, it will be either a human being or a created intelligence. (I am leaving the First Cause out of consideration for now, since here the discussion is mainly about created causes.) But if one follows natural reason, then this claim cannot be made about either of these two sorts of causes.

This is proved, first, for the case of the intelligences. They are known by natural reason only as the movers of the celestial orbs. But in that action they cannot be thought of as freely acting causes; otherwise, the motions in question would be neither necessary nor unavoidable, and the created intelligences would be able by their own choice to change the order of the universe. This is why the philosophers claimed that the secondary intelligences are as immutable as the First Intelligence. Therefore, since the same line of reasoning that holds for this effect holds for other effects as well, the intelligences—insofar as they can be known by natural reason—must be thought of as causes that act necessarily in all cases.

And on this basis the second part of the claim, which has to do with human beings, is proved a fortiori. For, first of all, acting without necessity pertains either to perfection or to imperfection. If it pertains to perfection, then, given that the intelligences do not partake of it, how will we attribute it to human beings? If it pertains to imperfection, then why will we attribute it to human beings rather than to brute animals?

Second, a human being is subject to celestial influences in the same way that other lower entities are. But from the influence of a celestial body lower causes acquire a kind of necessity /694a/ in their own effects. Therefore,

5. See §1 above.

6. This third argument, along with the fourth argument in §4 below, is discussed at length in *DM* 19. 5.

7. See *DM* 19. 1. 12–14.

human actions and practices partake of necessity because of that same influence—a conclusion that experience itself and the predictions of astrologers seem to support convincingly.

4. *Fourth argument.* The fourth argument is this: If any cause operates without necessity, then it must have some faculty or power that has the ability to hold back its own operation even when all the things required for acting have been posited. But there is no such faculty among created things. Therefore, neither is there freedom—that is, an absence of necessity—in their acting.

The major premise is clear from the converse of what was said in the preceding section. For a secondary cause does nothing except through some faculty of its own. But a faculty is the principle of a necessary operation if it exercises that operation necessarily once all the required things have been posited. Therefore, in order for an action not to be necessary, some faculty must have the opposite mode of operating.

The minor premise is proved from the fact that if there were a faculty of this sort, then it would be either the intellect or the will, since we have explained that there is no faculty of this sort among any of the lower things.

However, [the mode of operating in question] cannot be attributed to the intellect, since, as is obvious from experience, the intellect gives its assent by necessity once the truth has been sufficiently cognized. Therefore, the intellect is of itself a faculty that is terminated in one effect. And if at times it is not adequately determined, this is only (i) because of an insufficient application on the part of the object or (ii) because the reasons that are proposed conflict with one another and, as it were, resist one another—which is not enough for an indifference in operating, as we explained above, *mutatis mutandis*, in the case of the lower faculties.[8]

5. The will does not seem to have this mode of operating either. For the intellect is a more perfect faculty than the will. Therefore, if the intellect does not partake of this mode of operating, then neither does the will. Besides, the will does not operate unless it is moved and determined efficaciously by the intellect.[9] For the will is a blind faculty which (i) cannot issue in an act unless it is led by the intellect and which (ii) cannot resist the intellect if the latter moves and commands it efficaciously. Otherwise, there could be a defect in the will even if the intellect, for its own part, acted to direct the will—something that moral philosophers do not admit.[10]

6. This argument is confirmed, first, by the fact that the will (and the

8. See *DM* 19. 1. 5–11.

9. The relation between intellect and will in a free act is discussed below in *DM* 19. 6.

10. The source of defects in acts of will is taken up below in *DM* 19. 7.

same holds for the intellect) operates by necessity in its most important actions—namely, in loving the good as such and in intending the ultimate end; therefore, it acts by necessity in all its actions.[11]

The consequence is obvious, first, from the fact that a single faculty has a single mode of operating. It is obvious, second, from the fact that operating /694b/ by necessity is either better or not better than operating without it. If it is better, then if the will attains this mode of operating in its most important acts, it will attain it in all its acts. If it is not better, then for the very reason that the will does not have this more perfect mode of operating in all its acts, and especially in those that are proper to it, it will not have it in the rest of its acts either.

7. The argument is confirmed, second, by the fact that if the will is free in any of its operations, then it has that freedom either at the very instant it operates or else before it operates. But it does not have it at the very same instant it operates, since by then it is already necessarily operating. For just as a thing, once it exists, necessarily exists, so too once it operates, it necessarily operates. Nor does it have freedom before it operates, since it is not then exercising a nonnecessary action—and, besides, at that time it is necessarily not operating.[12]

REMARKS WHEREBY THE MEANING OF THE QUESTION IS EXPLAINED

8. *'Necessary' and 'free' are taken in several senses.* Even though the question under discussion is a general one about all created causes—in fact, it can even be extended to the Uncreated Cause—nonetheless, we will be treating it specifically as it concerns human actions, both because (i) these actions are better known to us and it is about them that the discussion is most often carried on, and also because (ii) as far as all lower agents are concerned, we are assuming, as was noted in the preceding section, that there is no room among them for any mode of acting other than by necessity, while as far as higher agents are concerned, we cannot philosophize about them except by a certain analogy with our own deeds, to the extent that we are similar to these higher agents in intellect and will.

Now in order to get clear about the terms, one must note that the terms 'necessity' and 'freedom', and 'free' and 'necessary', can be taken in various

---

11. The question of which of the will's acts are necessary and which are free is discussed below in *DM* 19. 8.

12. This argument is answered in *DM* 19. 9.

senses. For speaking properly and in the manner of logicians, the necessary is opposed both to the impossible and to that which is possibly not the case. In this sense, an action that is called necessary is one that is not able not to exist or come into existence—always presupposing the hypothesis that all the things required for acting have been posited. This is the sort of necessity on the part of an action that we talked about in the preceding section.

However, the necessary is often taken in another sense, according to which it is opposed to the voluntary. And in order for an action to be called necessary in this sense, it is not enough that it not be able not to be exercised; rather, it is also required that it not be voluntary. This can happen in two ways: namely, either by *negation* or by *contrariety*.

In the first way, all the actions of things that lack cognition are called necessary, even if those actions are wholly natural. For even though such actions can metaphorically be called spontaneous, given that /695a/ they conform to a natural and metaphorical desire, nonetheless, they are not properly voluntary, since they do not proceed from cognition, without which the voluntary cannot exist—as is clear from [Aristotle], *Ethics* 3.1 [1109b30–1111b3], and as St. Thomas says in *Summa Theologiae* 1–2, q. 6, a. 1 and 2.

In the second way, what is called necessary is that which is violent and coerced, since it is contrary to a proper elicited desire: either a perfect—that is, rational—desire or an imperfect—that is, sentient—desire.

And in this way, if a brute animal's action proceeds from a desire alone, then even though the action is necessary in the first sense, it is nonetheless not necessary in either of these two ways just mentioned. For it is neither a violent action nor a merely natural action but is instead a spontaneous action. However, the action will be necessary in the way in question if the animal is forced to do something contrary to its own desire, and as far as this point is concerned, the same holds for a human action. This is the sense in which it is said in 2 Corinthians 9:[7], "Not out of sadness or necessity . . ." —though, to be sure, human actions can be called necessary in other senses as well, even if they are voluntary (indeed, even if they are free): namely, by reason of their being done out of a necessity of precept. Concerning this latter necessity 1 Corinthians 7:[37] says, "Not having necessity, but having the power of one's will." For such actions are done out of a certain servile subjection, in the way that the actions of a servant are called necessary, especially if the servant does them out of fear.

9. Now since the free is opposed to the necessary, 'free' is said in almost as many ways as 'necessary' itself is. For if the term 'free' (*liber*) is thought of as taken from the verb 'to render free from' (*liberare*), so that an action that is called free is one that is free from every sort of necessity, then an action that is free in all respects will be one that has none of the aforementioned kinds

of necessity—something that is hardly found at all except in God's action, though it is also found in some human actions in their own way, especially in those actions that are upright and are done only on the basis of deliberation and out of a desire for rectitude and justice. And 'free' is taken sometimes in such a way that it excludes not only necessity in the proper sense but also servitude, in the way that in Scripture those who are sanctified by grace or glory are said to be especially free—that is, free from the servitude of sin.

Alternatively, an action that is called free is one that is not coerced but is instead voluntary. This sort of freedom does not exclude the first type of necessity, which consists in a determination to one effect with an inability to suspend the action; instead, it excludes only violence and coercion. On this interpretation, it is utterly obvious that there are nonnecessary actions not only among human beings but also among brute animals, even though such actions are more perfect in human beings /695b/ because the notion of the voluntary is realized more completely in them. Some writers, especially heretics, have taken this point as an occasion for claiming that human actions are free for no other reason than that they are perfectly voluntary, so that 'free' (*liber*) is taken not from the verb 'to render free from' (*liberare*) but from the verb 'it is pleasing' (*libet*).

However, lastly, and in the most proper sense, an action that is called free is one that is truly free from the sort of necessity that natural and nonrational things have in acting, as this was explained in the preceding section. This is the sort of freedom or nonnecessity that we are properly discussing in the present question, and it is on this interpretation that freedom was always discussed by earlier philosophers as well. For no one has ever doubted—or been able to doubt—that in many of their actions human beings operate spontaneously and by their own will, moving and applying themselves to action in the light of previous cognition; instead, what has evoked disagreement is the question of whether necessity and a determination to one effect are intermingled with this very voluntariness.

POSITIONS THAT DENY FREEDOM

10. Now on this matter there was the ancient error of certain philosophers who claimed that all the effects and actions of the causes in the universe, even those of human wills, proceed by a sort of fatalistic necessity that arises from the connection among all causes and from the influence of the celestial bodies and stars. This is what Augustine recounts in *Confessiones* 4, chap. 3, as well as in *De Civitate Dei* 5, chap. 1, where Louis Vives cites Democritus, Empedocles, and Heraclitus as favoring this position, which is also

commonly attributed to the Stoics—though unjustifiably, as I will explain below.[13] In later times this erroneous opinion was adopted by many heretics—for example, Simon Magus, Bardesanes, Priscillian, Manichaeus, and others—as is clear from Augustine and other early writers. What's more, this same error has been revived by the heretics of our own time, as is extensively recounted by the modern doctors who have argued against them very insightfully.

However, as I see it, [these philosophers and heretics] have not all propounded this error in the same way or by appeal to the same principles. For some have attributed the necessity in question to the influence of the stars, whereas others have attributed it to God's concurrence and moving action or to the efficacy of God's will or to grace. Again, some have denied freedom altogether and in all actions—both internal and external, both good and evil—whereas others /696a/ have denied freedom only in moral or just actions, but not in civil or indifferent actions.

11. Still, hardly any of the aforementioned philosophers or heretics has made sufficiently clear whether the necessity he attributes to human actions arises from the intrinsic nature of a human being or whether, instead, it arises solely from the action of some extrinsic cause. For it is only in the latter way that they explicate this necessity, and yet, if they are to speak consistently, they must hold that the necessity is also grounded in the intrinsic nature of a human being—namely, in the fact that there is within a human being no faculty that is of its own nature indifferent in its actions. For when things are moved in a way befitting their nature rather than violently, then each is moved in the way in which it is naturally apt to be moved. Therefore, since both the influence of the celestial bodies and God's concurrence are natural rather than violent, if human beings always operate necessarily because of causes of this sort, then this is an indication that they require such a mode of operating by their nature.

(I am leaving out of account the positions of those who have attributed this necessity to either divine grace or original sin, which are not natural causes but rather causes that are merely extrinsic and either preternatural or supernatural. A thorough discussion and refutation of these errors belongs to theology rather than metaphysics, since an inquiry into original sin, grace, and other similar causes exceeds natural reason.)

Therefore, there are two things that we must prove in opposition to the errors in question. The first is that there exists in a human being an active faculty that is not of itself and by its own intrinsic and particular nature determined only to one effect but is instead of itself indifferent as regards

13. See §12 below.

doing this or doing that, or indifferent as regards operating or not operating, given that all the things required for acting have been posited. Second, it must be shown that there is no extrinsic cause that always impedes this mode of operating. For in this way it will have been shown that (i) among created agent causes there are some that are able to operate with freedom rather than by necessity and that (ii) they often in fact operate in this way.

IT IS SHOWN THAT HUMAN BEINGS
OFTEN OPERATE FREELY

12. Thus, I assert, first, that it is evident to natural reason and evident from the very experience of things that in many of his actions a human being is led not by necessity but by his own will and freedom.

This thesis is proved, first, from the common consensus among the philosophers. For this is how Aristotle and the Peripatetics think of a human being's freedom, as is clear from Aristotle, *Metaphysics* 9.1ff. [1045b27ff.], /696b/ where he distinguishes rational faculties from nonrational faculties and grants only to the former the intrinsic power of doing contrary things *per se*—that is, by their internal freedom. Moreover, in *Ethics* 3, from the beginning [1.1109b30ff.], he establishes this freedom as the basis for the whole of moral doctrine. Plato acknowledged this same freedom, as is evident from the *Gorgias* and from the last book of the *Republic* [617D–620A]. Even the Stoics excluded human wills from the necessity of fate that they affirmed for all other things, as Augustine testifies in *De Civitate Dei* 5, chap. 10, where Vives, drawing from Plutarch, *Placita* 1, reports that the Stoics had the same view as Plato regarding human freedom. Likewise, in *De Divinatione* and *De Natura Deorum*, Cicero, in order to safeguard human freedom, rejected divine foreknowledge because he thought that it conflicted with human freedom, which he took to be evident from our very experience of things; and so, as Augustine puts it in the place cited above, "in order to make men free, he made them sacrilegious." This, then, is an indication that the truth in question is sufficiently clear by the natural light [of reason]. For it was accepted by the common consensus of the more astute philosophers and their schools.

In addition, the Fathers of the Church, as well as all the scholastics and Catholic philosophers, defend this truth with great constancy. Not all of them need be cited here but only those who discuss this truth by appeal to philosophers and philosophical principles—for example, Eusebius, in the whole of *De Praeparatione Evangeliae* 6; Gregory of Nyssa, in the last four books of *De Philosophia*, which are attributed to him and are found in Nemesius, *De Natura Hominis*, where˙ this issue is treated from chap. 32 to chap. 42; Damascene, *De Fide Orthodoxa* 2, chap. 25; and Augustine, vol. 1, in the three books of the *De Libero Arbitrio*. Moreover, in volume 7, where Augustine argues against Pelagius, defends free choice, reconciles it with grace, and proceeds from theological principles, he presupposes the natural truth in question as certain and shows that grace does not destroy nature but instead brings it to perfection. In addition, Prosperus, Anselm, Bernard, and the other Fathers who wrote about the reconciliation of free choice with grace and foreknowledge proceed in much the same way.

From this it is clear, incidentally, that when these and the other early authors defend free choice, they are talking about freedom not only insofar as it is opposed to coercion but also insofar as it excludes a necessity in operating. Otherwise, they would not have struggled to reconcile freedom with grace, providence, and predestination, since it is utterly obvious that the things we do by our will we do spontaneously and without coercion. Rather, the problem could only have had to do with /697a/ an indifference in operating. Thus, it is in defending this indifference and in harmonizing it with God's grace and moving action that they work so hard.

13. *The assertion is proved from experience.* Second, we can argue from experience. For it is evident to us from experience that it is within our power to do a given thing or to refrain from doing it; and we use reason, discourse, and deliberation in order to incline ourselves toward the one rather than the other. That is why choice is posited in our faculty of judgment. Otherwise, as Damascene correctly observed in the place cited above, this ability to ponder and deliberate would have been given to us in vain. Consider also the ordinary way of performing and guiding human actions through advice, through laws and precepts, through exhortations and censures, through promises of reward and threats of punishment. All this would be superfluous if human beings operated by a necessity of nature and not by their own freedom.

14. *An objection that weakens the experiential evidence.* Someone will object that the only thing that these indications and experiences prove clearly is that a human being is guided and moved by reason in his operations, not that he exercises those operations freely. For all the things proposed in the argument—namely, punishments and rewards, exhortations, deliberations, and so on—seem to contribute only to the conclusion that the actions in question, or their objects, are apprehended and judged as either things that are desirable or things to be avoided, and not to the conclusion that they are freely chosen. Consequently, one who is persistent on behalf of the contrary position will insist that (i) once the apprehension engendered by all the relevant causes and circumstances has been posited, a human being is necessarily determined to do this or to do that, and that (ii) the apprehension or

judgment is itself necessary once the causes in question have been applied. Now the application of these causes is oftentimes from without, and in such a case it likewise cannot be free but is instead necessary for the individual himself. On the other hand, sometimes the application comes from his own will, as when he voluntarily deliberates or investigates in order to choose, and in such a case the claim will be that (i) this very willing [to deliberate] arises necessarily from some other apprehension or judgment and thus that (ii) one must always arrive at some first apprehension or judgment that proceeds from external causes.

This way out [of the assertion] can be confirmed by the fact that even in the case of certain brute animals we see that they are kept from doing a given thing by punishments inflicted on them—so much so that oftentimes the memory of a past punishment is sufficient for this. Similarly, they are induced by kindnesses and by certain signs or words that serve as exhortations or incitements. All these things, as well as similar things, are done to animals not because it is within their power /697b/ to act or not to act but rather because they are moved in diverse ways corresponding to diverse apprehensions—moved spontaneously, to be sure, but nonetheless by necessity, in accord with what the apprehensions demand. Therefore, one can contend that it is in this same manner that a human being is moved to operate through exhortations, advice, and so forth—to be sure, with more perfection as regards the mind's reasoning and its perception of all the reasons that can determine the appetitive faculty or the will, but not with more perfection as regards indifference or an absence of necessity.

A second possible confirmation is this: If we imagine that at a given time God necessitated the will of some person who has the use of reason (for we are assuming that God can do this), then in such a case it would seem to that person that he was operating by his own choice and volition in just the way that he now operates. For he would feel that he was moving himself by his own reason and will, and he would have no basis for recognizing the necessity imposed by God from without. Therefore, one cannot adequately infer from experience alone that free operations exist in human beings.

15. *The objection is answered.* One may reply that these arguments establish that the experience in question is not so transparent and *per se* evident that there is no room left for an obstinate person to raise difficulties. Otherwise, it would have been impossible for there to be such a diversity of opinions and errors about this matter among human beings themselves.

Nonetheless, if we resolve to undertake a full investigation of our mode of operating, then we will easily counter the objections just raised. For our experience shows that it is not only when our cognition or apprehension of an object changes but also when it remains the same, that it is up to our own will whether to sit or stand, whether to enter by this way or that way, and so forth. This, then, is an indication that this versatile mode of operating consists formally and proximately not in reason's deliberation and apprehension but rather in freedom or indifference. Further, our experience shows that even after we apprehend a threat of punishment or a promise of reward, it is within our power to be moved or not to be moved by such a consideration. And the same holds for pleas, exhortations, and similar incitements. Finally, after deliberating about the means [to an end], we sometimes choose one means over another solely because we will to. And thus it is also clear that what was adduced above about brute animals is not analogous.

As for the confirmation that had to do with the divine power imposing necessity, we reply, first of all, that the natural evidence in question leaves aside miracles or extraordinary actions on God's part. Hence, it will be sufficient if we show, on the basis of the effects, that (i) the relevant mode of operating exists within our intrinsic faculty /698a/ and, consequently, that (ii) it is not connatural to this faculty or in keeping with the nature of things that it should be moved in some other way by God from without, and that (iii) unless [this sort of extrinsic divine movement] is clear from revelation, it cannot be affirmed of any of our operations, not to mention all of them.

16. Next, we can add experiential evidence derived from morally depraved human actions, which cannot, without a manifest impiety that is opposed to the light of nature itself, be attributed to a divine moving action that imposes necessity. Thus, such evil actions proceed from our own free determination. This is so especially in light of the fact that God not only prohibits these actions but also punishes them severely. But this would be utterly unjust if he imposed a necessity with respect to these same actions.

From this it is also clear that punishment and reward are conferred on a human being not only for the sake of future actions (that is, in order that he might be either attracted toward them or drawn away from them) but also precisely and *per se* because of the good or evil that he has done *within* the actions. And it is for the same reason that a human being is judged to be worthy of praise and honor because of his actions—all of which would be unintelligible in the absence of freedom.

What's more, the point in question is also confirmed by the fact that among all people this is the common way of thinking about human actions. For everyone believes that those who act badly deserve punishment by the very fact that acting in such a way has been placed within their own power and will. This is why people get indignant when they suffer an injustice inflicted by someone who has the use of reason but not when they suffer an injustice inflicted by someone who is insane or absentminded. Indeed, the harm inflicted by these latter is not even counted as an injustice. Hence, as Eusebius correctly points out in the place cited above, even those who deny free choice, when they reluctantly bear injustices inflicted on them by other people and try to avenge them, are acknowledging—whether they wish to or not—that those injustices were inflicted freely. For if it had not been within the power of those others not to inflict such harms, then in that case the notion of an injustice or of just anger or redress would not apply.

And it is also on this basis that in *De Fide Orthodoxa* 2, chap. 7, Damascene claims that there is neither virtue nor vice in that which occurs by necessity. This was also taught authoritatively by Dionysius in *De Divinis Nominibus*, chap. 4; by Augustine in *De Vera Religione*, chap.14, and in *Epistolae*, no. 46, where he says that if free choice were removed, then judgment and just punishment, and even scolding, would be removed; by Chrysostom in *Matthew*, homily 60, and in the sermons on providence; by Clement of Alexandria, *Stromaton* 1; and by many others.

17. Lastly, we can give an a priori argument, which will have to be taken from the mode and perfection of the cognition that belongs to an intellectual* nature: /698b/ Freedom has its origin from intelligence, since a vital appetitive faculty takes cognition as a guide, and so a more perfect sort of appetitive faculty accompanies a more perfect sort of cognition. Therefore, a cognition that is universal and in its own way indifferent guides an appetitive faculty that is likewise universal and indifferent. Now an intellectual cognition is universal and perfect in such a way that it perceives the proper notion of an end and of a means [to an end], and with respect to each thing it can assess that thing's goodness or badness, usefulness or unsuitability; likewise, it can judge that a given means is necessary for an end or that it is indifferent in the sense that other means can be used. Therefore, an appetitive faculty that takes this sort of cognition as a guide has a corresponding sort of indifference—that is, complete power—in its desiring, with the result that it does not necessarily desire every good or every means but instead desires each in accord with the degree of goodness that is judged to be in it. Therefore, a good which is judged to be indifferent and not necessary is loved freely and not necessarily. And it is in this sense, as I was explaining above,[14] that free choice follows upon rational deliberation.

The argument is confirmed as follows: God is a free agent by reason of the fact that he freely wills goods that are not necessary for himself; therefore, creatures who participate in the intellectual grade [of being] and who in some sense agree with God in this also participate in the free mode of operating.

14. See §15 above.

The antecedent will be proved below in the discussion of God's perfec-tions.[15] The consequence is proved, first, by the fact that the most perfect sort of freedom follows (in our way of conceiving it) upon the most perfect sort of intellectuality; therefore, corresponding to a participation in intellec-tuality there will also be a participation in freedom. It is proved, second, by the following analogue of the same argument: An intellectual creature can perceive a given good either as necessary or as indifferent or, alternatively, either as absolutely good or merely as good in a certain respect (that is, as having some evil or disadvantage or difficulty conjoined with it); therefore, a creature that participates in the intellectual grade [of being] participates in freedom as well.

IT IS SHOWN THAT THERE IS A FREE FACULTY IN A HUMAN BEING

18. From this first assertion there follows a second that is no less evident: namely, that within a human being there is an active faculty that is free by virtue of itself and of its own intrinsic nature—that is, an active faculty that has control over its own action in such a way that it has it within its power to exercise that action and not to exercise it and, consequently, to elicit one action or another—that is, opposite—action.

The parts of this assertion are all connected in such a way that /699a/ one follows upon another. Thus, in the preceding assertion we verified the exer-cise of freedom that we experience within ourselves, and a free faculty is inferred evidently from this exercise of freedom, in the way that a power is inferred from an act. We then add that this faculty, insofar as it is free, can only be an active faculty—or, conversely, that a faculty cannot be free unless it is active and except insofar as it is active. This part [of the assertion] must especially be kept in mind if we are to explicate and defend freedom of choice in the correct way. It is proved as follows: A passion *qua* passion cannot be free with respect to the patient as such but instead can be free only insofar as the action from which that passion derives is free with respect to the patient; therefore, freedom does not reside formally and precisely within a passive faculty as such but instead resides within an active faculty.

This consequence is obvious from the fact that a passion corresponds only to a passive faculty as such, just as an action corresponds only to an active faculty as such. Therefore, if a passion is free only by a denomination that is

15. See *DM* 30. 16.

derived from a free action, then the power or dominion of freedom cannot reside within a passive faculty as such but resides instead within an active faculty.

The antecedent, on the other hand, is proved by the fact that if an action is an action with respect to a subject (and it is of this sort of action that we are now speaking), then it necessarily introduces a passion;[16] and, conversely, a passion cannot exist except insofar as it is introduced by an action, and it cannot fail to exist if the action emanates from the agent. Therefore, all the freedom and indifference has to do with the action insofar as it is an action, whereas it does not have to do with the passion except insofar as the passion is introduced by the action. Therefore, a free faculty must be an active faculty *qua* active—and not *qua* passive.

19. *A passive power is not as such free.* You will object as follows: A passive power can of itself be indifferent as regards various acts or contrary modes, as is clear in the case of primary matter and in the case of a surface that is of itself indifferent as regards whiteness and blackness; therefore, for the same reason a passive power as such can be a free faculty.

One should reply by denying the consequence. For an indifference with respect to various acts or with respect to the absence of those acts is not sufficient for freedom. Rather, what is necessary is an internal power whereby a faculty of the sort in question is able to resolve that indifference into one or the other part. However, this sort of power cannot reside in a passive faculty as such but can reside [only] in an active faculty. The reason is that if a faculty is indifferent but lacks the internal power to determine itself, then as far as it itself is concerned, it will always and necessarily remain in that same condition and in that same indifference—that is, in that same lack of any act—until it is determined by some other faculty. Such a determination could, to be sure, be free with respect to this other cause that effects the determination but not with respect to the recipient [of the determination].

For example, if we assume that a celestial body is merely passively indifferent /699b/ to motion and rest, then it is inconceivable that motion or rest should be free with respect to the celestial body itself, since it itself has no power to determine either of these [states]. However, the motion in question could be denominated as free with respect to some other agent if it proceeded from a free volition. And the same holds in general for every passive faculty insofar as it is passive, since a passive faculty is not as such able to

---

16. In the act of creation *ex nihilo* something is produced but nothing is acted upon, and so there is no *passion*, since a passion is an accident had by that which is acted upon by virtue of the fact that it is being acted upon.

alter its own natural condition. Indeed, the reason why efficient causality is required over and above material causality is that what is passive cannot as such transform itself. Therefore, neither can a passive faculty, insofar as it is passive, have the power to initiate its own determination, since such a determination does not occur without a change and, consequently, does not occur without an instance of efficient causality either.

20. *An objection is refuted.* You will object as follows: A passive faculty as such is able either to resist an action or not to resist it. Therefore, it is in this sense that freedom can be thought of as existing in a passive faculty as such—namely, if we imagine that it is within the faculty's power to resist an agent or not to resist it. For example, those who claim that an act of loving is not elicited by the will but is instead impressed upon the will by the cognized object (or by the cognition itself) will still insist that even though the object (or cognition) acts necessarily for its own part, the act of loving is nonetheless free with respect to the will, since it is within the will's power to resist or not to resist the act of loving's being effected or impressed in this way.

One may reply, first of all, that since the will, taken in isolation, is of itself indifferent with respect to receiving or not receiving the act of loving, it is inconceivable that the will should through itself and through its own pure being and passive power resist the act of loving's being impressed. For resistance, formally speaking, can stem only from something that is contrary to or incompatible with [the relevant act] and not from a subject that is itself as such susceptible to [the act].

Second, from this it follows that resistance of the sort in question cannot be indifferent and free, since resistance arises solely from a formal incompatibility or opposition between entities. And so, for example, if it is ever the case that the will, through its very own being, formally resists an act of loving's being impressed, then it will always and necessarily resist it, since it will always have the same formal opposition to it. On the other hand, if it does not have this sort of formal opposition to the act, then it will never resist it unless there is some other thing adjoined to it by means of which it opposes and resists it—and in that case it will be in the effecting or non-effecting of that [other] thing that freedom can be discerned. For instance, in the posited example, if we grant that there is an active power of loving in the object or in the cognition, then the will will be able to resist that activity in just one of two ways: namely, either (i) by removing the object or the consideration of the object, and this /700a/ can occur only by the doing or willing of something, or else (ii) by not cooperating with the object or cognition, and this presupposes that the will itself is at least a partial efficient cause of the very act of loving. And so the sort of indifference that belongs to freedom is always traced back to a faculty of doing something insofar as it is a faculty of this sort.

21. *What sort of freedom divine freedom is; where created freedom resides.* Finally, you will object as follows: The most perfect sort of freedom exists in God, even though this freedom does not formally reside in a faculty of acting.[17] This is proved both by the fact that (i) in God there is a faculty of acting only with respect to actions directed outside himself, whereas the freedom resides formally and *per se* primarily in the very act of loving, which is immanent in God (as we say in our own manner), and also by the fact that (ii), as we will explain below,[18] the active power in God is conceptually distinct from his will, whereas it is the will alone that is a formally free faculty, as we will explain shortly.[19]

One may reply that we have been talking here about created freedom, which is proximately and primarily exercised in relation to the acts of the free faculty itself. For as Scotus correctly noted in *Sentences* 1, dist. 39 (the section that begins with the words "As for the first objection, I reply that the will"), freedom can be understood either (i) in relation to diverse immanent acts within the faculty itself or (ii) in relation to diverse objects [of willing] or (iii) in relation to diverse extrinsic effects.

This last relation or type of indifference is posterior to and, as it were, a consequence of freedom, to the extent that the faculty that wills freely is, in addition, efficacious with respect to the things that it wills: that is, able to apply the power that effects those things.

The second relation, on the other hand, is formally required for freedom, and it is by itself sufficient for freedom if there is an indifference in it. However, to have this sort of indifference immediately with respect to the

17. In God, who is Pure Actuality and hence imperfectible, there is no distinction between first act and second act: i.e., between a faculty capable of acting and its actually exercising its act. For God's act of will is perfect, necessary, eternal, and immutable. Divine freedom consists in the fact that God could have willed contingent objects other than those he in fact willed. Hence, divine freedom, unlike creaturely freedom, does not involve the power either to will or not to will (*freedom of contradiction*); rather, it involves the freedom either to will *this* object or to will *that* object (*freedom of contrariety*). It is for this reason that God does not have a 'faculty' (or power or potentiality) of will. For to have such a faculty implies having a perfectible power. By contrast, in creaturely free agents, whose volitional faculty (first act) stands in need of being perfected and completed by the exercise of its characteristic acts (second act), one finds both freedom of contradiction and freedom of contrariety.

18. See *DM* 30. 13.

19. See *DM* 19. 5.

objects—in the very act itself, without any addition or change—is proper to God alone, as we will show below when we discuss this topic.[20] And that is why the freedom of the divine will does not formally reside in either a faculty of acting or a faculty of receiving; instead, it resides solely in a certain eminence that belongs to the pure act itself.

A creature's freedom, on the other hand, cannot be determined to its objects except by means of intervening second acts which are added to the free faculty itself and with respect to which that faculty, taken in the mode of first act, is indifferent.[21] And our claim is that freedom with respect to these [second acts] resides in a faculty of the sort in question insofar as that faculty is an active [cause] of such acts and not, formally speaking, insofar as it is receptive either of the acts themselves or of any other thing that is related to them.

22. *The position of the philosophers.* And this is why all the philosophers, especially Aristotle, /700b/ explain our freedom by reference to the power to act and not to act or by the power to do the opposite. For example, in *Magna Moralia* 1.9 [1187a21–22], Aristotle says: "It is within our power to do good things or evil things," a point that he pursues at length in *Ethics* 3, especially 3.5 [1113b2–1115a6]. But the morally good and bad things spoken of in these places consist formally and properly in the acts of the will itself.

There are similar passages in Scripture that agree with this truth: "He was able to sin and yet did not sin, able to do evil things and yet did not do them" (Ecclesiasticus 31:10); and "Either make a tree good and its fruit good, or make a tree bad and its fruit bad" (Matthew 12:33). In discussing this latter passage in *Contra Adimantum Manichaei*, chap. 26, Augustine says: "It has been placed within the power of the will to alter itself in such a way that it can do good." Again, in *De Libero Arbitrio*, Methodius explains freedom in this way: "A human being is given the power to do the things that he wills to do." And one reads similar passages in Basil, in the homily entitled "God is not the author of evil things"; in Gregory Nazianzen, sermon 1; and in the other authors to be cited below.

And, lastly, the Council of Trent, session 6, chap. 5*,[22] and session 6, canons 4 and 5,[23] in order to safeguard the freedom of our will, teaches that the will does not behave merely passively in its acts but instead effects them

20. See *DM* 19. 3. 6 and 19. 4. 7.

21. Once again, the faculty taken in the mode of *first* act is just the faculty constituted as capable of various acts which bring it to completion; these acts, which are the actual exercise of the relevant capacities, are themselves called *second* acts.

22. See Denzinger, #1525.

23. See Denzinger, #1554–1555.

actively—thus intimating that the exercise of freedom consists in action, whereas the faculty of freedom consists in a certain power insofar as that power is active. And in this way it is simultaneously proved that among created efficient causes there are some that act freely—which is the main thing that we intended to prove in the present discussion.

23. Now certain points that have to be clarified have already arisen: What is this faculty that is thus free in its acting? Again, what sort of indifference does it have? And in what is this indifference posited? But we will discuss these questions below in the course of replying to the [four] arguments [proposed at the beginning of this section]. For each of the proposed arguments poses serious problems.

Section 3

Whether There Could Be Any Freely Acting Efficient Cause If the First Cause Operated by Necessity; and, in General, Whether the Freedom of an Action Requires Freedom in All the Causes That Influence It, or Whether Freedom in One of Them Is Sufficient

1. The first argument[1] raises, in the first place, the question of whether the First Cause operates freely or by a necessity of nature. However, this question will be dealt with below in the disputation that is properly concerned with the divine perfections.[2] Here we are presupposing that the First Cause effects freely, rather than necessarily, whatever he properly effects outside himself. Not only is this certain from the point of view of the Faith, but we believe that it can be sufficiently proved by natural reason, too, /701a/ as we will show in the place just mentioned. And so the first argument is refuted by denying the antecedent.

2. Nonetheless, as regards this same argument, a hypothetical question remains: namely, whether a freely acting created cause would still be conceivable even if God did act by a necessity of nature. This question is a source of controversy between Scotus and the principal disciples of St. Thomas. For Scotus denies unconditionally that it is possible for a secondary cause to act freely if the First Cause acts by a necessity of nature. And he thinks that Aristotle or any other philosopher who propounded these two claims together—namely, that God operates necessarily and that a human being operates freely—propounded contradictories.

Scotus's foundation was mentioned above in the first argument: namely, that a secondary cause does not act unless it is moved by the First Cause; hence, if the First Cause acts and produces motion necessarily, then it must be that the secondary cause is moved and acts by that same necessity. Scotus makes this claim in *Sentences* 1, dist. 1, q. 1; dist. 4, q. 4; dist. 38, ad 1; dist. 39, the section that begins "As for the first objection"; and *Sentences* 2, dist. 1, q. 3. The disciples of Scotus think the same thing, as one can see in Antonius Cordubensis, [*Quaestiones Theologicae*] 1, q. 55, problem 4. And the same position is adopted by some of the modern commentators on St. Thomas, *Summa Theologiae* 1, q. 19, a. 8.

3. However, other earlier authors believe that (i) from the hypothesis that

1. See *DM* 19. 2. 1.
2. See *DM* 30. 16.

God operates by a necessity of nature it does not follow that every secondary cause operates by necessity but that instead (ii) an effect can be contingent by reason of a proximate cause even if the First Cause influences it by natural necessity.

The foundation [for this position] is that when an effect depends on more than one cause, it can have a particular characteristic or defect by reason of the one cause and not by reason of the other. Thus, what is effected by two acts of assent with respect to the premises [of a syllogism], the one act certain and the other uncertain, is an uncertain act of assent with respect to the conclusion; and what follows from a perfect First Cause and a defective secondary cause is an imperfect effect, since, as they say, good comes from the complete cause and evil comes from any defect at all. So in order for an effect to be free or contingent, the freedom of the secondary cause can be sufficient, even if the First Cause operates necessarily. For given that the effect depends on both causes, the influence of both is required in order for the effect to follow, whereas in order for the effect not to follow, it is sufficient that one or the other of the causes be absent; and, by parity of reasoning, in order for the effect to follow necessarily, it is required that both causes act by necessity, whereas in order for the effect to be free or contingent, it is sufficient /701b/ that one or the other of the causes be able not to act.

This is pretty much the claim made by Cajetan, *Summa Theologiae* 1, q. 14, a. 13, comment on the reply to the first objection, and *Summa Theologiae* 1, q. 19, art. 8; by Ferrariensis, *Contra Gentes* 2, chap. 67, comment on arg. 5; and by Capreolus, *Sentences* 1, dist. 38. They attribute this position to St. Thomas because in the places just mentioned he claims that even though God's knowledge is a necessary cause, contingent effects proceed from it, since his influence is modified in the secondary causes. And the selfsame St. Thomas says similar things in *De Veritate*, q. 2, a. 14, ad 5, and q. 5, a. 9, ad 10. Gabriel holds the same view in *Sentences* 1, dist. 38, q. unica, a. 1, pt. 2, as does Palacios in disp. 2.

4. Both these positions contain some truth, but neither of them explains or argues the matter with precision. For the conditional or hypothetical question under discussion has several possible interpretations, which have to be distinguished from one another, and the question must be answered in different ways according to these different interpretations.

THE FIRST INTERPRETATION OF THE QUESTION AND THE ANSWER TO IT

5. The first interpretation is this: If freedom in acting did not exist in the First Cause, could it exist in any secondary cause? And on this interpretation

one should altogether deny that any secondary cause can be free if the First Cause is not free. Given this interpretation, what Scotus says is true: namely, that the philosophers who claimed that God acts by a necessity of nature whereas human beings act freely were talking nonsense—even though, as we shall see,[3] Scotus does not have the present interpretation in mind and his argument is not compelling on this interpretation.

The first argument [for my answer to the question] is that if God does not have freedom, then there is no source for a creature's participating in freedom.

You will object that one could argue in the same way that because God does not have sensation, there is no source for a creature's participating in sensation. I reply that there is no analogy here, since freedom as such pertains to a perfection *simpliciter*, a perfection such that if it does not exist formally in God, then it likewise cannot exist in a creature. Hence, a more comparable argument is that if there were no cognition in God, then there likewise could not be any cognition—or, consequently, any intellection or sensation—in a creature.

The second argument is this: If any secondary cause is capable of freedom, it will be an intellectual creature in particular. But if in God there is no freedom in acting, then neither can such freedom exist in an intellectual creature. Therefore, etc.

The minor premise is proved by the fact that God is intellectual through his essence, whereas a creature is intellectual [only] through participation; therefore, any perfection within the intellectual grade [of being] that can be thought of as a source of freedom exists in a more excellent way in God. Thus, for instance, the perfection /702a/ of understanding, the universal cognition of all goods, the immateriality of the [intellective] powers, a non-necessary connection with external goods (that is, an independence from external things), or any other perfection of this sort that could be a source of freedom, either on the part of the object or on the part of the subject or the subject's own nature—any perfection of this sort, I repeat, is found in a more excellent way in God. Therefore, if in the case of God all these things cannot be sufficient for his being free in acting, then they will likewise not be sufficient in the case of a creature.

6. *The genus of perfection that freedom belongs to.* You will object as follows: Freedom requires a perfection that is mixed with some imperfection—specifically, with potentiality or mutability—and for this reason the line of argument just presented may not be evident. This is also why we say that in a creature, but not in God, freedom is accompanied by an indifference as regards various acts.

3. See §§15 and 18–19 below.

One may reply by denying what is assumed. For freedom, taken simply and precisely, involves no imperfection at all, since it can be preserved in conjunction with an indifference as regards the objects or effects without any composition or any potentiality with respect to different acts. And freedom so taken bespeaks only a certain control and independence with respect to such things. And it is in this way that freedom exists in God, since God is freedom through his essence. In a creature, by contrast, freedom exists only through participation and thus has adjoined to it the sort of imperfection that an indifference as regards diverse acts involves.[4] Whatever there is of potentiality and composition in such indifference bespeaks an imperfection; however, granted such imperfection, this indifference and dominion over one's own act is itself a perfection which a creature could not participate in if the perfection of freedom just alluded to—pure and without any imperfections—did not exist in God.

Nor does the argument of the second position go through against this interpretation. For that argument assumes, of course, that given God's necessity in acting, there are free secondary causes—the opposite of which we have shown to follow from the stated hypothesis.

THE SECOND INTERPRETATION OF THE QUESTION AND THE ANSWER TO IT

7. The second interpretation of the question is this: If *per impossibile* God acted by a necessity of nature even while a creature had a faculty of acting that was by its nature free, would God, by virtue of his natural mode of acting, impede the exercise of freedom in the creature in such a way that the creature would not have free action de facto despite having a free faculty?

And, indeed, a negative answer seems clearly to follow /702b/ from the opinion of certain Thomists, who believe that in order for a creature to have a free action it is sufficient that (i) it operate through a faculty that is of itself free and that (ii) it be attracted by the object in a nonnecessary manner— that is, that it not be determined by the object to one effect. For God would not undermine these two conditions even if he both (i) acted by a necessity of nature with all the power of his will and (ii) acted along with the created will. Therefore, even given this mode of acting on God's part, the creature would still act freely.

8. However, this foundation is false and provides an abundant opportunity for going wrong on the matter at hand.

4. See *DM* 19. 2. 21 and n. 17 for more on this point.

For, first of all, it does not adequately distinguish between (i) having a free faculty and (ii) having the unimpeded free *exercise* of such a faculty—even though these two things are absolutely distinct from one another, since the former has to do solely with the power—that is, the first act—whereas the latter has to do with the second act. Now even though a free act cannot exist without a free faculty (for a second and vital act essentially presupposes a first act), nonetheless, a free faculty can exist without the exercise of freedom—not only when it is not operating but also in a case where, even though it is operating, it is prevented from having the sort of control over its own act which it is able by its nature to have. For such control consists in the power of not doing that which one does or of doing something else. But it is possible for an agent that of itself is otherwise indifferent to be led or determined to act by some other higher agent in such a way that with respect to a given action or mode of acting it does not have the power not to act; and in this way the agent, even while retaining its innate free faculty, can be deprived of its exercise of freedom.

This is confirmed by the fact that all theologians teach that God is able to impose necessity on our will. But in such a case he would not be taking away the *faculty* that is free, since this faculty is not distinct from the will itself; rather, he would be preventing a *free exercise* of that faculty and replacing it with a necessary exercise. Thus, the two things mentioned above have to be distinguished; and God can bring it about that a faculty which is of itself free and which remains free in first act with respect to a given object should be led toward that object not freely but by a necessary motion that hinders the exercise of freedom. Theologians seem to agree on this point in *Sentences* 2, dist. 15. In addition, St. Thomas presupposes it in *Summa Theologiae* 1-2, q. 6, a. 4, and Scotus holds to it in *Sentences* 4, dist. 49, q. 6, the section that begins "Thus there are two."

9. From this it follows further that what the position in question presupposes is false: namely, that in order for there to be a free exercise and a free act, it is sufficient that there be (i) a faculty that is of itself free and (ii) an object that is of itself indifferent—that is, an object that is not sufficient by itself to impose necessity on the faculty. For this position assumes /703a/ that no cause can impose necessity on the will except the object or except by the mediation of the object—which is false. For God, too, can impose necessity on the will, not as an object but as an agent of infinite power.

Indeed, if the will were able to receive necessity only from the object, then it could never be drawn out of its connatural mode of operating or be moved necessarily except when it was being led by its own nature and by its own intrinsic impetus. For an object *qua* object does not move the will in a preternatural way but moves it in an especially connatural and intrinsic way.

And so an object does not, within its own genus [of causality], move with necessity a power that is otherwise free, except when that power is not free with respect to the object in question. Therefore, if the will can be necessitated only by the object, then it is not in fact necessitated toward an object with respect to which it was of itself free. Thus it is that in heaven the will is necessitated by God, as by a clearly seen object, because the will is not of itself free with respect to such an act.

10. And so it follows that, according to the position in question, God can never necessitate the will toward an act with respect to which it is of itself free.[5] For either (i) God proposes an object that is sufficient of itself to move the will necessarily, in which case the will is in fact not of itself free with respect to such an action and so receives no extrinsic necessity, or else (ii) God proposes an object which, within its own genus [of causality], is incapable of moving the will necessarily, and the will would never be moved necessarily by force of such an object unless God imposed the necessity from elsewhere.

You will object as follows: An object that is of itself insufficient to move the will with necessity can nonetheless be proposed in such a way—or under such a judgment—that it imposes necessity on the will.

I reply, first, that this cannot happen without a false judgment—namely, the false judgment that something is the highest good or is a necessary good when it is not such—a judgment that God cannot impart.

Second, even if such a judgment were posited, the will would in that case be moved not as a power that is of itself free but as a power that is determined to one effect. For just as the will is led by its nature not only toward a real good but also toward an apparent good, so too it is apt by its nature to be led necessarily toward an apparent necessary good. And so it never turns out that the will can be necessitated by God toward an act that it might of itself elicit freely. But this is clearly false and contrary to the common position, and it derogates God's omnipotence. For because he is the author and lord of the will, he is able, as he wishes, to move and impel the will toward acting necessarily or prevent it from acting at all.

This is confirmed by the fact that /703b/ the power which the created will has either to will or not to will is not infinite in its efficacy, since it is commensurate with the finite capability of such a faculty. Therefore, in both [its willing and its not willing] it can be subdued and overcome by an extrinsic agent with infinite power, such as God is. Therefore, the created will can be moved by God to will an object—an object that is of itself otherwise indif-

---

5. This conclusion is problematic for Suarez's opponents, since they have already admitted, with Scotus and St. Thomas, that God is able, by virtue of his infinite power, to impose necessity on a created will.

ferent—in such a way that the will, thus moved, is altogether incapable of resisting or of using the power it has not to will such an object. (Indeed, the claim that this falls under God's omnipotence seems to be taught at times by Augustine—and not unjustifiably, since there is no contradiction involved in the effect or motion in question.) In such a case, therefore, even if the will is of itself free and is not moved necessarily by the object, nonetheless, the very exercise and act is not free for the will itself, since the higher agent does not permit it to exercise its free faculty; nor does the will itself have the power with respect to the higher agent to resist it when the latter exercises its own absolute power.

11. Therefore, in order for there to be a free act or free exercise of the will, it is not sufficient that there be a faculty that is of itself free along with an indifferent object or judgment, unless it is also the case that the higher cause is imposing no force or preternatural efficacy but is instead allowing the will itself to operate in the way connatural to it. This is also asserted by the Fathers of the Church whom I will name below. Therefore, there is no solid foundation for the position under discussion.

Thus it now remains to be seen whether, given the hypothesis that God acts by a necessity of nature and that a human being has a faculty that is of itself free, it nonetheless truly follows that in such a case there will be no free act or free exercise in the created will.

12. *If God acted by a necessity of nature, there would be no exercise of freedom on the part of [created] causes.* And on this interpretation one should reply, it seems, that given the hypothesis in question, no exercise of freedom remains in the created agent. And what Scotus claims is true on this interpretation as well: namely, that those philosophers were mistaken who held that God acts by a necessity of nature and who also countenanced free and contingent effects emanating from secondary causes.

Scotus's argument, however, does not go through on this interpretation; nor to my mind is it probative, as I will explain below. Therefore, the proper argument must be based on what was said a moment ago. For, as has been proved, through his infinite power God can move the will in such a way that he imposes necessity on it, and this same thing could still be true even if he acted by a necessity of nature, since in such a case he is being thought of not as having less *power* but only as having less *indifference* /704a/ or *freedom*. But if God were acting by a necessity of nature when he acted on the created will, then he would act with as much efficacy as he could. Therefore, he would always act by imposing necessity on the will, and so there would never be an exercise of freedom in the created agent.

The minor premise is evident from the fact that the condition of a natural agent is such that it does as much as it can. For it does not have a faculty for moderating its action: that is, for applying that action to a greater or lesser degree, since this is done only by a free faculty.

13. *An objection is answered.* But perhaps the philosophers were claiming that when God acts by a necessity of nature, he does not always do as much as he can absolutely speaking, but that instead he does as much as is required by the nature of the secondary causes, and it is the latter that determine whether he acts to a greater or lesser degree and whether he acts in this way or in that way.

First of all, however, we are speaking here only on the hypothesis that the divine power has an absolute necessity in acting.

We next add that if for any reason whatsoever God is said to act by a necessity of nature and not out of freedom, then the determination of God's own action cannot come from the natural capacity of a secondary cause. For God's power is related adequately not to that capacity but to a greater capacity. Therefore, it cannot be determined by that capacity. For how might God's power be limited by that capacity in such a way that it would never be able to do more, given that God has a greater power?

I admit, to be sure, that many impossibilities follow from the hypothesis in question when it is taken together with God's infinite power. Still, once the hypothesis is granted, it follows via an extrinsic medium[6] that through his own power God always moves the created will in such a way that he imposes necessity on it. This is why the holy Fathers say of God's wisdom and free providence that in acting on and moving the created will it accommodates itself in such a way that it does not coerce the will but instead allows it to move itself in its own way. One can see this in Augustine, *De Praedestinatione et Gratia,* chap. 15; Prosperus, *Ad Objectiones Gallorum,* chaps. 1 and 11; Cyril, *In Ioannem* 4, chap. 7; and Damascene, *De Fide Orthodoxa* 2, chap. 30.

14. Nor does the foundation for the second position militate against this resolution of the question on the present interpretation.[7] For in order for the act to be free and for the effect to be contingent, it is not enough that the secondary cause be a free or contingent cause in its own right. Rather, it is necessary that, insofar as it is such a cause, it be allowed to exercise its action, since otherwise it is free only materially (as I will put it) and does not

6. An extrinsic medium (or middle) is a principle that serves as the justification for an inference but does not itself contain any of the terms that appear in the premises. In this case the extrinsic medium is the principle that a necessarily acting cause acts to its full capacity. This principle takes us from the premise that God acts with absolute necessity in concurring with a created cause to the conclusion that he imposes necessity on the created cause.

7. The argument for the second position is found in §3 above.

act as a free cause. Now the action receives its designation and denomination not from the cause taken materially but from the cause insofar as it is having an actual influence. But the argument in question fails to prove that God's necessity /704b/ in acting does not prevent the free exercise of the created faculty.

Further, St. Thomas, who is cited [in the foundation for the second position], does not contradict [what I have said] on either this interpretation or the previous one. For he is not talking about an absolute necessity in acting on God's part; rather, he is talking about a necessity of immutability, which does not rule out absolute freedom, as I will explain below in the disputation concerning God.[8]

THE THIRD INTERPRETATION OF THE QUESTION AND THE ANSWER TO IT

15. *If God necessarily gave the concurrence that he now provides to free causes, they would remain free.* The third interpretation of the question is this: If (i) God acted by a necessity of nature and if (ii) he did nothing more [than he now in fact does] and provided the created will with no other concurrence or motion than he now [in fact] provides it with, would he in that case remove the contingency of the action and prevent the exercise of freedom?

This interpretation is very different from the previous ones and proceeds, as is rather obvious, from several presuppositions. Thus, in the last of the preceding assertions we claimed that a prevention of the exercise of freedom would follow from the necessity of God's action, because the relevant motion would [in that case] be greater than it is at present, when God concurs freely. But what we are now asking is this: If we assumed that the motion in question was no greater [than it now in fact is] and that it was different not in magnitude (as I will put it) but only in God's mode of giving it—so that, namely, the very same motion that is now [in fact] given freely would in that case be given by a necessity of nature—would it follow just from this that the exercise of freedom is prevented and that the contingency of things is removed? And it seems to be on *this* interpretation that Scotus's position and argument are advanced.

16. Now my own judgment is that one should claim that even if the First Cause acted by a necessity of nature in the way just described, he would not prevent the exercise of freedom or destroy all the contingency of the effects of secondary causes.

8. See *DM* 30. 9.

On this point I agree with the second position adduced above. For even though more than one cause might concur with respect to a given act, still, in order for that act to be free, it is sufficient that (i) the proximate cause be free and that (ii) it not be taken out of its natural mode of operating by the cooperation of the other cause; but this is how it would be in the case under discussion; therefore, etc.

The major premise is sufficiently proved by the foundation for the second position. For even if several causes concur and all of them except one operate necessarily in their own right, still, if that one is able by its own freedom alone not to elicit the act, then this is sufficient for the effect's being free or contingent, since the effect is absolutely able not to exist. Nor, given [just] what is assumed by the aforementioned hypothesis, does the necessary mode of acting on the part of the rest of the causes prevent the exercise of the relevant power in this other cause.

And this is easily explained by the proof /705a/ of the minor premise. For in the case at hand God would not move the created will more forcefully or more vehemently than he now [in fact] moves it. But God's act of effecting the motion does not now [in fact] take the will out of its connatural mode of operating. Therefore, neither would it change that mode of operating in the case under discussion. For the question of whether this motion or concurrence on God's part is given freely or given necessarily is irrelevant to the effect that it produces outside [of God], as long as the very motion or concurrence is in itself no greater [than it now in fact is].

17. Hence, I argue, second, that if this were not so, then it would follow that our act of will is now [in fact] free only because God concurs *freely* with respect to it. But the consequent is false, both because (i) it is not because of God's freedom but because of my own freedom that I have control formally and immediately over my own act and also because (ii) otherwise the appetitive act of a horse or a lion would [likewise] be free, since God concurs freely with respect to such an act. Therefore, an act that is free with respect to a given cause is one that is effected by that cause in such a way that the cause has the power and ability not to effect the act, regardless of the other causes that are concurring with respect to that same act—and this whether those other causes are concurring naturally or concurring freely in their own right. But this is the situation in which the created will would find itself in the case under discussion, as has been shown. Therefore, etc.

18. Third, the same thing can be proved not only by replying adequately to Scotus's foundation but also by turning it against itself. For if that foundation carried any weight, then it would prove that (i) even now the contingency of effects and the exercise of freedom are absent from all the acts of a secondary

cause insofar as they are from that cause and that (ii) nothing is free except by virtue of its relation to the freedom of the First Cause. But the consequent is not only contrary to natural reason but also contrary to the Faith, since if it were true, free acts could not be imputed to us.

The inference is proved by the fact that (i) even now a secondary cause acts only if it is moved by the First Cause—that is, only if the First Cause concurs[9]—and that (ii) even now the First Cause acts—that is, effects a motion—with the very same natural priority with which it would effect the motion if it acted by a necessity of nature. In addition, God's act of effecting the motion is equally efficacious even now—as we have been assuming and as can also be proved by Scotus's argument itself, since God's act of effecting the motion is incompatible with the creature's not being moved. Therefore, given God's act of effecting the motion, the created will is moved necessarily. Therefore, if such a motion, when given by God through a necessity of nature, would remove freedom from the act of the human will, then it removes that freedom even now, since [even now] it is prior to the act of the will in just the same way. Or, alternatively, if it does not now remove freedom—because even though it is in some way prior [to the act of the will], it is nonetheless given with a dependence on the created will itself, as we will explain shortly[10]—then for the very same reason it would not remove freedom in the case under discussion. For even if it were given necessarily on God's part, it would nonetheless also be given /705b/ with a dependence on created free choice.

19. Nor is Scotus's reply adequate—namely, that if God acted by a necessity of nature, then his act of effecting the motion would be absolutely necessary and so would remove all of the effect's contingency, whereas now his act of effecting the motion is free, and that is why it does not [in fact] remove the effect's contingency. This reply, I repeat, is inadequate, both because (i) at most what it makes clear is how the present contingency or freedom of the effect can be salvaged with respect to the divine will, not with respect to the secondary causes, and also because (ii) if Scotus means that, given the hypothesis in question, God's act of effecting the motion would be absolutely necessary—that is, that it would necessarily be posited in reality—then he is assuming something false. For the act would be necessary only on God's part; however, because it would at the same time depend on the created will and could not be posited in reality without the latter, it

9. Suarez ultimately denies that, strictly speaking, God acts *on* (rather than *with*) a secondary or created cause in concurring with it. See *DM* 22. 2. 47.

10. See *DM* 19. 4 and 22. 4.

would not be *absolutely* necessary.[11] And so in that case (i) God would be said to act by a necessity of nature, since he would be determined of himself and by his own intrinsic nature to concur with the will, but nonetheless (ii) this concurrence, given that it is posited in reality only when the will itself simultaneously cooperates, would not be posited in reality with *absolute* necessity but rather would be posited in reality in consequence of its being required by the cooperation of the free will.

20. And from this one may infer the following general rule, which confirms the position being proposed here: The fact that there is a cause that concurs by natural necessity with respect to a given act—that is, effect—does nothing to prevent that act from being free or contingent as long as there is some [other] cause that effects it with indifference, a cause with respect to which the effect is denominated as free.

The reason for this was adequately clarified when we explained the foundation for the second position. However, it can be further illustrated by a few examples.

One example is connected with the plausible position that an act of cognition (or an object as cognized) concurs as an efficient cause with respect to an act of the will. For this concurrence, insofar as it comes from the act of cognition, is natural and lacking in freedom, and yet the act [of the will] is absolutely free because of the will's indifference. Hence, even though the act of cognition, as far as it itself is concerned, has its influence by a necessity of nature, nonetheless, its actual influence is not absolutely necessary, since that influence is not posited in reality without the will's actual influence.

Something similar can be said about the influence of a habit that concurs with a free faculty, since the habit does not of itself have a proper indifference or freedom but instead operates by a necessity of nature when its faculty operates.

Another example has to do with the effects of natural agents insofar as they come both from those agents themselves and also from God. For such an action, even though it comes from the proximate agent by a necessity of nature, is nonetheless free with respect to the First Cause, since, according to the true doctrine, God /706a/ provides his concurrence freely. Hence, because of God's power the action in question is absolutely able to exist and able not to exist, even though this power does not exist in the proximate agent. However, as a matter of fact the action is denominated as simply natural, both because (i) just as the action takes its determination and specification from the proximate agent, so too it takes the type of denomination

---

11. I.e., in such a case a prerequisite for God's necessary action would be a free act of will on the part of the created cause.

in question from the proximate agent, and also because (ii) it is by a sort of general law and fixed volition that God now concurs with respect to the relevant actions in accord with the requirements of the nature—that is, of the secondary cause. It is in this sense that one should understand the common saying that the influence of the First Cause is modified in or by the secondary cause.

So, then, given the hypothesis that we are presently concerned with, the [created will's] action would be free because of its relation to the secondary cause even if the First Cause provided its own concurrence by a necessity of nature.

21. *Whether one and the same action can be free for one of the causes but necessary for the other.* For this reason, what Scotus assumed above—namely, that the same action cannot be necessary with respect to one cause and free with respect to another, because the necessary and the contingent are opposed as contradictories—is either untrue or else, in the sense in which it can be true, irrelevant.

For it has been demonstrated that two causes can influence the same act, the one freely and the other by the natural impetus of its nature. Therefore, in this sense it is not absurd that the same effect should be contingent and necessary with respect to different things. For the same reason, there is no contradiction, since contradictories have to be taken with respect to the same thing.

On the other hand, if 'necessary' is being taken not just in a relative sense but in an absolute sense for that which is absolutely not able not to be, then it is indeed impossible for an effect to be necessary and yet to have contingency from some cause. However, in this sense it is not true that a necessary effect is one that some necessarily acting cause concurs with respect to, since [for the latter] it is enough that the effect should be brought about necessarily in a relative sense and with respect to that [necessarily acting] cause. But it is consistent with this that the effect can have contingency or freedom from some other source—that is, with respect to some other cause.

Section 4

How Freedom or Contingency Abides in the Action of a Secondary Cause Despite the Concurrence of the First Cause and, Consequently, in What Sense It Is True That a Cause Is Free Which, Given That Everything Required for Acting Has Been Posited, Is Able to Act and Able Not to Act

1. This problem is raised in the second argument posited at the beginning of section 2,[1] /706b/ and Scotus touches upon it as well in the following argument. A secondary cause—specifically, a created will—cannot do anything at all unless it is moved by the First Cause. But when it is moved by God, it necessarily moves itself. Therefore, a created will's movement is never free and contingent with respect to the created will itself.

The major premise, in the very same terms, is found in St. Thomas, *Summa Theologiae* 1, q. 105, a. 1, ad 4 and 5, and it will be proved below when we discuss the dependence of secondary causes on the First Cause.[2] What's more, the minor premise is found in the selfsame St. Thomas, *Summa Theologiae* 1–2, q. 10, [a. 4], ad 3, where he says, "It is impossible that God move the will and that the will not be moved." In addition, this premise can be easily inferred both (i) from the efficacy and perfection of the divine act of effecting the motion and (ii) from the mutual relation between moving and being moved.

There is a second way to set forth the same problem. A free cause is one which, given that all the things required for acting have been posited, is able to act and able not to act. But one of the things required in order for a secondary cause to act is God's act of effecting the motion, an act which is such that (i) if it is posited, the secondary cause is not both able to act and able not to act but instead acts necessarily, just as it is such that (ii) if it is not posited, the secondary cause necessarily does not act. Therefore, the above definition [of a free cause] is incompatible with every secondary cause, and so there is no contingency or freedom with respect to such a cause; instead, there is contingency and freedom only with respect to the First Cause.

---

1. See *DM* 19. 2. 2.
2. See *DM* 22. 2, esp. §47.

A FIRST MANNER OF SPEAKING IS PROPOSED

2. This problem is one of the most important concerning this subject matter, and it provides us with an opportunity to explain more fully what a free cause is—that is, what conditions it requires. And at the same time the common, received definition of a free cause will be expounded upon.

Since the authors whom I cited above locate the whole nature of freedom in objectival indifference (as I will put it), they will quickly resolve the present problem by claiming that (i) a free faculty is one which, given that all the things required *on its part* have been posited, still remains indifferent—that is, not determined to one effect by the force of the object—and thus that (ii) no obstacle to the exercise of freedom is posed by the fact that, once the motion effected by the First Cause has been posited, the will is at that point determined to one effect in such a way that it is not able not to exercise the act toward which it is moved.

Given this interpretation, the common distinction between necessity in the composed sense and necessity in the divided sense is applied in order to resolve the first [formulation of the] problem. For the fact that the will, when moved by God, operates necessarily is a necessity only in the composed sense and so is not incompatible with the freedom of an act that is necessary in that sense.[3]

As for the second [formulation of the] problem, they will reply by placing a restriction on the major premise and [thus] on the common definition of a free faculty, so that a free faculty is one that is able to act and able not to act, given, that is, that all the things required /707a/ on the part of the *intellect* and of the *will* itself have been posited—but not all the things required on *God's* part. Prior to these modern authors, Almain had suggested this modification in his *Morales*; however, he does not endorse it there, even though he does not adequately impugn it.

3. Hence, these new theologians have produced an alternative definition of a free act: namely, that a free act is a movement of the will made on the basis of a judgment of reason that is not sufficient, either in itself or by virtue of the object it proposes, to determine the will to one effect.[4]

They confirm this definition, first, as follows. The will's entire freedom arises from the judgment of reason. Therefore, a free act is optimally and

---

3. In this case the composed sense is: *Necessarily, if God moves the will, then the will operates;* while the divided sense is: *If God moves the will, then the will operates necessarily.* The proponents of the position in question claim that their view entails only the composed sense, not the divided sense.

4. For Suarez's criticism of this alternative definition, see §§5–7 below.

adequately defined by its relation to such a judgment or, what amounts to the same thing, by its relation to all the things that are required on the part of the intellect and the will.

Second, an indifference on the part of the *object* is sufficient for freedom, and an indifference on the part of the *faculty* is not required. This is obvious in the case of the divine will, which of itself is always determined to one effect, and yet the fact that created objects are indifferent to it is sufficient for its willing them freely.[5] Therefore, the same thing will be sufficient for a free act of the [created] will.

THE POSITION JUST STATED IS REFUTED

4. This whole doctrine proceeds from a false foundation, as I proved in the preceding section,[6] and the occasion for going wrong seems to have been a failure to distinguish adequately between (i) the *formal freedom* of the faculty and act and (ii) the *root of freedom*. The indifference of the judgment is the root of freedom; this was mentioned above and is the common position of theologians. However, the indifference of the judgment is not formal freedom itself, since the judgment is not in itself free and does not proceed proximately from a formally free faculty, as I will explain below.[7] Rather, the judgment is said to be *objectivally* indifferent—that is, indifferent on the part of the object—because it proposes an object that is indifferent in the sense that it does not attract the will by necessity. And from this it follows that an indifferent judgment is a sufficient indicator that there is a formally free faculty in a nature capable of judging in this way and, consequently, a sufficient indicator that there is also a free exercise or free act as long as that faculty is allowed to operate in the mode proper to itself and is not subject to any extrinsic force by which it might be coerced or, properly speaking, necessitated to tend toward an object that is of itself otherwise indifferent. For it was proved above[8] that such necessitation is possible, and from this we justifiably inferred—absolutely and without the aforementioned restriction—that it is not sufficient for the exercise of freedom that there be an indifferent judgment and a faculty that is of itself free.

5. *First inference.* From this we infer further /707b/ that it is wrong to restrict the received description of a free faculty—namely, "a faculty which, given

---

5. See *DM* 19. 2, n. 17.
6. See *DM* 19. 3. 8–11.
7. See *DM* 19. 5. 11–12.
8. See *DM* 19. 3. 7–14.

that all the things required for acting have been posited, is able to act and able not to act"—it is wrong, I repeat, to restrict it to those things that are required on the part of the judgment and of the will itself. For even if all the things required on the part of the judgment are present concurrently and the faculty is of itself free, it is still possible for that faculty not to be free in its very exercise, or, what amounts to the same thing, it is still possible for the act not to be free. Therefore, in order for the definition to encompass not only the free faculty in its very self (as I will put it)—that is, the free faculty in first act—but also the free exercise or act [of that faculty], the required things in question are not sufficient.

That is why the heretics of our time, even though they see that we operate on the basis of reason's judgment and consideration and that we are not led along or determined of necessity by the objects themselves, nonetheless claim that we do not operate freely because we are subject to necessity from *God himself*. To be sure, they are mistaken in asserting that God in fact always operates in us in this way—an assertion that is contrary to the Faith, to Sacred Scripture, and to sound reason. Still, they are not mistaken about the inference—namely, that *if* God imposes an extrinsic necessity on the act, then the act is not in fact free; nor, again, would they be mistaken if all they were claiming was either that this mode of operating on God's part is possible or that, given this mode of operating, the indifference of the judgment is not sufficient for the free exercise [of the will].

6. *Second inference.* Indeed, one may infer further that the problems set forth above are not resolved by this position's replies. For even though, as we will see below,[9] the distinction between the composed and divided senses by which the first [formulation of the] problem is resolved does indeed, if explained correctly, resolve the problem, nonetheless, that distinction cannot be sufficient when taken so generally. For we will show that there is a sort of necessity, even in the composed sense, which is incompatible with the exercise of freedom and which destroys it.

This is easily seen from what has been said. For God is able, by effecting a certain motion and by his own activity, to impose necessity on the will, and in such a case (i) the act would not be necessary in the divided sense, since the will, of itself and prescinding from that motion, would be able not to exercise the act, whereas (ii) the act would be necessary in the composed sense, since once that motion has been posited, the act is not able not to be exercised. And yet this necessity in the composed sense would still remove the free exercise [of the will], since we are assuming that in the case under discussion God is necessitating the will to as great an extent as he

9. See §16 below.

can. Therefore, something more has to be added in order for the distinction in question to be adequate.

Further, the restriction of the common definition of freedom whereby the second [formulation of the] problem is resolved has already been disproved, even apart from the fact that this restriction is arbitrary and provides an occasion for the introduction into this matter of any similar restriction you please. For by parity of reasoning someone could claim /708a/ that once a certain influence on the part of a celestial body has been posited, or once some special movement by a demon has been applied, (i) our will is not able not to operate in a way that conforms to that motion and yet that (ii) it nonetheless operates freely in such a case, because, given that all the things required on the part of the judgment and of the intrinsic faculty have been posited, the operation does not follow necessarily—even though it does follow necessarily on this further assumption.

7. *Third inference.* Finally, it is obvious from what has been said that this new definition of a free act—namely, that a free act is one that is effected by the will on the basis of a nonnecessitating judgment of reason—is falsely conceived. For, as has been explained, it is possible for there to be some other source of the act's being necessary with a necessity that prevents the free exercise [of the will]. Therefore, the definition in question can apply to an act that is absolutely necessary.

Now the first argument[10] on which this definition is based proves only that an indifferent judgment is the *root* of freedom. But it does not follow from this that the definition of a free act is completed by saying that a free act proceeds from such a judgment. Rather, one must add that it proceeds from a faculty which, in consenting to the judgment, is neither impeded nor subject to any extrinsic necessity; the common definition makes this clear with the words "given that all the things required have been posited, it is able to act and able not to act."

Further, in the second proof[11] something false is assumed when it is claimed that an indifference on the part of the object is sufficient for a free act, so that an indifference on the part of the faculty is not necessary. For how will the act be free if the faculty is not indifferent with respect to exercising it? Alternatively, why is the object, in its role as an object, called indifferent except because it does not impose necessity on the faculty but instead leaves it indifferent?

Moreover, the example concerning the divine will either assumes something false or else is irrelevant by reason of the fact that it turns on something

---

10. See §3, par. 2, above.

11. See §3, par. 3, above.

that is disanalogous. For the divine will, though in a higher and more perfect way, is nonetheless of itself truly indifferent with respect to willing created objects, since it is not naturally determined to do this. Otherwise, how would it be free? And even though it has determined itself from eternity and necessarily perseveres forever in that determination, nonetheless, that very determination (whatever it might be) proceeds from the will's freedom, and its necessity is not a necessity of nature but rather a necessity of immutability, which does not destroy the proper indifference that a free thing has of itself. However, because in God's will there is no efficient causality with respect to its own act and no composition of potency and act, it follows that the indifference in question does not exist in the faculty with respect to its act but instead exists in a pure act with respect to its objects.[12] And so in this respect the indifference of created freedom is not comparable to God's indifference. /708b/

THE DEFINITION OF FREEDOM IS EXPLICATED

8. In order to deal adequately with the problems posed above we must, first of all, retain and explicate the description of a free faculty in which two things are postulated: (i) the first is that it is an active faculty that of itself and by its own internal ability has the power to exercise its action and the power to withhold its action; (ii) the second is that when this faculty exercises its act, it is disposed and proximately prepared (as I will put it) for its work in such a way that, with all the things required for acting having been posited, it is able to act and able not to act.

There is no problem with the first part of this position, and a new explanation is almost unnecessary, given what was said in section 2, where we showed that freedom consists in an active faculty as such.[13] For it manifestly follows from this that freedom requires an active faculty that is indifferent with respect to acting and not acting. Hence, for the sake of clarity we can distinguish within a free power two separate powers or, as it were, two parts of a single power. One is the power to will—that is, to exercise the act; the other is the power not to will—that is, to withhold the action. For this second part of the power, even though it is in itself a certain positive perfection, cannot be brought into exercise except through a negation—that is, through the absence of an act of the faculty in question, if we are speaking of that faculty's absolute power. This is taken from St. Thomas, *Summa Theologiae* 1–2,

12. See *DM* 19. 2, n. 17.
13. See *DM* 19. 2. 18–22.

q. 6, a. 3, and from other theologians in the same place. For not-willing can as such be free, but not-willing, taken just by itself, includes not an act but instead the absence of an act, an absence that will be free as long as it exists together with a complete consideration on the part of reason and the full power to will. However, I added the qualification "if we are speaking of the faculty's absolute power", because morally—that is, ordinarily—speaking, this absence of an appetitive act will not be exercised without some positive act that is either (i) an act of willing against, whereby one rejects either the proposed object or some other act with respect to that object—for example, an act of loving it or an act of intending it—or else (ii) an act of turning to some incompatible or diverse object, as is sufficiently obvious from experience. For given a complete practical consideration on the part of reason, it would be extremely difficult to withhold every act of the will.

9. From this one sees in passing that a free faculty's indifference is preserved in a satisfactory way primarily and precisely through the faculty's relation to the act or to the absence of the act. This is usually called freedom with respect to *exercise*, since it is by virtue of this freedom that the very exercise of the act is indifferent.[14]

However, since the free faculty in question is a vital faculty, and since it is perfect and spiritual in such a way that it can reflect upon itself and upon its own movements, /709a/ it follows that as often as it is able freely not to exercise a given act, it is also able, by means of some other positive act, to will that absence—that is, to will against exercising such an act. And in this sense freedom with respect to exercise never exists without a certain freedom with respect to *specification*. For as often as the will is able freely not to love, it is also able to elicit some act which by its own nature and species is incompatible with an act of loving, and so in such a case there is an indifference with respect to the specification of the act.

In addition, another sort [of indifference] can be found in relation to contrary acts regarding the same object, since the object is able either to be loved freely or to be held in contempt. A free faculty, taken by itself and absolutely, includes this sort of twofold power as well, even though it need not have it with respect to each and every object.[15] For, as we will explain below, it

14. This is a sort of freedom that is lacking in God, since the divine act of will is exercised necessarily and eternally. However, as noted above, there are no created objects that God wills necessarily.

15. There are, then, three modes of freedom or indifference: (i) freedom of *exercise* with respect to an object, O, where one is able to will (i.e., desire, intend, choose, etc.) O and also able not to will O; (ii) freedom of what we might call *reflexive specification*, where one is able to will O and also able to will not to will O—in such a case the object of the latter act is

need not be equally free with respect to all such objects. These remarks will suffice for the first part of this position.[16]

10. The second part of the proposed position explains not only the nature of a free faculty but also that which is necessary for the exercise of freedom—that is, for a free act. For the aforementioned definition of freedom encompasses all this—and justifiably so, since the whole problem regarding freedom, as well as the utility of freedom, is centered in the very use and exercise of freedom.

However, one should carefully note that there are two ways in which something can be said to be required for an act. In one way, it can be required as a prerequisite for the action; in the other way, it can be required as something intrinsically and essentially included in the action itself. The former sort of thing is commonly said to be required *antecedently*—that is, required on the part of the *first* act, whether it be a proper principle of the action or [merely] a condition that is required beforehand in one or another way or in one or another genus of cause. The latter sort of thing, on the other hand, can be said to be required *concomitantly*—that is, in the *second* act itself, since it is not distinct from the free action itself, which is the second act of a free faculty.

Thus, when it is said that what is free is such that it is able to act and able not to act, given that all the things required for acting have been posited, this should be understood as referring to the things that are required antecedently and in the first act, and not to the others. This very point is suggested in the position under discussion when it is claimed that a free faculty must be disposed and proximately prepared for its work in such a way that, given that disposition, it is able to act and able not to act. For the preparation in question includes all those things that are required in the first act for operating.

11. And, indeed, it can easily be shown that for the free exercise [of the will] it is necessary that the aforementioned indifference /709b/ and, as it were, full twofold power should exist together with all the required things.

For, first of all, if this were not so, then the withholding of an act, for example, might result not from the intrinsic power and faculty but instead from the absence of some required condition. But an absence of this sort contributes nothing to freedom, since there is no natural power that acts necessarily to such an extent that it cannot sometimes fail to act because of the

---

not *O* itself but the absence of a willing of *O*; and (iii) freedom of *specification with respect to the same object*, where one is able to will (love, desire, intend, choose, etc.) *O* and also able to will against (hate, abominate, reject, etc.) *O*.

16. See *DM* 19. 8. 15–18.

absence of some required condition—for example, proximity to the patient or some other similar condition. Indeed, if one correctly reflects upon the matter, this is not an ability not to act but rather an inability to act—that is, a case of not being able to act when a given defect is present. By contrast, the indifference that belongs to freedom is based not on an inability to act but rather on an ability not to act. Hence, when the will itself fails to act because of a natural inattention on the part of reason, this absence of an act proceeds not from an ability not to act but rather from an inability to operate or to will in a given way, and so an absence of this sort cannot be free. Therefore, in order for a faculty to have free exercise, it is necessary that by its own internal force and power it be able to act and able not to act, given that all the things that are antecedently required—that is, required in the first act— have been posited.

Now in order to forestall objections, when we say "by its own internal force and power" we are ruling out neither God's concurrence nor the greater [divine] assistance required by the specific character of the acts. However, we leave this [last] matter to the theologians.[17]

12. Now the claim that the definition in question should not be understood as referring to what is required *concomitantly* is proved as follows. These [concomitant requirements] are, as we have said, included within the action itself. For just as the action is required for acting, so too whatever is included in the action can be said to be required. Now the action is required as that whereby the faculty is formally determined and as that whereby it is constituted as actually acting; and for this reason the action cannot be included among those conditions in the presence of which the faculty has to be indifferent with respect to acting or not acting, since this involves an obvious contradiction. Therefore, neither should one include among those required things anything at all that pertains to the intrinsic nature of the action or is essentially included in the action. For the same argument that applies to the action itself applies to all these things as well.

This interpretation of the definition in question is taken from the common position of theologians in *Sentences* 1, dist. 38 and 39, and *Sentences* 2, dist. 24, as well as from Anselm's teaching, which we will explicate in a moment.[18]

17. What Suarez has in mind here are the various elements of the doctrine of divine grace.

18. See §16 below.

REPLY TO THE FIRST PROBLEM

13. *The twofold movement of our will by the divine will.* On the basis of this interpretation, the two problems mentioned at the beginning are easily resolved.

The reply to the first problem[19] is that /710a/ God's movement of our will can be understood to be of two types. One type is antecedent to God's actual concurrence with respect to the will's action; the other type consists in the actual concurrence itself.

The first type is not at all known in metaphysics or on the basis of the principles of nature alone, though it is a certitude in theology.[20] And whatever sort of motion it might be, it is contained under the conditions that are antecedently required for an act, whether in the manner of a principle or in the manner of a first act. For even though this motion is effected through an act that is vital with respect to the faculty in which it exists and that is thus a second act, it is nonetheless related as a principle with respect to the other act for the sake of which the motion is given; and for this reason the motion is said to exist in the manner of a first act. In the same way, a judgment about a good thing to be done is a principle of that act of the will whereby such a good is loved; hence, even though this judgment is a second act in the intellect, it is nonetheless related to the will as a first act. And the same thing holds for other similar cases.

The second type of motion is better known to the natural light [of reason], since, physically speaking, it is more necessary intrinsically for a creature's action. However, this sort of motion is numbered among the things that are required concomitantly for the act, since God's concurrence is essentially included in the creature's action.[21]

14. Therefore, as far as the first type of motion is concerned, one should claim that even when it is posited, the will is still able not to do the act for the sake of which the motion is given. For since that motion is one of the prerequisite conditions for a free act, if it did not leave the will unimpeded, then it would remove the free exercise [of the will]; for it would determine the faculty to one effect. But, as Evodius correctly asked Constantius (according

---

19. See §1, pars. 1, 2, above.

20. The sort of antecedent movement in question here is called *prevenient* grace and may involve an antecedent movement of either the will or the intellect. But, as Suarez insists, this movement, even though it itself is an actual modification of the intellect or will, does not necessarily result in the will's consenting to the exercise of freedom for the sake of which the grace has been given.

21. Suarez is talking here about God's *actual*, as opposed to *aptitudinal*, concurrence. See *DM* 19. 1. 4.

to Turrianus, *Pro Epistolis Pontificianis* 4, chap. 2), what sort of freedom or choice would there be in a case where only one part [of the contradiction] was allowed? And this is why the Council of Trent, session 6, canon 4,[22] decreed, regarding this sort of antecedent motion even in the case of the works of grace, that when this motion is posited, it is still within the will's power not to consent. Nor does this contradict the efficacy of God's act of effecting the motion, both because (i) it stems not from a lack of power but from the wisdom, providence, and will of the First Mover himself and also because (ii) when God wishes to, he also brings it about efficaciously that the will consents infallibly even though it is able not to consent. Still, it is not a *per se* and absolute contradiction that this motion should exist and yet that the will not be moved via the free act or movement for the sake of which the motion in question is being given. And in this regard moving and being moved are not correlatives: namely, when a motion is related to another act as its principle and not just as a path to its terminus.[23] Otherwise, how is it that Augustine claimed that one who is moved in this way is unable not to feel the motion /710b/ but is nonetheless able not to consent to it?

Now within theology this matter is the subject of a momentous and extended debate. We are deliberately abstaining from this debate here, and, abstracting from all the various opinions, we are content with that reply which, as expressed in the words just cited,[24] is embraced by all the parties— even though there is disagreement over the interpretation of those words. We are not at present passing judgment on that disagreement.

15. Now it is in regard to the second type of motion that the problem we are discussing properly arises. For this is the motion by virtue of which a secondary cause's action depends *per se* and essentially on the First Cause; and, as I have said, this motion is none other than God's concurrence itself. (As for why it is called a motion, we will have more to say below˙ when we discuss the secondary cause's dependence on the First Cause in its operating.[25]) Thus, it is true of this motion that once it has been posited, it is impossible for the will not to be moved. However, we deny that this is incompatible with the exercise of freedom, since the motion in question is not numbered among the conditions that are required antecedently for an act but is instead

22. See Denzinger, #1554.

23. I.e., the motion in question is not the act toward which God is prompting one but is instead the very prompting itself, which in turn is ordered toward some good free act.

24. The relevant point of general agreement is this: God's antecedent movement of the intellect and the will is such that the will is still able not to consent to the act toward which God is prompting it.

25. See *DM* 22. 2–4.

essentially included in the will's very action. Now in the place cited just a moment ago we will explain (i) what sort of thing this divine concurrence or motion is, (ii) the way in which it exists simultaneously with the influence of the created will itself, (iii) whether it can in any way be called a prior motion without doing prejudice to freedom, and, finally, (iv) the way in which it is within the power of a human being to have or not to have this motion from God (for this is also true, and it is necessary for freedom).

REPLY TO THE SECOND PROBLEM

16. Lastly, the second problem[26] has already been resolved by what has been said. For once we put aside the first type of motion, which does not concern us here and which is not the subject of the argument in question, we may, as we have already explained, deny that the second type of motion—that is, God's concurrence—is numbered among the antecedent prerequisites spoken of by the definition of freedom. And so we acknowledge that once this latter type of motion has been posited, it is impossible for the will not to be moved, since this motion is already presupposed as included within the will's action though not without the will's free determination.

And this is the sense in which one may also best reply by appeal to the distinction between the composed and divided senses. For once this motion has been posited, it is impossible in the composed sense for the will not to operate, since the will is already assumed to be operating. Hence, this is not incompatible with freedom, since the exercise of freedom is included and already presupposed in this very assumption. And it is true to say of the exercise of freedom, as of any other thing whatsoever, that when it exists, it is necessary that it exist—even though simply and absolutely (this is said in the divided sense) it is able not to exist.

This is the very thing that Anselm said in *De Concordia*, at the beginning, and in *Cur Deus Homo* 2, chaps. 17 and 18: namely, that what removes freedom is necessity on an *antecedent* supposition, /711a/ not necessity on a *consequent* supposition. For what he calls an antecedent supposition is anything that is required antecedently for a free act: that is, anything that is required on the part of the first act. That is why he calls this antecedent supposition a cause of the thing, and so if the act necessarily follows from such a supposition, then this removes freedom, the nature of which is such that in the presence of all these prerequisites the full power to act or not to act remains—even in the composed sense with respect to such anteced-

26. See §1, par. 3, above.

ent conditions, as has been explained. On the other hand, what he calls a consequent supposition is everything that includes the creature's very action itself, since a supposition of this sort already presupposes the free exercise [of the will], as has been explained. Thus, the necessity that arises from this sort of supposition cannot remove the free exercise itself, since it is not a real necessity but merely a necessity of inference—as St. Thomas explained in *De Veritate*, q. 24, a. 1, ad 13, and confirmed in *Physics* 2, lect. 15, at the beginning. Also, St. Augustine endorses this view in *De Civitate Dei* 5, chap. 10.

Section 5

Which Faculty the Freedom of a Created Cause Formally Resides In

1. *All and only rational agents are capable of freedom.* In the third and fourth arguments for doubt proposed in section 2,[1] we are asked to explain more distinctly (i) which created causes are such that in acting they are not subject to necessity and (ii) through which faculty they have this sort of control [over their own acts].

To be sure, with respect to principal causes—that is, causes that operate as principles *quod*[2]—it is easy to answer this question on the basis of what has been said. For we have shown that all things that lack reason also lack freedom because of their imperfection. From this it follows, conversely, that all agents that are rational or intellectual are also free. For the denial of the use of reason is a sufficient and adequate reason for the lack of freedom; therefore, the opposite affirmation [of the use of reason] is likewise an adequate reason for the opposite affirmation [of freedom].

This is confirmed as follows. It has been shown that human beings in particular are free agents, even though within the intellectual grade [of being] human beings are the lowest of all; therefore, a fortiori, one should claim that all created agents that have an intellect also have freedom. (We will return to this point as it concerns created intelligences in particular when we discuss them below.[3])

Nor does the argument taken from the motions or influences of the celestial bodies count against this claim. For as far as the intelligences that move the celestial bodies are concerned, even if they are free in other matters, /711b/ they can be led by some sort of necessity in moving the celestial bodies, either because of a higher agent's motion and command or because of some preconceived end that they immutably love and intend. On the other hand, as far as the influence of the celestial bodies [themselves] is concerned, one should claim that this influence does not extend directly and *per se* to spiritual and immaterial entities, both because (i) the celestial bodies have their influence only through physical motion, which a spiritual entity is not sus-

---

1. See *DM* 19. 2. 3–4.

2. For Suarez's explanation of the distinction between a principal cause *quod* and a principal cause *quo*, see *DM* 17. 2. 7.

3. See *DM* 35. 5. 6–8.

ceptible to, and also because (ii) a spiritual entity is of a higher order, and so a material entity cannot act upon it directly. But the minds of human beings are in themselves immaterial, and they have freedom to the extent that they are immaterial and operate through an immaterial faculty. And so the influence of the celestial bodies cannot deprive human beings of the exercise of freedom, even if this influence can, by the mediation of the body and its affections, incline them indirectly toward one of the two parts [of a contradiction] to a greater or lesser degree. A human being can overcome this inclination by his freedom and [thus] dominate the stars.

2. *A spiritual substance is the root principle of free action.* From this it is obvious, further, that the principal principle *quo* of a free action is always some spiritual substance or spiritual substantial form. This is proved by the fact that a principle of this sort is either a rational soul or some higher substance; but a rational soul is immaterial, and every higher substance is all the more so; therefore, etc. And this is confirmed by the fact that every material form, insofar as it is material, operates without intelligence and reason, and so it operates in a merely natural manner; therefore, a form that is a principle of a free action must be spiritual.

3. *The proximate principle of a free action is always a spiritual faculty; a free act is either elicited or commanded.* Third, from this it is also obvious that the proximate principle of a free action is some faculty that belongs to a spiritual substance insofar as it is spiritual or intellectual. (I add this qualification because of the human soul, which, though it has a plurality of faculties, is nonetheless such that many of those faculties are material, since they do not belong to it insofar as it is intellectual. And so those faculties are not the proximate principle of a free action.)

The argument for this assertion is that the proximate principle has to be accommodated to the principal principle. Likewise, an entity has control over its own act only insofar as it is intellectual; therefore, it has this control only through a faculty that pertains to the intellectual grade [of being]; but this grade is immaterial both with respect to itself and with respect to all the faculties that are proximate to it; therefore, etc.

The only thing to note is /712a/ that there are two ways in which an action can be denominated as free: namely, either (i) as an *elicited* act—that is, one that is denominated as free *proximately* vis-à-vis the faculty that effects the action, in the way that an act of willing is itself free—or (ii) as a *commanded* act—that is, one that is denominated as free *remotely* vis-à-vis the faculty that moves or applies a lower faculty to its act, in the way that walking is free. Thus, when we speak of the proximate principle of a free action, this should be taken to refer to an action that is properly free vis-à-vis its immediate principle, and it is in this sense that we are claiming that the proximate principle of a free action is a spiritual faculty. For the proximate principle of an action that is free only as commanded can sometimes be a material faculty—as is the case with the faculty for effecting local motion that exists in the members of the body, since this faculty can be subordinated to a higher spiritual substance in which there exists a proper faculty that has control both over its own act and also, by the means of that act, over the lower faculty and its act. Hence, one can also claim that even though an action that is free as commanded is, speaking physically and with respect to its own being, brought about proximately by this other [lower] faculty, nonetheless, it has the denomination 'free' only from the higher faculty by the mediation of the higher faculty's act; therefore, this higher faculty, which is the proximate principle of an act that is free *per se* and immediately, must as such be spiritual and belong *per se* to the intellectual grade [of being].

FREE CHOICE CONSISTS NOT IN AN ACT OR A HABIT BUT IN A FACULTY

4. And from this we conclude, fourth, that created free choice consists directly and formally in the sort of faculty that has the aforementioned power and control over its own act. Nor is it necessary to tarry long over a refutation of the opinion of those who have claimed that free choice consists (i) in an act or (ii) in a habit or (iii) in a faculty insofar as it is affected by some habit. The first of these opinions was held by Hervaeus in *Quodlibeta* 1, q. 1; the second by Bonaventure in *Sentences* 2, dist. 25, a. 1, q. 4; and the third by Albert in *Sentences* 2, dist. 24, a. 5. However, these opinions either lack plausibility or else use the words in a different sense.

For a human being has free choice even when he is not acting. Otherwise, he would lose free choice just by ceasing to act—which is absurd. Therefore, free choice cannot consist in an act.

Likewise, a human being has free choice by reason of the fact that he is able to act and able not to act, once all the things required for acting have been posited. But it is proximately through some faculty that he is able to act. Therefore, /712b/ it is proximately through some faculty of the soul that he has freedom. Therefore, free choice will be a faculty of this sort.

Finally, if freedom of choice consists in an act, then I ask whether or not that act is elicited from a free faculty. If the answer is yes, then the freedom already exists prior to the act; therefore, it is in the faculty itself prior to the act. On the other hand, if the answer is no, then the act is necessary; in that case, how can freedom of choice consist in that act?

5. *An objection is answered.* Perhaps someone will object that even if the act

in question is necessary, it can still be the principle of a free act of choosing or deliberating. This is the way that Hervaeus seems to have philosophized. For he thought that a faculty is apt to elicit a free act only if the free act is preceded by a necessary act that is its principle. For a free act (he says) is preceded by an act of deliberating, and an act of deliberating is preceded by an act of willing to deliberate.

Now this claim may be taken to apply either to an act of the intellect or to an act of the will.[4] Thus it is true that before the first freely elicited act there must necessarily be a prior act of the intellect that is not free or properly voluntary but is instead natural. For since nothing can be willed without being previously cognized, every volition must be preceded by some judgment. Therefore, the judgment that precedes the first volition cannot have arisen from the will and, consequently, cannot be free.

However, it is false and absolutely improper to claim that this judgment, by reason of the fact that it can, within its own genus, be the foundation and root of a free exercise, just is free choice itself. For the judgment is merely a condition—namely, the application of the object—that is required in order for the free faculty to be able to exercise its own power. And even if we granted that this judgment concurs as an active cause with respect to an act that is freely elicited by the will, nonetheless, the freedom would not consist in the judgment. Rather, the judgment of itself has a natural influence, but it awaits (as I will put it) the consent or influence of the will, which has the power to grant or withhold that consent or influence. Therefore, it is incorrect to attribute freedom to this judgment or act of the intellect as if it were the principle in which freedom proximately resides.

6. On the other hand, if the claim in question is meant to apply to an act of the will, it is not universally true that every free act of the will is preceded by some natural act [of the will] that is a principle of the free act. For which act is like this, and what necessity is there for it to precede [the free act]?

Someone may reply that it is an act of willing to deliberate. But against this: First of all, in God there is perfect freedom without any such act of willing, since in his intellect there preexists (in our way of conceiving it) /713a/ a perfect knowledge of things which is merely natural and necessary.

Again, an angel, even in his first instant, had a free act of will in the absence of any previous act of willing to deliberate by means of his intellect. Instead, all that was presupposed was an actual cognition on the part of the intellect, a cognition that he possessed as something co-created [with him]

---

4. I.e., the necessary act posited by the objector could conceivably be either an act of the intellect or an act of the will. Suarez now proceeds to impugn this position on each of the two alternatives.

and received [from without], rather than as something acquired by his own volition.

And, similarly, if a human being has within his intellect a sufficient representation and consideration of an object, then even if he does not have this representation because of an application of his will but has it instead because he is stimulated by a proposed object or because someone else talks or communicates with him, he is immediately able to freely will the object or freely not will it. Besides, even though in a human being there often is an antecedent act of willing to deliberate—that is, to find out or take into account something further concerning a given object—this act of willing to deliberate is in fact not natural but free, since there is nothing that necessitates one's having it. Therefore, it is not the case either that (i) this sort of willing to deliberate always precedes that other, free act in the case of every object or that (ii) when it does precede it, it itself is always natural and necessary. And the reason is that in order for the will to will an object, it is not necessary that it should have previously willed to consider the object; rather, it is sufficient that it should have the relevant sort of consideration, regardless of whether it has that consideration from nature or from the will or from some other source. For all that is necessary as regards the object to be willed is that it be previously cognized; the fact that such a cognition comes from this or that source is incidental. And for the same reason, even if it often happens that the intellect's deliberation or inquiry is directly willed, it does not have to proceed from a natural or necessary volition. Instead, it is possible for it to proceed from a free volition—indeed, this is what happens, ordinarily speaking. And the reason why a failure to deliberate is often culpable is that the deliberation could have been had through a free volition.

For these reasons, then, it is not necessary that a natural act of the will should precede a free act.

7. *Whether every intending of an end is necessary.* Alternatively, one could object as follows. It is always the case that an act of intending the end precedes the choice of a means [to that end]. But an act of intending the end is necessary, since, as Aristotle and St. Thomas affirm, there is freedom only in the choice of the means. This, then, is the reason why a free act is always preceded by some necessary act that is the proximate principle and ground of free choice. Therefore, free choice must be posited first and foremost in that [necessary] act.

I reply both that (i) something false is being assumed here and that (ii) the inference is invalid. For not every act of intending an end is necessary, since there are many particular ends /713b/ that we will freely, not only with respect to exercise but also with respect to specification. It is only the ultimate or highest end that we love necessarily, and this only with respect to specification and not, at least in this life, with respect to exercise.[5] We will touch on this a little later, and there we will explain the sense in which freedom is said to be concerned with choice.[6]

Next, even when there is an antecedent act of intending the end, the freedom that exists in the choice of the means should not be attributed to the act of intending the end as to a proper principle; rather, it should be attributed to the faculty from which the intending and the choosing proceed. This is so both because (i) it is still uncertain whether the act of intending is a proper and *per se* principle of the effecting of the choice or whether it is merely an antecedent disposition—that is, a necessary condition for the choice—and especially because (ii) even if the act of intending does concur, along with the faculty, as an active cause with respect to the choice, nonetheless, the determination to choose this means rather than another proceeds not from the act of intending but from the power of the will itself; and it is because of the will's influence that the choice itself is intrinsically voluntary and hence determined to this means rather than to some other means.

Therefore, it is wholly unintelligible that the power of freedom should properly reside in some act. Instead, it resides in the faculty from which the free act proximately proceeds.

8. By similar arguments it can be readily shown that free choice is not a habit. For, first of all, such a habit would be either (i) natural and generated along with the faculty or else (ii) acquired through acts. (I am leaving aside infused habits, since we are now talking about natural freedom and about acts in the natural order.[7]) The first answer cannot be given, since according to the true teaching, there is no natural habit with which the will is naturally endowed—given that we are speaking properly about a habit as a quality that is distinct from the faculty and that adds to the faculty a certain facility or inclination. For it is not nature but exercise that yields such a habit. Nor does either experience or reason teach anything else. For the inclination or power with which nature endows a faculty is not distinct from the faculty

5. I.e., in the case of a universal or highest good, we are able to refrain from loving it, and so we have freedom of exercise with respect to it; however, we are not able to hate it, and so we lack one sort of freedom of specification with respect to it. (For background here, see *DM* 19. 4, n. 15.) Suarez makes the stipulation "at least in this life" because the standard scholastic view is that we lack not only freedom of specification but also freedom of exercise with respect to God as clearly seen in the beatific vision.

6. See *DM* 19. 8.

7. The infused habits alluded to here are, first and foremost, the theological virtues of faith, hope, and charity. However, some scholastics claim that these theological virtues are accompanied by infused moral virtues, which serve to transform and bring to perfection the naturally acquired moral virtues. For more on this, see St. Thomas, *Summa Theologiae* 1–2, q. 63, a. 3.

itself. (Thus, if it turns out that St. Bonaventure and St. Albert mean by the word 'habit' the connatural ability or power of such a faculty, then they differ from us only verbally.) Likewise, the second answer cannot be given, since a free faculty acquires habits through free acts. Therefore, the exercise of free choice precedes this sort of habit. Therefore, free choice cannot itself consist in such a habit.

Further, there is a general argument. A habit can be a principle of a free act only to the extent that we are able to exercise it when we will to. Therefore, the habit itself does not confer freedom but instead receives freedom (as I will put it) from the faculty in which it resides. For it is the faculty that /714a/ exercises the habit, and it is within the faculty's power to exercise the habit or not to exercise it.

The third argument is that a habit does not confer the ability to act but instead confers a facility in acting. Hence, there is no act in the natural order that the will is able to effect when it has a habit that it cannot effect absolutely in the absence of the habit. But free choice does not necessarily require this sort of facility in acting but instead requires [only] the absolute power to act and not to act, once all the required things have been posited. Thus, a human being who has the use of reason is free from the beginning, prior to acquiring this sort of facility. Therefore, freedom does not consist either in a habit or in the faculty taken together with a habit. For the faculty itself has this absolute power *per se*.

It is only in the case of habits that are infused *per se* that the claim in question seems plausible, since such habits confer not only a facility [in acting] but also an ability [to act]. Hence, one can grant that in this regard these [infused] habits complement the [faculty's] intrinsic freedom with respect to supernatural acts—though with regard to such acts the faculty can be called free unqualifiedly even in the absence of the [infused habits] as long as it has appropriate assistance in other respects. For the faculty is sufficient by itself for *not* eliciting those acts, whereas in order to elicit them, it can be complemented not only by the habits but also by the aids [of grace]. And there is no problem with this teaching; nor does St. Bonaventure or St. Albert pose any objection that requires a reply from us.

FREE CHOICE IS NOT A FACULTY DISTINCT FROM THE INTELLECT AND THE WILL

9. *Alexander of Hales's position is refuted.* Therefore, assuming that a free power is proximately posited in some faculty of a soul or intellectual substance, it remains to investigate which faculty this is.

And, first of all, there have been some who claim that it is a faculty distinct from the intellect and the will. Alexander of Hales holds this position in his *Summa Theologica* 2, q. 72, memb. 2, a. 1, §3, where he claims that free choice, taken properly and specifically, is a certain moving faculty distinct from the intellect and the will.

However, this position is neither provable nor intelligible. For either (i) he is talking about the faculty that effects local motion, or else (ii) he is talking about the faculty that moves the other faculties to their own acts.

As for the former, it is probable that in the soul and even in the intelligences this faculty is distinct from the intellect and the will, regardless of whether it is a faculty for moving oneself or a faculty for moving other things; this was touched upon above and will also be treated below when we discuss the created intelligences.[8] However, freedom cannot be formally constituted in this faculty. For, first of all, what the faculty in question properly elicits is not /714b/ an immanent act but instead a *transeunt* action; and so it is less perfect than it needs to be in order to be capable of formal freedom. Second, this faculty does not issue in an act unless it is applied by the will, since an angel or human being moves himself or other things when he wills to. (Indeed, in general, the principle of motion in the more perfect living things is an appetitive faculty.) Therefore, the faculty in question is not actively free (as I put it)—that is, free as eliciting—but is instead passively free—that is, free as commanded. Therefore, it is not in itself a free faculty but is instead subject to a free faculty. Hence, its act is voluntary only through a denomination that is taken from the act of another faculty, and it is not intrinsically voluntary in its own right—which is what is required for a formally free faculty, as I will explain a little further on.[9]

On the other hand, if [Hales] is talking about a faculty that moves the other faculties, then such a faculty in an intellectual creature is not distinct from the will and the intellect. For if one is talking about the [cognized] object's moving something, then in this sense the intellect moves the will. On the other hand, if one is talking about a motion that effects something or that applies something to its act, then in this sense the will moves both itself and the other faculties. For we are applied to acting freely only because we will to be. Therefore, it is both superfluous and unintelligible to conjure up some other faculty, since it is only by desiring and willing that we are inclined toward acting and applied to acting.

10. But if perchance Hales is drawing a conceptual, rather than a real, distinction between the will and this faculty that moves the other powers, and if it is in this sense that he is calling free choice a faculty distinct from the will, then, first of all, he differs from us only verbally. Second, he is not

adequately explaining the function of free choice, since this function consists not just in moving the other faculties but also in willing a given object while having the power not to will that object. Therefore, it is evident and certain that the faculty in which formal freedom resides is not distinct from the intellect and the will. However, it remains to be seen which of these faculties it is.

FORMAL FREEDOM IS NOT IN THE INTELLECT BUT IN THE WILL ALONE

11. *Freedom is not formally composed of reason and will together.* On this question there are three possible replies. The first is that the intellect and the will together formally constitute free choice in such a way that (i) each of these faculties is formally free in its own acts and that (ii) the complete freedom of a human being, along with his human acts, consists in the freedom of both of the faculties.

Durandus held this position in *Sentences* 2,. dist. 24, q. 3, where he first claims that the intellect along with the will /715a/ is a formally free faculty, and he thinks that this is Aristotle's position in *Metaphysics* 9.2˙ [1046a35–1046b24], where Aristotle says indiscriminately that rational˙ faculties are free. Durandus then adds that the intellect is free in a prior and more perfect way, since, given that it is proper to a rational faculty to be free, a faculty that is more perfectly rational will be more perfectly free. But the intellect is the more perfect rational power. Indeed, it alone is properly and, as it were, essentially rational, whereas the will is rational only by virtue of a certain participation or subordination because it is apt to be directed by reason. Therefore, it is also the intellect that is primarily free.

And this is confirmed as follows. The intellect is not only free but is also the root of the will's freedom, since the indifference of the judgment, which pertains to the intellect, is the root of the indifference of the choice, which pertains to the will. Therefore, there is a prior and more perfect freedom in the intellect. For that by virtue of which a given thing is such and such is itself such and such to a greater degree.

Finally, from this Durandus seems to infer implicitly that free choice is, as it were, formally composed of the intellect and the will—and it is for this reason that the Master, in the same place, and St. Thomas, in *Summa Theologiae* 1–2, q.1, a. 1, define free choice as a power of reason and will. For the word 'and' should be taken not conjunctively but collectively.[10] Hence,

---

10. I.e., according to the position under discussion, when free choice is said to be a power of reason and will, this does not imply that either the intellect or the will is a free

the function of free choice consists neither in judging alone nor in choosing alone but in both of them together.

12. *Freedom does not exist formally in the intellect alone.* The second possible reply is that freedom exists formally in the intellect alone and not in the will. I do not find this reply in any particular author, but it can be grounded plausibly enough, it seems, in a certain view that is accepted by many: namely, that the will is completely determined to its choice by the judgment of the intellect, in such a way that (i) in the absence of that judgment the will cannot be determined to choose anything and that (ii), once that judgment is posited, the will is unable to be at odds with it—that is, unable not to conform to it.

Now from this principle it plainly follows, first, that the faculty of will is not formally free. For, first of all, [it follows that] it is never within the will's power to act or not to act once all the things that are antecedently required have been posited, in the sense that was explained above. For one of the required things is the judgment of reason, which [on this view] is such that, once it has been posited, either (i) it is not within the will's power not to act (if it has been judged that it should act) or else (ii) it is not within its power to act (if it has been judged that it should not act).

Second, [it follows that] the will, in its own determination, behaves passively rather than actively, since it conforms to the motion of another faculty by a sort of necessity. But formal freedom cannot reside /715b/ in a faculty insofar as that faculty is moved; rather, as has been shown,[11] formal freedom resides in a faculty insofar as that faculty moves itself.

Third, this last point is made clear by an analogy with the executive faculty: the faculty that effects local motion. For that faculty is able to effect motion and able to refrain from effecting motion, and it is able to effect either this motion or some contrary motion. Yet it is not formally free, since it is unable to do this by moving or determining itself; instead, it is able to do it [only] by being moved and by necessarily conforming to the will's motion. Therefore, the same thing will have to be said of the will, since [on the view in question] it obeys the judgment of the intellect with an equal necessity.

Now from this part [of the position in question], thus argued for, the other part necessarily follows: namely, that freedom exists formally in the intellect to the extent that it has the power to make the judgment and not to make the judgment. For otherwise there would be no place left for formal freedom. And this latter part of the position can also be confirmed by Durandus's arguments.

faculty in its own right. Rather, it implies only that they are free when taken in conjunction with one another.

11. See *DM* 19. 2. 18–22.

13. *Freedom formally resides in the will alone.* The third reply is that freedom exists formally in the will and not in the intellect. This is the position of St. Thomas in *Summa Theologiae* 1, q. 83, a. 3, in *Summa Theologiae* 1–2, q. 13, a. 1 (and a. 6 as well), and in *Sentences* 2, dist. 24, q. 1. The same thing is held in these same places by Cajetan, Capreolus, Conrad, and other Thomists; and it is also endorsed by Richard, *Sentences* 1, dist. 24; Scotus, *Sentences* 1, dist. 25; and Henry, *Quodlibeta* 1, q. 16.

I judge this position to be absolutely true. And it will be adequately proved in opposition to the preceding position if we show that formal freedom does not exist in the intellect, since in that case there will be no faculty left in which it can exist except the will.

Now the claim [that formal freedom does not exist in the intellect] can be demonstrated as follows: The intellect is not of itself free either (i) with respect to the specification of its own act or (ii) with respect to the exercise of its own act; therefore, it is not free in any way, since no other mode of freedom is conceivable.

14. The first part of [the antecedent] is proved from the fact that the intellect is determined by its nature to assent to what is true and to dissent from what is false. But if neither of these traits is present in the object, or if the intellect does not perceive the trait, then the intellect is unable to elicit either an act of assenting or an act of dissenting, since it is unable to operate in the absence of an object.

You will object that there is a third possible alternative between these two: namely, that the intellect does not clearly see truth or falsity in the object but that truth or falsity is apparent in some degree because of probable arguments or because of someone's testimony. In such a case the intellect could be free with respect to the specification of its act.[12]

I reply, first of all, that the intellect cannot on its own be determined to a species of act unless it can also determine itself to the exercise of the act. For a faculty does not determine itself to a given act except by exercising that act, and, as we said above, freedom is found primarily and *per se* /716a/ in the exercise of the act.[13] Therefore, if we show that the intellect is not of itself free with respect to the exercise of the act, then it will also be obvious that, as regards the sort of objects [mentioned in the objection], it does not have formal freedom with respect to the specification of the act either.

15. What's more, this can be clarified and proved a priori as follows. It is not because the intellect has an intrinsic power and control over its own

___

12. Suarez's opponent is here claiming that when there is evidence, but not compelling evidence, for a given proposition, then the *intellect itself* is free to accept that proposition, reject it, or withhold both acceptance and rejection.

13. See *DM* 19. 4. 9.

act that it remains, as it were, suspended and undetermined with respect to objects proposed in the way in question; rather, it is only because the object is not applied in a way that is sufficient for the intellect's being led toward it necessarily by the natural impetus that inclines it toward what is true. One sees in this a major difference between the will and the intellect. For the intellect cannot be undetermined with respect to its own act for any reason other than that the object is proposed in an imperfect way. By contrast, even with respect to a precisely proposed object, the will can remain indifferent as to the fittingness of the object. And it is for this reason that in the divine intellect there is no indifference, properly speaking, with respect to the act of judgment; for the divine intellect is invariably an evident act of knowing and is accompanied by a perfect manifestation of the object. In the divine will, by contrast, there is an indifference with respect to the objects, even though they are proposed in an absolutely perfect way.

16. An argument that is a priori to a greater degree can be taken from the difference between the objects of the intellect and the will. The formal object of the intellect is truth, and truth and falsity cannot exist in the same object, since truth consists in something indivisible, as was explained above.[14] And so the intellect—both of itself and as regards the merits of the object—is always determined to one effect with respect to the species of its act. Hence, if in some cases it is not adequately determined, this is only because the object is not sufficiently proposed or sufficiently apparent, and not because the intellect itself has an internal power or control over its own act. By contrast, the object of the will is the good, and one and the same object can be simultaneously both good and evil—that is, both fitting and unfitting in relation to different things or under different aspects. And so even if the object is perfectly proposed or cognized, the appetitive faculty can be indifferent, as far as specification is concerned, with respect to pursuing or rejecting such an object. Therefore, indifference with respect to specification is found *per se* and formally not in the intellect but in the will.

17. The second part [of the antecedent],[15] which concerns necessity with respect to exercise, is proved as follows: (i) No faculty whose act is not intrinsically voluntary can be formally free with respect to exercise, and yet (ii) an act of the intellect is not intrinsically voluntary; /716b/ therefore, the intellect is not a formally free faculty.

To clarify the antecedent [of this argument], I am assuming that there are

---

14. Suarez deals with truth and falsity in *DM* 8 and 9.

15. The antecedent referred to here is found in §13, par. 3, above. The whole antecedent is: "The intellect is not of itself free either (i) with respect to the specification of its own act or (ii) with respect to the exercise of its own act." Suarez is here trying to prove (ii).

two ways in which an act can be voluntary. The first is *extrinsically*, through a denomination taken from the act of a different faculty that moves or applies another faculty to its act, in the way that walking is voluntary when someone spontaneously moves himself. In the second way, an act is voluntary *intrinsically* and through itself, in the way that an act of loving is voluntary. For what is more spontaneous than an act of loving? And yet, speaking *per se*, such an act is voluntary not through a denomination taken from another act but through itself. For in order for someone to love, it is not necessary that by a prior and distinct act he should will to love. And even though at times one is able by his freedom to do this, it is still accidental to a voluntary act of loving. For one is able, immediately and in the absence of any prior act, to elicit an act of loving, and the very act of loving is itself intrinsically a willing to love.

Now the difference is that in the first mode of voluntariness, the act that is denominated as voluntary because of another act is the object and effect of that other act. It is its object because that prior act tends toward it, whereas it is its effect because such an act is not only willed as an object but is also caused (at least mediately). For it is by an act of the will or appetitive faculty that the lower power is applied to its act. By contrast, an act that is intrinsically voluntary through itself is not related as either a proper object or an effect to the act by virtue of which it is voluntary, since it is voluntary by virtue of itself and it is not properly either an object or an effect of itself. Therefore, it has some other object toward which it directly tends, and it is an effect of the faculty that elicits it—and it is voluntary solely because of a sort of virtual reflexivity that it includes within itself. That is why such an act is commonly said to be willed in the manner of an act and not in the manner of an object.[16]

18. *An act that is in itself voluntary is always elicited by an appetitive faculty.* From this one can see that no act can be voluntary intrinsically and through itself unless it is an act elicited by an appetitive faculty.

This is proved from the fact that what is properly voluntary, as opposed to what is connatural, proceeds formally from an act elicited by a vital appetitive faculty. And so in the first mode of voluntariness, the act that is extrinsically called voluntary receives this denomination from an act elicited by the vital appetitive faculty that commands the extrinsically voluntary act. Therefore, necessarily, an act that is voluntary through itself, since it does not receive this denomination from any other act elicited by an appetitive faculty, must itself be elicited by a vital appetitive faculty. /717a/

And on the basis of the very nature and manner of such an act one can

---

16. This corresponds to the distinction between an *elicited* act and a *commanded* act.

formulate the following argument also: An act elicited by the will exists in the manner of an intrinsic and spontaneous tendency or inclination toward the object, and so such a tendency is itself spontaneous as well. But this sort of tendency is proper to an appetitive faculty. Therefore, it is also proper to such a faculty that its act be intrinsically voluntary through itself. Therefore, since the intellect is not an appetitive faculty, it is obvious that its act is not intrinsically voluntary through itself—which was the second part of the assumed antecedent.[17]

19. The first part [of that same antecedent]—namely, that only a faculty whose act is intrinsically voluntary can be free with respect to exercise— is explained as follows. The exercise of an act—or (what amounts to the same thing) the determination of a faculty to its operation—must be either (i) *natural*, due to the force of nature alone, or (ii) *voluntary*, due to an elicited inclination on the part of that which is operating. For there is no conceivable reason why a cause should issue in an act other than that either (i) it is of such a nature that it is of itself determined to that act or (ii) it wills and desires such an operation. But a faculty that is free with respect to exercise is not determined to an act by the force of nature alone. Therefore, it has to be determined voluntarily. Therefore, either (i) it is determined extrinsically through a voluntary act elicited by another faculty, in which case it will not be a formally free faculty but rather a faculty that is free as commanded, since it does not move itself with respect to exercise but is instead moved and determined by another; or else (ii) it is determined through an intrinsically voluntary act, in which case the faculty in question must be an appetitive faculty. Therefore, in order for a faculty to be formally free with respect to exercise—that is, in order for it to be able to determine itself with respect to exercising a free act—it is necessary that it be a faculty that operates in an intrinsically voluntary way through its own act. Therefore, since the intellect is not a faculty of this sort, as is evident *per se*, it is correct to conclude that it is not a faculty that is formally free in the exercise of its own act.

20. This can be confirmed, first, from the common way in which all people think and speak. For given that a man is able to think about this or about that, if he is asked why he is occupied with thinking about this thing rather than some other thing, he will reply that he is doing it because he wills

17. See §17, par. 1, above. The whole antecedent is: "(i) No faculty whose act is not intrinsically voluntary can be formally free with respect to exercise, and yet (ii) an act of the intellect is not intrinsically voluntary." Suarez has just argued that the intellect's act is not intrinsically voluntary. In §19 he will argue that only a faculty whose act is intrinsically voluntary can be free with respect to exercise. This will bring to a conclusion his argument for the second part of that other antecedent found in §13 and quoted in n. 15 above.

to. Indeed, one who believes things that he does not see clearly likewise believes because he wills to—where his will is regulated by reason if he is believing prudently. That is why theologians claim that an act of faith is meritorious and that it depends on a pious disposition of the will. This, then, is an indication that the intellect is never freely determined to one or the other part except through the will. Therefore, /717b/ the intellect is not in itself formally free.

And, finally, this is confirmed by the fact that when an act of the intellect—that is, the exercise of an act of the intellect—is not had by a necessity of nature, it can be appropriated by someone—that is, preferred to the absence of such an act or exercise—only through a choice whereby the one is preferred to the other. But choice is an act of the will. Therefore, the determination of the faculty to the exercise of the act is always by means of a command or motion on the part of the will as choosing. And so all the freedom of such an act is formally from the will and not from the intellect.

And the same conclusion is reached, a fortiori, when the act of choice in question has to do not only with the exercise of the intellect's act but also with the species of that act—as when someone chooses to believe firmly rather than to disbelieve or to doubt. For this must necessarily be accomplished through the will's determining the intellect, as St. Thomas correctly claimed in *Summa Theologiae* 2-2, q. 2, a. 1, ad 3.

21. *The use of reason is the root of freedom*. First of all, then, on the basis of the proof of this part [of the antecedent] Durandus's opinion is sufficiently disproved. For if the intellect is not *formally* free, then free choice cannot formally consist in a combination or aggregation of the faculty of intellect and the faculty of will. I say 'formally', however, because the intellect— that is, reason—does pertain to free choice as its *root*; this is the sense in which it is claimed that free choice is a power of the will and of reason. For free choice belongs to the will formally, whereas it belongs to reason as to a presupposition or a root.

What's more, there is no need to dispute with Scotus, Henry, and the others who claim that reason should not be called the root of freedom but should instead be called merely a necessary condition for freedom. These authors seem to be arguing about a way of speaking rather than about the thing itself. For because cognition is only a necessary condition that precedes volition, they want to call the relevant mode of cognition merely a necessary condition for that mode of willing which consists in freedom.

Nonetheless, it is absolutely correct to claim that the root of freedom is the use of reason or understanding. For if we are speaking of the faculties themselves, the appetitive faculties follow the cognitive faculties in such a way that, even though the root of them [all] is the soul, nonetheless, the soul is immediately the root of a cognitive faculty and [only] mediately the root of an appetitive faculty. And so a more perfect appetitive faculty is rooted proximately in a more perfect knowing faculty. Therefore, the perfection of formal freedom likewise arises from the perfection of understanding or reasoning. Therefore, just as one attribute is the root of another, so the will's freedom will be said to be rooted in the reason's understanding.

Moreover, /718a/ this same relation obtains among the acts, since just as there is a *per se* ordering among the faculties, so too there is a *per se* ordering among their acts. And since this relation is one of *per se* moral causality, whereas the foundation of all moral being is freedom, it also follows that the indifference in the will's acts proceeds from the judgment of reason, as St. Thomas correctly teaches in *Summa Theologiae* 1, q. 83, a. 1, and in the other places cited above. The Thomists follow him in those same places, as do Soncinas, Javellus, and others in *Metaphysics* 9.

22. The only thing that must be noted is that the authors just mentioned often say that the indifference of the act of the will arises from the indifference of the judgment of reason—a locution in which one must avoid equivocating on the word 'indifference'. For indifference as attributed to the will [as a faculty] signifies a formal freedom within the faculty itself—that is, a power with respect to both parts—while indifference in the will's act signifies an immediate relation to the faculty as eliciting the act, along with a proximate power with respect to the opposite part. Hence, if the indifference of the act of the will is said to arise from the indifference, in the same sense, of the judgment, then the position in question is not true, since, as has been demonstrated,[18] this sort of formal indifference cannot exist in the judgment insofar as it precedes the volition.

Therefore, the indifference attributed to the judgment as the root of freedom has to be understood in another sense, and one can call it an *objectival* indifference but not a *formal* indifference. For the judgment of reason is the foundation for the will's act of free choice because, by virtue of its own perfection and breadth, that judgment proposes within the object various aspects of fittingness and unfittingness; and it likewise proposes the means [to the end] not as necessary in all cases but instead as indifferent, since it discerns the level of usefulness and difficulty of the means and at the same time discovers or proposes other means. Moreover, the claim that no other sort of indifference or freedom is required in the judgment is sufficiently proved by what was said above against Hervaeus's position.[19] And this is readily obvious in the case of God's freedom. For given a merely natural

18. See §§12–20 above.
19. See §§5–7 above.

knowledge of all possible objects, the divine will freely wills this or that thing outside itself solely because of the indifference or nonnecessity of the objects, an indifference or nonnecessity which it clearly and necessarily grasps through its natural knowledge.

23. And in this way the foundations of Durandus's position are all sufficiently answered.[20] For being a formally free faculty is not the same as being a rational faculty. Nor is being a formally free faculty necessarily concomitant with being a rational faculty; instead, it is concomitant only with being an *appetitive* rational faculty. For from a faculty's being rational as such it follows only that it is either formally free or free as a root. And this is how Aristotle should be understood in *Metaphysics* 9,[21] /718b/ where he speaks indiscriminately about the rational faculties as a unit, and where he intends to teach only that in the rational part [of the soul], which we call the mind, there is an indifference in operating. He does not, however, discuss the question of how each of the faculties of that higher part [of the soul] contributes to this indifference—though we have now explained this.

24. Second, the proof of the same part [of the antecedent][22] leaves in its wake a disproof of the second position,[23] which denied that formal freedom exists in the will. For if, as has been shown, formal freedom does not exist in the intellect, then it must exist in the will. Otherwise, it would not exist anywhere.

Besides, the position in question is in its own right utterly implausible and foreign to all human sentiment. For everyone believes that a human being is free by reason of the fact that he acts if he so wills and refrains from acting if he so wills. Accordingly, Sacred Scripture, too, attributes this indifferent power especially to the will: ". . . who, not having necessity, but having the power of his own will . . ." (1 Corinthians 7:37). And so, too, all goodness and badness, along with every ground for reward or punishment, is judged to be in the will, as theologians widely hold. And, in an eloquent manner, the Council of Trent (session 6, canon 5),[24] having taught that it is within the

20. See §11 above. Briefly, Durandus's position is that freedom resides formally in the combination of the intellect and the will.

21. See §11 above for this reference to Aristotle.

22. The "same part [of the antecedent]" is the second part of the antecedent found in §17. It reads as follows: "(i) No faculty whose act is not intrinsically voluntary can be formally free with respect to exercise, and yet (ii) an act of the intellect is not intrinsically voluntary."

23. See §12 above. The second position is that according to which freedom resides formally only in the intellect and not in the will.

24. See Denzinger, #1555.

power of a human being to freely cooperate with or resist grace, expressly declares that a human being does this "by his own free will"—either by his own free will alone (if he resists the grace) or else by his own free will as aided by God's grace (if he cooperates with it). And, lastly, it is for this reason that the ancient Fathers often call free choice itself 'free will', as one can see in Augustine, *De Libero Arbitrio* 3, chap. 1ff., and in Damascene, *De Fide Orthodoxa* 2, chap. 25—though sometimes they call it 'free choice of the will', as is clear from Augustine, *De Civitate Dei* 5, chap. 9, and from Ambrose, *De Fide* 2, chap. 3.

25. And on the basis of the one part—namely, that the will is formally free—one can confirm the other part—namely, that the intellect is not formally free. For acts elicited by the two faculties should not be posited as *per se* free in a human being solely by virtue of their relations to their own faculties. Otherwise, there would be *two* sorts of moral disorder in such acts of the intellect and the will. For as soon as the intellect judged that a given evil object is able to be chosen, there would be badness in this act taken precisely as such and prior to any other act of consent on the part of the will, since [this act of judgment] would of itself be both (i) in conflict with reason and also (ii) formally free in other respects. In turn, there would be a new badness in the act of choosing such an object, since this act would be both (i) a new free act that the human being in question would be able to avoid and also (ii) an act with respect to an object that is contrary to reason. But if, while the relevant judgment remained, the will were as yet not to consent, the person in question would nonetheless deserve /719a/ to be reprehended because of such a judgment—not by reason of any prior act, formal or virtual, on the part of the will but precisely on account of the intellect's freedom. And for the same reason deliberation or error could be culpable because of the intellect alone without any intervention on the part of the will. But all these things are absurd, since nothing is more repugnant than for there to be a sin in the absence of anything voluntary. Therefore, just as there is no formal moral goodness or badness in a human being other than that which proceeds from the will, so neither is there any faculty that is formally free other than the will.

Nor is this contrary to the perfection of the intellect. For, absolutely speaking, it is a greater perfection to be a rule with respect to the will. However, this perfection is incompatible with the existence of formal freedom in the same faculty, both because (i) a rule must be certain and of itself immutable and also because (ii) the operation that constitutes this rule does not exist through an inclination or tendency toward the thing that is being regulated but rather exists through a sort of measuring of that thing, a measuring that is not indifferent but is instead certain and determinate. By contrast, since the will is, as it were, blind, it stands in need of the intellect's rule or direction. However, because it tends toward its object through a perfect voluntary inclination, it is capable of freedom, and in this it can exceed the intellect in a certain respect—even though, absolutely speaking, it is inferior to the intellect in perfection.

Section 6

How a Free Cause Is Determined by the Judgment of Reason

1. However, we have yet to reply to the problem proposed on behalf of the second position,[1] a problem that raises another question: namely, how the will, when it wills freely, is determined by reason.

On this question the disciples of St. Thomas cited above,[2] along with other more recent disciples, contend that it is altogether impossible for the will to be determined to a free act unless there is antecedently in the intellect a definitive practical judgment—or, as others put it, a command—by which (i) the intellect, here and now with all things considered, pronounces the definitive verdict that the person is to choose this, or by which (ii) the intellect effects an impulse that is expressed by the words 'Do this!'

One can argue for this claim as follows: Since the will is a rational appetite (*Ethics* 6˙.2 [1139b4]), it can be led only toward an object that is cognized and proposed by reason. Therefore, until reason judges determinately what is to be chosen, the will cannot choose; otherwise, it would tend toward an uncognized object. For in the absence of a judgment there is no cognition that is true, since through a mere apprehension [of a thing] one does not yet cognize /719b/ whether the thing is or is not such and such. Therefore, conversely, once the definitive judgment 'This is to be chosen' is in place, the will is unable not to choose, since otherwise it would be led without reason in that case as well, and it would be led formally or at least virtually toward an uncognized object. For in not choosing, the will—through either a formal or a virtual act—would reject the object or would will not to embrace a given means in the absence of any reason or judgment.[3] Therefore, it is repugnant to the will to operate in such a way.

Perhaps this is why Bernard, in *De Gratia et Libero Arbitrio*, claimed that an act of the will always has an associated reason, since even though the will is not always moved in a reasonable manner, it is nonetheless never moved in the absence of a reason.

---

1. See *DM* 19. 5. 12. This problem was first broached in passing in *DM* 19. 2. 5.

2. Suarez apparently means to refer here to Cajetan, Capreolus, and Conrad, who are cited in *DM* 19. 5. 13.

3. I.e., even if in such a case the will simply withholds its act and does not formally reject the object by a positive act of, say, hating the object, nonetheless, its withholding its act is virtually equivalent to its positively rejecting the object. This is the force of the qualification "through either a formal or a virtual act."

2. However, this position does not please Henry, and neither does it please Scotus or his disciples, as is evident from the places already cited and from Antoine André, *Metaphysics* 9, q. 2. And, indeed, the argument suggested in the preceding section with reference to the second position seems irrefutable to me.[4] For if this judgment of reason is a prerequisite for acting in the sense that, within its own genus, it is a necessary cause with respect to a free act of the will, and if, once this judgment has been posited, the will is unable not to consent to it, then the will is not the sort of faculty that is able to will and able not to will, given that all the things that are absolutely required for acting have been posited. Therefore, it is not a free faculty.

This whole line of reasoning seems evident in conjunction with the principles demonstrated above. And it is further explicated as follows: Once the judgment has been posited, the will wills by a necessity in the composed sense (as they put it). This is a point that the authors of the position in question will readily concede, so much so that in *Summa Theologiae* 1–2, q. 9, a. 1, dub. 2, after the second conclusion, Medina claims that for as long as an efficacious command exists on the part of the intellect, no freedom to contradict it remains within the will. And he adds that the command does not have this efficacy from the will, speaking *per se*. For because there is no infinite regress, one must necessarily arrive at some command on the part of the intellect that comes before any action on the part of the will and that efficaciously carries the will along with it. Again, Bellarmine, who holds this position, claims, in *De Gratia et Libero Arbitrio* 2, chap. 8, that just as the will of the blessed in heaven is determined with respect to loving God once the vision of God has been posited, so too, in choosing any particular thing, the will is determined to one effect as regards both specification and exercise, and it will indeed choose necessarily in the presence of a particular practical judgment dictating that here and now, absolutely and all things considered, this is to be chosen.

3. But in that case I ask, once again, whether (i) the judgment in question /720a/ is absolutely and unqualifiedly necessary, so that it proceeds from the intellect either solely by virtue of an evident object and middle term or by virtue of some other cause that necessitates the intellect with respect to such a judgment or whether instead (ii) the judgment is an act that is unqualifiedly free.

If the first answer is given, the exercise of freedom is obviously destroyed, since such an exercise is found neither in the making of the judgment itself nor in the act of the will that necessarily follows upon that judgment. Nor does the composed sense help at all here, since the hypothesis with which

4. See *DM* 19. 5. 12.

the act is composed in a necessary manner is in itself unqualifiedly necessary and nonfree, and it precedes the act of the will as a cause that necessitates the will with respect to the subsequent act.[5] This is the mode of composition that is found in a beatific act of love, and there is no other way in which an act of the will can be necessary.

If, on the other hand, one replies that the judgment in question is free (as Javellus, *Metaphysics* 9, q. 4, finally concedes after making some useless and obscure distinctions), then I ask again whether (i) the judgment is free as elicited by the faculty of the intellect or whether (ii) it is free as commanded by the will. The first answer cannot be given according to the position accepted by those of us who on this point argue that the intellect is not a formally free faculty.[6] On the other hand, if the second answer is given, then either there is an infinite regress or else the position in question is completely destroyed. For I ask, concerning the act of will that determines the intellect to such a judgment, whether it itself is determined by another judgment of the intellect—and [if so, then] the same argument will return with respect to the latter judgment, and one will proceed in this way ad infinitum. On the other hand, if this free act of the will does not proceed from the determination of a similar antecedent judgment, then this entails two things contrary to the position under discussion. The first is that the will is not determined in *all* its free acts by a judgment of the intellect; the second is that it is never thus determined except because of some prior free volition by virtue of which the rest [of the acts] follow and because of which they participate in freedom.

4. Perhaps someone will object that even though, as long as the judgment remains, it is impossible for the will not to consent to it, it is nonetheless possible for the will to remove the judgment, and it is because of this that its act is free and not necessary. However, this is not a sufficient reply to the proposed argument. Rather, it tacitly and implicitly admits that the judgment in question is free—otherwise, the will could not remove it—but it does not make clear just which volition it is through which the judgment is free in the first place.

Nor is it sufficient to claim that the judgment is *indirectly* free by virtue of

5. The composed sense does not help preserve freedom here because if the antecedent as well as the consequence is necessary, then the consequent is necessary too. But in the case at hand, what is necessary is not only the consequence—viz., *If the intellect judges in such and such a way, then the will wills in accordance with that judgment*—but also the antecedent—viz., *The intellect judges in such and such a way.* For according to the position under discussion, the intellect's judgment issues from its cause by a necessity of nature.

6. Suarez's argument for the claim that the intellect is not a formally free faculty is found in *DM* 19. 5. 13–23.

the fact that the will has not impeded it. For the will was at least able to have a free volition by which it might impede the judgment, a volition with respect to which the same argument returns. Further, even if /720b/ an indirect voluntariness might be sufficient for the *absence* of an act, it is nonetheless not sufficient for the *positive exercise* of a free and commanded act; instead, what is required is a formally free act that commands and determines the faculty in question.[7]

Moreover, a second way out, which can be gleaned from Javellus in the place cited above, fails to weaken the force of the argument. For he claims that the judgment in question is free as a root, a feature it gets from the intellect and not from the will. However, to say this is not to respond to the proposed dilemma but to evade it. For to be free as a root is nothing other than to be the root of the freedom that is in the will. But this is not what we are asking about; instead, we are asking about *formal* freedom. For this very act of the intellect, which is the root of the act of the will, is truly and formally elicited by its own faculty; and we are asking, with respect to *this* act, whether it is elicited necessarily by its faculty or whether instead it is elicited with indifference.

Others reply by distinguishing between the speculative judgment and the [corresponding] practical judgment, since it is not the speculative judgment but the practical judgment that determines the will. And they claim that the practical judgment is free even if the speculative judgment happens to be natural. However, this does not weaken the force of the proposed difficulty. For if, after a complete speculative judgment has been made about the fitness, usefulness, and rectitude or turpitude of the object and about the other aspects or circumstances, the practical judgment that a given thing is to be loved or chosen is free, then the whole argument made above returns with respect to this practical judgment. For what is it that determines the intellect to such a judgment? If it is determined by the intellect, then the intellect is free. If it is determined by the will, then what determines the will? And in this way one reaches the conclusion that the first free determination of the will takes place without a judgment of the sort in question, and that there is no judgment that completely determines the will to any act except in virtue of some prior free volition.

5. Finally, there are some who claim that (i) this practical judgment is free because of the will's loving the object, that (ii) the will itself loves the object

7. Suarez is claiming that because the judgment itself is a *positive* commanded action (rather than just the absence of an act), it follows that if the judgment is free, then it must have a *positive* free act in its causal ancestry. The mere absence of an act, even if this absence is due to the free withholding of an act, does not suffice.

because of a judgment of this sort, and that (iii) these two acts are causes of one another within diverse genera of causality, since (a) the will determines the intellect to judge practically in the way in question and (b) the intellect determines the will to will the relevant thing. And (they say) it is not impossible that these two acts should mutually precede and follow one another, since this happens within different genera of causality.[8] For the will determines the intellect as an efficient cause, whereas the intellect determines the will as a final cause.

However, to my mind this doctrine is unconvincing. For, first of all, it is wholly groundless and unnecessary for anything. And, from another angle, the mind can scarcely conceive of this sort of mutual priority and motion between the two acts in question. /721a/

Further, I prove as follows that this doctrine is impossible. In every vital act, the sufficient application of the object required for the act precedes such an act absolutely and in every genus of causality, and it cannot happen that the very application of the object proceeds from the act toward which that application is ordered as from an efficient cause. But the judgment of reason, insofar as it applies the object, is required for the act of the will. Therefore, it is impossible that the judgment of reason that is required for the act of the will should proceed from that same act as from an efficient cause.

The major premise can be proved by an induction over all the other vital acts besides the one we are talking about. And an analogous argument can be drawn from natural acts, since it is impossible that (i) an agent that requires a patient in order to act should not presuppose—absolutely and in every genus of causality—the application of the patient to such an action or that (ii) such an agent should apply the patient to itself through that very action. Also, one can make the argument that an agent is unable to act except with respect to a matter that has been applied; therefore, it is impossible for the agent to effect the application through that very action itself—instead, it must altogether presuppose such an application. Likewise, if this were not so, then such an action, insofar as it applied the patient, would be directed not toward the patient as applied, but rather toward the patient as distant.

8. The claim is that the will determines the intellect as an efficient cause of the practical judgment, while the judgment determines the intellect as a final cause. So suppose I decide to raise my hand in order to draw someone's attention. Then, on the view in question, (i) my willing to raise my hand causes the practical judgment that, given my end, I ought to raise my hand in these circumstances, and (ii) the judgment that I ought to raise my hand, given my end, provides the reason or final cause of my act of willing to raise my hand. Incidentally, there is some reason to believe that the position Suarez here outlines and rejects is St. Thomas's position.

This point will be further clarified in a moment with respect to the topic we are dealing with.

6. The minor premise of the original syllogism[9] is certain by reason of the principle that nothing is willed unless it has been previously cognized. And if one contends that the judgment of reason is not only a [necessary] condition and an application of the object but also a principle which, along with the will, effects the act of the will, then this does not weaken the argument but instead adds to its force.[10] For it will be all the more impossible for that judgment to proceed from the motion of the will's act as from an efficient cause, given that the very judgment itself is claimed to be a principle that effects this act of the will.

This is further confirmed, first, as follows. The will does not apply any faculty to its act except by willing that act. Therefore, if the will directly applies the intellect to the judgment in question, then it will do this through an act whereby it wills that the intellect make this judgment. What, then, moves the will to will this? Is it some distinct prior judgment about whether the judgment in question is to be willed? If it is a distinct judgment, then the will is determined to the act in question not by the judgment which it wills but rather by the judgment which precedes the act. [On the other hand], if it is the very same judgment, then that judgment moves the will in the manner of an object before there has been any sort of judgment about that object.

Second, it is confirmed by the fact that if it were not so, then the very first act of the intellect could proceed from the will itself—which is contrary to the position that is held by everyone and that is grounded on the principle "Nothing is willed unless it has been previously cognized." And the inference is proved from the fact that /721b/ one could say, even with respect to this very first act of the intellect, that (i) it is free and voluntary because of the will's motion and yet that (ii) within its own genus it is a cause of that same act of the will by virtue of which it is voluntary. But if such a thing is impossible in the case of the first act, as indeed it is, this is not because that act is the absolutely first act but rather because it is a cause of the will's act in such a way that it is presupposed by the latter absolutely and in every genus of causality. But this line of reasoning goes through in the case of every other act [as well]. Therefore, it can never happen that the intellect's

9. See §5, par. 3, above for the original syllogism. The minor premise is this: "But the judgment of reason, insofar as it applies the object, is required for the act of the will."

10. This line of criticism is in a way unfair, since it was not part of the position outlined in §5 that the judgment is an *efficient* cause of the act of will. Rather, on the most obvious interpretation the judgment was supposed to serve as the *final* cause (and hence as the teleological explanation) for the act of will.

judgment is free by virtue of an act of the will that is subsequent to it. Or, alternatively, it can never happen that the will is determined to a free act by a judgment that arises from that same free act. And so it follows that either (i) the will is determined by a judgment that is altogether necessary, which is incompatible with freedom, or (ii) the free determination does not arise from such a judgment, which is what I intended to prove.

THE RESOLUTION OF THE QUESTION

7. Because of these problems, my own view is that in order for there to be a free determination of the will it is not necessary that there be a practical judgment of the sort that completely determines the will. In addition to the line of reasoning already presented (which seems to proceed a posteriori and from absurdities), this view can be explicated a priori and on the basis of the thing itself. The judgment of the intellect does not move the will except by means of the object that it proposes. But the proposed object does not always impose necessity on the will or determine it to one effect, nor is this required in order for the will to be able to tend toward the object. Therefore, such a determination on the part of the judgment is not required or, indeed, even possible.[11]

The major premise is proved by the fact that either the judgment moves [the will] only by reason of the object, or else the judgment itself, by its very nature, has a special sort of efficient causality with respect to determining the will. This latter cannot be claimed, because (i) an efficient causality of this sort would be incompatible with the will's freedom, as has been explained,[12] and because (ii) such a manner of moving is foreign to the intellect's function, which is to illuminate, direct, and regulate the operations of the will, and, finally, because (iii) this manner of moving is proper to the will, which is conferred specifically for the purpose of moving the other faculties as an efficient cause with respect to their exercise. Therefore, it cannot be the case that the intellect, which is moved by the will as by an efficient cause, should in turn move the will in the same manner. And this is what St. Thomas explicitly teaches in *Summa Theologiae* 1–2, q. 9, a. 1 and 3.

8. However, there are some who object that the intellect moves the will to its act by means of a practical *command* [rather than a judgment]. /722a/ The reply is that the practical 'command' of the intellect whereby someone

---

11. The major premise of this argument is defended in the rest of §7 and in §8, while the major premise is defended in §9.

12. See §§2–4 above.

is thought of as commanding himself or his own will is nothing other than a *judgment* that is completely practical and wholly definite with regard to all the circumstances. Nor can one conceive of any act in the intellect that impels the will except in the manner of a judgment—just as, with respect to other acts, a command is thought of only in the manner of a pronouncement that declares what is to be done. And anything else that is imagined to exist in the intellect (i) is posited gratuitously, (ii) is such that what it is cannot be explained and (iii) falls outside the nature of the intellect, which is essentially and adequately a cognitive and judicative power and so cannot have an act except in the manner of either an apprehension or a judgment. Therefore, since the command we are now speaking of is not merely an apprehension, as is obvious *per se*, it cannot be anything but a practical judgment. What's more, neither Aristotle nor St. Thomas ever explains the nature of a command in any way other than as a wholly practical judgment, as is explained at length in *Summa Theologiae* 1–2, q. 17.

Therefore, as has been explained, it is only on the part of the object that this judgment on its own moves [the will]. And if the judgment sometimes seems to impel [the will] as an efficient cause, this is only because of some prior efficacious act on the part of that same will. For if the will has efficaciously resolved or intended to pursue a given end, or if it has chosen to employ a given means, then, when the occasion arises, the intellect here and now judges that such and such must absolutely be done—presupposing the prior volition. In such a case the will is completely determined not so much by the judgment as by itself. An indication of this is that the will is not *absolutely* determined but only, as it were, *conditionally* determined—that is, determined on the condition that it should will to persist in the intention or choice that has been made. This is why it can, if it so wills, back away from the prior volition and impede a command of the sort in question. However, when no such efficacious volition occurs beforehand, it is impossible for the intellect's command to have this kind of efficacious impelling force. Otherwise, it would destroy the will's freedom, and praise and blame would have to be attributed not to the will but to the intellect. In the end, Medina concedes this point because of the authority of St. Thomas, *Summa Theologiae* 1–2, q. 17, a. 5.

9. The second part [of the argument][13] remains to be proved: namely, that the will is not always determined to one effect by the proposed object. This is certain and accepted by everyone, and St. Thomas expressly argues for it in *Summa Theologiae* 1–2, q. 10, a. 2. For, as the arguments given above show, to say that the will is not necessitated by another is the same as saying that

---

13. See §7, par. 1, above for the original argument.

it is not determined by it to one effect. But it is certain that the will is not necessitated by all /722b/ objects. Therefore, neither is it determined to one effect.

This is why, according to the received teaching, with respect to *exercise* the will is determined to one effect only in heaven by the clearly seen infinite goodness of God, whereas with respect to *specification* it is determined to one effect by the good in general or by other similar objects, as we will explain below.[14] However, the will is not thus determined by all objects, since it is not the case that some necessary type of goodness appears in all objects— that is, it is not the case that what appears is a goodness that has no badness or unfittingness or defectiveness mixed in with it.

Yet even if an object does not determine the will in this way, it can still be sufficient to excite and attract it to such an extent that the will is determined or led toward that object by its own freedom. For if any aspect of goodness is represented in the object, that aspect is of itself enough to move the will. Therefore, the sort of determination described above is not required in order for the will to be moved.

REPLY TO THE CONTRARY FOUNDATIONS

10. Not only is our own position proved by these considerations, but the foundation for the opposite position is answered as well.[15] For from the fact that the will cannot be led toward what is uncognized one may infer only that the intellect's judgment is necessary in order for the will to be able to choose; it does not follow that this judgment must determine the will to one effect. This point is elegantly expressed by Bernard, *De Gratia et Libero Arbi- trio*, in the following words: "Reason has been given to the will in order to instruct it, not in order to destroy it; but it would destruct it if it imposed any necessity that prevented it from turning itself by its own choice."

Thus, when it is assumed in the argument that the intellect must judge beforehand what is to be chosen, this proposition can have two meanings. If it means that the intellect judges beforehand how much goodness or use- fulness or fittingness is had by the means to be chosen and by the choice itself, then the proposition is true. However, if it means that the intellect has to judge beforehand, absolutely and completely, that such and such *must* be chosen, then the proposition is false. For in that case what it means is that,

---

14. See §8 below. For more background on the different modes of freedom see *DM* 19. 4, n. 15, and 19. 5, n. 5.

15. The foundation for the opposite position is found in §1 above.

all things having been considered and taken into account, it is here and now for some given reason necessary to choose this, and so this must absolutely be chosen. But there is no reason why a judgment of this sort should be required prior to every choice; indeed, such a judgment is incompatible with freedom of choice, as has been shown.

Therefore, what suffices is a judgment whereby a given means is judged to be useful and, all things considered, appropriate in the sense that it is able to be chosen; and the same thing holds in the case of any good object whatsoever—namely, that it be judged sufficiently good to be lovable. For just as, in order for it to be possible for the faculty of vision to be led /723a/ to an object, it is required that the object be applied not as something that is already seen or as something that must be seen but rather as something that is able to be seen, so too in order for the will to be moved by an object, it is sufficient that the object be proposed as something that is able to be loved, even if it is not judged to be something that must absolutely be chosen.

11. This is made clear, first, in the case of the divine will and intellect, since in order for God in his eternity to will something outside himself determinately and freely, it is not required that prior to (in our way of conceiving it) every free determination there should first exist in the divine intellect the judgment 'This must absolutely be loved or chosen by me.' For such a judgment would be temerarious, groundless, and strictly false, since it entails that a given object outside of God is in some way necessary for him. Thus, all there is beforehand is the judgment that a given object is appropriate or able to be chosen. Therefore, the same should be thought to hold in the case of the created will.

It is confirmed and clarified, second, as follows. In order for the will to choose a given means, the intellect does not have to judge with respect to that means in such a way that it makes no judgment about any other means. For the will requires only the cognition of the object toward which it is led, whereas ignorance of, or inattentiveness to, another object is irrelevant to it, speaking *per se*. Therefore, if the intellect judges that this means is useful or able to be chosen, then even if it simultaneously judges that some other means is useful, the will is able to choose the former; nor is it required that the intellect should first judge determinately, with respect to one of the two, that it must be chosen or even that it is more worthy of being chosen than the other.

12. *Reply to an objection.* You will object: If the intellect's judgment is indeterminate, then how can the will's choice be determinate?

The reply is that a judgment cannot be called indeterminate when by means of it one judges that an object is such and such and that it has such and such a degree of appropriateness and lovableness. Instead, it can be called either (i) a multiple judgment, as when one judges, with respect to more than one object, that they are such and such, or else (ii) a determinate judgment with respect to an indifferent object—that is, an object that does not have a necessary connection with the will, though it does have some goodness or appropriateness. Even though this sort of determinateness on the part of the judgment is not sufficient to impose necessity on the will, it is nonetheless sufficient for the will's being able by its own freedom to determine itself and to follow that judgment.

13. But you will persist: If only one judgment is present, then the will will follow it absolutely, since it has no other judgment to turn to. On the other hand, if there is more than one judgment, then it will necessarily follow the one that relates to the more useful means or the better object. So the will will always be determined /723b/ by some judgment.

One may reply, first of all, that it is possible for the [two] judgments to be about means that are equal to one another. In such a case the will cannot be determined by a judgment, nor will it necessarily be suspended; rather, its freedom is just its being able to choose the one and dismiss the other. If it cannot do this, then I do not see how it can be called free. However, it can in fact do this, since it is free in order that it might be able to will what is good and not to will what is not necessary. And the shining exemplar of this freedom is the divine will, which, from among this matter and another altogether equal and similar matter, and from among these celestial bodies and other altogether equal celestial bodies (and so on for the other things), chose to create these in preference to the others—something that cannot be traced back to a differentiating judgment, since there is no ground, either on the part of the things themselves or on the part of God, upon which a true judgment of this sort could be based. Therefore, that primeval act of choice proceeds solely from the free determination of the divine will.

Again, even when the objects or means are judged to be unequal, I deem it more probable (though by no means certain) that the will is not, by dint of that judgment, determined necessarily to will the one that is better. This is proved as follows. By the very fact that neither of the objects is proposed as necessary, the will is able not to love either of them; therefore, it is also indifferently able to love either one of them while dismissing the other. And to many this seems necessary in the case of the divine will, since the divine will was able to produce better things than those it has in fact produced, and yet it did not will to do so. Thus, all theologians teach that (i) God's incarnation was the best means for redeeming human beings and that (ii) God must have made a judgment to that effect conceptually prior to choosing this means, and yet that (iii), despite the judgment, God was able not to have willed the Incarnation but to have willed some other means instead. And so a judgment concerning a better or more useful means does not determine the will to will that means. However, I said "by dint of that judgment," since it can happen, by dint of a prior act or intention on the part of the will, that the will is absolutely determined to choose the more useful means if this greater usefulness is necessary for pursuing the end insofar as it has already been intended. For in that case the means is no longer just useful but also necessary for fulfilling such an intention. On the other hand, if this greater usefulness is not necessary relative to the intending of the end, then a judgment concerning it will not determine the will to will the relevant means absolutely.

14. Finally, from this it is obvious what should be said when only one judgment is present. For even if the intellect (i) thinks about only one object, (ii) judges it appropriate and worthy of being desired, and (iii), by a practical judgment, incites the will as much as it can to desire it, still /724a/ the will is able in its freedom not to love that object. For the will does not need another judgment just in order not to exercise its act; rather, for this it is sufficient that the person not judge, through the judgment he now has, that the good in question must here and now necessarily be loved by him. Hence, in such a case the will is able either (i) to withhold its act or (ii) to divert the intellect from thinking about the object or (iii) to apply the intellect to investigating more carefully, regarding that object, how much goodness it has and whether it has conjoined to it some evil or inappropriateness in light of which the will is able not only not to love it but even to hate it. Therefore, it is never the case that the judgment as such completely determines the will, unless the object has this kind of force in other respects because of the excellence of its goodness. We will touch upon this last point below.[16]

It is in this way, then, that the whole problem proposed above is best resolved, that our freedom is excellently defended, and that one sees clearly how freedom exists formally in the will and how the intellect operates in relation to it and to its exercise.

16. See *DM* 19. 8. 7–21.

Section 7

What the Source or Origin of a Defect in a Free Cause Is

1. However, we must still resolve the three problems that were mentioned in the fourth argument proposed in section 2 and in the confirmations of that argument.[1] The first problem is this: If the will is able, as it pleases, to will something contrary to the judgment of reason, then how is the doctrine true that is held by many philosophers and theologians: namely, that there cannot be a defect in the will unless there is an antecedent defect in the judgment, in the sense that the latter is erroneous or at least imprudent and rash?

Aristotle propounded this principle in *Ethics* 3.1 [1110b16–1111b3], 3.3 [1112a18–1113a14], and 3.5 [1113b2–1115a6]; *Ethics* 6.12 and 6.13 [1143b18–1145a12]; *Ethics* 7.3 [1146b6–1147b19]; and in *On the Soul* 3, text 58 [434a16–21]. From these places one gleans the axiom "Everyone who sins is ignorant." The Wise Man also seems to have taught this in Proverbs 14 when he said, "They are in error who do evil." And the same thing can be confirmed by the fact that otherwise it would be possible for a person always to judge prudently by means of his intellect and yet to be vicious in his will—which is contrary to all moral philosophy and to experience.

2. As for this problem, Scotus and other authors do not deem it absurd to grant that there can be a moral defect in the will without any preexisting defect in the intellect, since the created will's freedom is sufficient for being morally defective, regardless of what the intellect might do. This position is clearly Scotus's in the places cited above. Gabriel and the nominalists generally agree with him in *Sentences* 3, dist. 36, and so does /724b/ Almain, *Morales*, tract 3, chap. "On Prudence."

3. And Adrian, *Quodlibeta* 4, holds almost the same position. However, he qualifies or explains it by saying that one who acts badly always has a practical judgment by which he judges absolutely, in a way consonant with his own desire, that such and such is to be done by him—that is, that it is necessary for him to do such and such, given a desire of that sort—even if he is not otherwise ignorant of anything or mistaken in his judgment about the rectitude or badness of the object or deed in question.

4. However, it seems neither appropriate nor wholly satisfactory to add this qualification, since it is not necessary that every perverse desire of the

---

1. See *DM* 19. 2. 5–7. The first problem is treated in the present section, the second in sec. 8, the third in sec. 9.

will should proceed from the sort of practical judgment whereby one judges absolutely that something is to be done in conformity with a prior desire. For the desire or appetitive act that precedes this sort of practical judgment is such that either (i) it is elicited by the will or else (ii) it signifies only a natural, or even habitual, propensity on the part of the will. But it is not necessary that such a desire, or a practical judgment conforming to it, should exist antecedently in either of these ways. For I take the very first perverse volition that exists in a human being or angel who was antecedently well-inclined and well-disposed even in his natural or habitual inclinations; in him the practical judgment does not proceed˙ from any prior affective act that is evil or that inclines him toward evil.

5. One can reply that even in this case there is an antecedent natural or elicited inclination which, though not evil in itself, can nonetheless be an occasion of sin because the person allows himself to be led by it in such a way that he judges rashly, and not prudently, that something is to be done or loved by him. For instance, to cite an example used by Adrian, if someone has a desire to save a man from death and then realizes that he cannot save him except by lying, then even if that prior actual and elicited desire is not evil, the person is able to judge absolutely, in a way consonant with that desire, that he should lie. Likewise, because of a natural love for himself that is not evil or perhaps not even elicited, someone might judge that he should pursue a given pleasurable good. And in this way, prior to any morally evil act and prior to the first perverse desire, there is always an antecedent practical judgment whereby an object that is less good is proposed absolutely as something to be loved or to be chosen or even to be preferred to some other greater good. Such a judgment is called false from a practical point of view, since it does not conform to an upright desire.

6. But a problem still remains, since /725a/ it is never adequately proved that this judgment must be absolute in such a way that the will is moved. For I explained above[2] that (i) what is required is not a judgment about an object that *has* to be loved but rather a judgment about an object that is *able* to be loved, not a judgment about an object that *must* be chosen but rather a judgment about an object that is *able* to be chosen, and that (ii) a comparative judgment (as I will put it) is not always required—that is, a judgment to the effect that a given object is worthy of being chosen in preference to other objects. Rather, it is sufficient that there be a non-comparative judgment to the effect that the object is useful or able to be chosen—or, if the judgment is indeed comparative, it can be a judgment to the effect that the objects are equal or a judgment to the effect that the one object exceeds the other not in

2. See *DM* 19. 6. 7–14.

an unqualified way but with regard to this or that aspect of goodness—for example, pleasurableness, and so forth.

For instance, if, on the basis of an intention to pursue health, someone deliberates about two means [to this end] and judges that both of them are appropriate and useful but that the one is more upright while the other is more pleasurable, and if at the same time he makes the explicit judgment that according to reason or the rule of virtue the former is to be preferred whereas according to the inclination of the body or the senses the latter is to be favored, then no further practical judgment seems to be required in order for the will to select one of them by its own choice. For it cannot be shown that there is any necessity for another judgment, since the object has already been sufficiently proposed by the judgments we have described, and a judgment is required only in order to propose an object—as was explained above[3] by appeal to St. Thomas's position, a position one also finds in *Summa Theologiae* 1˙, q. 82, a. 4, and especially in *De Veritate*, q. 22, a. 11, ad 5, and a. 12.

7. This can be further clarified as follows. As Adrian observes in the place cited above[4] and as must be kept in mind in order to understand all the things we have said, the absolute judgment 'This is to be done' has three possible interpretations.

The first is that it expresses only the futurity of the act, as when we say that Peter is to be chosen for the episcopate.[5] And this sense is irrelevant to moral actions, as is *per se* obvious.

The second interpretation is that the judgment signifies a demand of the law and of rectitude. And this sense is also irrelevant in the present case, since it is clearly not necessary that everyone who acts freely should make a judgment of this sort. Otherwise, in order to do an evil act, one would have to make a heretical judgment—which is what it would be to judge, with respect to such an act, that it is to be done in this sense.

The third interpretation is that the judgment signifies a necessary succession of one thing from another: that is, a necessary connection between a subsequent act and an antecedent proposal or intention. It is in this sense that one who has decided to take vengeance on an enemy immediately judges, once the occasion has presented itself, that the enemy is to be killed. This interpretation is more to the point, and yet it also seems evident that such a judgment is not always required in order to do either good or evil, since

---

3. See *DM* 19. 6. 7.

4. See §3 above.

5. In English this meaning is usually expressed by the locution 'is *going* to be done'.

there is not always a necessary connection of this sort /725b/ between an act judged as that which is to be done and some antecedent desire—a point that is sufficiently proved by the arguments made above.[6]

8. We can further add a fourth interpretation: namely, that the judgment in question signifies the person's absolute (as I will put it) resolution to execute a given act or to will a given object. And if the matter is considered carefully, this act [of judging] cannot *precede* the will's free decree but must instead be *subsequent* to it. For, first of all, the judgment taken in this sense cannot, by dint of the deliberation, be inferred from any premises that display only the goodness or usefulness of the object and not the person's resolution. Second, the resolution is a free [act] and is, in fact, nothing other than the free choice or free execution [itself], since there is no other conceivable object for the judgment taken in the present sense. Yet the person could not make a true judgment about this free resolution unless he already had the resolution.[7] Finally, since the judgment in question is absolutely free, it must arise from some free volition. But there is no free volition from which it could arise other than the one whereby the person decides to do what he judges is to be done (in the present sense) by him.[8]

Therefore, it is in no sense the case that a judgment that is false from a practical point of view must precede every perverse determination* of the will.

THE RESOLUTION OF THE QUESTION

9. As for the proposed problem, then, I think one should reply that we might be discussing a judgment, disposition, or defect of the intellect that is *antecedent to* the will's free determination* or else one that is, at least in the order of nature, *subsequent to* the will's free determination. Likewise, the discussion might concern that which is *physically and absolutely* necessary for

6. See §§4–6 above.

7. The sequence, then, is this: First, there is an act of will, which Suarez here calls the resolution—say, an act of choosing a certain means; then there is a judgment to the effect that this resolution is to be carried out. So the resolution is part of the object or content of the judgment.

8. It is worth comparing this account of the practical judgment 'This is to be done' with that presented in *DM* 19. 6. 5. On both views the act of will is an efficient cause of the judgment, and the judgment has the act of will as its object. The difference is that Suarez insists that this sort of judgment must be consequent to, and not concomitant with, the act of will.

the will's being able to act or that which is *morally* necessary in keeping with those things that, for all practical purposes, always occur.

10. First of all, then, I do not believe that in order for one to do evil by means of the will, it is absolutely necessary that there should be an antecedent defect of erroneousness either in the intellect's speculative judgment or in its practical judgment. The arguments made above prove this to my satisfaction. And we grant that this follows from the principle that no judgment of the intellect is of itself sufficient to determine the will.

Nor can the opposite claim be based on the words of Aristotle, since he is talking about *ignorance* and not about *error*. Neither can it be based on the words of the Wise Man [in the book of Proverbs], both because (i) he is not talking about an error that precedes the volition but can instead be understood to be talking about an error that is subsequent to the volition, as I will explain in a moment, and also because (ii) Adrian expounds those words, and not incorrectly, as having to do with a moral error and not an error of understanding—as when someone is said to err when he deviates from the right /726a/ path, even if he does not have a false judgment in his intellect.

11. *Morally speaking, some defect in the intellect precedes a defect in the will.* Second, I claim that, *morally* speaking, the will never lapses unless there is some antecedent defect in the intellect—at the very least a failure to take into consideration some of the many reasons or motives that can hold the will back from the desire in which it sins. This claim is sufficiently proved from experience. And the Philosopher can be understood to be talking about such a lack of consideration, since this lack of consideration is said to be a kind of practical ignorance. Indeed, in *Summa Theologiae* 1–2, q. 78, a. 1, ad 1, St. Thomas interprets the Wise Man's words as having to do with this practical ignorance. For a judgment about what is to be done or desired absolutely, when made with such a lack of consideration, is a kind of practical error, since it is an act that is imprudent and of itself at odds with upright desire.

However, I do not mean that it is so much as morally necessary, or necessary in keeping with what ordinarily occurs, that this judgment should be either (i) a formally comparative judgment—that is, a judgment to the effect that a given thing is to be chosen in preference to something else—or (ii) a judgment that is formally about the object as something that is absolutely to be loved or done under one of the interpretations posited above. For the arguments made above are sufficiently telling against this claim. Rather, I mean that, morally and ordinarily speaking, there is a judgment whereby one judges absolutely that (i) a given object or act is appropriate here and now because of pleasure or honor or some other similar reason and that (ii) the object is worthy or sufficient to be sought after here and now. For this sort of judgment suffices in order for the will to be able to be moved, as was proved at length above and as I will explain below in the disputation on the final cause.[9]

Now oftentimes such a judgment is had in an absolute and unqualified way, since it does not ordinarily happen that more than one judgment is had at the same time or that various objects—or several aspects of good and evil in the same object—are compared with one another. In fact, even if a comparison of this sort does sometimes occur antecedently, still, at the very moment that the person freely wills a perverse object, he ordinarily averts his mind's eye from other considerations and attends [only] to that consideration which moves the will toward the act in question; and it is in this way that he formulates a judgment of the sort mentioned above. And this is sufficient in order for that judgment to be counted as erroneous from a practical point of view. For the judgment virtually contains a comparison of, and preference for, that object in relation to other objects, and it consequently includes a lack of harmony with upright desire.

12. *A practical judgment follows upon the free act of the will.* However, I add, third, that it is plausible to think that from the free consent of the will regarding the things to be done there necessarily follows in the intellect a practical judgment regarding those same things /726b/ whereby one judges absolutely that (in the third and fourth senses described above[10]) such and such is to be done. And if this is true, then, by reason of such a judgment, those who do evil can always be justifiably said to err with respect to the intellect as well [as with respect to the will]—not by a speculative error but instead by a practical error, and not by an error that precedes the free consent but instead by an error that is subsequent to it.

You will object: If such a judgment in no way precedes the free consent, then it is not posited in order that it might represent the object to the will or in order that it might induce the will to consent. Why, then, is such an act [of judging] necessary?

One may reply that the judgment seems necessary, first, because of the natural sympathy and agreement between the faculties in question,[11] a sympathy and agreement that were necessary in order that the person might be better able to execute what he decides should be done. Second, prior (in time or in nature) to his consenting he does not know that he will consent, and

9. See *DM* 19. 6. 10–14 and also 23. 3. 3–17. *DM* 23 is the first of the *DMs* dealing with final causality.

10. See §8 above.

11. The two relevant faculties are, of course, the will and the intellect.

so it is necessary that, as soon as he does consent, he should know about his own consent and (as I will put it) make known or promulgate his consent to himself. But this is done by means of the judgment in question.

13. And from this it follows further that if this free consent concerns something to be done, and if the consent is thus to be handed over for execution through some action, then the intellect immediately makes the absolutely practical judgment that the thing in question is to be done. And this is the *command*, which St. Thomas posits in the intellect subsequent to the will's efficacious choice.

On the other hand, if the will's consent takes place through a simple act of love or delight that is not ordered toward executing some other action, then in the intellect there is no subsequent judgment concerning a thing to be done—that is, no judgment that impels one, as it were, toward an action. However, there is a subsequent judgment concerning the consent as now having been exhibited, and this judgment can be called a sort of knowledge of approbation through which, by dint of the perverse free consent, the person, as if approving of that consent, makes the practical judgment that the thing in question is to be loved by him. However, this latter judgment cannot be called a command with respect to such a consent on the part of the will, since a command is as such ordered toward a subsequent act. For one does not command what has already been done but instead commands what is yet to be done—as St. Thomas correctly notes in *Summa Theologiae* 1–2, q. 17, a. 3.

These remarks about the first problem seem sufficient for the present occasion. (See St. Thomas, *Contra Gentes* 2, chap. 48, and Ferrariensis, in the same place, on the third argument.)

Section 8

Which Acts a Free Cause Has Indifference with Respect to

1. The second problem adumbrated above[1] was how it is that the will is called a formally free faculty, given that in its principal acts it is /727a/ not free. There are two questions suggested by this problem. The first is whether it is possible for the will to elicit certain acts freely but others by necessity. The second is this: If the will is able to elicit acts in both these modes, then which acts does it exercise freely and which necessarily?

THE FIRST QUESTION:
THE WILL'S TWO MODES OF OPERATING

2. As for the first question, one can here call to mind Scotus's opinion in *Sentences* 1, dist. 2, q. 7, and dist. 10, q. 1, and in *Quodlibeta*, q. 16. In these places he asserts that a single faculty can have only a single mode of operating, and that thus, since the will is by its nature free in operating, it cannot have any other mode of operating in its acts. And so he concludes that the will exercises *all* its acts freely—so much so that he asserts that God, too, loves himself freely and that the Father and the Son (for the same reason) produce the Holy Spirit freely.[2]

However, on this matter there can be no disagreement among Catholics unless there is an equivocation on the word 'freedom'. Thus, in the place just cited Scotus is taking 'free' not in the sense in which it is opposed to what is necessary but rather in the sense in which it is opposed to what is coerced or nonvoluntary. For he explicitly grants in that place (nor could he have denied it without heresy) that the procession of the Holy Spirit is altogether necessary, so that it implies a contradiction for that procession not to exist or for God not to love himself. Yet he contends that (i) necessity is not incompatible with freedom but rather strengthens and perfects it and, conversely, that (ii) the mode of operating naturally is repugnant to the will,

---

1. See *DM* 19. 2. 6.

2. As Suarez points out in the next paragraph, according to the Catholic Faith the relations among the divine persons—specifically, the generation of the Son by the Father and the procession of the Holy Spirit from the Father and the Son—are constitutive of the divine persons and hence necessary rather than contingent.

since the free and the natural are not only diverse modes of operating but also opposed modes of operating.

3. Still, Scotus's whole line of reasoning is based on an equivocation of terms. For he is clearly using 'free' for what is perfectly voluntary, where the latter follows upon intellectual cognition and indisputably admits of necessity in some cases. And we willingly grant to Scotus that this interpretation of the word 'free' is not altogether uncommon. For St. Thomas, too, sometimes makes use of it, as is clear from *De Potentia*, q. 10, a. 2, ad 5, where he says that God loves himself freely.

However, as we noted in section 2,[3] we ourselves are not taking the word 'free' in this sense but are rather taking it in the sense in which it adds something over and beyond the voluntary. For in *Ethics* 3.4 and 3.5, the Philosopher distinguishes the free from the voluntary. But they are distinct from one another in the case of the human will only if the free precludes a necessity in operating—as has been taught by other theologians in *Sentences* 2, dist. 24 and 25; by Alexander of Hales in [his *Summa Theologica*] 2, q. 72, memb. 3, a. 5; and /727b/ by St. Thomas in *De Malo*, q. 6. This point is obvious enough from the considerations by which we proved above that we are free from a necessity to act.[4]

4. *One and the same will is able to love some things freely and others necessarily.* Therefore, given this authentic understanding of 'free', one should say in the case under discussion that it is not contradictory for one and the same will to love some things freely and other things necessarily and not freely.

This is evident by induction. For the divine will loves God himself necessarily, whereas it loves other things freely and not necessarily. And the same is true, *mutatis mutandis*, of the created will.

Moreover, there is an a priori argument that simultaneously undermines Scotus's foundation if it is deployed against it: namely, that the two [modes] in question do not involve an opposition, since they do not hold with respect to the same thing. For even though it plainly involves a contradiction for one and the same act to be both free and necessary at the same time and in the same respect, it is nonetheless not impossible for acts that are diverse and that have diverse objects (or involve diverse means) to be such that the one proceeds freely and the other necessarily from one and the same faculty. Nor is it required that one or the other of these two modes of operating should be precisely proper to the faculty in question, since it is possible for the faculty to be a logical superior of, and more universal than, [either of the modes

3. See *DM* 19. 2. 8–11.
4. See *DM* 19. 2. 12–17.

of operating].[5] Likewise, it is possible that with respect to one act the faculty should have a twofold power—namely, the power to act and the power not to act—but that with respect to another act it should have only one of these powers—namely, the power to act. And, finally, this difference can be grounded in the objects themselves, and it is here that the a priori argument finds its source, as will be explained shortly in the promised second part of this section.[6]

5. From these considerations it is clear what to say about this same topic when using the terms 'freely' and 'naturally', since there is likewise an equivocation regarding the latter of these terms in what Scotus said above. For in some cases what is said to operate naturally is not only that which operates by the impetus of its nature but also that which operates without any antecedent cognition and hence without any elicited desire; and 'natural' in this sense excludes not only what is free but also what is voluntary. In this sense, we will say that [the element] earth moves [downward] naturally and that fire produces warmth naturally, and so on. And on this interpretation what Scotus claims is true: namely, that the will cannot operate both freely and naturally even with respect to diverse acts, since it is necessary for it to operate voluntarily and by means of an antecedent cognition.

However, in a no less frequent sense, what is called a natural operation is an operation that proceeds from the inclination of a nature insofar as that nature is wholly determined to one effect, even if the operation proceeds at the very same time from an antecedent cognition and a vital desire—and, in a word, voluntarily. This is the sense in which brute animals are said to move themselves naturally or to desire something naturally. And it is in this sense that in *Summa Theologiae* 1, q. 41, a. 2, and *Summa Theologiae* 1–2*, q. 8, a. 1 and 2, /728a/ St. Thomas correctly claims that it is not a contradiction for the same faculty of will that exercises many acts freely to elicit certain acts naturally, since the will itself has its own proper nature whereby it can be determined to certain acts even though it is not determined to all its acts—and this because of a difference among the objects, as we will soon see.[7]

6. *Why the will cannot be moved except voluntarily.* But given that the will operates both voluntarily and freely, someone will ask why it is repugnant to the will to have a mode of operating other than the voluntary, whereas it is not repugnant to it to have a mode of operating other than the free.

5. I.e., as Suarez will explain below, it is *voluntariness* which is the will's adequate mode of operating, whereas the modes of operating freely and operating necessarily are species of voluntariness.

6. See §§7–21 below.

7. Ibid.

One may reply that this is so because the first of these modes, but not the second, is precisely proper to the will. For the will is precisely a will but is not precisely a faculty of free choice, since free choice is, as it were, a logical inferior—that is, more determinate.[8] For, as was explained above,[9] free choice necessarily includes the will—that is, the principle of a voluntary act—and adds to it freedom—that is, indifference or the power not to operate.

Next, this argument can be further expounded by appeal to the objects. The precise object of the will is the good, which must necessarily be assumed to be cognized, since the will is essentially an elicitive appetitive faculty and so must operate in light of an antecedent cognition and in the manner of a desire; this is what it is to act voluntarily. However, subordinated to this precise object there can be various objects which differ greatly from one another in goodness and which are thus likewise lovable in different ways as regards freedom or necessity.

Finally, the voluntariness of an act elicited by an appetitive faculty is a positive mode of such an act, a mode that is intrinsic in such a way that it is not distinct from the act and is thus inseparable from it. By contrast, the freedom of an act adds only a denomination that is taken from the faculty insofar as the latter is able not to elicit the act or able to withhold it. This denomination cannot belong to an act if the will does not have the relevant sort of power with respect to that act.[10]

THE SECOND QUESTION: WHICH OBJECTS THE WILL
IS NECESSITATED TOWARD

7. As for the second part [of this section], there are various questions that could be discussed regarding the will's necessary acts in either the present life or the future life as well. However, these questions have their proper place either in the science of the soul or in theology. Here they will be

8. There is an appeal to etymology here, since the Latin term *voluntas* (will) is the root for the term *voluntarius* (voluntary) but not for the term *liberum arbitrium* (free choice).

9. See *DM* 19. 2. 9.

10. This is an ontological point. Voluntariness is a positive accident—more specifically, a mode—of a voluntary action, whereas an act's freedom is not a positive accident of it. Rather, a free act is one that has the mode of voluntariness and is, in addition, elicited in circumstances in which it could have been withheld or in which a contrary act could have been elicited. So a free act does not differ *intrinsically*—i.e., in its inner ontological constitution—from a merely voluntary act.

touched upon only to the extent that they are necessary for (i) explaining in general the various modes of efficient causality and the necessity or contingency of effects in the universe and (ii) resolving problems that arise concerning this topic. /728b/ For this is what the whole of the present disputation is aimed at.

What we are principally going to discuss is the position held by the many thinkers who claim that the will is free only in choosing the means and not in loving or intending the end. This position can be grounded in Aristotle, *Ethics* 3.2 [1111b25–27] and 3.3 [1112b11–19], where he says that deliberation is not about the end but only about the means. On this basis the following argument can be formulated. Everything that is free can be subject to deliberation. But only the choice [of the means] can be subject to deliberation. Therefore, only the choice [of the means] is free.

The major premise is evident from the fact that in everything that is free there is a certain indifference along with a reason for tending or not tending. Therefore, the question of whether or not a given object or a given act is appropriate can be subject to deliberation.

And [the argument] is confirmed, first, by the fact that the will is related to free choice in the way that the intellect is related to discursive reasoning. But the intellect, insofar as it is [a faculty of] discursive reasoning, is concerned not with the principles but with the things that it infers from the principles. Therefore, the will, insofar as it is [a faculty of] free choice, is concerned not with the end but with the things that it chooses for the sake of the end. For as Aristotle said in *Ethics* 6.2, "Ends are related to what can be done in the way that principles are related to what can be known speculatively."[11]

It is confirmed, second, by the fact that everything that is variable and movable must be grounded in something invariable and immovable. But free choice is of itself variable. Therefore, it must be grounded in something invariable. But it is grounded in the intending of the end. Therefore, the latter must be invariable and not free.

8. *The sense in which the intending of the end is necessary.* This position, however, stands in need of qualification and clarification. Therefore, let us take for granted, first of all, the common distinction between two types of necessity and freedom: namely, (i) necessity and freedom with respect to the *exercise* of an act and (ii) necessity and freedom with respect to the *specification* of an act. The explanation of these terms is sufficiently evident from what has been said above.[12]

---

11. This passage is not found in *Ethics* 6.2, though a similar passage is found in Ethics 7.8 (1151a16).

12. See *DM* 19. 4. 9.

Again, let us take for granted the distinction between two types of end: namely, (i) a *proximate* or *particular* end and (ii) an *ultimate* or *universal* end. This division will be explicitly discussed below in the disputation on the final cause.[13] For now, briefly, any individual good that is loved for its own sake—for example, health or knowledge—is called a particular end. By contrast, human happiness itself is called an ultimate end, regardless of whether this happiness is posited in some determinate thing or whether it is understood in general, either simply under the formal notion of beatitude or under the more universal notion of the good in general.

Further, let us leave aside for now the state of the future life and especially the state of already attained supernatural happiness, the consideration of which does not pertain to metaphysics. Theologians argue at length about whether in this latter state /729a/ the will is determined necessarily to love God, even with respect to exercise. For in *Sentences* 1, dist. 1, q. 4, Scotus claims that even within this state the necessity in question has no place in any of the will's acts, whereas the contrary position is taught by St. Thomas in *Summa Theologiae* 1, q. 82, a. 2; by Capreolus in *Sentences* 1, dist. 1, q. 3; by Cajetan in the just cited a. 2; by Ferrariensis in *Contra Gentes* 3, chap. 62; and, in general, by many others. We take this second position to be closer to the truth, but here we will be discussing the will only insofar as it operates according to its own nature and, specifically, in the state of the present life.

9. *First Assertion.* Given this understanding, we assert, first, that the will has no act, regarding either the end or the means, that is absolutely necessary with respect to exercise. This is what St. Thomas claims (in the place just cited from *Summa Theologiae* 1 and in *Summa Theologiae* 1-2, q. 10, a. 2), along with the Thomists in general. However, St. Thomas's argument is that in this life the will is always able to avert the thought of any good that is proposed to it, an argument which does not seem to be universal—that is, true without exception—and which is thus not sufficient to prove the assertion. For a human being's first thought is merely natural, and he is not able to avert it. Therefore, it is not always within the human will's power to avert a given thought.

Cajetan touches on this problem in the article just cited and grants that the first thought is not within the will's power. And he likewise grants that the first act of loving—that is, the first act of the will—is necessary with respect to exercise, as he had taught in *Summa Theologiae* 1-2, q. 9, a. 4. However, he does not think that this is contrary to what St. Thomas says in the first of the places just cited, since St. Thomas (he claims) is not denying absolutely that the will has any act that is necessary with respect to exercise but is denying

---

13. See *DM* 23. 2. 14–16.

instead that the will receives this necessity from the object—which [Cajetan claims] is true, because the necessity arises solely from the will's own natural condition and propensity. Similarly, he claims that as far as the force of the object [alone] is concerned, the will is able to avert any thought, and that this is all that St. Thomas is asserting—an assertion that does not rule out its being the case that sometimes, because of some disposition or other cause, the will is unable to avert a given thought.

10. But I myself believe, first of all, that this interpretation is contrary both (i) to St. Thomas and (ii) to the truth.

The first point is evident from the fact that in *Summa Theologiae* 1, q. 82, a. 2, St. Thomas denies absolutely that outside the beatific vision there is any necessity in our will with respect to exercise. And he is not talking only about what comes from the side of the object but is instead talking in an unqualified way about the will itself.

The second point is evident from the fact that just as the will has no act unless the object concurs within its own genus [of causality], so too the will receives no necessity /729b/ in its act—I am talking about intrinsic and connatural necessity—unless this necessity is caused by the object within its own genus—namely, in the manner of a final cause that attracts and that moves metaphorically. Hence, even in the state of beatitude, God, as clearly seen, moves the will in such a way that it is in the manner of an object and an ultimate end that he determines it of necessity to one effect. For even this sort of necessity is intrinsic and connatural to the will as informed by charity.

This is not incompatible with what St. Thomas says in the other place—namely, *Summa Theologiae* 1–2, q. 10, a. 2—since there he is talking about the will of a wayfarer who is [still] on the way to happiness. To the contrary, this doctrine is taken from the selfsame St. Thomas in *Summa Theologiae* 1, q. 82, a. 2, obj. 2, along with the reply. For the objection was this: The [will's] object is related to the will in the way that a mover is related to a movable thing; but the motion in a movable thing follows necessarily from the mover. He replies, however, as follows: "A mover causes motion necessarily in a movable thing when the mover's power exceeds the movable thing in such a way that all the latter's potentiality is subject to the mover. However, since the will's potentiality pertains to a universal and perfect good, it is not the case that all its potentiality is subject to anything that is a particular good; and so it is not moved necessarily by that sort of good." So St. Thomas clearly believes that all the will's potentiality is subject to a universal and perfect good and so is moved necessarily by such a good. Hence, whenever St. Thomas gives an explanation of any intrinsically necessary act of the will, he always assigns that explanation to the side of the object, as one can see in the places cited.

11. *The first act of the will in one who has the use of reason is not necessary with respect to exercise.* And on this basis I believe, further, that what Cajetan says is false: namely, that the first act of the will in a human being who only now has the use of reason is necessary with respect to exercise—even though other Thomists hold the same view on this point: for example, Ferrariensis, *Contra Gentes* 1, chap. 23, and more clearly in *Contra Gentes* 3, chap. 89; and Capreolus in *Sentences* 2, dist. 24, q. 1, ad 7. Capreolus even adds that the act in question does not proceed actively from the will but instead proceeds from it only passively—which is implausible, as we mentioned above in the discussion of efficient causality.[14] Moreover, as Scotus (*Quodlibeta*, q. 21) and Henry (*Quodlibeta* 12, q. 26) correctly taught, it is likewise false that this act is unqualifiedly necessary; Conrad says the same thing in *Summa Theologiae* 1–2, q. 9, art. 4, as do other commentators in the same place.

And this is proved by the fact that the will is never moved necessarily with respect to exercise unless the object itself, within its own genus, concurs in a way sufficient for that necessity and completely subjects the will to itself; /730a/ but the object proposed by the first thought is not of this sort, since it is often some particular and deficient good; therefore, etc. What's more, if this were not so, then an angel's first volition would have been necessary with respect to exercise and, as a result, there would have been no merit in it—which is contrary to the common teaching of theologians, especially in the school of St. Thomas.

Likewise, if the foundation proposed by Cajetan and Ferrariensis were solid, then not only would the will's first act in its whole life be necessary with respect to exercise, but also its first act each day or its first act each time the person begins to advert to something through his intellect and to consent to it through his will. But this consequent is plainly false and contrary to experience. The inference, on the other hand, is evident from the fact that (i) the first thought each day is likewise natural and that (ii) the will's first act proceeds from that thought alone when the will tends toward the object by its own efficient causality. However, neither of these two points carries any weight, because even if a thought is natural, it may still be applying a nonnecessitating object, and even if the will alone effects the act in question, it is able to effect it freely. For through its very being the will has (i) a certain eminent power to effect the act, (ii) a natural inclination toward it, and also at the same time (iii) a power by which it is able to refrain from it and withhold it.

12. *A person's first act of will when he first begins to have the use of reason is not necessary with respect to specification.* On this basis I add, further, that the

14. See *DM* 18. 1. 12 and 19. 2. 18–21.

[will's] first act is nonnecessary not only with respect to exercise but also with respect to specification. This is proved by an analogous argument. For the object that is applied by the first thought may not be sufficient to impose necessity even with respect to specification, since it can happen that this object is not beatitude or the good in general but is instead some particular good that is closer to the senses—for example, health or some sort of sensual pleasure. Thus, in discussing the final cause below,[15] we will show that it is not necessary that the human will's first act should concern an absolutely ultimate end.

And this is confirmed by the fact that this first act in the human will can be either morally good or morally evil. For the first object that is proposed can be a perverse object such that the will can either reject or embrace it, and in so doing can either act well or act badly. (However, the question of whether the same thing holds true for an angelic will is another matter.)

13. As for the objection made against St. Thomas's argument, then, one may reply that even if a human being's first thought is natural and even if it is thus /730b/ not within his power not to have that thought at the moment he receives it naturally, it is nonetheless within his power to remove it as soon as he sufficiently adverts to it. And this is sufficient for the will's not being necessitated with respect to exercise, since it has the freedom either to consent or else not to consent and instead to divert the thought.

Next, even if the first thought is natural, the judgment about whether to love or not to love the object might nonetheless not be completely natural. For when this natural thought is present, the will can apply the intellect to a further consideration and investigation of the thing in order to make a judgment. On the other hand, if the intellect has not yet sufficiently adverted to the idea in order for this to be within the will's power, then there is not yet a sufficient actual use of reason, and so neither is there full freedom— and thus the movements that follow are of the kind that theologians call indeliberate.

14. Finally, I add that even if a full and complete thought were entirely natural, still, if the thought did not propose the object as an absolutely necessary good—indeed, not only the object but the very act [of will]—then the will would not be moved of necessity. I take this to be an a priori argument for the proposed assertion. For when the will is led toward an object, it not only wills the object but also virtually wills the exercise of its own act, since the act is intrinsically voluntary, as was explained above.[16] And so in order for the will to be necessitated with respect to exercise, the person

15. See *DM* 24. 2.
16. See *DM* 19. 5. 7.

must apprehend and judge that such an exercise is, here and now, a good that is absolutely necessary, so that the absence of such an act cannot be apprehended as having any aspect of goodness. But this never happens in the present life with respect to any act of the will, as is clear both from experience and from the fact that there is no argument or pretext for such a necessity. However, if one were to imagine that, because of some error, a person had such a judgment here and now concerning an object and concerning the exercise of an act with respect to that object, then I willingly concede that, given this hypothesis, such a person would act necessarily. However, I maintain that the hypothesis is, humanly speaking, impossible in the case of a person who is not stupid or who does not lack a sufficient* use of reason.

15. *Second assertion.* Second, one should claim that even though (i) the will is led necessarily, with respect to specification, toward an end that is proposed under the concept of a universal good, nonetheless, (ii) when the will loves or intends other ends that are particular, this is done freely even with respect to specification. I take this assertion to be consonant with what St. Thomas teaches in the places cited above.

The first part [of the assertion] is explained and proved, first, by the fact that /731a/ when the good in general is proposed, even though the will is not forced to actually love it, it is nonetheless unable to hate it, since it finds no aspect of evil in it. So if it wills to exercise an act, then the act must be an act of loving and not an act of hating—and this is necessity with respect to specification. The same holds true for happiness in general. For, as Augustine often says, if people are asked whether they will to be happy, there is no one who replies or is able to reply that he wills against it. Instead, either he will remain silent or else he will respond that he especially wills happiness; but this is necessity with respect to specification. The reason is that no aspect of evil is discerned in these or similar objects, and we are assuming that nothing can be hated except under a concept of evil, just as nothing can be loved except under a concept of goodness.

16. As for the second part of the assertion, this thesis, too, is readily evident from induction and argument. For anyone who intends to pursue knowledge, health, or similar goods does not love them to such an extent that he is not also able to hate or reject them. For sometimes within these particular goods there is some defect or inconvenience or difficulty by reason of which they can be displeasing to the will. Indeed, it is for this reason that even an act of loving God is free not only with respect to exercise but also with respect to specification. For even though God is of himself a universal good, he can nonetheless be apprehended in the manner of a particular good, and so some aspect of evil or inconvenience can be apprehended in

him, at least in relation to his effects. And this sort of inconvenience or difficulty can be found all the more in an act of intending or loving God himself, and so such an act can easily be rejected by the will; and sometimes even God himself can be hated.

17. *An objection derived from St. Thomas.* But someone will bring up St. Thomas, who claims, in *Summa Theologiae* 1–2, q. 10, a. 1, that there are some particular goods that a human being naturally desires through his will—for example, existence, life, the cognition of truth, and similar goods. But a natural desire involves necessity at least with respect to specification. That is why in the same place, in replying to the first objection, he says that in this sort of desire the will operates in the manner of a nature. But when the will operates as a nature, its activity has a determination to one effect, since this is a nature's mode of operating.

18. *A reply, along with an exposition of St. Thomas.* One may reply, first, that in the place in question St. Thomas is not talking about necessity at all, not even necessity with respect to specification. /731b/ Instead, he is talking about the mode of operating naturally, as is obvious from the title of the article.[17] But here the term 'naturally' does not signify the same thing as the term 'necessarily', since St. Thomas is clearly distinguishing these two terms both in this article and in article 2. Hence, in this place the phrase 'to be moved naturally' signifies the same thing as 'to be moved by a natural propensity'. For here St. Thomas wants to teach that the will has a natural propensity not only toward its own peculiar goods but also toward the goods that are proper to the other faculties or parts of the whole human being. And this is the sense in which he is claiming that the will naturally desires knowledge, life, and so forth. However, freedom with respect to specification in an elicited desire for such goods is compatible with this sort of natural propensity. For, as I said above, the will has the power either to withhold an act toward which it is inclined or even to elicit a contrary act when the object contains some other aspect on which an act of this sort might be grounded.

That this is what St. Thomas means is obvious from the reply to the third objection, where, notwithstanding the sort of natural movement or propensity in question, he adds that the will is not determined to any of the particular goods but is determined only to the good in general. Here he is talking about determination with respect to specification. For, as he immediately goes on to explain in article 3, even in the case of the good in general the will is determined not with respect to exercise but only with respect to specification.

17. The title of *Summa Theologiae* 1–2, q. 10, a. 1, is: "Is there anything to which the will is naturally moved?"

However, it can further be added that with regard to the [particular] goods in question one can countenance a certain necessity with respect to specification, as long as he is speaking *per se* and prescinding from all extrinsic considerations. For some of these goods are so suited to [human] nature that they can scarcely—or not at all—be hated unless they are hated wholly *per accidens* and for wholly extrinsic reasons. Indeed, it is extremely rare for these goods to be hated in themselves even for reasons of this sort; it is rather the pursuit or procurement of them that is displeasing, either because it is arduous or because it interferes with other enjoyments that are sensual in nature. In fact, these goods can even be loved necessarily if they are apprehended as absolutely necessary for happiness—although in such a case they would be loved not so much as ends but as means to, or parts of, a necessary and universal end.

19. *Third assertion.* Third, one should claim that the will's freedom is more clearly and more perfectly exercised in the choice of the means—so much so that every free act as such (i) participates somehow in the notion of choice and (ii) is able, under that notion, to be subject to deliberation.

This thesis is supported by the arguments formulated at the beginning [of the discussion] of the present question. In addition, it is clarified succinctly as follows. The will is led toward intending an end /732a/ only by˙some natural inclination, even though it is led freely, whereas it is led toward choosing a means by force of its desire for the end, a desire that the will itself has adjoined to the inclination that is natural to it. And so the will is said to move itself more specially and more properly in choosing the means than in intending the end. But it operates freely in a more perfect way when it moves itself in a more perfect way. Therefore, etc.

The second part of the thesis is further explicated as follows. The freedom of an act derives from (i) the various aspects [of goodness and evil] that exist within the object or within the act itself and from (ii) a formal, or at least virtual, comparison of these aspects with one another. For if there is freedom with respect to specification, then within the object there must be some aspect of goodness by reason of which the object can be loved as well as some defect or aspect of evil by reason of which it can be hated. On the other hand, if there is freedom only with respect to exercise, then within the object (or at least within the act itself) there must be some defect or lack of goodness by reason of which [the act] can be apprehended as here and now inappropriate or at least unnecessary. And so whenever an act or its omission is free, some sort of comparison, explicit or implicit, is being made among these aspects [of goodness and evil], and so some sort of choice is also being made of one act over another or of a given act over its omission, or vice versa.

20. Now in this choice of the one over the other, a comparison must be made relative to some third thing or common aspect to which the will is in some way, either formally or virtually, attracted, in order that the will might be able to have a principle or ground for making the choice. This was insisted upon by the arguments at the beginning and is evident from the thing itself. For whenever someone is choosing between a righteous good and a pleasurable good, a desire for the good as such is obviously being presupposed—otherwise, the person would not immediately choose from among the specific goods but would instead first deliberate with himself about whether he should pursue the good [as such]. And the same holds true in all similar cases. So, then, even though the tendency toward a particular end, insofar as it is a movement toward a given object because of its goodness and toward other things for the sake of that object, is an act of loving or intending an end, nonetheless, since it is a free act whereby one good is preferred over others, it is a virtual choice of this good as a means to, or indeed as a part of, the happiness that the will intends in its acts. And even the very act of intending or loving ultimate happiness, since this act is here and now exercised freely and preferred to its own absence or to an act of hatred, is a virtual choice whereby such an act is chosen here and now as a means to initiating or obtaining happiness. And /732b/ this is why it is commonly said that every act of intending a particular end is a virtual act of choosing happiness, an act of choosing that does not always have to be preceded by an elicited act of intending happiness itself; rather, it is enough that it be preceded by a natural and necessary propensity [toward happiness].

So, then, every deliberation has to do with choice in some proportionate way, and every free action participates in some notion of choice. This is why a formal and proper act of choosing, which proceeds from a proper and elicited act of intending the end, is thought of as the maximally free action. And for this reason free will (*liberum arbitrium*) is said, by a sort of antonomasia, to be concerned with choice, even though it includes several other types of free act as well, as has been explained.

21. *Whether it is more perfect to operate freely or to operate necessarily.* Through these points we have replied adequately to the arguments adduced at the beginning [of the discussion] of this question. And as for the problem remitted to this place from section 2, the problem that occasioned our writing the present section, we have now explained how one and the same will is capable of both ways of acting: namely, freely and necessarily.

Now if someone asks why, given that the mode of operating freely is more perfect than the mode of operating necessarily, the will follows the former mode in some of its acts but not in all of its acts, and in its less perfect acts but not in its more perfect acts, the reply should be that operating freely is not always or in every way better than operating necessarily. Rather, the rule of perfection is that an object be loved in proportion to its worthiness and capacity; so that if a given object is the highest and most necessary good, then it is loved with complete necessity, whereas if it is a lesser or nonnecessary good, then, correspondingly, an act with respect to it is under the control of the one who loves it. And it is for this reason that God loves himself necessarily and other things freely, even though his act is absolutely perfect in every respect. Therefore, the same should be said, *mutatis mutandis*, about the created will.

Section 9

Whether a Cause's Freedom Exists While It Is Actually Operating

1. The last problem stemming from section 2 is this: Does a free cause have actual freedom *while* it is operating or *before* it operates?[1] For if the cause is already operating, then it is necessarily operating, so that it is impossible that it should not be operating at this time—and the same argument can be made about the absence of an operation. On the other hand, if freedom always has to do with the future, then no act that exists in reality will be free, since a future act as such does not exist, and so, de facto, no effect will be free. Furthermore, it is impossible /733a/ for a future act as such to be free and for it afterwards not to be exercised freely in the present. For the future is the future for no reason other than that it will at some time be present.

2. As for this problem, in *Sentences* 1, dist. 38, Ockham, Gabriel, and other nominalists teach that with respect to an act that it is already exercising, the will is not free at the very instant at which it exercises that act, except either in the sense that (i) the act proceeds from the freedom and indifference that the will had immediately before that instant or in the sense that (ii) at the instant in question the will has the power to desist from the act in the time immediately following that instant, even if all the other conditions or causes that concur for the act persist. It is in this, they claim, that a free cause differs from a natural cause. The Master seems to embrace this position in *Sentences* 2, dist. 25, chap. 2, where he says that free choice has to do not with the present or the past but with the future.

The foundation for this position was touched upon above. In the present the will is already determined to one effect, and that which exists, when it exists, exists necessarily, as the Philosopher says in *On Interpretation* 1, last chapter [9.19a22–25]. This is why, in *De Consolatione* 1, last prose, Boethius says: "The sun's rising and a man's walking agree in the fact that while they are taking place, they are not able not to be taking place; but they differ in that the sun's rising, even before it occurred, was necessarily going to occur, whereas the man's walking was not like that."

3. *The will exercises freedom most properly at the instant at which it acts.* But this position is false and to my mind plainly implausible. Therefore, one should claim that the will's freedom is properly exercised at the very instant in question and with respect to the very same act that it is eliciting or exercising as

---

1. See *DM* 19. 2. 7.

present. This was taught by Scotus in *Sentences* 1, dist. 39; by Hervaeus in *Quodlibeta* 1, q. 1, dub. 6; and by Gregory in *Sentences* 1, dist. 39. Gregory, however, added something false, as I will show in a little while.[2]

This latter position is proved, first, by an argument, suggested above, which to my mind constitutes a demonstration. If the will, at the instant it elicits an act, does not proceed freely into that act, then it was never free beforehand in relation to that act, since [beforehand] the will was free only because of its relation to the instant at which it was going to freely effect such an act.

Likewise, if at that very instant it has the act necessarily and not freely, then, by parity of reasoning, in the whole preceding temporal interval when it lacked the act, it lacked it necessarily and not freely. And the same argument will hold for future time. Therefore, there is never in fact any exercise of freedom.

4. Second, this position is explained a priori. The authors of the first position err /733b/ in not distinguishing between temporal priority and natural priority and in not distinguishing the composed sense, which is true, from the divided sense. Thus, at the very instant it elicits a free act, [but] prior in nature to eliciting it, the will is thought of as having the power to elicit the act; and it is next thought of as eliciting the act by that power. Therefore, prior in nature at that same instant the will must be thought of as being capable of eliciting such an act and capable of not eliciting it—otherwise, it is not really being thought of as free to elicit the act.

This is confirmed and clarified as follows. In the time immediately preceding the instant in question, the will is assumed to have the power to elicit the act and the power not to elicit it. And at the instant itself, naturally prior to the faculty's determining itself to the act, nothing has taken away its power not˙ to elicit the act. Therefore, the will retains its twofold power at that instant, and by that power it either elicits or does not elicit the act at that very instant. Therefore, if the will is taken simply and absolutely at that instant along with all the prerequisites for acting, then it is really able at that instant not to elicit the given act. This is power in the divided sense, or power that is prior in nature—which is necessary and absolutely sufficient for freedom.[3] On the other hand, if the will is viewed at that [same] instant [but] now later in nature, when it has already elicited the act, then it can no longer go backward within that same instant. But this is only a necessity of

2. See §8 below.

3. The divided sense that is true is equivalent to this: The will elicits the act (later in nature) at instant *t* and is able, earlier in nature at *t*, not to elicit the act.

composition based upon a hypothesis that is consequent to the will's own determination or action.[4]

5. And this is confirmed by the fact that God freely loved creatures from eternity, and yet there was no instant or real interval in which he lacked that free determination—a determination that is related to the divine will in the way that a free act is related to our will. Therefore, the will has freedom not only (i) with respect to an act that is later in some real durational measure but also (ii) with respect to an act that exists at the very same instant, though later in nature (if such an act is truly elicited and caused by the faculty), or only logically or conceptually later (if there is merely a free determination of the same act).[5] Otherwise, God's act of loving could not be thought of as being free. For he would not have loved freely from eternity, since he has always loved unceasingly; nor would he have loved freely after the instant of eternity, since he is all the less able to begin to love what he has never loved or to cease loving what he has loved and has thus loved from eternity.

The same argument can be based on the free action that angels had at the first instant of their creation, since, according to the position that is closer to the truth, they had merit at that instant.[6] And what Ockham suggests carries no weight: /734a/ namely, that the act in question was meritorious because the angel had the power to prolong or not to prolong it in the immediately subsequent time. For though such a power could have made it the case that the *continuation* of the act would be meritorious and that its *discontinuation* would be lacking in merit˙, nonetheless, it had nothing at all to do with the merit [earned] at the first instant. For this power was not being exercised at the first instant, and yet we merit formally not through our free power but through the *exercise* of that power. Furthermore, the discontinuation of the particular act in question could not confer merit, and yet the bad angels, who discontinued that act immediately after the first instant, nonetheless earned merit at the first instant. Therefore, the act was free at that very instant, at least with respect to exercise. In addition, the same argument can be made

4. The composed sense is this: Necessarily, if the will elicits the act (later in nature) at instant *t*, then the will elicits the act at *t*. This is true but trivial.

5. This latter alternative applies to the divine will. For since the divine act of will is eternal and necessary in its essence (though not in the external objects toward which it is directed), it is not elicited or caused. The first alternative applies in the case of human wills, which elicit new acts of will.

6. The common assumption shared by all sides of this debate is that every angel loves God meritoriously at the instant he is created. It is only afterwards that some angels discontinue this act of loving.

about Christ's merit, with regard to which it is more certain that it began from the first instant of his conception.

6. Finally, analogous arguments can be made in the case of human beings. For, as I was saying above, at the first instant of his use of reason a human being is able to have a free act—either a good one or even an evil one.

Likewise, as is *per se* evident, when a human being sins, he does not demerit or lose grace in the time immediately prior to the instant at which he exercises his sinful act. For one sins or demerits not in that which he is *going* to do but rather in that which he in fact *does*—as Augustine explains at length in *Epistolae*, no. 107. Therefore, a sinful act has to be free at the very same instant at which it is exercised, since no one truly sins except at a time when he is able to avoid what he does or able to do what he fails to do.

Likewise, there is a similar argument concerning the time at which a sinner repents. For he acquires grace neither before nor after the instant of contrition but˙ at the very moment at which he elicits the act of contrition. And it is only at that same moment that he sufficiently disposes himself, and yet the disposition has to be free; and it is at that same moment that he merits glory. Therefore, he exercises the free act *at* that same moment and *for* that same moment.

7. *The argument for the contrary position is refuted.* The foundation for the first position has already been dissolved. For Aristotle is clearly talking about a necessity that is conditional and that follows from a hypothesis. And Boethius should be interpreted as talking about the same thing, since what he says—namely, that the sun's rising was necessary beforehand—should be understood as having to do not only with temporal priority but also with natural or causal priority. Indeed, the reason it was true to say at a prior time that the effect in question was going to occur by necessity is that it had necessity in its cause.

On the other hand, the claim they make: /734b/ namely, that one and the same faculty is not at the same time able to effect something and not to effect it, is a sophism that rests on an equivocation of terms. For this twofold power exists all at once at the same instant, though not in order to exercise the two acts together but in order to exercise them separately—that is, in order to exercise either the one or else the other, depending on the faculty's choice. Hence, even if the faculty exercises one part of the power—for example, by eliciting the act—it still retains its power for the opposite, a power which it was able at that same instant to exercise—not, to be sure, along with the other act or by forming a compound act together with it, but rather absolutely speaking.

8. *An act of the will does not necessarily have temporal duration.* Now in the place cited above Gregory adds that if one assumes that the will has [already]

elicited the act, then it is impossible for it to discontinue the act not only at that same instant but even in the time immediately following that instant. For he thinks that it is impossible that an act should cease to exist at the same instant at which it begins to exist.[7]

However, this position has no foundation in either philosophy or theology. For it is not impossible for a thing that comes into existence to last just for a single instant, since one and the same instant can be both the first instant and the last instant of the thing's existence. For what impossibility is there in this?

He will reply that it is impossible for the thing to simultaneously begin to exist and cease to exist. But if the beginning takes place through an intrinsic instant while the ceasing takes place through an instant that is extrinsic to the ceasing itself—that is, intrinsic to the existing itself—then there is no impossibility. For it does not follow that the thing exists and does not exist at the same time. Rather, it follows only that the thing is such that it neither existed immediately beforehand nor will exist immediately afterwards. It is in this way that an instant itself has existence, and it is in this way that God could create an angel without further conserving him. Therefore, there is no necessity on these [philosophical] grounds for prolonging a free act.

Nor is there any such necessity on the other, [that is, theological], grounds. For it is probable that the bad angels persisted in their good acts for only a single instant. Also, one who sins is not forced by any necessity to persevere in his sinning; otherwise, in this life it could happen that, for some temporal interval, a human being necessarily sins and necessarily fails to desist from sinning—which is absolutely absurd. And, conversely, one who begins to merit perseveres in merit freely; otherwise, nothing would be merited by persevering in one's good works. But this is a matter that is discussed more extensively by theologians. /735a/

---

7. One way to approach this debate is to ask how the propositions 'S begins to exist at t' and 'S ceases to exist at t' are to be expounded. On one standard view, each implies that S exists at t. Thus, 'S begins to exist at t' is expounded as 'S exists at t and S did not exist immediately before t,' whereas 'S ceases to exist at t' is expounded as 'S exists at t and will not exist immediately after t.' It is clear that on this account there is no contradiction involved in a thing's beginning to exist and ceasing to exist at the same moment.

Section 10

Whether Contingency in the Effects of the Universe Arises from the Freedom of the Efficient Causes, or Whether It Could Exist in the Absence of Such Freedom

1. *Two senses in which an act is called contingent.* Lest there be any ambiguity in the word 'contingent', it should be noted that there are two senses in which an effect can be called contingent. In one sense, an effect is contingent because it happens by chance and apart from the agent's intention. It is in this sense that the word 'contingency' is taken most strictly and rigorously, but we are not speaking in this way right now, since we will be discussing chance effects in the last section of this disputation.[1] In the other sense, 'contingent' is understood as expressing something in between the necessary and the impossible. It is in this sense that logicians claim that the contingent comprises that which is at one and the same time able to exist and able not to exist. This is the signification in which 'contingent' is being taken at present, and this is also how Aristotle seems to take it in *On Interpretation* 1, last chapter [9.18b10–19b4], where he discusses future contingents.

2. Second, one should note that a given effect can be considered either (i) in relation to its proximate cause only as regards the latter's intrinsic power or (ii) in relation to that same proximate cause as conjoined with the concurrence or opposition of the other causes which, within the whole order of the universe, are able to obstruct it or concur with it. Among these latter causes we can either include the First Cause or else include only the succession and arrangement of secondary causes. It is in this second way that we are now speaking. For we are assuming that relative to the First Cause no effect in the universe occurs by absolute necessity, since all such effects depend on the First Cause's concurrence, which he is able to withhold from them because of his freedom. And so relative to the First Cause there is no entity that is so necessary—or, alternatively, there is no effect that has a cause that acts so necessarily—that it is not both able to exist and able not to exist; and in this sense [each such entity or effect] is contingent.

However, even though God acts freely, we are assuming for the present that he is prepared to concur with secondary causes and that he grants his concurrence by a fixed law. And so we are now considering the contingency or necessity of natural effects in relation to secondary causes as if

1. See *DM* 19. 12.

384

they did not depend on the First Cause, or as if the First Cause were unable to withhold his concurrence from those causes or unable to impede or alter their actions. For philosophy does not take account of the miracles that God can perform in this way, though neither does it deny them if they are real. Rather, it claims that they are exceptions to a general rule—exceptions that do not pertain to philosophy. /735b/

THE RESOLUTION OF THE QUESTION

3. *First assertion*. Given these assumptions, the resolution of the present question is very easy. Thus, one should assert, first, that relative to a proximate cause that is operating by a necessity of nature, (i) there is no effect that is contingent by virtue of the intrinsic power of such a cause, but that nonetheless (ii) the effect can be contingent because of the imperfection or deficiency of such a cause, which is able to be impeded by the concurrence or opposition of some other cause.

The first part of this assertion is clear. For if a cause is determined by its nature to one effect, then its capacity for acting is such that it is unable, by its own intrinsic power, not to act. Therefore, on this score the effect has necessity and not contingency. Thus, if someone were to consider merely the cause's intrinsic power and its natural mode of acting, then on this basis he could infer neither that the effect is not going to exist nor that it is able not to exist. Instead, he could infer only that the effect has a necessity to exist as far as this consideration is concerned. Therefore, an effect cannot have contingency by virtue of its relation to the sort of cause in question.

Nonetheless, the second part of the thesis is equally true and straightforward. For even if a proximate cause acts necessarily, it may be unable to resist all the contrary causes opposed to it or to overcome and surmount all the resistance that can be effected by other causes. So, because of this, it can turn out that an effect does not occur which would otherwise have occurred necessarily, as far as the proximate cause's power and mode of acting are concerned. Therefore, such an effect is contingent, not because of its cause's power, but rather because of its cause's lack of power, once the possible concurrence or opposition of other causes is taken into account. Among these latter causes we are including not only efficient causes but also material causes and causes that in any way resist or impede the natural action of a cause. And this is the sense in which philosophers correctly admit of contingency among the effects of natural causes. For a contingent effect is one that is able to be effected and able not to be effected by its cause. But the sort of effect in question is, absolutely speaking, able to be effected and able not to be effected by its cause—regardless of whether this stems from the latter's power or from its lack of power in the face of possible impediments. Therefore, etc.

4. *Intrinsically and extrinsically contingent effects.* However, on this basis one may, for the sake of greater clarity, correctly distinguish two sorts of contingent effects: namely, (i) *intrinsically* contingent effects and (ii) merely *extrinsically* contingent effects.

As for the first sense, an effect is called intrinsically contingent because it emanates from a cause that can confer contingency on the effect by its intrinsic force and power. This does not mean that the relevant contingency /736a/ is ever an intrinsic mode that inheres in the effect itself, since the contingency is nothing other than a denomination taken from the cause's power and mode of acting. Rather, it means that this denomination stems solely from the intrinsic power and perfection of the cause itself. And this sort of contingency exists only in relation to a free cause.

By contrast, an effect is called contingent in the second sense—that is, extrinsically—when the lack of necessity that exists in it stems solely from extrinsic impediments. From this one also sees that contingency of this sort does not depend on the freedom of any cause, even the First Cause, since it consists only in a relation to a proximate cause that is able to be impeded. This relation remains the same whether or not free causes intervene. Indeed, it would remain the same even if God acted by a necessity of nature, provided that he had produced the very same natural causes that now exist.

5. *Second assertion; if free causes are excluded, there is no contingent effect in the whole succession and collection of other causes.* My second assertion is this: If (i) an effect that is contingent relative to a naturally operating proximate cause is considered in relation to the whole order or succession of causes in the universe, and if (ii) among these latter causes there is none that acts freely, at least insofar as it applies other causes or removes impediments, then the effect in question has necessity and not contingency.

This assertion is taken from St. Thomas, *Contra Gentes* 1, chap. 67, arg. 3, where he says, "Just as an effect follows with certitude from a necessary cause, so too an effect follows with certitude from a complete contingent cause if the latter is not impeded." In the same place Ferrariensis correctly comments that this claim must be understood to apply to the effects of natural causes. The assertion is likewise taken from Durandus, *Sentences* 1, dist. 38, q. 3, and from Scotus, *Sentences* 1, dist. 1, q. 1, and dist. 8, q. 2, and dist. 38; however, Gabriel propounded it more clearly in *Sentences* 1, dist. 38, q. unica, art. 1.

It is proved by the fact that if all the causes which concur for a given effect within any genus of causality and which can either promote or impede the production of that effect act by a necessity of nature, then any sort of effect that *can* follow from all those causes, thus disposed and applied, *will* follow with the same necessity. This is clarified as follows. Just as an unimpeded natural cause that has an appropriate and sufficiently applied matter necessarily produces a proportionate effect, so too, if that same cause is wholly impeded, then with the same necessity it will do nothing at all—or, alternatively, if it is partially rather than wholly impeded, then with the same necessity it will produce an imperfect or deviant effect. Therefore, if (i) all the causes, both acting and impeding, come together in a given way solely by a natural and necessary succession, and /736b/ if (ii) each of them likewise operates with necessity in its own mode—so that an impeding cause necessarily impedes, a cause that applies the matter does so necessarily, and so on for the others—then the effect in question, considered in relation to the whole series and collection of such causes, has necessity and not contingency.

6. I find no reason for doubting this assertion. For, as we assumed at the beginning,[2] all this necessity is being thought of as subordinated to the divine will. And relative to the divine will each of the effects in question has contingency—that is, the possibility that it might not occur; yet it is at this very point that the divine freedom also comes into play. And so it is true, absolutely and without doubt, that there can be no contingency in the effects relative to the whole order or collection of agent causes unless a free cause intervenes in that collection of causes.

7. From these [first] two assertions one sees in passing how difficult it is to foreknow with certitude those future contingent effects, even merely natural ones, which (i) have contingency relative to one or another cause or even relative to several causes and which (ii) have inevitability or necessity only relative to all the causes taken together. For it is extremely difficult—at least for human beings, since we are not taking account of angels—to know all such causes. For (i) some of these causes are very far removed from the senses and quite hidden, as are the stars or their powers, and (ii) there are a great number of them, and their concurrences and oppositions are varied and multiple, and, lastly, (iii) these causes do not act without matter, the dispositions of which are likewise varied and often unknown. And so it is very hard to integrate all these things with one another and to observe them all in such a way that on that basis one might pre-cognize a particular future effect with [even] a tolerably plausible conjecture, not to mention infallible certitude. On this matter one should read Benedict Pererius, *In Genesim* 2, chaps. 2 and 3.

---

2. See §2 above.

8. *Third assertion; if there is any way in which a free cause intercedes in the series of natural causes, the effect can be contingent.* My third assertion is this: If a free cause contributes to a given effect, even an effect of natural causes, then—regardless of whether it contributes as a *per se* cause, a *per accidens* cause that applies the agent, a material cause, or a cause that removes an impeding cause—this is sufficient for the effect to be absolutely contingent, even if it is considered in relation to the whole collection and series of causes.

This is proved by the fact that a contingent effect is one which, by virtue of its cause, is able to exist and able not to exist. But effects of the sort in question, /737a/ when considered in relation to the whole collection of their causes, are without qualification able to exist and able not to exist—and this because of the mere fact that among those causes there is a free cause by whose choice it can happen either that the matter is not disposed for the given effect or that some proximate and *per se* cause is absent or that there is some other similar impediment sufficient for the effect's not following. For example, if the farmer neglects to plow the earth, which is a free act for him, then the natural crop is impeded, even if there is the right amount of rain and even if all the other causes concur. And the same line of reasoning holds true for any other effect that requires on the part of a free cause some concurrence without which the effect is not able to exist.

9. *The distinction between natural effects and nonfree contingent effects.* And from this one can infer the difference between these latter contingent effects, which in a broad sense we can call free, and natural effects of the prior sort.[3] The latter are contingent only *secundum quid*, relative to one or more of their causes, but they are not contingent relative to all their causes taken collectively. By contrast, the former—that is, the free effects—are absolutely contingent regardless of whether they are considered relative to their causes taken one by one or relative to their causes taken all together.

From this it also follows that these free effects are much less able to be foreknown in their causes than are the others. For even though a natural effect, insofar as it is contingent, is formally unable to be known with certainty as future in its cause—that is, in just its proximate cause considered in itself—nonetheless, it can be known [with certainty] in the collection and

---

3. See §§5–6 above. Note that in the heading of this paragraph effects that are both (i) contingent relative to all created causes taken collectively and yet (ii) not themselves directly free are identified as 'nonfree contingent' effects. On this acceptation, the only 'free' effects are those brought about directly by free agents—e.g., free acts of will. However, in the paragraph itself Suarez says that we can call such nonfree contingent effects free in a broad sense, and this because they must have a free cause somewhere in their causal ancestry.

integration of all its causes, since it is then being known not as contingent but as necessary. By contrast, an absolutely contingent effect cannot be foreknown with certainty as future either in one of its causes or in all of its causes taken together, since it is absolutely contingent in both respects and is thus, in virtue of its causes, indeterminate and indifferent with regard to existing or not existing. And so unless there is some other source from which one knows of a free determination on the cause's part that is sufficient to determine the effect, there is no way in which such an effect can be foreknown with certainty on the basis of its causes.

10. An occasion has just presented itself here for discussing the foreknowledge and prediction of these [absolutely] contingent effects insofar as they are future. For if, before they come to exist, they do not have within their causes either a determination to exist or a determination not to exist, then there cannot be any determinate truth in the propositions by which the one or the other of these is asserted to be future—a consequence that Aristotle seems clearly to have conceded and indeed to have argued for explicitly /737b/ in *On Interpretation* 1.9˚. However, from this concession it follows further that neither part [of the contradiction]—be it the part that affirms that an effect of this sort is future or the part that denies this—can be foreknown as determinately true, even by God. For what is not true is not knowable; therefore, what is not determinately true likewise cannot be known as determinately true. And so it is that Cicero conceded the point in *De Fato* and *De Divinatione*, as Augustine recounted in *De Civitate Dei* 5, chap. 9.

11. *The determinate truth of future contingents.* However, this problem requires a deeper and more extensive discussion of the sort that theologians provide in *Sentences* 1, dist. 38, and in *Summa Theologiae* 1, q. 14, a. 13. For present purposes, one may reply briefly that the determinateness of the truth in a future contingent proposition does not have to derive from its being the case that the cause from which a given effect will proceed is already, in its own power and ability, determined to that effect at the time or instant when it is true to say that the effect is going to occur. Rather, this determinateness derives solely from the fact that at some [future] time the cause in question will be determined in its action to a given free effect. For this is all that is being asserted by means of the proposition in question—and it is *not* being asserted that the cause, of itself and by its own power, is already determined to such an effect. Therefore, the truth or falsity of the propositions in which the effects in question are asserted to be future is compatible with the absolute contingency of those effects, since this sort of determinate truth is no more incompatible with contingency than in the case of a present-tense proposition. For even if a given effect is able to be brought about and able not to be brought about, from which it follows that it is contingent, nonetheless,

one or the other will in fact determinately occur, and from this it follows that it is determinately a future contingent. And on this point we believe that Aristotle was mistaken and that what he said was contrary to the principles of our Faith, even though there are some Catholics who try to interpret and defend him.

From what has been said it follows further that it is not absolutely impossible for these free effects to be foreknown with certainty before they come to exist—at least by means of a type of knowledge which, because of its infinity, comprehends and intuits every truth and every knowable object in the way in which it exists. On this point Cicero erred rather shamefully when he denied that God foreknows all future things. For such knowledge does not destroy the contingency in question, both because (i) it does not change or alter (as I put it) its object—or else it would render itself false if, by knowing that an effect was going to be contingent, it made it necessary—and also because (ii) this sort of knowledge of future things as future is not a cause of them but a pure intuition. But more on this elsewhere.[4] /738a/

12. There are two remaining problems concerning the last assertion. The first is whether the freedom of a secondary cause would by itself suffice for the sort of contingency in question, even if *per impossibile* freedom did not exist in the First Cause. This problem was dealt with above.[5] For to ask whether, given the relevant hypothesis, contingency in an absolute sense can arise among natural effects, is the same as asking whether, given this hypothesis, freedom and the exercise of freedom are possible in a creature. For if the exercise of freedom exists, then contingency in the absolute sense will also exist, whereas without the exercise of freedom such contingency will not exist. And so the reply given above should be applied here.

The second problem is whether, conversely, the First Cause's freedom would by itself be sufficient for the contingency of an effect even if no secondary cause were free. However, this problem has a straightforward answer on the basis of what has been said. For in whatever way an effect is free, it can be called contingent in the sense in which we are now speaking. But when we discuss God and his free will below,[6] we will deal with the question of whether one should say without qualification that effects can be called contingent by virtue of the fact that they come to exist freely relative to God.

13. *Which free agent the root of contingency exists in.* And on this basis another

4. Suarez deals with these questions at length in two places in his commentary on *Summa Theologiae* 1–2, both of which occur in the tract *De Gratia*, prolegomenon 2 and opus 2, books 1–2.

5. See *DM* 19. 3.

6. See *DM* 30. 16.

problem that is normally dealt with here is also cleared up: namely, the problem of which cause the root of contingency is posited in—more specifically, whether that source is in the freedom of the First Cause or in the freedom of the secondary cause or in both together.

Now if we are talking only about the sort of contingency that is extrinsic and *secundum quid,* then one should claim that its source is not posited in *any* sort of freedom, be it the freedom of the secondary cause or the freedom of the First Cause. Instead, it is posited proximately in the nature and condition of a secondary cause that is able to be impeded, taken together with the order and succession of other natural things and causes because of which a given impediment is wont to occur. Now the First Cause, or God, can be called the primary root of this sort of contingency only insofar as he is the First Cause of all the effects in the universe—that is, only by reason of the fact that such secondary causes were both created by him and also disposed and ordered in such a way that contingent effects of the sort in question might proceed from them. However, as far as the present point is concerned, the fact that the First Cause produced all these things *freely* is, formally speaking, irrelevant. For this same sort of contingency would follow even if he had created them all by necessity, provided only that he had ordered them in the same way and had afterwards concurred with them.

By contrast, if we are speaking of contingency in the absolute sense, then, as has been explained, its immediate source is posited in the freedom of the proximate cause and in some exercise of that freedom, whereas its primordial source is the freedom of /738b/ the First Cause, in just the way this was explained in section 3˚ above.

Section 11

Whether There Is Any Good Reason for Numbering Fate among the Efficient Causes in the Universe

1. There was an old position held by certain philosophers who attributed all the effects in the universe to fate. They identified fate with a given relation and ordering of the causes of the universe, from which, they claimed, all things issue forth by necessity—as is reported about the Stoics by Cicero, *De Divinatione,* near the end, and by Diogenes Laertius, *Lives of the Philosophers* 7, in the life of Zeno. They attributed this power principally to the stars and their position and arrangement, taken together with the motions of the celestial bodies. For from these sources the myriad appearances and conjunctions of the causes in the universe issue forth with an unavoidable necessity; and from these causes, they claimed, the effects in this lower world of ours proceed with the same necessity. Hence, they defined fate as "an assemblage of causes that gets its efficacy from the motions and power of the stars," as Albert recounts in *Physics* 2, tract 2, chap. 19, drawing from Apuleius and others.

Now many of them asserted this position not only with respect to natural effects but also with respect to human actions, both virtuous and depraved. For they thought that the celestial bodies influence the human will with the same power and immediate action as those with which they influence other things—as Augustine recounts in *Confessiones* 4, chap. 3, and *De Civitate Dei* 5, chap. 1. Augustine also notes in these places (as Plotinus does, too, in *Enneads* 3) that some of them were so obtuse as to deny that the arrangement of the causes in the universe, to which they ascribed this fatalistic necessity, stems from God's wisdom or will, claiming instead that the causes have of themselves an absolutely unavoidable intrinsic necessity.

2. But others, even though they did not deny that this ordering of secondary causes proceeded from the divine will, nonetheless attributed to it an absolutely unavoidable necessity, even with respect to God—perhaps because they believed that God acts by a necessity of nature. In *Contra Haereses,* under the entries 'Freedom' and 'Future Contingent', Castro relates that, among the heretics, Peter Abelard held this position; and he likewise relates the same thing about Wycliffe—namely, that he claimed that (i) all things happen with such an unavoidable necessity that even God himself could not have created things in any way other than he did create them or govern them in any way other than he does in fact govern them and that (ii) from these

things, thus created and governed, no actions can proceed other than those that do in fact proceed.

In addition, there are many other /739a/ heretics who have held this position concerning fate in the way in which it was asserted by the philosophers mentioned above.

3. By contrast, there are others who have located the necessity of fate not in the stars but in the divine will. Here is what Seneca says in *Naturales Quaestiones* 2, chap. 35: "Just as the water of rapid torrents does not in itself run backwards or even hesitate, since the water that comes afterwards hastens along the water that went before, so too the order of fate is regulated by an eternal succession whose first law is this: 'Let it be fixed by decree.'" And shortly afterwards in chap. 36, when he defines fate, he says that it is "the necessity of all things and actions, a necessity that no force may interfere with." He says the same thing very elegantly in *De Beneficiis* 4, chap. 7. Plato, too, seems to have held the same position in the last book of the *Republic* [12.616B-617D].

Certain recent heretics (we can attribute this to Calvin and his followers) have likewise introduced this type of fate, though perhaps not by that name. For they teach that all things happen by necessity, not because of the influence of the celestial bodies alone but because of the higher influence of God, who moves and applies all secondary causes to their actions in such a way that they do by necessity what they are impelled to do, and nothing else. But they subject this necessity to the divine will and claim that, absolutely speaking, it is changeable relative to the divine will—even though the eternal ordinance by which God decided to establish, govern, and impel things is now immutable, with the result that all things happen by a necessity which is an absolute necessity relative to the creatures and a necessity of immutability relative to God.

THE RESOLUTION OF THE QUESTION

4. This doctrine of fate, thus explained, contains many errors that are contrary not only to the Catholic Faith but also to natural reason, as can easily be seen from what has been said thus far. Because of this, not only has the thing itself been condemned by the Church in several Councils and very assiduously attacked by the holy Fathers, but it is even the case that the very term 'fate' is odious to all Catholics—though there are some who believe that if a sound interpretation is attached to the term, then it need not be rejected altogether.

THE AFOREMENTIONED ERRORS ARE
LISTED AND REFUTED

5. *First assertion*. First of all, it is plainly stupid and contrary to natural reason to attribute to secondary causes a fatalistic necessity that is independent of God. There is no other way to prove this than by demonstrating that all things depend upon God in their coming to exist, in their existing, and in their operating—a demonstration that we will present in the next three disputations.[1]

6. *Second assertion*. Second, it is repugnant to natural reason to subject the necessity of fate to a divine causality and influence that is unavoidable even relative to God himself. /739b/ This is proved by the fact that such a position involves either both of the following erroneous claims or just one of them—namely, that (i) God is not omnipotent or, at the very least, that (ii) he does not freely bring about whatever he brings about outside himself. For if God has these two perfections, then what sort of arrangement, influence, or necessity can there be on the part of secondary causes that he himself is unable to change or impede by his own omnipotent and free will? But we will demonstrate below, when we discuss God and his attributes, that there is [indeed] omnipotence and free will in God.[2]

The present assertion, however, must be understood as having to do with unavoidable necessity in the absolute sense. For if we are talking only about unavoidability *secundum quid*—namely, the sort that stems from God's immutability—then, as we will explain below,[3] there is no error on that score unless it gets mixed in from some other source.

7. *Third assertion*. Third, it is likewise an error repugnant to natural reason to posit a sort of fatalistic necessity that emanates from the influence of the stars and other natural causes onto *all* lower causes, including even human wills among the latter. (This thesis is meant to hold even if the necessity in question is assumed to be dependent on the divine will and to be changeable through that will.)

The assertion is proved by the fact that a fatalistic necessity of this sort destroys free choice. It is on this score that the position in question is condemned by the Council of Braga 1, chap. 9, and by Leo I, *Epistolae*, no. 91, chaps. 11 and 13. In addition, Eusebius brings many arguments to bear

---

1. *DM* 20 deals with creation, *DM* 21 with conservation, and *DM* 22 with God's general concurrence.

2. See *DM* 30. 16 and 17.

3. See §§9–10 below.

against it in *De Praeparatione Evangelii* 6, chap. 5ff., and Chrysostom also writes about it at length in his sermons *De Providentia*, as does Augustine, in almost the entirety of the already cited *De Civitate Dei* 5; Gregory of Nyssa (that is, Nemesius), *Philosophia* 6; Boethius, *De Consolatione* 6; and many others. Indeed, philosophers, too, have opposed this sort of fate, as is seen from Aristotle, *Ethics* 1.1 [1094a1–17], and *On Interpretation* 1, last chapter [9.18b10–19b4] (along with Ammonius and other interpreters of Aristotle in the same place), and *Physics* 2.6 [197a35–198a12] (along with Simplicius, Themistius, and others in the same place); and from Alexander of Aphrodisias, *On Fate;* and from Plutarch, *De Fortuna*. (See also the others listed in Julius Sirennus, *De Fato*.)

The foundation for this position also includes a second error: namely, that the influence of the celestial bodies falls directly and *per se* upon human souls and wills—which is contrary to the immateriality of the soul and consequently contrary to its immortality.

8. *Fourth assertion*. Fourth, it is an error contrary both to the Faith and to natural reason to posit fate by attributing it to the efficient causality and influence of the First Cause as one who necessitates all secondary causes, even rational wills, with respect to particular effects. /740a/

This is proved by what has already been said, since free choice is destroyed by this mode [of positing fate], too. Hence, fatalistic necessity has been condemned in this sense as well—although in the Council of Trent, session 6, it is not condemned under the name 'fate'.

The assertion is also made clear by a philosophical argument. For among secondary causes either (i) there are some that by their nature do not need a necessitating motion on God's part in order to act or (ii) there are none of this sort. If the second answer is given, then there is no secondary cause that is of itself a free and indifferent cause. On the other hand, if the first answer is given, then either (i) the First Cause is always pulling the secondary cause away from its natural mode of operating—which is contrary to any correct way of thinking, since in the ordinary mode of providence the First Cause cooperates with the secondary cause only as much as the latter requires, as we will explain below[4]—or else (ii) it is not always the case that the secondary cause is necessitated to act by the First Cause in the way in question— which is what we intended to prove. Therefore, from this it follows that it is altogether wrong to posit fate in the way just mentioned.

4. See *DM* 22.

IN WHAT SENSE FATE, AS REGARDS THE THING
ITSELF, CAN BE COUNTENANCED

9. *Fifth assertion.* Fifth, (i) to posit fate in such a way that it extends only to those effects of natural causes that neither angelic nor human creatures contribute to in any way by their freedom and (ii) to posit within those effects either (a) a fatalistic necessity, stemming from the succession and ordering of the causes in the universe, that is unavoidable both because of the secondary causes and because of the First Cause as regards his ordinary power and the mode of operating and concurring that is connaturally due to [secondary] causes of the sort in question, or even (b) a fatalistic necessity that stems from the immutability of some decree or predetermination on the part of God himself, though not from his absolute power and will—to posit fate in this way, I say, does not contain any error but instead contains true doctrine. Still, as we will explain below,[5] circumspection in the use of words is required here.

This whole assertion is obvious from what was said in the preceding section, and it is unnecessary to add any further proof or clarification. Louis Vives, drawing from Plutarch and others in his commentary on *De Civitate Dei* 5, chaps. 1 and 10, relates that it was in this sense that Plato and the Stoics posited fate, since they excluded human wills and free actions from the necessity of fate. Thus, in *De Fide Orthodoxa* 2, chap. 25, Damascene likewise reports, without naming names, that the philosophers posited fate not with respect to human actions, which are contingent, but with respect to necessary actions. Similarly, in *De Anima*, chap. 20, Tertullian says that even the philosophers distinguished between fate and freedom of choice; and he then adds, expressing his own opinion, /740b/ "And we now know, in accordance with the Faith, that they must be kept distinct with their own names."

10. But you will ask: "Is fate with respect to such effects an efficient cause? Or just what is it?"

Some believe that the term 'fate' formally signifies a certain relation, because in *De Consolatione* 4, [prose 6], Boethius defines fate as "an ordering among secondary causes that executes divine providence." But 'ordering' connotes a relation. Likewise, this view is taken from St. Thomas, *Summa Theologiae* 1, q. 116, a. 2, ad 3.

However, one should reply that fate in this sense is not just the relation, since such a relation does not contribute toward effecting anything. Nor is fate any single efficient cause, since no single cause is by itself sufficient to impose the sort of necessity that fate implies. Instead, it is a collection of

5. See §12 below.

causes arranged by divine providence in the way required in order for a given effect to follow. This is clear from the very explanation of fate we have given and from the posited assertion.

Now the arrangement of causes that the others call an ordering or a succession is not a relation but instead bespeaks, within each and every cause, the application that is appropriate in order for a given effect to be able to follow. This application is not really a relation, even though it might be the foundation of a relation, or even though it might be explained by us in the manner of a relation. And thus St. Thomas, in the place just cited, can be understood to be using the term 'relation' for the term 'foundation'—and this on the basis of the selfsame St. Thomas's opusculum *De Fato* (that is, Opusculum 28), chap. 5, where he says that 'fate' connotes something causal. And those who number fate among the efficient causes are making the same claim; see Alexander in the aforementioned opusculum *On Fate*, chap. 2.

From what has been said one can see that not only efficient causes but also material causes are included within this collection of causes, since the necessary propagation of a given effect depends in large part on the material causes. Still, fate is traced back in greater measure to the efficient cause, since it is the efficient cause that *per se* induces the effect, given the relevant matter along with the other conditions required for acting.

Again, from what has been said one may infer that fate is not, on the present interpretation, always a *per se* cause of all its effects. For there are some *per accidens* effects which (i) are chance effects with respect to their particular causes, as we will explain below, and which (ii) do not have a *per se* cause, as will be proved in the same place.[6] Hence, these effects occur necessarily relative to the collection of all natural causes, and yet they cannot be attributed to any *per se* natural cause that might be called fate. Thus, the stated assertion has to be qualified along these lines. /741a/

WHAT ONE SHOULD SAY ABOUT THE TERM 'FATE'

11. *Sixth assertion.* Sixth, (i) it is not an error, as far as the thing itself is concerned, to posit fate in the arrangement of natural causes insofar as they are subject to divine providence and operate infallibly in accord with its predetermination (or permission) and foreknowledge; rather, this is a Catholic doctrine that is also consonant with natural reason; still, (ii) it is necessary to qualify, or to explain adequately, this way of speaking.

This whole assertion is taken from St. Thomas, *Summa Theologiae* 1, q. 116,

6. See *DM* 19. 12.

a. 1, and from Augustine, whom St. Thomas himself cites, in *De Civitate Dei* 5, chap. 1, where he says, "If anyone calls God's will and power by the name 'fate', he should hold on to the opinion and correct the language."

The first part of the assertion is what Boethius has in mind in the place cited above, when he attempts to trace the term 'fate' back to its fitting and authentic signification. And many claim that the positions of Plato and Seneca, recounted above, can be traced back to this same signification, since Plato and Seneca did not mean to deny our freedom of choice. This also seems to be what Plutarch has in mind in *Placita* 1, chap. 27, and Aristotle, too, in *On the Universe to Alexander*, near the end [6–7.397b10–401b30], where he talks very eloquently about this matter. Indeed, as was mentioned above, in *De Civitate Dei* 5, chap. 10, Augustine tells us that even the Stoics thought the same thing about fate and did not deny freedom of choice.

Finally, this is made clear by the fact that the term 'fate', thus construed, signifies nothing other than that secondary causes are subordinated to divine providence insofar as all those causes are ordained by God to produce the effects in question—which is absolutely certain. In addition, 'fate' signifies that (i) these secondary causes do nothing that God does not foresee and promulgate beforehand—that is, utter beforehand (since the term 'fate' is thought to be derived from *fandus*, 'to be uttered') and that (ii) they do nothing that God does not in some sense also foreordain (or permit) and, generally speaking, provide for—which is also absolutely certain and consonant with natural reason, as we will show below when we discuss the attributes of God.[7] And from this it follows that relative to divine providence there is a certain infallibility or, as Boethius puts it, immovability in the effects of secondary causes, since these causes are never at all able to subvert the order of God's providence. And the term 'fate' expresses this immovability, an immovability that does not rule out the contingency or freedom of certain causes, because it does not consist in an absolute necessity but instead consists in the infallibility of God's foreknowledge and providence and its immutability. And corresponding to this immutability there is a similar necessity in the effects of secondary causes, /741b/ a necessity that is called hypothetical necessity or the necessity of the consequence. For it is impossible for things to turn out otherwise than as they have been foreknown, as St. Thomas explains in the place cited above, a. 3.

However, one should note that, even given this signification, it is not correct to attribute fate to God, as St. Thomas notes in the same place, drawing from Boethius in the place cited above. For fate is the arrangement of causes insofar as it is subject to God, but fate is not properly God himself or the

7. See *DM* 30. 17.

divine will except by way of causality—as is asserted by Augustine here and there in *De Civitate Dei* 5, chap. 1, and by Seneca and Aristotle in the places cited above. This is consonant with the term 'fate' itself, which is taken from *fandus*, 'to be uttered', and thus signifies that which is uttered and not the one who does the uttering. What's more, fate, in the sense that has been explained, likewise cannot be properly attributed to the free acts of the created will, since free choice is subject immediately to God, and it is not subject to other causes or to the arrangement of those causes except remotely and *per accidens*. And so either the proper acts of free choice cannot be attributed to fate in any sense at all, or else they can be attributed to it only in a very improper sense—namely, by calling God's very providence and his immediate influence fate.

12. And, finally, the last part of the assertion, the part that has to do merely with the use of the word 'fate', is obvious from what has been said. For St. Thomas says that the holy Fathers objected to the use of this word because of those who situated fate in the influence of the stars. That this is true is clear from the places cited above and from Augustine, *De Civitate Dei* 5, chap. 1, and *In Ioannem*, tract 37; from Gregory [the Great], *In Evangelia*, homily 10; and from Gregory of Nyssa, *Philosophia* 6, chap. 2 (or, alternatively, Nemesius, *De Anima Eiusque Facultatibus*, chaps. 35 and 36). And the reason is that, in its original imposition, the word 'fate' was instituted to signify the source of a fatalistic necessity which those who invented the term 'fate' thought of as an absolute necessity. And so in its proper signification it cannot be attributed to all secondary causes, even insofar as they are subject to divine providence.

From this it also follows that not even the natural effects that occur in this lower world of ours should be said to happen by fate in the proper sense. For, as a general rule, they never occur without the intervention of some free cause, be it angelic or human. Thus, not even rain and wind and other similar effects, which seem to be especially natural effects, should be said to occur with a fatalistic necessity. For, by God's permission or ordinance, these effects are often either impeded or stimulated by some action on the part of good or evil spirits. Because of this, then, the term 'fate' must not be taken over by us without qualification. However, if someone wants to use the term while correcting its signification, then no one should argue with him. And the relevant clarification or correction is that /742a/ the term 'fate' signifies merely a succession of causes, subject to divine providence, which does not impose necessity on those causes but instead allows each of them to act in the way appropriate to it.

In *On Fate*, chap. 3, Alexander of Aphrodisias adds that 'fate' sometimes signifies the nature of each thing; and this signification has a foundation in

Aristotle, *Physics* 5.6, text 57,[8] where he calls natural generation and corruption fatalistic. According to this signification, fate has neither more necessity nor more universality than nature does. Hence, just as it is not the case that all things happen by a natural order or by natural necessity, but rather some happen freely and others by chance, so, too, it is not the case that all things happen by fate. However, this signification of the term 'fate' does not seem to be in common use or to have a foundation in the etymology of the word, according to which—as we have already noted, drawing from Augustine— 'fate' comes from *fandus*, 'to be uttered'. Thus, in order for something to be fate, divine foreknowledge and providence must not be excluded from it.

8. This citation seems to be incorrect.

Section 12

Whether Chance and Fortune Should Be Numbered among the Efficient Causes

1. The discussion of chance and fortune is connected with the discussion of fate by virtue of the fact that if fatalistic necessity is denied, then it seems to follow as a consequence that many effects in the universe occur by chance and by fortune. And since nothing can occur unless it has an efficient cause, it likewise seems to follow that such fortuitous or chance effects must have an efficient cause that is named 'fortune' or 'chance'.

So we are now asking, concerning this [putative] cause, whether there is such a cause and what sort of cause it is. For it seems that it is not one of the causes that act either necessarily or freely, and thus that it cannot be a cause at all. The assumption is evident from the fact that a cause that operates necessarily is such that it attains to its effect always or for the most part, whereas chance effects are said to be among the things that happen infrequently. Therefore, chance effects do not stem from a cause that operates necessarily. Again, a free cause always operates purposefully and by virtue of intending an end, whereas chance is said to exist when something unintended happens. Therefore, chance is not a free cause. Therefore, chance cannot be an efficient cause.

ON THE CHANCE EFFECT

2. Even though the terms 'chance' and 'fortune' are often used for the same thing, nonetheless, strictly speaking, they have diverse significations. And so we will first talk about chance and then about fortune. /742b/

The term 'chance' properly signifies the effect rather than the cause, and it is predicated of any unexpected effect. Boethius noted this in *De Consolatione* 1, prose 1, where he claims that 'chance' signifies not the cause but rather the effect. However, there was once a usage according to which 'chance' is predicated of the cause as well, since the sort of effect in question cannot exist without a cause. And this is the sense in which Aristotle talked about chance in *Physics* 2, and with him the other philosophers. Still, it is when the effect has been explained that the cause will be better understood.

Now a chance effect is said to be one that is joined *per accidens* and unexpectedly or unintentionally to the *per se* effect of some cause, as, for instance, when someone who is digging up some ground discovers a treasure. This is clear from the common signification of the word 'chance', since a chance effect is one that occurs infrequently and unintentionally.

And so there seem to be two aspects to the notion of a chance effect. The first is that such an effect occurs infrequently, as Aristotle said in *Physics* 2.8˙ [199b19–26], along with Averroës, Alexander of Aphrodisias, St. Thomas, Albert, and others in the same place—though, as I will explain below,[1] Avicenna wished, without good reason, to qualify this claim. Now when such an effect is said to occur infrequently, this must be taken in the composed sense (as I will put it)—that is, on the assumption that the cause has been posited. For in many cases an effect is infrequent because its cause is rarely posited—even though, given that the cause has been posited, the effect always or regularly follows. And in such a case the effect is not a chance effect but instead can be a *per se* effect, as long as the positing of the cause or of the confluence of several causes does not itself occur by chance. Thus, in the alternative sense, an effect follows infrequently even given that the cause has been posited. And it is in this sense that a chance effect is said to occur infrequently. However, since such an effect always proceeds from the confluence of more than one cause, it is required that this confluence not have a fixed and definite cause within the universe—from which it likewise follows that it occurs infrequently. Because of this, an eclipse is not a chance effect; nor is any other effect that is regularly conjoined with a given *per se* effect.

3. Second, it is part of the notion of such an effect that it occurs outside the intention of the agent cause. For instance, when a rock falls on Peter as he is passing by, this is said to be a chance accident, since it happened outside the intention of both (i) the man who was passing by and (ii) the falling rock or the generating thing that was moving the rock toward the center [of the earth]. However, if this confluence of causes had been intended by someone, then relative to that person it would not be called a chance effect; instead, it would be called a *per se* effect within its own genus. Thus, it is part of the notion of chance that it be an effect that falls outside the agent's intention. For it is a *per accidens* effect.

4. From this explanation one can see that within the universe there are no chance effects /743a/ relative to God. Instead, there are chance effects only relative to secondary—that is, particular—causes. And the reason is that nothing can happen outside God's intention, since nothing can undermine his foreknowledge.

You will object that at times something does happen in given things that

---

1. See §8 below.

falls outside God's intention: for example, sins in the case of human acts. And perhaps even among natural effects some can occur which, even though they are foreknown by God, are nonetheless not intended by God.

One may reply, first of all, that in order for an effect to be a fortuitous or chance effect relative to a cause that operates through intellect and will, it must fall not only outside the agent's volition but also outside the agent's knowledge or expectations. For if something I foresaw as future follows from my action, then that thing cannot be said to be a fortuitous or chance effect relative to me—even if it is not willed but is merely permitted or is even in some sense contrary to my will. Hence, in *Magna Moralia* 2.8 [1270a4–5], Aristotle says, "There is less of fortune where there is more awareness." Therefore, in order for it to be the case that nothing happens by chance relative to God, it is sufficient that nothing should happen outside his knowledge and foreknowledge.

We add further that it is one thing to talk about the *effect* that exists in the sin, which is always some entity, and another thing to talk about the *defect* [in the sin], which is merely a lack of the appropriate moral perfection. For if we are talking about the *effect*, it cannot be a chance effect relative to God—not only because it is foreknown but also because it is caused *per se* and not merely *per accidens* by God himself and can thus in some sense be said to be intended, at least as regards God's having willed to concur with respect to that effect when the secondary cause also concurred. And for this reason no natural effect can be called a chance effect relative to God—not only because of his foreknowledge but also because of his *per se* efficient causality and because of his having intended the given effect by the very fact that he willed to create the natural causes appropriate for such an effect and to concur with those causes. Also, certain effects—for example, freaks and some other things that are said to be generated *per accidens*—which are judged to be chance effects relative to particular causes are not chance effects relative to universal causes such as celestial bodies (if the latter in fact concur *per se* with respect to such effects).

On the other hand, in order for the *defect* conjoined to the effect in a sinful act not to be a chance effect, it is not required that that defect be intended *per se*. For this lies outside the notion of [such a defect], since no one acts intending evil [as such]. Rather, it is sufficient that the defect be foreseen and permitted, especially given the fact that such a defect is always ordered by God either toward some punishment /743b/ or in such a way that it might be an occasion for some greater good. It is ordered in this way, I repeat, not by means of a preordination that is conceptually prior to the foreknowledge but rather by means of a preordination that follows upon the foreknowledge.

And so, absolutely speaking, such an effect can never be a fortuitous or chance effect relative to God—a point that is made correctly by St. Thomas in *Summa Theologiae* 1, q. 103, a. 7, ad 2, and q. 116, a. 1, ad 2; by Augustine in *83 Quaestiones*, q. 24; and by Boethius in *De Consolatione* 1, prose 1.

ON CHANCE INSOFAR AS IT SIGNIFIES A CAUSE

5. On the basis of what we have said about chance effects it is easy to explain what chance is insofar as the word 'chance' signifies the cause of a chance effect. For one should claim that there is no distinctive cause that is instituted *per se* for such an effect, but that the cause can be any created efficient cause whatsoever insofar as there is a second effect, infrequent and altogether adventitious, which is conjoined accidentally and unintentionally to that cause's *per se* effect.

This is the position held by Aristotle and the other philosophers in the places already cited. And in *Summa Theologiae* 1, q. 116, a. 1, St. Thomas clarifies this position as follows: An effect that is contingent in the way just explained[2] is not as such a being or unity absolutely speaking but is instead a being or unity *secundum quid*—that is, a *per accidens* unity; therefore, it is not necessary that it have an absolute and *per se* cause, at least not a natural one, but instead it need only have a *per accidens* cause—and so chance is not a determinate *per se* cause but is only a *per accidens* cause.

The antecedent is evident from the fact that it is a contingent effect that, say, someone who is digging a grave should discover a treasure, and yet this is not any one unified thing.[3] And so, says St. Thomas, "There can be no cause in nature which tends *per se* toward this effect, since a natural cause always tends toward something that is properly a unified thing." However, it is with justification that we say '*natural* cause', since an intellectual cause can intend *per se* as a unity something that exists *per accidens*: for example, the confluence of given causes or effects. And so among intellectual causes there can be a *per se* cause of the sort of effect in question, as we explained a short while ago with respect to God. In such a case, however, the effect will not be contingent relative to the relevant [intellectual] cause, since it will not fall outside that cause's intention.

---

2. The sort of effect in question is such that it supervenes upon the coincidental conjunction of two distinct effects.

3. The reason why it is not a 'unified' thing is that it results from the coincidental conjunction of two separate 'first-level' effects: viz., the effect brought about by the digger and the effect brought about by the agent who buried the treasure.

Hence, the argument can be concluded as follows: If chance were a *per se* cause, it would be either an intellectual cause or a natural cause. It is not the former, since an intellectual cause is a *per se* cause at [just] those times when it acts from its knowledge and intention, whereas a chance effect occurs outside the agent's intention. But neither is it the latter, since nature does not tend toward /744a/ a *per accidens* unity in the way in question. Therefore, chance is not a *per se* cause of any effect.

6. *The sense in which God is the cause of a chance effect.* You will object as follows: If that is so, then neither is God a *per se* cause of a chance effect. The consequent is false. For being a chance effect is something that exists in the effect, but there is nothing that exists in the effect that is not *per se* from God.

One may reply that being a chance effect adds no entity to the effect but instead adds [only] a denomination that is taken from the effect's conjunction with, or relation to, a given cause, through the mediation of that cause's *per se* effect. Then one argues as follows. God is a *per se* cause of the contingency of the effects, since he willed that certain given effects should be brought about by chance. However, it is not the case that they are constituted as chance effects by virtue of their relation to God—for that would be a contradiction. Rather, they are constituted as chance effects by virtue of their relation to created causes, a relation that is likewise such that God himself causes it in whatever way it is capable of existing or of being brought about.

7. You will object again as follows: Just which effect is it that in events of this sort comes to be wholly *per accidens* and without a *per se* cause, given that everything that exists *per accidens* has to be traced back to a *per se* cause?

One may reply that it is not necessary for every effect, of whatever kind it might be, to have a *per se* cause; instead, it is sufficient that it be adjoined to the *per se* effect of some cause. It is this interpretation that one should have in mind when [an effect] is said to be traced back to a *per se* cause. And so it is in the present case. For instance, in the example of the discovery of the treasure, the fact that the gold was generated in that place stemmed *per se* from some cause or other; likewise, the digging up of the earth is itself brought about *per se* and intentionally by the man. By contrast, the conjunction [of these two effects] is *per accidens* in such a way that it has no created cause, and this is why the discovery of the treasure that stems from that conjunction is called a fortuitous effect, the *per accidens* cause of which is in part the man who is digging up the ground and in part the [agent] that deposited the gold in that place. And the same is true of similar cases.

8. However, one should note further that contingent and *per accidens* effects of this sort stem not only from the confluence of efficient causes but also from the fortuitous confluence of an efficient cause with a material cause. For

freaks, which occur infrequently, are generated because of the disposition of the matter. In such a case, however, the effect is not a chance effect relative to the material cause but rather a chance effect relative to some efficient cause.

Avicenna did not pay enough attention to this point in *Sufficientia* 1, chap. 13, and that is why he claimed that chance effects include not only those which occur infrequently but also those which may turn out in either of two ways: that is, those which are equally able to occur and not to occur to a given subject—as, for instance, in the case of a surface which is such that it might become either white or black. /744b/ However, it is incorrect to say this. For 'chance' signifies the efficient cause and not the material cause, and relative to an efficient cause there is no effect that is contingent with respect to two outcomes, except in the case of free causes.[4] For natural causes are determined to one effect, whereas in the case of free causes a [two-way contingent] effect is as such a free effect and not a chance effect. Still, it will be a chance effect if it falls outside the agent's intention—something that is found, properly speaking, only in the case of those effects that are infrequently conjoined to the *per se* intended effects. By contrast, the indifference of a material potentiality is completely irrelevant to the effect's being called a chance effect—both because (i) the effect does not follow by the power of the material cause and also because (ii) it is not on the part of the material cause that the effect is *per accidens* or unintended; for this pertains, properly speaking, to the efficient cause, as is obvious *per se*.

9. *What fortune is.* From this it is readily evident what one should say about fortune, a topic on which many things were concocted by the pagans, who, ignorant of the cause of many of the chance effects that happen in human affairs, invented a sort of goddess, whom they called Fortune, in order that she might be the cause of these effects. However, this fabrication was impugned by, among others, Augustine in *De Civitate Dei* 4, chap. 18, and Lactantius in *De Vera Sapientia* 3, chaps. 28 and 29; also, one can read Albert, *Physics* 2, tract 3, chap. 10, and Scotus, *Quodlibeta*, q. 21.

Thus, one should claim that an effect of fortune is of the same type as a chance effect and that they differ solely in that the term 'fortune' is used specifically in the case of human affairs—that is, relative to one who acts purposefully from reason and from a proper and elicited intention. Hence, fortune, too, is a *per accidens* cause of the same type as chance, and all that [the term 'fortune'] does is express determinately that there is a purposefully acting cause which is a *per accidens* cause with respect to an effect that has ensued outside of the agent's intention. Hence, it can happen that one and the same effect is both a chance effect and an effect of fortune; that is, it can

4. See *DM* 19. 1. 5–11 for a related discussion.

happen that it proceeds from both chance and fortune, in different respects. For example, the discovery of the treasure is an effect of fortune relative to the man who is digging up the earth, whereas it is a chance effect relative to the natural cause that generated the gold. However, if the gold was not generated there but was instead buried there by some other man, then that man is likewise a cause in the sense of fortune—though it will be called bad fortune relative to him and good fortune relative to the first man. For the terms ['good fortune' and 'bad fortune'] do not signify diverse *per se* causes or diverse supernatural causes; instead, they signify denominations taken from propitious or adverse effects. This is the way Aristotle explicated the notion of fortune in *Physics* 2.5 [197a25–32] and in the book *On Good Fortune*.

10. *The effects of fortune are subject to the divine will.* There are just two things to be noted. One /745a/ is that fortune is understood by some philosophers in such a way that its effects are not subject to any providence at all and are likewise not intended, foreseen, or ordained by any supreme cause. And this is why St. Augustine reproaches himself in *Retractationes* 1, chap. 1, for having used the term 'fortune'. We, by contrast, subject all fortune to divine providence, since nothing happens to us by chance which has not been either ordained or permitted by God. This was made clear above and was elegantly explained in the following words by Augustine, in *De Trinitate* 3, chap. 4: "Nothing happens visibly and perceptibly which is not either commanded or permitted from the interior, invisible, and intelligible court of the most high Ruler, in accord with the ineffable justice of rewards and punishments and of graces and retributions in that most expansive and immense republic of all creatures." He touched on the same point in *83 Quaestiones*, q. 24.

The other thing to be noted is that there are certain effects brought about within us which we believe to be effects of fortune because we are ignorant of their causes, even though they are not effects that arise *per accidens* from us but are instead brought about *per se* in us by some higher cause. For example, someone, not intending or foreknowing any such thing, experiences within himself some good movement of the mind; or someone, about to embark on one road, is suddenly seized, as it were, by a desire and volition to take another road and thereby avoids an ambush by his enemies. Men call this fortune, and yet it has a cause that intends it *per se:* namely, some angel or God himself. And this is why, in *Retractationes* 1, chap. 1, and in *Contra Academicos* 1, Augustine said that what is popularly called fortune is ruled by a hidden order and has a concealed reason and cause. The Philosopher also mentions this in *On Good Fortune*, chap. 2.

So much for fortune and for created efficient causes.

Selected Bibliography

Other Parts of the Disputationes Metaphysicae *Available in English Translation*

Disputation 5: *Suarez on Individuation: Metaphysical Disputation V, Individual Unity and Its Principle.* Translated with introduction, notes, glossary, and bibliography by Jorge J. E. Gracia. Milwaukee: Marquette University Press, 1982.

Disputation 6: *On Formal and Universal Unity.* Translated, with introduction and notes, by James F. Ross. Milwaukee: Marquette University Press, 1964.

Disputation 7: *On the Various Kinds of Distinctions* (Disputationes Metaphysicae, Disputatio VII). Translated by Cyril O. Vollert. Milwaukee: Marquette University Press, 1947.

Disputations 10 and 11 and part of 23: *The Metaphysics of Good and Evil According to Suarez: Metaphysical Disputations X and XI and selected Passages from Disputation XXIII and Other Works.* Translated, with introduction, notes, and glossary by Jorge J. E. Gracia and Douglas Davis. Munich: Philosophia Verlag, 1989.

Disputation 31: *On the Essence of Finite Being as Such, On the Existence of That Essence and Their Distinction.* Translated from the Latin with an introduction by Norman J. Wells. Milwaukee: Marquette University Press, 1983.

Secondary Literature

Burns, J. P. "Action in Suarez." *New Scholasticism* 38 (1964):453–472.

Clarke, William N. "The Notion of Human Liberty in Suarez." *Modern Schoolman* 19 (1942): 32–35.

Cronin, Timothy J. "Eternal Truths in the Thought of Descartes and of His Adversary." *Journal of the History of Ideas* 21 (1960):553–559.

——. *Objective Being in Descartes and Suarez.* New York: Garland Publishing, 1987.

Davis, Douglas P. "Suárez and the Problem of Positive Evil." *American Catholic Philosophical Quarterly* 65 (1991):361–372.

De Scorraille, Raoul, S.J. *François Suarez, de la Compagnie de Jésus.* 2 vols. Paris: Lethiellieux, 1912–13.

Doig, James C. "Suarez, Descartes, and the Objective Reality of Ideas." *The New Scholasticism* 51 (1977):350–371.

Doyle, John P. " 'Extrinsic Cognoscibility': A Seventeenth-Century Supertranscendental Notion." *Modern Schoolman* 68 (1990):57–80.

——. "Heidegger and Scholastic Metaphysics." *Modern Schoolman* 49 (1972):201–220.

——. "*Prolegomena* to a Study of Extrinsic Denomination in the Work of Francis Suárez, S.J." *Vivarium* 22 (1984):121–160.

——. "Suarez on Beings of Reason and Truth." *Vivarium* 25 (1987):47–75 and 26 (1988):51–72.

——. "Suárez on the Analogy of Being." *Modern Schoolman* 46 (1969):219–249 and 323–341.

——. "Suarez on the Reality of the Possibles." *Modern Schoolman* 45 (1967):29–48.

——. "Suárez on the Unity of a Scientific Habit." *American Catholic Philosophical Quarterly* 65 (1991):311–334.

——. "The Suarezian Proof of God's Existence." In *History of Philosophy in the Making*, edited by Linus J. Thro, pp. 105–118. Washington, D.C.: University Press of America, 1982.

Ewbank, Michael. "The Route to Substance in Suarez's *Disputationes Metaphysicae*." *Proceedings of the American Catholic Philosophical Association* 61 (1987):98–111.

Ferrater Mora, Jose. "Suarez and Modern Philosophy." *Journal of the History of Ideas* 14 (1953):528–547.

Fichter, Joseph H., S.J. *Man of Spain: Francis Suarez*. New York: Macmillan, 1940.

Freddoso, Alfred J. "God's General Concurrence with Secondary Causes: Why Conservation Is Not Enough." *Philosophical Perspectives* 5 (1991):553–585.

——. "Medieval Aristotelianism and the Case against Secondary Causation in Nature." In *Divine and Human Action: Essays in the Metaphysics of Theism*, edited by Thomas V. Morris, pp. 74–118. Ithaca, N.Y.: Cornell University Press, 1988.

——. "The Necessity of Nature." *Midwest Studies in Philosophy* 11 (1986):215–242.

Grabmann, Martin. "Die *Disputationes Metaphysicae* des Franz Suarez in ihrer methodischen Eigenart und Fortwirkung." In *Mittelalterliches Geistensleben*, vol. 1, pp. 525–560. Munich: Max Hueber Verlag, 1926.

Gracia, Jorge J. E. "Evil and the Transcendentality of Goodness: Suarez's Solution to the Problem of Positive Evils." In *Being and Goodness: The Concept of the Good in Metaphysics and Philosophical Theology,*, edited by Scott MacDonald, pp. 151–179. Ithaca, N.Y.: Cornell University Press, 1991.

——. "Francisco Suárez: The Man in History." *American Catholic Philosophical Quarterly* 65 (1991):259–266.

——. *Introduction to the Problem of Individuation in the Early Middle Ages*. Munich: Philosophia Verlag, 1984.

——. "Suárez's Conception of Metaphysics: A Step in the Direction of Mentalism?" *American Catholic Philosophical Quarterly* 65 (1991):287–309.

Iturrioz, Jesús, S.J. "Fuentes de la Metafísica de Suárez." *Pensamiento* 4 (1948):31–89.

Kainz, Howard P. "The Suarezian Position on Being and the Real Distinction: An Analytic and Comparative Study." *Thomist* 34 (1970):289–305.

Kronen, John D. "Essentialism Old and New: Suárez and Brody." *Modern Schoolman* 69 (1991):123–151.

——. "The Importance of the Concept of Substantial Unity in Suárez's Argument for Hylomorphism." *American Catholic Philosophical Quarterly* 65 (1991):335–360.

Maurer, Armand. "St. Thomas and Eternal Truths." *Medieval Studies* 32 (1970):91–107.

McCullough, Laurence B. "Leibniz and Traditional Philosophy." *Studia Leibniziana* 10 (1978): 254–270.

Mullaney, Thomas U. *Suarez on Human Freedom*. Baltimore: Carroll Press, 1950. (Reprint of four articles that appeared in *Thomist* 11 (1948):1–17, 331–369, and 449–502, and 12 (1949):48–206.)

Noreña, Carlos. "Ockham and Suarez on the Ontological Status of Universal Concepts." *New Scholasticism* 55 (1981):159–174.

———. "Suárez and the Jesuits." *American Catholic Philosophical Quarterly* 65 (1991):267–286.

Owens, Joseph. "The Number of Terms in the Suarezian Discussion on Essence and Being." *Modern Schoolman* 34 (1957):147–191.

Peccorini, Francisco L. "Knowledge of the Singular: Aquinas, Suarez, and Recent Interpreters." *Thomist* 38 (1974):606–655.

———. "Suarez's Struggle with the Problem of the One and the Many." *Thomist* 36 (1972):433–471.

Robinet, Andre. "Suarez in Werk von Leibniz." *Studia Leibniziana* 13 (1981):76–96.

Ross, James F. "Suarez on 'Universals.'" *Journal of Philosophy* 59 (1962):736–747.

Wells, Norman J. "Material Falsity in Descartes, Arnauld, and Suarez." *Journal of the History of Philosophy* 22 (1984):25–50.

———. "Objective Being: Descartes and His Sources." *Modern Schoolman* 45 (1967):49–61.

———. "Objective Reality of Ideas in Descartes, Caterus, and Suarez." *Journal of the History of Philosophy* 28 (1990):33–61.

———. "Suarez on the Eternal Truths." *Modern Schoolman* 58 (1981):73–106 and 159–174.

Werner, Karl. *Franz Suárez und die Scholastik der letzten Jahrhunderte.* 2 vols. Ratisbonne: 1861 and 1889. Rept., New York: B. Franklin, 1962.

Index of Names and Works

Abelard, Peter (1079–1142): 392

Abulensis [Alphonsus Tostatus] (1400–1455): *Matthew*, 144; *Paradoxes*, 202

Adrian [Pope Adrian VI] (1459–1523): *Quodlibeta*, 358–60, 362

Albert of Saxony (c. 1316–1390): *On Generation and Corruption*, 232, 237; *Physics*, 144

Albert the Great, St. (c. 1193–1280): *De Animalibus*, 179; *Metaphysics*, 209; *On the Heavens*, 118; *On the Soul*, 153; *Physics*, 37, 144, 186, 252, 392, 402, 406; *Sentences*, 61, 329, 333

Alexander of Aphrodisias (fl. c. 205): 8, 32; *Metaphysics*, 179; *On Fate*, 395, 397, 399; *Physics*, 158, 186, 402; *Quaestiones Naturales*, 209; *Sense and Sensibilia*, 58

Alexander of Hales (c. 1186–1245): *Summa Theologica* (his own), 334, 366

Almain, Jacob (d. 1516): *Morales*, 315, 358

Ambrose, St. (339–397): *De Fide*, 344; *Hexameron*, 45, 212

Ammonius Hermiae (6th century): *Physics*, 395

Anselm of Canterbury, St. (1033–1109): 291, 322; *Cur Deus Homo*, 325; *De Concordia*, 325

Antoine André (d. 1320): *Metaphysics*, 134, 170, 258, 271, 347

Apuleius (b. c. 125): 392

Aristotle [The Philosopher] (384–322 B.C.): 6–7, 9–11, 27, 54, 128, 137–38, 142–43, 150, 152, 154, 157, 160, 188, 195, 202, 204, 231, 234, 244, 262–63, 283, 301, 331, 353, 399, 404; *Ethics*, 42, 118, 299, 358, 362, 366, 369, 382, 390; *History of Animals*, 180; *Magna Moralia*, 299, 403; *Metaphysics*, 5, 8, 12, 28, 40, 58, 118, 131, 163, 175–76, 252, 280, 290, 335, 343; *Meteorology*, 190, 236; *On Generation and Corruption*, 58, 63, 71, 86, 146, 172, 175–76, 186, 225, 237, 278; *On Good Fortune*, 407; *On Interpretation*, 379, 384, 389; *On the Generation of Animals*, 58, 80, 125; *On the Heavens*, 42, 144, 146, 148, 182, 229; *On the Movement of Animals*, 156; *On the Parts of Animals*, 26; *On the Soul*, 18, 58, 148, 358; *On the Universe to*

Alexander, 398; *Physics*, 5, 8, 28, 40, 58, 63, 67, 118, 133–34, 139, 144, 146, 151, 158, 178, 182, 186, 225–26, 265, 400–402, 407; *Posterior Analytics*, 13; *Problems*, 179, 203, 235–36; *Sense and Sensibilia*, 58

Astudillo, Diego de (16th century): *On Generation and Corruption*, 237

Augustine of Hippo, St. (354–430): 47–48, 211, 289, 307, 324, 374, 400; *Confessiones*, 288, 392; *Contra Academicos*, 407; *Contra Adimantum Manichaei*, 299; *De Civitate Dei*, 39, 41, 118, 210, 288, 290, 326, 344, 389, 392, 395, 398–99, 406; *De Libero Arbitrio*, 291, 299, 344; *De Praedestinatione et Gratia*, 308; *De Trinitate*, 40, 407; *De Vera Religione*, 294; *Epistolae*, 294, 382; *In Ioannem*, 399; *83 Quaestiones*, 404, 407; *Retractationes*, 407

Aureoli, Peter (d. 1322): 69

Averroës [The Commentator] (1126–1198): 40, 61; *Metaphysics*, 32, 37, 59; *On the Heavens*, 81, 134, 144, 207; *On the Soul*, 153; *Physics*, 67, 144, 159, 186, 207, 402

Avicebron (1021–1070): *Fons Vitae*, 38

Avicenna (980–1037): 50, 53, 60, 87, 402; *De Anima* (his own), 179; *Metaphysics* (his own), 39; *Sufficientia*, 39, 406

Bardesanes (154–222): 289

Basil the Great, St. (c. 329–379): *Hexameron*, 212; *Homilies*, 45, 299

Bassolis, John of (d. 1347): *Sentences*, 179

Bellarmine, St. Robert (1542–1621): *De Gratia et Libero Arbitrio*, 347

Bergamo, Peter of (d. 1482): *Concordantia*, 147

Bernard of Clairvaux, St. (1090–1153): 291; *De Gratia et Libero Arbitrio*, 346, 354

Boethius (c. 480–524): 382, 398; *De Consolatione*, 379, 395–96, 401, 404

Braga, Council of (563): 394

Buridan, John (c. 1300–1358): *Physics*, 144

Cajetan [Thomas de Vio] (1469–1534): 104, 109, 371–72; *Summa Theologiae*, 25, 55, 58, 61, 63, 94, 95, 102, 118, 144, 169, 186, 302, 337, 370

Index of Subjects

228, 245, 248, 272–73, 281, 297, 319, 342, 350–52, 369, 372, 386, 394–95, 399, 403. *See also* Action; Cause: efficient cause
—causality of the efficient cause: what it consists in, 3, 5, 8–10, 114–15, 249–58
—causality of the form: what it consists in, 5, 10, 254, 256–57, 297
—causality of the matter: what it consists in, 5–6, 10, 256–57
—corruptive causality: 259–68
—moral causality: 342

Cause (*causa*). *See also* Agent; Principle
—advising cause: is a true efficient cause, 8; sense in which it is a moral cause, 16–17
—agent cause: 87, 171–72, 225–26, 228, 252, 290, 387, 402. *See also* Cause: efficient cause
—cause that acts by necessity: is distinguished from free cause, 33; which causes act by necessity, 270–82. *See also* Necessity; Will
—conditions required for cause to act: 131–32, 270–79; comparison to *per se* causes, 14–16; required distinction between agent and patient, 131–77; required proximity between agent and patient, 178–221, 271; required dissimilarity between agent and patient, 222–48, 271–72
—corporeal cause: 48–50, 75, 196, 214; not equivalent to physical cause, 16; some deny that there are any, 37–39
—corruptive causality: 259–68. *See also* Corruption
—efficient cause: 35–37, 52, 54, 59, 68, 71, 131, 135, 151, 157, 162, 168, 171–78, 186–87, 190, 194, 196–97, 206, 209, 211–12, 214, 219, 222, 224, 227, 237, 269, 301, 312, 350–53, 384–85; its existence is obvious, 3; causality of efficient cause, 3, 5, 8–10, 114–15, 249–58; Aristotle's definition of, 5–10; how it differs from formal, material, and final causes, 5, 8, 10, 256–57; does not give its own *esse* to effect, 10; types of, 11–36; conditions required for efficient cause, 14–16; whether created things are efficient causes, 37–50; efficient cause of substances, 51–90; efficient cause of accidents, 91–130; which accidents can be efficient causes, 111–20; corruptive efficient causality, 259–68; which efficient causes act by necessity, 270–82; whether

any efficient causes act freely, 283–300; whether fate, chance, and fortune are efficient causes, 392–407
—equivocal cause: 42, 51, 224, 227; how it differs from univocal cause, 32
—extrinsic cause: 143, 256, 276, 289–90; efficient cause and final cause are extrinsic causes, 3, 6–7, 9–10, 256
—final cause: 3, 93, 129, 177, 214, 350, 363, 370–71, 373; its influence is obscure, 7; how it differs from efficient cause, 7, 10
—First Cause: 18, 21, 39, 44, 46, 49–50, 60, 62, 76, 82, 88–89, 100, 124, 127, 171, 172, 283–84, 386, 390–91, 395; how it falls under the definition of an efficient cause, 7–8; its mode of acting, 17; its general concurrence with secondary causes, 17, 28–29, 37, 100, 169, 172, 273, 279, 281–82, 289, 313, 384–85, 396, 403; how it differs from a secondary cause, 31–32; created things are instruments of the First Cause, 40; whether created causes could act freely if the First Cause acted by a necessity of nature, 301–13; how the First Cause's concurrence is compatible with creature's exercise of freedom, 314–26. *See also* Concurrence; God
—formal cause: 3, 43, 59, 177, 250, 256, 267; is the (formal) terminus of change, 5; how it differs from the efficient cause, 5, 8, 10, 254, 256–57; gives its own being to effect, 10. *See also* Principle: formal principle
—free cause: 177, 263, 269, 272–73, 309, 314–15, 346, 358, 365, 386–88, 399, 401, 406; is a physical cause, 17; is distinguished from cause that acts by necessity, 33; whether there any free causes, 283–300; whether created causes could act as free causes if God acted by a necessity of nature, 304–13; definition of free cause, 286–88, 315–22; how a free cause is determined by the judgment of reason, 346–57; source of a free cause's defects, 359–64; which acts a free cause has indifference with respect to, 365–78; whether a free cause's freedom exists while it is actually operating, 379–83. *See also* Free Choice; Freedom
—instrumental cause: 56, 78, 89, 127, 130, 227; is counted as an efficient cause, 7–8; how it differs from principal cause,

the will has freedom with respect to exercise, 369–78

—freedom with respect to specification: 320, 331–32, 337–38, 341; in which acts the will has freedom with respect to specification, 369–78

—root of freedom: 280, 316, 318, 328, 330, 335, 341–43, 349

Future contingents (*futura contingentia*): 387; nature of truth of future contingents, 388–90

Generation (*generatio*): 5, 19, 49, 89–90, 98–99, 101, 103–6, 113, 125, 135, 145–46, 148–49, 155, 169, 171–72, 175–76, 181, 186, 225–26, 229, 232–33, 236–37, 248, 251, 257–58, 400; as conjoined necessarily to the corruption of another substance, 14, 259–68; some claim that all generations are effected by the lowest spiritual substance, 39; generation by putrefaction, 39, 60, 76, 79, 86, 179; principles by which substances are generated, 51–88; proximity of agent and patient in substantival generation, 200–201

God (*Deus*): 39, 40–42, 45–48, 54, 57, 68–69, 71, 76–77, 96, 99, 101, 104, 120, 125, 132–33, 178, 186–87, 197, 213, 218–19, 281–83, 288–89, 292–95, 314–15, 317, 322–23, 325, 330, 344, 347, 354, 365, 370–71, 374–75, 378, 381, 383; is a physical cause when he creates, 16; effects the motion of secondary causes as a concurring principal cause, 17–19, 28–29, 37, 100, 169, 172; why the denomination 'seeing' is not attributed to God when he effects a human being's act of seeing, 18–19; whether creatures should be called God's instruments, 27–28; existence of, 32; uniqueness of, 32; some claim that God is the only efficient cause, 37–38; whether God does more when he acts with secondary causes than when he acts alone, 43–44; produces the forms of living things as a particular cause, 88; God's providence, 190, 291, 308, 324, 395–400, 407; God and corruptive causality, 259–68; God's foreknowledge, 290, 389–90, 402–3; nature of God's freedom, 298–99, 316, 318–19, 338, 342–43, 355–56; whether creatures could act freely if God acted by a necessity of nature, 301–13, 390; God loves himself voluntarily

but necessarily, 366; God and contingency, 384–91; God and fate, 392–400; God and chance, 402–5. *See also* Cause: First Cause; Concurrence

Gold (*aurum*): 77, 84, 212, 250, 405, 407

Grace (*gratia*): 45–46, 120, 283, 288–89, 291, 324, 344, 382

Gravity [heaviness] (*gravitas*): 57, 95, 108, 110, 174, 198, 208–9, 228, 271; motion of heavy and light bodies, 143–50

Habit (*habitus*): 114–15, 119–20, 237, 239, 312, 329, 332–33; whether languid acts can intensify a habit, 243

Having [as a category] (*habitus*). *See* Category: category of having

Health (*sanitas*): 119, 146, 360, 370, 373–74

Heart (*cor*): 152, 174, 182, 201, 212–14; explanation of the heart's motion, 151, 153–56

Heat (*calor, caliditas*): 13, 20–21, 26, 28–29, 33, 41–42, 44, 49, 55–58, 62, 70–71, 74, 76–79, 98–100, 102–3, 116, 119–20, 124–25, 128–29, 140–42, 147, 149, 154, 169, 180–84, 193–94, 199, 203–5, 207–9, 222–23, 229, 234–35, 239, 241–46, 266–67, 278

Heaviness (*gravitas*). *See* Gravity

Imagination (*phantasia*): 121–22, 182; alteration of a body by imagination, 179, 201–2; action of, 212–13

Immediacy of power (*immediatio virtutis*): 25, 85, 215

Immediacy of suppositum (*immediatio suppositi*): 25, 85, 215

Impediment (*impedimentum*): 14, 70, 95, 140, 150, 160, 191, 233, 244–45, 275, 277, 281–82, 388, 391

Impetus (*impetus*): 29, 34, 112, 137, 145, 147, 157, 198, 208, 212, 215; natural impetus of a rational faculty, 305, 313, 338

Indifference (*indifferentia*): 270, 292, 296, 298, 300, 303–4, 307, 312, 335, 338, 349; of natural agents, 273–79; indifference in operating, 281, 285, 291, 293–94, 379; nature of the will's indifference, 315–22; two senses of, 342–43; which acts a free cause has indifference with respect to, 365–78. *See also* Freedom

Inherence of an accident (*inhaerentia accidentis*): 100, 175

CPSIA information can be obtained
at www.ICGtesting.com
Printed in the USA
LVHW080059230119
604844LV00002B/4/P

9 780300 060072

CPSIA information can be obtained
at www.ICGtesting.com
Printed in the USA
LVHW080059230119
604844LV00002B/4/P